BCBA® EXAM REVIEW

Rondy Yu, PhD, is a licensed clinical and educational psychologist, nationally certified school psychologist, and board-certified behavior analyst. Dr. Yu previously served as an assistant professor of teaching in school psychology and the director of the applied behavior analysis training program at the University of California, Riverside. He has experience in public schools and nonpublic agencies as a psychologist, behaviorist, clinical supervisor, and researcher. Dr. Yu has presented at professional conferences at the local, national, and international levels on topics related to behavioral consultation, treatment fidelity, and programming for children and adolescents with emotional and behavioral disorders.

Aaron Haddock, PhD, is an associate professor of practice in the Department of Education and director of behavioral health initiatives and programs in the Mosakowski Institute for Public Enterprise at Clark University. Dr. Haddock is a credentialed multiple subject teacher and nationally certified school psychologist. He has experience in school and community settings as a teacher, school psychologist, program evaluator, and consultant. Dr. Haddock's areas of expertise include social–emotional learning, child and adolescent behavioral health, and school-based prevention and intervention.

BCBA® EXAM REVIEW
SECOND EDITION

Rondy Yu, PhD
Aaron Haddock, PhD

SPRINGER PUBLISHING

First Springer Publishing edition 978-0-8261-8628-7 (2024)

Springer Publishing Company, LLC
902 Carnegie Center/Suite 140, Princeton, NJ 08540
www.springerpub.com
connect.springerpub.com

Acquisitions Editor: Jaclyn Koshofer
Development Editor: Libby Ornstein
Production Editor: Susan White
Compositor: Thomson Digital

ISBN: 978-0-8261-5717-1
e-book ISBN: 978-0-8261-5937-3
DOI: 10.1891/9780826159373

25 26 27 28 / 5 4 3 2 1

Library of Congress Control Number: 2025009498

Printed in the United States of America by Gasch Printing.

This book is dedicated to all those who strive to make a meaningful impact through behavior analysis—students, practitioners, and educators alike. Your dedication to learning, teaching, and applying evidence-based practices is the driving force behind progress and innovation in our field. Your passion and commitment inspire change, foster growth, and positively affect the lives of many. It is with deep respect and admiration that this work is dedicated to you and your enduring contributions.

Contents

Preface

Over the past 20 years, the United States has witnessed significant growth in the field of behavior analysis—both in terms of the number of behavior analysts and the demand for these professionals across various industries. As the recognition of and need for BCBAs® continue to rise, so too does the need for high-quality training materials. This book aims to prepare candidates for the certification exam and help meet this growing demand.

Purpose of This Edition

Since the first edition, the field has continued to evolve, and with it the requirements and expectations for aspiring behavior analysts. This second edition has been carefully updated to align with the new BCBA Test Content Outline (TCO; 6th ed.; www.bacb.com/wp-content/uploads/2022/01/BCBA-6th-Edition-Test-Content-Outline-240903-a.pdf), ensuring it remains a relevant and reliable guide for all candidates preparing for their certification exam. Each chapter has been revised to reflect the latest updates in the field, and this edition includes new practice questions designed to enhance understanding and retention of the material, helping bridge the gap between theoretical knowledge and practical application.

Intended Audience

This book is designed for students of behavior analysis and candidates preparing for the BCBA certification exam. However, it may also be of interest to those preparing for other certifications in behavior analysis (e.g., Board Certified Assistant Behavior Analyst [BcaBA]), as well as educators and field-based supervisors. The content can be extremely useful for teaching and mentoring, providing a comprehensive resource that supports the increasing emphasis on evidence-based practice in various settings, including education and healthcare. Thus, this book can prove to be an invaluable resource for many in the field.

Final Thoughts

The journey to becoming a certified behavior analyst is rigorous and demanding, but it is also immensely rewarding. This book is a testament to our commitment to supporting you through this journey, and provides you with the resources and guidance necessary to achieve your goals. Whether you are a first-time candidate or seeking recertification, this second edition is designed to be a trusted companion on your path to success.

As you embark on your preparation, we encourage you to approach your studies with curiosity, diligence, and a commitment to excellence. The field of behavior analysis holds great potential to make a meaningful impact on the lives of individuals and communities, and your dedication to mastering its principles is a vital part of this mission.

Rondy Yu
Aaron Haddock

Acknowledgments

We would like to extend our deepest gratitude to the many professionals, colleagues, and students whose collective wisdom and experiences have greatly influenced this book. Your ongoing contributions to the field have enriched the content and scope of our work. We also wish to acknowledge the dedicated editorial team at Springer Publishing Company, with special thanks to Jaclyn Koshofer, Libby Ornstein, and Susan White, for their exceptional support and guidance. Last but not least, our heartfelt appreciation goes to our families and friends for their steadfast support throughout this endeavor. Your encouragement has continually inspired us to strive for excellence and has been instrumental in bringing this book to life.

Pass Guarantee

If you use this resource to prepare for your exam and do not pass, you may return it for a refund of your full purchase price, excluding tax, shipping, and handling. To receive a refund, return your product along with a copy of your exam score report and original receipt showing purchase of new product (not used). Product must be returned and received within 180 days of the original purchase date. Refunds will be issued within 8 weeks from acceptance and approval. One offer per person and address. This offer is valid for U.S. residents only. Void where prohibited. To initiate a refund, please contact Customer Service at csexamprep@springerpub.com.

Overview of the Certification Process

1

LEARNING OBJECTIVES

- Review requirements of qualifying training components for BCBAs®.
- Assess your eligibility status for the BCBA Exam.
- Identify next steps required to submit your initial application for certification.
- Examine the structure and scoring of the exam.

THE BCBA CERTIFICATION PROCESS

MEETING DEGREE, COURSEWORK, AND EXPERIENCE REQUIREMENTS

Prior to submitting your application for initial certification, you must meet the current eligibility requirements. This includes obtaining a qualifying degree and successfully completing qualifying coursework and supervised experience requirements.

Qualifying Degree

This is a graduate-level degree from a qualifying institution. In the United States, this means a master's or doctoral degree from a college, university, or program that is accredited by the Council for Higher Education Accreditation.

- If you are unsure of the accreditation status of your institution, simply search for it at https://www.chea.org/search?search_api_fulltext=accreditation+status. If it is listed, then it is accredited.
- If you earned a graduate-level degree outside of the United States, Canada, Australia, or the United Kingdom, an equivalency evaluation will be required to determine whether your degree is equivalent to a master's degree or higher in the United States. The equivalency evaluation is conducted as a part of the certification application. If it is needed, the Behavior Analyst Certification Board® (BACB®) will notify you and provide instructions for the next steps.

Qualifying Coursework

This refers to graduate level coursework from a qualifying institution that you received academic credit for within the last 10 years. A passing grade ("C" or better; "pass" or equivalent for pass/fail grading) must be earned for each course to be counted. Table 1.1 summarizes the content that the qualifying coursework must cover, along with the minimum hours for each area.

Table 1.1 Required Hours of Coursework by Content Area

CONTENT AREAS	REQUIRED HOURS
BACB Ethics Code and Code-Enforcement System; Professionalism	45
Philosophical Underpinnings; Concepts & Principles	90
Measurement, Data Display & Interpretation; Experimental Design	45
Behavior Assessment	45
Behavior-Change Procedures; Selecting & Implementing Interventions	60
Personnel Supervision & Management	30
Total	315

Note. Content area 1 (BACB Ethics Code...) must be taught in one or more "freestanding courses" (i.e., course[s] with a majority focus on a single content area). For Content area 2 (Philosophical Underpinnings...), 45 hours of Concepts & Principles must be taught in a freestanding course. Content area 3 (Measurement...) must be taught in one freestanding course.
Source: Behavior Analyst Certification Board. (2024, September). *Board Certified Behavior Analyst® handbook*. https://www.bacb.com/wp-content/uploads/2022/01/BCBAHandbook_240925-a.pdf.

- If you completed all your coursework through an Applied Behavior Analysis International (ABAI) verified course sequence (VCS), then the qualifying coursework requirement will be met. If you are uncertain about the VCS status of your institution, search for it on ABAI's directory of verified programs at www.abainternational.org/vcs/directory.aspx.
- Another method that may be used to evaluate your coursework involves having your coursework reviewed by your BCBA-certified VCS coordinator. If the review indicates that all requirements are met, the VCS coordinator can then complete the VCS Coordinator Coursework Attestation form at www.bacb.com/wp-content/uploads/2022/01/BCBA-VCS-Coursework-Attestation-2022-Coursework-Requirements-240209-a.pdf, which is then directly submitted to the BACB.
- If you completed coursework that covers behavior analytic content outside of a VCS, you can request that the department chair at your institution complete a Nonverified Course Content Attestation, which is available at www.bacb.com/wp-content/uploads/2022/01/Course-Content-Attestation-2022-240208-a.pdf and submit the document with your application for certification. You may also consider submitting a request for a preliminary review of your coursework by the BACB for a fee; the application for this service is available at www.bacb.com/wp-content/uploads/2022/01/2022-Preliminary-Coursework-Evaluation-Application-240606-a.pdf.

Qualifying Supervised Experience

This is a defined practical supervised experience in behavior analysis. Fulfilling this requirement means you have completed a supervision contract with one or more qualified supervisors and accrued at least the minimum number of supervised experience hours in behavior analytic activities *within 5 consecutive years*. Remember—only hours accrued after you have attended your first class session of your first qualifying course in behavior analysis can be counted to meet this requirement!

A qualified supervisor is (a) an active BCBA, not subject to disciplinary sanction, who has been certified for at least 1 year and meets continuing education requirements for supervision; (b) an active BCBA, not subject to disciplinary sanction, who has been certified for less than 1 year but receives monthly consultation from a qualified supervisor and meets continuing education requirements for supervision; (c) a psychologist certified in behavioral and cognitive psychology by the American Board of Professional Psychology (ABPP) who was tested in behavior analysis; or (d) an authorized instructor of a VCS.

Experience hours are classified as supervised fieldwork (SF) or concentrated supervised fieldwork (CSF). An applicant can accrue experience hours under just one type (e.g., only SF) or both (i.e., SF and CSF). CSF hours are weighted more heavily than SF hours. When calculating your total supervision hours, multiply CSF hours by 1.33 to convert them to SF-equivalent hours (e.g., 1 hour of CSF = 1.33 hours of SF). The requirements for each type of experience are provided in Table 1.2.

Table 1.2 Supervision Requirements by Experience Type

	SF	CSF
Fieldwork hours required	2,000	1,500
Fieldwork hours that can be counted in a supervisory period	20 to 130 hours	20 to 130 hours
Required # of contacts with supervisor in a supervisory period	4	6
Required # of times supervisor must observe you with a client in a supervisory period	1	1
Minimum % of hours spent in supervision in a supervisory period,with no more than 50% in group supervision	5	10

Note. Supervisory period = 1 calendar month. A minimum of 60% of the hours accrued must have been spent engaged in *unrestricted activities* (i.e., what a behavior analyst does; assessment, developing behavior-change programs, etc.); a maximum of 40% of the hours accrued can be from *restricted activities* (i.e., what an interventionist does; delivering instructional procedures).

CSF, concentrated supervised fieldwork; SF, supervised fieldwork.

Source: Adapted from Behavior Analyst Certification Board. (2024, September). *Board Certified Behavior Analyst® handbook*. https://www.bacb.com/wp-content/uploads/2022/01/BCBAHandbook_240925-a.pdf. ©Behavior Analyst Certification Board®. All rights reserved. This information was adapted from the BCBA Handbook. The most current version of this handbook is available at www.bacb.com.

- You can use the BACB Certificant Registry available at www.bacb.com/services/o.php?page=101135 to find/verify the qualifications and status of supervisors.
- Experience requirements may be subject to change, and it's your job to remain current on what they are to ensure you meet them for certification. Any changes made are published in the BACB newsletters and summarized in a table available at www.bacb.com/upcoming-changes.
- Ensure that you have all required documents. These include a copy of your (a) signed supervision contract, (b) documentation of fieldwork (i.e., detailed record of your qualifying experiences), and (c) completed monthly and final fieldwork verification forms.

OTHER PATHWAYS TO BCBA CERTIFICATION

The process described is referred to as *Pathway 2* for meeting eligibility requirements by the BACB and serves as the most traveled path to certification. There are, however, three other options (i.e., pathways) that the BACB offers:

Pathway 1

If you obtained a master's or doctoral degree from a behavior analysis training program accredited by ABAI or the Association of Professional Behavior Analysts (APBA), then you have met the qualifying degree and coursework requirements. Now, it's just a matter of also meeting the *qualifying supervised experience* requirements.

- ABAI-accredited programs are listed at accreditation.abainternational.org/accredited-programs.aspx.
- As of June 2024, the APBA has yet to launch its accreditation program. Please visit www.about-accreditation for more information.

Pathway 3

This pathway requires the same degree and supervised experience requirements of *Pathways 1 and 2*. But unlike those other pathways, this one throws out the need for *qualifying coursework* and instead requires you to have obtained at least 3 years of full-time work experience as a faculty member at a qualifying institution during which you taught at least five graduate level behavior analytic-focused courses in at least two content areas (i.e., applied behavior analysis, concepts/principles, ethics for behavior analysis, and single-case research). Additionally, at any point in your career, you must have been named as the first, second, or corresponding author of a behavior analytic article involving at least one experimental evaluation that was published in a high-quality, peer-reviewed journal (e.g., *Journal of Applied Behavior Analysis*).

Pathway 4

The requirements of this pathway overlap the least with those described for *Pathways 1, 2, and 3*. This one is for those of you who earned a doctoral degree at least 10 years ago from a qualifying institution, and since then accrued at least 10 years of experience practicing behavior analysis under a relevant national or state/provincial credential. To meet the *qualifying supervised experience* requirement of this path, you will also need to have accrued at least 500 hours under a qualified supervisor after you have already accrued at least 10 years of postdoctoral practice experience in the field. At least 5% of the 500 experience hours must be from supervision.

Once you've met the requirements under at least one of the four previously described pathways, the next step is to complete your initial certification application!

SUBMITTING THE CERTIFICATION APPLICATION

Currently, the certification application can be accessed through the BACB Certification Gateway at gateway.bacb.com/Account/Login.aspx. Look for the "Certification Applications" tab and follow the on-screen instructions. Once the online application is completed, you will need to pay the application fee and provide the BACB with supplemental documents, as outlined in Table 1.3.

Table 1.3 Supplemental Documents Required by Certification Pathway

CERTIFICATION PATHWAY	SUPPLEMENTAL DOCUMENTATION
1	▪ Official Transcript(s) ▪ Final Experience Verification Form(s)
2	▪ Official Transcript(s) ▪ Final Experience Verification Form(s) ▪ VCS Coordinator Coursework Attestation (if applicable) ▪ Nonverified Course Content Attestation (if applicable)
3	▪ Official Transcript(s) ▪ Final Experience Verification Form(s) ▪ Letter from Department Chair re: Faculty Appointment ▪ Syllabi for Relevant Courses Taught ▪ Copy of Published Behavior Analytic Article
4	▪ Official Transcript(s) ▪ Final Experience Verification Form(s) ▪ Curriculum Vitae ▪ Signed Attestation(s) from Current/Former Employers ▪ Proof of Professional Credentials

Note. Supplemental documentation must be submitted within 90 days of the application fee payment.
Source: Adapted from Behavior Analyst Certification Board. (2024, September). *Board Certified Behavior Analyst® handbook*. https://www.bacb.com/wp-content/uploads/2022/01/BCBAHandbook_240925-a.pdf. ©Behavior Analyst Certification Board®. All rights reserved. This information was adapted from the BCBA Handbook. The latest version of this handbook is available at www.bacb.com.

After you submit your online application, application fee, and supplemental documents for your certification pathway, the BACB will need to review your application and supplemental documents to determine whether you meet the requirements for certification. This process can take up to 45 days—or longer if there are any problems in your application—so be patient. Assuming everything is in order, and you do indeed meet eligibility requirements, the next step will be to schedule an appointment to take the BCBA Exam!

STRUCTURE OF THE EXAM

The BCBA Exam is a computer-based exam administered at Pearson VUE test centers. The questions are presented in multiple-choice format and cover the current 6th Edition of the BCBA Test Content Outline (TCO; BACB, 2024). Table 1.4 provides a breakdown of the domain areas and number of questions allocated to each on the exam.

Table 1.4 Number of Exam Items by Content Area

DOMAIN	NO. OF QUESTIONS
Behaviorism and Philosophical Foundations	8
Concepts & Principles	24
Measurement, Data Display, & Interpretation	21
Experimental Design	13
Ethical & Professional Issues	22
Behavior Assessment	23
Behavior-Change Procedures	25
Selecting and Implementing Interventions	20
Personnel Supervision and Management	19
Total	175

Source: Behavior Analyst Certification Board. (2024, September). *BCBA test content outline* (6th ed.). https://www.bacb.com/wp-content/uploads/2022/01/BCBA-6th-Edition-Test-Content-Outline-240903-a.pdf (Original work published in 2022).

During the exam, you will be presented with 185 questions (not 175) because there are 10 extra pilot questions that are not scored. There are four answer options for each question. Some questions may involve opening an "exhibit" or "figure." For a sneak peek at what the test screens will look like and practice navigating through them, Pearson VUE offers a computer-based testing demonstration that can be accessed at www.pearsonvue.com/us/en/test-takers/demo-test.html.

If you have a disability as defined by the Americans with Disabilities Act (ADA), you can submit a request for testing accommodations to the BACB at www.bacb.com/accommodations-documentation. The review process for this request can take as long as 2 weeks—or more if the BACB requires additional supporting documentation—so ensure any such request is submitted at least 15 days before the date of the exam. Possible accommodations can include extra time for completing the exam, access to a scribe/reader, use of a separate testing room, and so on. Pearson VUE test centers are wheelchair accessible, and the text presented on the computer screen during the exam can be enlarged.

SCORING OF THE EXAM

You may be wondering, "How well do I need to do to pass the exam?" Well, the BACB uses the Modified-Angoff method to score the exam. This means that a panel of experts went through the exam questions and, for each one, provided an estimate of the probability that a "minimally competent" examinee will answer correctly. These estimates were then used to determine what the minimum passing score would be.

After you complete the exam, you will receive a scaled score (i.e., a number between 0 and 500 representing the number of questions you answered correctly; Figure 1.1). A scaled score of 400 or higher is a passing score on the exam!

Figure 1.1 Exam Score Range

So now that you know the minimum score needed for passing, let's focus on more important matters—like implementing strategies that will help maximally prepare you for the exam.

CONCLUSION

This chapter focused on orienting you to the certification process. To that end, we provided some background information about the Behavior Analyst Certification Board and reviewed the process for obtaining the BCBA certification. Because the process for acquiring certification is rather involved, we included information about meeting degree, coursework, and supervised experience requirements; the multiple pathways to obtaining certification; and preparing and submitting the application. In addition, to give you a general idea of what to expect on the exam, we also described the structure and scoring of the BCBA Exam. We hope that, at this point, you have a clear understanding of what the steps are to this process and can plan to move forward in meeting one of the certification pathways.

REFERENCE

Behavior Analyst Certification Board. (2024, September). *BCBA test content outline* (6th ed.). https://www.bacb.com/wp-content/uploads/2022/01/BCBA-6th-Edition-Test-Content-Outline-240903-a.pdf (Original work published in 2022).

BIBLIOGRAPHY

Applied Behavior Analysis International. (n.d.). *Accredited programs*. https://accreditation.abainternational.org/accredited-programs.aspx

Behavior Analyst Certification Board. (n.d.). *BACB annual data report*. https://www.bacb.com/about/bacb-certificant-annual-report-data

Behavior Analyst Certification Board. (n.d.). *Examination information*. https://www.bacb.com/examination-information

Clauser, B. E., Margolis, M. J., & Case, S. M. (2006). Testing for licensure and certification in the professions. In R. L. Brennan (Ed.), *Educational measurement* (4th ed., pp. 701–731). American Council on Education/Rowman & Littlefield.

Pearson VUE. (2024, November 13). *BACB certification examinations*. https://home.pearsonvue.com/bacb

2

Preparing for the Exam

LEARNING OBJECTIVES

After reading this chapter, you will be able to:

- **Implement recommended practices for effective studying.**
- **Develop a study plan with SMART (Specific, Measurable, Achievable, Relevant, and Time-bound) goals.**
- **Evaluate and implement test-taking strategies for multiple-choice questions.**
- **Describe the structure and scoring method of the exam.**
- **Describe the structure of this book and common notations used.**

You've worked hard to meet those Board Certified Behavior Analyst® (BCBA®) eligibility requirements and now have one final task: passing the certification exam. Congratulations! Give yourself a pat on the back and take a moment to let that sink in. BCBAs help people around the world live more fulfilling and successful lives every day, and you're about to join their ranks.

To help you prepare for the exam, this chapter will review research-backed and time-tested studying tips and test-taking strategies that can improve your performance. The studying tips include recommendations for making the most out of the time you have to study, creating a strategic study plan, setting goals for studying, and monitoring your progress. Test-taking strategies include effective techniques for tackling multiple-choice questions, as well as common mistakes to avoid.

TIPS FOR STUDYING

CULTIVATE A GROWTH MIND-SET

B. F. Skinner may have conceptualized thoughts and feelings as behaviors (i.e., "private events"), but he never denied their importance—and neither should you! How you're thinking and feeling about preparing for and taking this exam is critical.

Take a minute to ask yourself: Are you optimistic, pessimistic, or neutral about studying for and taking the exam? Do you expect to do well and pass or are you concerned that you won't? How do you feel about taking high-stakes exams like this? Is it an exciting challenge, a daunting task, or perhaps something in between? What's your previous experience with exams like this? How are those previous test-taking experiences informing your approach to this exam? Do you expect that you'll be able to set aside enough time to study and prepare or are you concerned that other responsibilities or procrastination will get in the way? Does studying for the exam feel like a chore or like an opportunity to develop real mastery of your field?

Let's try this activity: Fill in Table 2.1 with your response (in the second column) to each of the six questions posed (in the first column). Using the example responses and their interpretations (in columns 3 and 4), determine whether your responses support a growth mind-set. If you identify any negative mind-set responses, check out the rightmost column for example statements that reframe negative mind-set responses.

Table 2.1 Growth Mind-Set Activity

QUESTION TO ASK YOURSELF	YOUR RESPONSE: *TAKE A FEW MOMENTS AND WRITE IN YOUR ANSWERS HERE*	EXAMPLE RESPONSES:	DOES YOUR RESPONSE SUPPORT A GROWTH MIND-SET?	LET'S REFRAME!
How do you feel about taking high-stakes exams like this?		Response A: *I am super nervous. I have heard this is a hard test.*	This is a common response and one that is normal under the circumstances but does not show the potential for growth and improvement.	*Pass rates show this is a challenging exam, but with the right preparation, I have a high chance of passing.*
		Response B: *I dread taking these types of exams. For real.*	No. An honest response but somewhat pessimistic and "fixed" in nature with no space for future change in outlook.	*Test-taking is a learned skill that can improve over time and with the right preparation and study plan. I look forward to this challenge!*
		Response C: *I am pretty good at taking high-stakes tests and will be ready.*	Yes. Sounds like you are up to this challenge. You are all set to put in the work and be ready to pass.	
What's your previous experience with taking exams like this?		Response A: *I tend to stress about exams, but manage to do okay on them.*	Somewhat. This response holds some tension about the experience but also offers a semipositive outcome.	*I embrace the anticipation and nervousness that comes with studying, as I know it is a part of high-stakes testing. Some test anxiety can even improve performance!*

(continued)

Table 2.1 Growth Mind-Set Activity (*continued*)

QUESTION TO ASK YOURSELF	YOUR RESPONSE: *TAKE A FEW MOMENTS AND WRITE IN YOUR ANSWERS HERE*	EXAMPLE RESPONSES:	DOES YOUR RESPONSE SUPPORT A GROWTH MIND-SET?	LET'S REFRAME!
		Response B: *I never do well on tests like these—they don't capture all that I know.*	No. The word "never" does not leave any wiggle room for a new, improved experience.	*Despite having negative test-taking experiences in the past, I know that with the right preparation and study plan, I can set myself up for a better testing experience.*
		Response C: *My previous experience has shown that I can do well on exams.*	Yes. You are in the right frame of mind, but still must put in the work in order to be ready for this exam!	
How are those previous test-taking experiences informing your approach to this exam?		Response A: *I cannot stop thinking about other times I have studied and still done poorly.*	No. This is a "fixed and narrowly focused" view that you are allowing to extend to all future test-taking experiences.	*Previous failures are an opportunity to grow in new ways. My increased study effort will make me a better service provider no matter what.*
		Response B: *I know that it is a long shot that I will pass this exam. My colleague took it three times.*	No. Just because others have had a particular experience with this exam, that does not mean you will have the same one.	*Yes, this is a hard test, but my effort and my mind-set can really contribute to my performance. LEARNING the material is the true goal.*
		Response C: *My previous experiences give me the confidence to believe I can study and will pass this exam.*	Yes. Your previous experiences are setting the stage for a positive outcome, but you still must execute your study plan to be ready for this exam!	

(*continued*)

Table 2.1 Growth Mind-Set Activity (*continued*)

QUESTION TO ASK YOURSELF	YOUR RESPONSE: *TAKE A FEW MOMENTS AND WRITE IN YOUR ANSWERS HERE*	EXAMPLE RESPONSES:	DOES YOUR RESPONSE SUPPORT A GROWTH MIND-SET?	LET'S REFRAME!
Do you expect that you'll be able to set aside enough time to prepare or could other responsibilities or procrastination get in the way?		Response A: *I am just not sure I have the time, but I will plan the best I can.*	Somewhat. This honest answer acknowledges the limited time we all have as professionals, but also indicates the need to plan accordingly.	*Despite being busy, I will find windows of time (e.g., wake up 1 hour earlier, set aside every Sat morning, etc.) to make sure I have study time.*
		Response B: *I am a very busy person. I cannot really envision having enough time to study properly.*	No. This offers a limited and fixed view of your calendar with little room for expansion and creative scheduling.	*I am a very creative person, and I can certainly find time in my schedule to do fun things, so I am sure I can find the time I need to study.*
		Response C: *Yes, I will carefully plan my calendar for the next months to ensure I have enough time.*	Yes. You are all set; you just need an open calendar and your highlighter!	
Do you expect to do well and pass or are you concerned that you won't?		Response A: *I expect that I might not pass and will have to take it again.*	No. This sets up the expectation of failure right from the beginning.	*I will have to push through my fear of failure and try some new ways of studying and exam preparation.*
		Response B. *I am not sure what to expect, I have heard such varied outcomes about this exam.*	No. This view leaves you in a very unsure space with no real direction on how to move forward.	*I expect I will have to put in the time, effort, and energy to adequately prepare for this exam.*

(*continued*)

Table 2.1 Growth Mind-Set Activity (*continued*)

QUESTION TO ASK YOURSELF	YOUR RESPONSE: *TAKE A FEW MOMENTS AND WRITE IN YOUR ANSWERS HERE*	EXAMPLE RESPONSES:	DOES YOUR RESPONSE SUPPORT A GROWTH MIND-SET?	LET'S REFRAME!
		Response C: *I expect to do well on this exam.*	Yes. Go ahead and put your positive vibes out there! Get started on the execution of your study plan!	
Does studying for the exam feel like a chore or like an opportunity to develop real mastery of your field?		Response A: *Yes, it feels like just another thing on my already full plate.*	No. This perspective does not allow for the connection to future growth in your work.	*Studying for this exam will better prepare me for the challenging work I will face as a BCBA.*
		Response B: *It feels like a lot of work, but hopefully will pay off.*	Somewhat. This response acknowledges the work involved in studying, but also some future benefit.	*I enjoy opportunities to further develop my skills and, with focused effort, I can be prepared for this exam too!*
		Response C: *Studying for this exam will ensure I am on the cutting edge of my field.*	Yes. Let's get started studying!	

Making note of these thoughts and feelings and, if appropriate, challenging them or reframing them can help set yourself up for success. Cultivating a growth mind-set that appreciates how success is a function of hard work, sound strategies, and accurate feedback can be empowering and motivating and enhance your ability to study, learn, and pass the test. When you have a growth mind-set, you understand that you'll face setbacks and challenges, but that these are markers of progress and part of a process that will ultimately bring you success.

BEGIN BY TAKING A PRACTICE TEST

At the outset, it can be helpful to take the Practice Exam located in Chapter 12 to obtain baseline information on your readiness for the exam, identify any areas of weakness that will require additional focus, and get a sense of how the exam is organized and what to expect. Taking practice exams is also a helpful way to frontload the material that you will be learning more about as you make your way through each chapter. They add another learning format and are a great study tool that can be used to enhance the fluency in which you apply what you have learned to various situations. Practice tests require you to process and review data so you can continue to tailor and appropriately sequence your strategic study plan. Lastly, these practice opportunities can reduce anxiety as you become more familiar with the test format. With each administration of a practice exam, make note of the types of questions you struggled with (definition or application) and how long it took you to complete the exam.

DEVELOP AND STICK TO A STUDY SCHEDULE

As the title of this guide makes clear, it's not focused on helping you take the BCBA Exam—it's focused on helping you PASS! While we've strived to provide a study guide that is both comprehensive and succinct, there's no getting around the fact that there is a lot of content to master to be ready for the exam. As with any significant undertaking, doing so requires a solid plan. We recommend you create a study schedule with goals and target completion dates for each goal or section of the book.

While it's tempting to plan to study when you can squeeze it in, this rarely works well. There's likely always something else you would prefer to do when you have some time to study—which leads to procrastination. Research on procrastination among college students indicates its prevalence to be somewhere between 25% and 50% of students or even higher. So don't deceive yourself when it comes to delaying studying for the exam. Instead, be proactive and add studying on a consistent basis to your schedule just like any other task you need to complete. When you make regular appointments with yourself to study, you're more likely to do it. This will help you get into a rhythm which, in time, will become a habit.

To help yourself prevent procrastination and get into a rhythm, use self-management techniques to give yourself instant consequences that will thwart the consequences supporting procrastination. For instance, consider giving yourself a reward of some kind after you study as planned. It doesn't have to be huge, just something significant enough to facilitate your motivation. Take a minute now to think about how you might reward yourself each time you stick to your study schedule (e.g., time to watch your favorite show, check social media, or play a video game). Alternatively, you may find that you're more responsive to punishment. If so, consider fining yourself a dollar or two paid to your favorite charity each time you fail to study for the exam when you planned to.

In order to make the most of your study sessions, proactively remove all potential distractions from your environment. Paramount here is to turn off your smartphone, or at the very least turn off all notifications. Research has shown that continuously taking little breaks to respond to texts or check social media negatively impacts studying efficiency and effectiveness. Instead of continually being distracted by your phone, turn it off and then reward yourself with a certain amount of time on your phone after you've successfully completed your study session.

The first step in creating a study schedule is to determine what is realistic given your current responsibilities, commitments, and goals. Determine precisely when you can study each week. Write down the days and times in your calendar. If your schedule seems too full to fit in as many study sessions as you'd like or need, have a critical look at what is getting in the way. Are there activities you could take off your schedule to create more space for studying?

Once you've set a study schedule, do your best to adhere to it. You may find that you need to make adjustments to get it dialed in. That's okay. What's critical is that you're setting aside time on a regular basis to study and getting into a rhythm.

We generally recommend studying for the BCBA Exam from 10 to 20 hours a week for 3 to 4 months. The Essential Guide strategic planner (Table 2.2) aims for users to master one content area each week. You can modify the strategic planner to fit your time frame.

Table 2.2 Strategic Planner: Study Schedule & SMART Goals Worksheet

WEEK 1: __/__/__					
ACTIONS	SCORE	COMPLETION GOAL	COMPLETION DATE	REVIEW BY GOAL	DATE REVIEWED
Study Task Items ___ - ___	N/A	__/__/__	__/__/__	__/__/__ __/__/__ __/__/__	__/__/__ __/__/__ __/__/__
Practice Test #		__/__/__	__/__/__	__/__/__ __/__/__	__/__/__ __/__/__
WEEK 2: __/__/__					
ACTIONS	SCORE	COMPLETION GOAL	COMPLETION DATE	REVIEW BY GOAL	DATE REVIEWED
Study Task Items ___ - ___	N/A	__/__/__	__/__/__	__/__/__ __/__/__ __/__/__	__/__/__ __/__/__ __/__/__
Practice Test #		__/__/__	__/__/__	__/__/__ __/__/__	__/__/__ __/__/__
WEEK 3: __/__/__					
ACTIONS	SCORE	COMPLETION GOAL	COMPLETION DATE	REVIEW BY GOAL	DATE REVIEWED
Study Task Items ___ - ___	N/A	__/__/__	__/__/__	__/__/__ __/__/__ __/__/__	__/__/__ __/__/__ __/__/__
Practice Test #		__/__/__	__/__/__	__/__/__ __/__/__	__/__/__ __/__/__
WEEK 4: __/__/__					
ACTIONS	SCORE	COMPLETION GOAL	COMPLETION DATE	REVIEW BY GOAL	DATE REVIEWED
Study Task Items ___ - ___	N/A	__/__/__	__/__/__	__/__/__ __/__/__ __/__/__	__/__/__ __/__/__ __/__/__
Practice Test #		__/__/__	__/__/__	__/__/__ __/__/__	__/__/__ __/__/__
WEEK 5: __/__/__					
ACTIONS	SCORE	COMPLETION GOAL	COMPLETION DATE	REVIEW BY GOAL	DATE REVIEWED
Study Task Items ___ - ___	N/A	__/__/__	__/__/__	__/__/__ __/__/__ __/__/__	__/__/__ __/__/__ __/__/__
Practice Test #		__/__/__	__/__/__	__/__/__ __/__/__	__/__/__ __/__/__

(*continued*)

Table 2.2 Strategic Planner: Study Schedule & SMART Goals Worksheet (*continued*)

WEEK 6: __/__/__					
ACTIONS	SCORE	COMPLETION GOAL	COMPLETION DATE	REVIEW BY GOAL	DATE REVIEWED
Study Task Items ___ - ___	N/A	__/__/__	__/__/__	__/__/__ __/__/__ __/__/__	__/__/__ __/__/__ __/__/__
Practice Test #		__/__/__	__/__/__	__/__/__ __/__/__	__/__/__ __/__/__
WEEK 7: __/__/__					
ACTIONS	SCORE	COMPLETION GOAL	COMPLETION DATE	REVIEW BY GOAL	DATE REVIEWED
Study Task Items ___ - ___	N/A	__/__/__	__/__/__	__/__/__ __/__/__ __/__/__	__/__/__ __/__/__ __/__/__
Practice Test #		__/__/__	__/__/__	__/__/__ __/__/__	__/__/__ __/__/__
WEEK 8: __/__/__					
ACTIONS	SCORE	COMPLETION GOAL	COMPLETION DATE	REVIEW BY GOAL	DATE REVIEWED
Study Task Items ___ - ___	N/A	__/__/__	__/__/__	__/__/__ __/__/__ __/__/__	__/__/__ __/__/__ __/__/__
Practice Test #		__/__/__	__/__/__	__/__/__ __/__/__	__/__/__ __/__/__
WEEK 9: __/__/__					
ACTIONS	SCORE	COMPLETION GOAL	COMPLETION DATE	REVIEW BY GOAL	DATE REVIEWED
Study Task Items ___ - ___	N/A	__/__/__	__/__/__	__/__/__ __/__/__ __/__/__	__/__/__ __/__/__ __/__/__
Practice Test #		__/__/__	__/__/__	__/__/__ __/__/__	__/__/__ __/__/__
WEEK 10: __/__/__					
ACTIONS	SCORE	COMPLETION GOAL	COMPLETION DATE	REVIEW BY GOAL	DATE REVIEWED
Study Task Items ___ - ___	N/A	__/__/__	__/__/__	__/__/__ __/__/__ __/__/__	__/__/__ __/__/__ __/__/__
Practice Test #		__/__/__	__/__/__	__/__/__ __/__/__	__/__/__ __/__/__
WEEK 11: __/__/__					
ACTIONS	SCORE	COMPLETION GOAL	COMPLETION DATE	REVIEW BY GOAL	DATE REVIEWED
Study Task Items ___ - ___	N/A	__/__/__	__/__/__	__/__/__ __/__/__ __/__/__	__/__/__ __/__/__ __/__/__
Practice Test #		__/__/__	__/__/__	__/__/__ __/__/__	__/__/__ __/__/__

(*continued*)

Table 2.2 Strategic Planner: Study Schedule & SMART Goals Worksheet (*continued*)

WEEK 12: __/__/__					
ACTIONS	**SCORE**	**COMPLETION GOAL**	**COMPLETION DATE**	**REVIEW BY GOAL**	**DATE REVIEWED**
Study Task Items ___ - ___	N/A	__/__/__	__/__/__	__/__/__ __/__/__ __/__/__	__/__/__ __/__/__ __/__/__
Practice Test #		__/__/__	__/__/__	__/__/__ __/__/__	__/__/__ __/__/__
WEEK 13: __/__/__					
ACTIONS	**SCORE**	**COMPLETION GOAL**	**COMPLETION DATE**	**REVIEW BY GOAL**	**DATE REVIEWED**
Study Task Items ___ - ___	N/A	__/__/__	__/__/__	__/__/__ __/__/__ __/__/__	__/__/__ __/__/__ __/__/__
Practice Test #		__/__/__	__/__/__	__/__/__ __/__/__	__/__/__ __/__/__
WEEK 14: __/__/__					
ACTIONS	**SCORE**	**COMPLETION GOAL**	**COMPLETION DATE**	**REVIEW BY GOAL**	**DATE REVIEWED**
Study Task Items ___ - ___	N/A	__/__/__	__/__/__	__/__/__ __/__/__ __/__/__	__/__/__ __/__/__ __/__/__
Practice Test #		__/__/__	__/__/__	__/__/__ __/__/__	__/__/__ __/__/__
WEEK 15: __/__/__					
ACTIONS	**SCORE**	**COMPLETION GOAL**	**COMPLETION DATE**	**REVIEW BY GOAL**	**DATE REVIEWED**
Study Task Items ___ - ___	N/A	__/__/__	__/__/__	__/__/__ __/__/__ __/__/__	__/__/__ __/__/__ __/__/__
Practice Test #		__/__/__	__/__/__	__/__/__ __/__/__	__/__/__ __/__/__
WEEK 16: __/__/__					
ACTIONS	**SCORE**	**COMPLETION GOAL**	**COMPLETION DATE**	**REVIEW BY GOAL**	**DATE REVIEWED**
Study Task Items ___ - ___	N/A	__/__/__	__/__/__	__/__/__ __/__/__ __/__/__	__/__/__ __/__/__ __/__/__
Practice Test #		__/__/__	__/__/__	__/__/__ __/__/__	__/__/__ __/__/__

SMART, Specific, Measurable, Achievable, Relevant, and Time-bound.

USE DISTRIBUTED AND INTERLEAVED STUDYING

Spreading out your studying over time is significantly more effective than cramming. Research has documented how engaging with material to be learned multiple times and in different forms over a period of time engenders a distributed-practice effect that greatly enhances long-term retention of information. Moreover, studies have shown that incorporating longer, rather than shorter, lags between revisiting material to be learned is also more effective.

Using a study schedule will enable you to take advantage of the distributed-practice effect and prevent the human tendency to procrastinate and then steadily increase studying as the exam approaches, which is less effective. Instead, you want to study consistently in shorter, intensive study sessions over a longer period of time. It is especially helpful if you're able to study a section and then take some time away from it (e.g., 2 weeks) before reviewing it. This is known as spaced practice, and it's an incredibly effective approach to enhancing your ability to remember information for the test. When you review previously studied material just as you're about to start forgetting it, it strengthens memory and facilitates your ability to retain the information. This is why it's important to keep track of when you studied what in your study schedule.

Based on when you last studied the material, use your strategic planner to set dates to review the material again at increasingly spaced intervals in time. Specify target completion dates for each section of the book in the "Completion Goal" column of your study schedule, then note the date when you finished studying the section in the "Completion Date" column. Based on this date, set a goal to revisit this section of the book later (e.g., 2 weeks) and note it in the "Review by Goal" column. When you review the section, note the date in your study schedule in the "Date Reviewed" column. Aim to increase the lags between revisiting each section of the book over time.

A related effective technique is to alternate studying different kinds of items or content (i.e., interleaved practice). This is in contrast to focusing on one subtopic at a time (i.e., blocked studying). Given the interrelation between concepts and skills covered in different items within a section, alternating study of the items within a section and across sections will enable you to take advantage of interleaved studying. This is one of the greatest advantages of using a study schedule: It enables you to plan when you'll study certain items as well as when you'll revisit those items for maximum effect.

CREATE SMART GOALS

Creating clear goals that are actionable and effective can help you stick to your study schedule. At first, it can be difficult to know how long it will take you to learn all of the material you need to master to be successful on the exam; however, as you become more familiar with the material, you'll get a better sense of what's reasonable. It's also important to identify content areas that may require more time to achieve competency so that you can allot additional time to master those areas.

In your training as a behavior analyst, you've learned how important it is to set SMART goals for clients. Do the same for yourself. To develop clear and attainable goals, ensure each goal is **S**pecific, **M**easurable, **A**chievable, **R**elevant, and **T**ime-bound.

REINFORCING STUDYING BEHAVIOR

Studying for the BCBA Exam affords an excellent opportunity to practice self-management, which is the personal application of behavior change tactics to produce a desired change in behavior. You can use self-management strategies to develop study habits, achieve study tasks and goals, and prepare for the exam efficiently and effectively. Here are some ways you can incorporate self-management strategies into your approach to preparing for the exam:

- Schedule appointments with yourself to study accompanied by reminders on your phone.
- Dedicate a specific place to studying.

- When the time comes, sit down in your dedicated place and take out your study materials to create motivation to study.
- Remove all items from the environment that could distract you from studying.
- Reward yourself for studying with access to preferred activities and/or items, such as watching TV or using your phone.

Using your study planner as previously described will facilitate self-monitoring, which is another strategy to support helpful habits and goal acquisition.

GENERAL APPROACH TO PREPARING FOR THE EXAM

Your success on the BCBA Exam will be determined by a few factors that we recommend you keep in mind during every study session. While it isn't everything, your mastery of the content assessed by the exam is of paramount importance. While test-taking strategies can help a lot, they can only get you so far. At the end of the day, you're going to have to know your stuff! Think of this as the foundation upon which your success on the exam is built. This book will help you ensure your foundation is solid. Spend time reading and reflecting on each of the items in the guide to ensure that you truly understand and can apply all of the concepts and skills covered therein. While you may still occasionally encounter unfamiliar questions, a sound knowledge base will enable you to confidently figure out correct answers.

ACTIVE AND INTENSIVE STUDYING

All of the information you need to know to be successful on the BCBA Exam is contained in this book. However, as obvious as this may seem, simply reading through it will not prepare you for the exam. You need to study actively and intensively. In this section, we share the most effective study strategies based on psychologic and educational research.

As you study, you'll want to keep two different though equally important types of information processing in mind. Surface-level processing emphasizes operation learning and involves memorization and repetition, whereas deep-level processing emphasizes comprehension learning and involves relating what you're learning to the landscape of what you know and critical thinking and application. When actively and intensively studying for the exam, you'll want to aim to engage in both types of information processing.

Summarize It

Research has shown that creating summaries or brief structured outlines that synthesize and rephrase information facilitates focus and boosts learning and retention. While this book has condensed everything you need to know to pass the exam, it is still possible to summarize the information further and extract the gist of each section or item. To write a successful summary, identify the main points, key concepts, skills, and supporting details in a brief summary or an at-a-glance guide you can use to review and refresh your memory. Ensure your summary is accurate and captures the key information.

This book includes copious tables, figures, and memory aids (i.e., mnemonics) to help synthesize the information and make it easier to comprehend and remember. You can also use this approach as you study! Develop figures, tables, diagrams, concept maps, and mnemonics of your own to actively engage with the material and enhance your ability to remember it on the exam.

Create and Use Flashcards

The use of flashcards has also been shown to be an effective approach to studying. Actively read an item once through identifying the key concepts, skills, and supporting details. Then, when you read it a second time, develop a flashcard either using paper flashcards or a flashcard app for each key concept or skill contained therein. This is an exercise in summarizing what you've read and learned, so be concise (e.g., aim for 15 words or fewer) without sacrificing accuracy. You can then turn your flashcards into your own practice test using a flashcard app.

Employ the SAFMEDS (**S**ay **A**ll **F**ast **M**inute **E**very **D**ay **S**huffled) approach to learn the content more efficiently and effectively and increase your retention of the information (McDade et al., 1985; Potts et al., 1993). Here's how to do it:

- **S**ay—Look at the front of the flashcard and say the answer.
- **A**ll—Study all of the flashcards in your deck each time.
- **F**ast—Run through the entire deck fast to accelerate learning.
- **M**inute—Practice for 1 minute at a time or an alternate timed unit (e.g., 30 seconds or 2 minutes).
- **E**very **D**ay—Practice with the SAFMEDS procedure every day.
- **S**huffled—Shuffle the deck between practice sessions.

Test Yourself

Even though we provide you with sample questions for each section and a comprehensive practice exam, don't let this deter you from coming up with your own questions and quizzes based on the material. In fact, there's research to suggest that you'll perform optimally if you use this book to develop your own study materials and practice tests. After studying a section, write out your own set of exam questions along with complete answers for those questions. If you have a study buddy, quiz each other using your custom questions. Similarly, regularly use active recall as you study. Periodically, put away your study materials and simply talk yourself through or write down what you've been studying.

Teach It to Others

Teach the information to others. If you have a study buddy or study group, arrange to take turns teaching the material to one another. However, if you don't have others to teach it to, pretend you're the instructor and record yourself teaching the material—with or without notes or the book. Then watch your recording. If you can provide a clear and understandable description of the concept or skill—complete with your own original examples—it's safe to say you're well on your way to mastering it! If you're not keen on recording yourself, teach the material aloud without recording it.

Use Mental Imagery and Mnemonics

The use of mental imagery is one of the oldest and most well-studied learning techniques. It is a powerful technique that has been shown to significantly boost learning and retention. Using mnemonics in the form of an acronym, rhyme, song, phrase, image, or sentence is one of the most popular mental imagery tools used to recall information or an order of operations. For example, many use the phrase "Please excuse my dear aunt Sally," and the acronym PEMDAS to remember the order of math operations or the name ROY G. BIV to recall the spectrum of colors. This book includes some mnemonics you can use, but we encourage you to come up with your own as well. The process of developing a mnemonic will increase your ability to remember it and the information it represents. While the use of mnemonics is likely the most familiar, creating simple and clear mental images of information as you study is also a powerfully effective learning technique. For some, creating drawings to represent the information may also prove effective.

Take Practice Tests

A large body of research has shown that regularly taking practice tests is one of the most effective techniques for improving learning and enhancing retention. This is because repeated testing fosters transfer of learning and generates testing effects that change how you encode and mentally organize information in ways that boost retention and test performance.

This book includes practice questions at the end of each chapter as well as a full practice exam consisting of 185 questions. Practice testing also includes any approaches you use while quizzing yourself, such as using physical or virtual flashcards or covering information and forcing yourself to recall it before looking. After you take a practice test, it's important for you to actively study the questions you missed. Dig into the question and answer to determine why you responded incorrectly. Was it because you didn't possess the knowledge needed to provide a correct response? If so, identify and actively study the content that will enable you to answer this question and similar questions correctly. Was it because you didn't read the question and/or response options carefully enough? If so, note what you could have done differently and aim to avoid this mistake in the future.

Diversify

As outstanding as this book is, don't solely rely on it as you prepare for the exam. It can be beneficial to have the information repeated and presented in different terminology and modes. As you begin studying a section of the guide, gather other materials on the topic from classes or books to review as well. Have a look online to see if there are podcasts you can listen to and videos you can watch to experience the information presented in a different mode.

Active and Close Reading

In everyday life, we often read rapidly and skim texts for the gist or general idea. This usually works just fine when reading emails, instructions, news stories, and social media posts, but it doesn't work well when you're studying for or taking an exam. In order to really learn the information presented in this book, you'll need to actively engage with the content as you read it and make it meaningful to you. Reading actively will significantly increase your understanding and retention of what you read.

Highlight and Underline

Highlighting and underlining are not the highest utility study techniques; however, students are more likely to remember what they highlighted or underlined when studying. In order to select what to highlight or underline, a reader has to consider the text carefully and determine what is most important. Once this has been determined, the isolated and emphasized text stands out and facilitates retention.

Research indicates that the key to using highlighting and underlining effectively is the degree to which this practice is engaged in actively and accurately. Consequently, to be effective, carefully consider what you're reading and only highlight or underline the most important points. If you overdo it or emphasize the wrong things, it will defeat the purpose. Some people prefer to read a printed copy so that they can physically write notes, thoughts, connections, and questions on the text, as well as highlight and underline; however, for others who are accustomed to reading on a computer, using these same techniques in a digital format also works just fine. Consider which format works best for you and go with it!

Read With Pauses

It's helpful to take periodic breaks to reflect on what you just read, such as at the end of a sentence, paragraph, or table. When you pause, restate or summarize what you just read aloud or in your mind. Some find it helpful to write a short note or bullet points. Next, skim over what you just processed to ensure you got it right and didn't leave out any important details. If you overlooked something, note it, and then resume reading. This practice will significantly improve both your retention and understanding of what you've read.

Reread

Rereading is one of the most popular study techniques, and there is research to support its utility for improving learning and information retention. It's also easy to employ—simply read sections of text multiple times. Rereading can be *massed* (i.e., repeatedly reading a section of text without a break) or *spaced* (allowing some time to pass between readings). Since spaced rereading appears to be more effective than massed rereading, it's best to allow a few days to pass before rereading the same material. When it comes to massed rereading, research indicates that it's the second time one reads something that is most helpful, so there's likely little benefit to be had from successively rereading the same material more than twice.

Apply It to Your Experiences

As you read, find ways to apply what you're reviewing or learning to your lived experience. Apply the concepts to your own life and come up with your own examples. The helpful thing about studying for the BCBA Exam is that it's all about behavior, which is ubiquitous, so it shouldn't be too difficult to think of numerous examples and applications. You'll want to strive to make connections between what you're reading about and other concepts and skills. This strengthens your overall understanding of the discipline and aids in retention.

Read Like a Detective

Exams call for "close reading." This means paying careful attention to and considering every word of a question and the response options. When reading closely, the reader also carefully attends to syntax or the arrangement of words and phrases and the order in which they appear. You're like a detective, focusing on each detail to accurately determine the precise meaning of each question and response option. Practice this skill as you're reading the guide and taking practice tests until it becomes habitual. The authors have made every effort to be as clear and as succinct as possible, which will require you to practice this form of close reading while working your way through the book.

Think Like a Detective

You'll also want to practice slow and careful thinking. Don't rush it. Reading closely will help you slow down and really consider each concept presented in the guide and on practice tests. Again, imagine you're a detective critically and analytically examining each detail of a case. Stay sharp and clear and don't let anything get by you. It's careful attention to detail coupled with lucid, logical thinking that will help you crack it every time!

TEST-TAKING STRATEGIES

If you've made it this far in your education, chances are you've studied for and taken a number of high-stakes standardized tests and learned the strategies one should always employ on such tests. In the event these strategies are rusty or unfamiliar, we'll briefly review the most helpful techniques you can use to boost your score.

READ QUESTIONS FULLY AND CAREFULLY

The close reading skills you've practiced while studying will pay off when taking tests—both practice tests and the real thing. This is important because misreading and, as a result, misinterpreting questions is the most common error test takers make on multiple-choice tests. In our everyday lives, we often skim texts without issue; however, when it comes to tests, carefully reading the full question before answering is critical. The test aims to test your knowledge of concepts and skills *and* your ability to comprehend questions about what you know. Use the following approach to avoid this all-too-common mistake:

- *Step 1:* Obscure the answers with a piece of paper or your hand before reading the question.
- *Step 2:* Read the question carefully, then ask yourself: "What is this question getting at? What is it asking?" Don't make hasty assumptions. Really think about it.

- *Step 3:* Be on the lookout for key words and phrases for insight into what the question is about and the body of knowledge you'll need to draw upon to answer it correctly. Carefully attend to adjectives and nouns that describe terms or words you may be less familiar with or do not know. Substituting a difficult word with a synonym that you're more familiar with may increase your comprehension of the question. Analyze words' prefixes and suffixes to assist your understanding and add context.
- *Step 4:* Questions often include information that is irrelevant and intended to lead you astray from the correct answer—these are called "distractors." Don't fall for it! Take time to carefully consider and define what the question is asking and the information you need to focus on to answer it correctly.
- *Step 5:* Rephrase the question to yourself in a way that makes sense to you. Put it in your own words and, if relevant, come up with an example.
- *Step 6:* Consider what you know about the topic the question is probing. Ask yourself: "What are the key ideas or components of this concept or skill? What would I say if I had to briefly explain what this is about?" Write down your thoughts on a piece of paper. This process facilitates access to your long-term memory. You'll likely be surprised to find that you know and/or remember more about a topic than you thought!
- *Step 7:* Before you look at the possible answers, formulate a potential response to the question.
- *Step 8:* Next, carefully and critically review the possible answers. Determine precisely why each possible answer is correct or incorrect. Eliminate the response options you're certain are wrong. Be suspicious of answer choices with words like *never*, *always*, *must*, and *all* as they're usually wrong. If it's a really difficult question and you're struggling to eliminate answers, take a little time to review each answer choice again. For each choice, consider whether it offers a satisfactory answer to the question independently of the other choices. Try to narrow it down to two answers.
- *Step 9:* Now, revisit step 4 for just these two answers. Ask yourself what you know about this subject.
- *Step 10:* Select the best answer from the two choices. If you're unable to discern which of the two is best and are forced to guess, at least you've significantly improved your odds and likely given yourself a 50/50 chance of getting it right.

HOW TO SELECT THE CORRECT ANSWER WHEN MULTIPLE ANSWERS SEEM CORRECT

Avoid trying to talk yourself into making an answer true. If a response option does not fully address the question, is only somewhat true, relies on significant assumptions that are not obvious, or is true only under certain narrowly defined conditions, it's likely the wrong choice. It's helpful to apply your practical experience when evaluating possible answers, but you should avoid dreaming up obscure scenarios to talk yourself into a certain answer. Most of the time, when test takers think they're dealing with a trick question, they're actually just reading too much into it or have yet to develop an accurate understanding of the question.

THREE TRUTHS AND A LIE

Sometimes questions require test takers to select the response that is *false* or *not correct*. Questions structured in this way can be tricky because they flip the logic typically used on multiple-choice tests. That is, instead of identifying the most correct response out of a set of incorrect responses, the test taker is tasked with identifying the incorrect response out of a set of correct responses. When you encounter questions organized in this way, recall the old party game Three Truths and a Lie and remember that you've got to figure out which statement is false.

HOW TO INTERPRET UNFAMILIAR QUESTIONS

If you've used this book, you'll be prepared to answer all of the questions on the exam. However, you may encounter some questions that, at first blush, make you feel unprepared to answer. This is because the test makers occasionally present the information in an uncommon or indirect manner that test takers are not used to, or they'll come at a concept from an unfamiliar or uncommon angle. Consequently, you'll need to be prepared to interpret parts of the question in order to answer it correctly. Slow down and work your way through the question piece by piece. Making sense of smaller pieces of the question will gradually build your understanding of the whole question. Stay calm and use the multiple-choice test-taking strategies detailed earlier to select the correct answer. Remember: On occasion, information presented in previous questions can help you answer subsequent questions. This is yet another reason to read and think carefully about each question!

MAKE PREDICTIONS

We've already discussed the importance of reading slowly and carefully. Another advantage of this technique is that it enables your mind to focus on and begin to process the information in the question. This is a great time to predict what the correct answer will be before you look at the answer choices. With your prediction in mind, look over the answer choices provided. If your prediction is among the possible answer choices, it's quite likely that it is the correct answer. However, you should still read and think critically about the other answer choices before selecting the choice that matches your prediction.

HOLD A KNOCKOUT TOURNAMENT

In a knockout tournament, individuals or teams play against one another and the loser of each match-up is eliminated from the tournament. As you read through the possible answer choices to a question, from first to last, mentally note whether or not an answer strikes you as correct and begin to construct a rank order in your mind of best to worst possible answers. Hold the first answer choice that seems correct in your mind to benchmark the other answer choices against. The answer is the current leader, but it must beat out all the other possible answers to emerge victorious. If it loses to a stronger contender, that answer becomes the new standard to beat. Continue this process until one answer choice is crowned tournament champion!

LOOK OUT FOR FACT TRAPS

A fact trap is an answer choice that is factually accurate, but nevertheless incorrect because it (a) fails to answer the question or (b) fails to answer the question better than another correct answer choice. Sometimes this is because the response contains both correct and incorrect information. Fact traps are some of the most persuasive and tempting wrong answers, so be especially careful of these! To successfully navigate fact traps, continually measure seemingly correct answer choices against what the question is asking. Remember: The correct answer is the answer that best answers the question.

DON'T GET TOO FAMILIAR

Test takers often succumb to familiarity traps when they don't understand a question very well and/or they don't know some of the words or concepts included in the question. As a result, the test taker selects an answer choice with a word or concept they do know just because it's familiar—but nevertheless wrong. Instead of immediately selecting the answer choice that is the most familiar, evaluate it critically. Consider whether or not it is accurate and the best answer to the question. If it's not, eliminate it. You may still not know the answer to the question, but at least you've improved your odds of guessing correctly. See the previous section on *How to Interpret Unfamiliar Questions.*

Occasionally test developers will exactly duplicate a piece of a question in an answer choice. Be careful with answer choices like this! While it could be true, more often than not it's a trap designed to lure you in by its air of familiarity. Correct answers usually summarize, paraphrase, or briefly reference aspects of the question rather than simply repeating it.

ELIMINATE RESPONSES

After carefully considering the question and the answer choices, eliminate answer choices that you're certain are incorrect or extremely unlikely. You should also eliminate responses that are synonymous (e.g., "multielement design" and "alternating treatments design"); if the two responses are, in effect, the same, one of them can't be correct and the other incorrect, so they both must be incorrect. Simply eliminating answer choices down to two possible answer choices greatly increases your odds of answering the question correctly—even if you have to guess! If, after reviewing all of the answer choices carefully, they all seem wrong, go back over them again and carefully consider each one. Test takers often discover something they missed on a second pass.

BEWARE THE HEDGE

Be on the lookout for hedge terms! See Table 2.3.

Table 2.3 Hedge Terms

not	usually	likely	will often
if	almost	may	sometimes
none	generally	can	often
all	except	mostly	rarely

Test developers often use these words to make a question more challenging since, if you fail to attend to the hedge word or phrase, you'll likely select an incorrect answer. Hedge phrases are also used to make statements all-encompassing and without exceptions. Answer choices with decisive words like *always* and *exactly* are often incorrect for this reason.

DON'T OVERTHINK IT

Sometimes test takers read too much into questions when they would be better off accepting the situation presented in a problem at face value. It's best to use your common sense and to refrain from engaging in mental gymnastics to justify an answer choice for a question. If you find yourself in the air performing acrobatic logic, draw on your common sense to bring yourself back down to earth, eliminate the answer choice, and move on. Remind yourself that the test addresses common skills and concepts behaviorists need to know to do their job well—not sit in a cafe theorizing. If your answer is getting too complicated, it's probably because you've overlooked something in the question or haven't thought about it carefully enough.

NEW INFORMATION HAS COME TO LIGHT

Sometimes test developers include new information in an answer choice. This should make you suspicious. Questions typically contain everything you need to know to answer them correctly, though you may need to engage in some additional reasoning. As such, responses that include new information are often incorrect; look suspiciously at them and, if warranted, eliminate.

MIND THE CURVE

Pay close attention when words or phrases are used that indicate changes in thought or meaning. *But* is the reversal word you'll come across most frequently, but stay alert for other reversal words and phrases, like those appearing in Table 2.4.

Table 2.4 Reversal Words and Phrases

however	although
on the other hand	nevertheless
even though	regardless of
in spite of	despite

RESPONSE CHOICE GROUPS

This is a lesser-known test-taking technique, but one that often pays dividends. A response choice group is a set of two or three answer choices that are constructed in a very similar manner, but usually mean nearly the opposite. Sometimes the set of answer choices provided contains two or more answer choices that are opposites or parallels; typically, one of these answers is correct. For example, suppose a set contains a response that states an intervention increases a behavior as well as responses that indicate that an intervention decreases a behavior or a different intervention increases a behavior. When you're presented with a response choice group such as this, the correct answer is usually one of the answers in the group—not an answer choice that does not fit how the response choice group has constructed the choices. Consequently, you can often eliminate answers outside of the response choice group and focus on determining which answer in the group is the correct answer.

GO WITH YOUR FIRST GUESS—IF YOU REALLY HAVE TO GUESS

If you've followed this book's test prep plan, it's unlikely that you'll need to guess or go with a hunch on what the correct answer is. Nevertheless, in the event that you find yourself in this situation, you should go with your first hunch as it's most likely to be correct. If you don't have a solid, well thought out reason to change answers, it's best to stick with your first guess. That said, if you realize that you misread the question or recall helpful information from a previous question that offers insights into which is the correct answer, by all means change your answer.

CHECK YOUR WORK

We know you've heard this since you were in elementary school, but that doesn't make it any less true or important. If you have time, look back over your test to ensure you've provided an answer to every question and not made any careless mistakes. It can be hard to force yourself to look back over every question one more time when you just want to be finished, but it'll be worth it if you catch mistakes or incorrect answers!

TIME MANAGEMENT

The practice exam in this book will help you get a feel for the pace you'll need to keep to successfully finish the test in time. You should work on your timing and endeavor to speed up your pace without sacrificing accuracy. Honing your ability to identify and eliminate incorrect answers is one of the best ways to quicken your pace. Remember—there's no advantage to finishing early. Pace yourself and use the time you've been given to read and think carefully.

STAY CALM: COPING WITH TEST ANXIETY

Anxiety is the tense emotional state that occurs when you can't predict the outcome of a situation or guarantee that the outcome will be to your liking. It's no wonder then that tests are one of the most common sources of performance anxiety. Fortunately, there are several strategies you can use to overcome it. Before we consider behavioral and psychologic strategies, we should note the importance of simply feeling well prepared and confident. Our aim in this guide is to provide you with a game plan and all of the information you'll need to be successful on the exam. Mastering the content of the exam and feeling like you're ready to ace it will go a long way toward staving off test-taking jitters.

However, even when very well prepared, some test takers continue to experience high levels of stress and performance anxiety. This can tax their cognitive faculties and ability to regulate negative emotions, which in turn impacts their performance. Anxiety can also lead to avoidance behaviors that prevent students from studying; in some cases, it could even prevent them from taking the exam. The good news is that learning and practicing skills to manage worried thoughts and regulate negative emotions significantly improves performance on tests.

Managing Worries

Anytime you take a test, there's a chance that you'll fail to perform well. The possibility of failure can generate worried thoughts, which is the cognitive aspect of test anxiety. Sometimes we're aware of our concerns, but more often than not our worries are running in the background, draining our mental energy and impinging on our focus and ability to think.

Get to know your anxiety. How do you experience it? Where do you feel it in your body? Knowing how you experience anxiety will help you recognize the feelings early—before they feel overwhelming. Simply acknowledging that you are worried and writing about your concerns can assuage worries and facilitate emotion regulation. Research has shown that thinking and writing about your anxiety before taking tests can reduce the symptoms of anxiety and engender a sense of control that leads to improved performance on exams.

These worries can also stem from the stories we tell ourselves. As human beings, we have an inner world made up of our thoughts and feelings. We all have an inner voice that's talking to us all the time. It's important to pay attention to how you talk to yourself because it influences how you feel and what you do. Self-talk can be helpful and positive or unhelpful and negative. Embracing a narrative that one is not good at tests or fails tests due to an inability to effectively cope with the associated stress and anxiety can become a self-fulfilling prophecy. Instead, talk to yourself like you would to a good friend or someone you love. Say encouraging and comforting things to yourself when you're feeling anxious and stressed. Show yourself compassion and remind yourself that you're not alone.

Regulating Negative Emotions

Since our thoughts and emotions are tightly connected, worried thoughts can generate negative emotions and stress, which register in the body as physiologic arousal (e.g., a racing heart, dizziness, sweating, stomachache). For some people, these signs of stress are seen as an indication that they're not going to perform well, which feeds into their already worried mind.

To counteract this, the test taker can reframe their physiologic arousal as energizing and facilitative of performance rather than as harmful. Rather than interpreting the signs of stress as harbingers of imminent doom, it helps to view them as the body and mind gearing up for a challenge in order to be successful. This is an example of a broader strategy of talking back to one's worries and replacing irrational, worried thoughts with more rational, calming thoughts.

The key is to get ahead of anxiety by proactively doing things that will keep it at a manageable level, like practicing deep breathing and mindfulness and getting regular exercise. Regularly practicing breathing techniques has been shown to lower stress and anxiety and promote a sense of well-being and relaxation. Try this. Take a deep breath through your nose, counting to 3 or 4 in your mind while you're inhaling. Then, exhale more slowly through pressed lips while you count to 5 or 8. Do this for 2 minutes. You can also try holding your breath for a count of 4 or 7 before exhaling.

It's important to remember that worrying isn't necessarily bad. Moderate, manageable levels of anxiety can increase performance because it provides energy to face and overcome challenges. Fear that you might fail a test can be highly motivating and help you stay focused on studying when other activities seem more enjoyable. Anxiety becomes a problem when it gets so high that it feels overwhelming and lowers performance. The key is to manage your level of anxiety and stress so that it facilitates rather than harms your performance.

PRIOR TO THE EXAM

In addition to studying consistently using this book, there are a number of things you can do to enhance your performance on test day.

- Take time to plan out your test-taking day. What time will you wake up? Where is the testing location? How will you get there? How much time do you need to get there? What do you need to bring with you?
- Sound sleep is one of the most important things you can do to be at your best on test day. Stick to your study schedule so that you're not up late at night cramming the week before the test. Instead, build in several rest days prior to test day during which you'll allow all of your hard work to settle in.
- Like sleep, hydration is critical. Drink plenty of water while you study and, especially, in the days leading up to the test. Coupling hydration with sleep will enhance your mental acuity and enable you to perform optimally on the exam.
- Eat a balanced meal of carbohydrates and proteins before you take the test. This will give you endurance and cognitive energy to perform your best.

YOU'VE GOT THIS!

We're here to tell you that you have every reason to be optimistic about your potential for success. Preparing for the exam will have its challenges, but this book contains everything you need to be successful.

USING THIS BOOK

The BCBA Exam is challenging. Fortunately, you're using the best study guide available to prepare. It explains the Test Content Outline (TCO) Tasks comprehensively but concisely and provides practice opportunities throughout and a full mock exam. The chapters of the book cover all essential content areas of the certification exam. Each content area chapter begins with coverage of the relevant TCO Tasks and concludes with practice questions to assess and support content uptake. A brief overview of the chapters to follow are presented in the text that follows.

CHAPTER 3: BEHAVIORISM AND PHILOSOPHICAL FOUNDATIONS

The field of applied behavior analysis (ABA) is grounded in a robust philosophical and scientific framework that distinguishes it from other approaches to behavioral research, defines its focus and goals, and informs its approach to analyzing and intervening in behavior. Familiarity with the field's scientific and philosophical foundation facilitates the behavior analyst's understanding of the interrelations among the discipline's defining elements and its highly specific use of key terms, concepts, and principles. To that end, Chapter 3 offers a clear and concise guide to

ABA's conceptual foundations, defining dimensions, and overall aims. This includes helpful explanations of the philosophical assumptions underlying the science and what distinguishes the perspective of radical behaviorism from other approaches to understanding behavior. In this chapter, you'll also learn about ABA's manifestations as both a science and a practice, including how to tell the difference between behaviorism, experimental analysis of behavior, ABA, and practice guided by the science of behavior analysis. It sounds like a lot, but don't worry—you'll find handy mnemonic aids to help you remember the content covered.

CHAPTER 4: CONCEPTS AND PRINCIPLES

As a professional applying science to analyze and intervene in behavior, the behavior analyst must understand, utilize, and be able to clearly communicate a variety of concepts, technical terms, and principles that define behavior and the environmental events that govern it. Chapter 4 covers the fundamental elements of the scientific analysis of behavior, specific concepts derived from ABA, basic skills, and key terminology and principles employed by behavior analysts. This includes a description of what makes respondent and operant behavior functionally distinct, and a clear illustration of how the environment influences each type of behavior in the form of respondent and operant conditioning. This chapter also reviews positive and negative reinforcement and punishment, the various schedules of reinforcement, stimulus control, and other processes central to behavior analysis. As you'll find, easy-to-remember examples that facilitate conceptual clarity, comprehension, and retention are provided throughout.

CHAPTER 5: MEASUREMENT, DATA DISPLAY, AND INTERPRETATION

In your graduate training, you've learned how to select behaviors for intervention and then develop and deliver interventions that foster quantifiable alterations and improvements in clients' lives. BCBAs utilize systematic measurement to document behavioral changes, monitor the progress of interventions, and communicate results to key stakeholders. As such, selecting, defining, and measuring behavior and displaying data are critical skills integral to the competent practice of ABA. Chapter 5 provides a clear and concise review of the current TCO Tasks focused on measurement, data display, and interpretation. It provides guidance on developing well-written operational definitions of behavior and distinguishing among different types of behavioral assessment measures. You'll also find reviews of the various dimensions of behavioral measurement (e.g., occurrence, temporal), as well as methods for designing and implementing sampling procedures, evaluating the validity and reliability of measurement procedures, and selecting a measurement system.

CHAPTER 6: EXPERIMENTAL DESIGN

As applied behavior scientists, behavior analysts design, conduct, and evaluate experiments to analyze the effects of their interventions and determine the factors driving behavior change. Designing single-subject experiments that identify the functions of behavior and document change is a highly valued skill that distinguishes the BCBA from other behavioral health professionals. As such, experimental design was an important component of your training program. Chapter 6 revisits the essential aspects of experimental design that may be covered on the BCBA Exam, including the distinction between dependent and independent variables, internal and external validity, and the defining features, advantages, and use of single-subject experimental designs.

CHAPTER 7: ETHICS

Behavior analysts study human behavior with the aim of modifying it. Consider the implications of this. While the desire for agency and autonomy is universal, behavior analysts apply behavioral science to influence the choices their clients make. Exercising influence over another person's behavior carries significant ethical consequences. Recognizing this, the Behavior Analyst Certification Board® (BACB®) requires that BCBAs understand and adhere to the Ethics Code for Behavior Analysts (BACB, 2020/2024) in practice. Chapter 7 reviews the core principles underlying the Code and delves into critical standards related to the behavior analyst's responsibility as a professional, responsibility in practice, responsibility to clients and stakeholders, responsibility to supervisees and trainees, responsibility in public statements, and responsibility in research.

CHAPTER 8: BEHAVIOR ASSESSMENT

Systematically assessing clients' behavior and interpreting the data gathered are integral skills of the behavior analyst. Chapter 8 delves into the comprehensive process of behavior assessment, starting with the essential records review. It covers the methods for conducting thorough assessments of preference, skill strengths and deficits, and problem behaviors. In addition, the chapter outlines criteria for determining the need for behavior analytic services and explores the common functions of problem behavior. Emphasizing the importance of identifying socially significant behaviors as targets for change, this chapter provides the critical questions and criteria behavior analysts use to assess the social significance of potential target behaviors and establish meaningful behavior-change goals.

CHAPTER 9: BEHAVIOR-CHANGE PROCEDURES

Behavior analysts are recognized as professionals that possess specialized expertise in designing and implementing behavior-change procedures. Chapter 9 covers the effective and efficient application of these procedures, which are essential for helping clients acquire new skills, refine existing ones, and maintain behavior changes. Given the importance and breadth of this domain, a comprehensive review is provided of key behavior-change procedures, including reinforcement strategies, differential reinforcement, and time-based schedules. It will also review procedures for promoting generalization and maintaining behavior change. Clear examples that foster understanding and retention are provided throughout.

CHAPTER 10: SELECTING AND IMPLEMENTING INTERVENTIONS

Behavior analysts carefully select and implement interventions to maximize their effectiveness. Chapter 10 reviews the various strategies involved in this process, such as developing intervention goals in observable and measurable terms and recommending interventions based on assessment results, scientific evidence, and client preferences. It also addresses essential factors for successful intervention implementation, including planning for and mitigating unwanted effects of reinforcement, extinction, and punishment procedures, as well as making data-based decisions about procedural integrity and intervention effectiveness. Furthermore, the chapter highlights the importance of selecting socially valid alternative behaviors and collaborating with others to support and enhance client services, ensuring comprehensive and effective behavior change.

CHAPTER 11: PERSONNEL SUPERVISION AND MANAGEMENT

Behavior analysts often undertake supervisory roles to ensure the effective implementation of behavior-analytic services and to support the professional growth of their supervisees. Chapter 11 explores the multifaceted nature of behavior-analytic supervision. It reviews the benefits of using behavior-analytic supervision, strategies for establishing effective supervisory relationships, culturally responsive performance management procedures, and function-based approaches to assess and improve supervisee behavior. Emphasizing the importance of data-based decision-making, this chapter also provides guidance on evaluating the efficacy of supervisory practices to ensure continuous improvement and optimal outcomes.

CHAPTER 12: PRACTICE EXAM

Test your knowledge and skills with a full-length practice exam consisting of 185 questions! The answer to each question, along with an explanation, is provided in Chapter 13.

CHAPTER 14: AFTER THE EXAM

In this final chapter, we provide valuable information about the many professional development resources available to behavior analysts. Chapter 11 also includes helpful tips for acquiring your first job as a professional behavior analyst and recommendations for those who have tried but have not yet passed the exam. Regardless of where you stand after taking the exam, there will be content here that is relevant to you!

COMMON NOTATIONS

Throughout the book, notations will be used in explanations of various concepts, examples, and so on. Table 2.5 can serve as a helpful reference for the notations used and their associated meanings. It is recommended that you familiarize yourself with these commonly used notations (from the behavior analytic literature) and refer back to the table as needed.

Table 2.5 Notations Used Throughout the Book

Notation	Meaning
S	Stimulus
R	Response
US	Unconditioned stimulus
UR	Unconditioned response
CS	Conditioned stimulus
CR	Conditioned response
S^{R+}	Unconditioned positive reinforcer
S^{r+}	Conditioned positive reinforcer
S^{R-}	Unconditioned negative reinforcer
S^{r-}	Conditioned negative reinforcer
S^{P+}	Unconditioned positive punisher
S^{p+}	Conditioned positive punisher
S^{P-}	Unconditioned negative punisher
S^{p-}	Conditioned negative punisher
S^{D}	Discriminative stimulus ("s - dee")
S^{Δ}	Stimulus delta ("s - delta")

CONCLUSION

In this chapter, we shared guidance on strategies that will help maximally prepare you for the BCBA Exam, including how to master the content tested by the exam and enhance your test-taking skills. Mastering the content on the exam requires a considerable amount of active and intensive studying, so this chapter described numerous evidence-based recommendations for studying. Since time management and planning are key when preparing for an exam like this, this chapter shared guidance on setting goals and creating a study schedule coupled with a strategic plan worksheet for planning weekly study sessions and tracking progress on your goals.

To help you optimize your performance on the exam, this chapter also taught multiple-choice test-taking strategies and shared tips on coping with test anxiety and preparing for exam day.

REFERENCE

Behavior Analyst Certification Board. (2024). *Ethics code for behavior analysts.* https://www.bacb.com/wp-content/uploads/2022/01/Ethics-Code-for-Behavior-Analysts-240830-a.pdf (Original work published 2020).

BIBLIOGRAPHY

Bednall, T. C., & Kehoe, E. J. (2011). Effects of self-regulatory instructional aids on self-directed study. *Instructional Science, 39*, 205–226. https://doi.org/10.1007/s11251-009-9125-6

Benjamin, A. S., & Tullis, J. (2010). What makes distributed practice effective? *Cognitive Psychology, 61*(3), 228–247. https://doi.org/10.1016/j.cogpsych.2010.05.004

Blanchard, J., & Mikkelson, V. (1987). Underlining performance outcomes in expository text. *The Journal of Educational Research, 80*(4), 197–201. https://www.jstor.org/stable/40539623

Bretzing, B. H., & Kulhavy, R. W. (1979). Notetaking and depth of processing. *Contemporary Educational Psychology, 4*(2), 145–153. https://doi.org/10.1016/0361-476X(79)90069-9

Bromage, B. K., & Mayer, R. E. (1986). Quantitative and qualitative effects of repetition on learning from technical text. *Journal of Educational Psychology, 78*(4), 271–278. https://doi.org/10.1037/0022-0663.78.4.271

Brooks, L. W., Dansereau, D. F., Holley, C. D., & Spurlin, J. E. (1983). Generation of descriptive text headings. *Contemporary Educational Psychology, 8*(2), 103–108. https://doi.org/10.1016/0361-476X(83)90001-2

Butler, A. C. (2010). Repeated testing produces superior transfer of learning relative to repeated studying. *Journal of Experimental Psychology: Learning, Memory, and Cognition, 36*(5), 1118–1133. https://doi.org/10.1037/a0019902

Cepeda, N. J., Pashler, H., Vul, E., Wixted, J. T., & Rohrer, D. (2006). Distributed practice in verbal recall tasks: A review and quantitative synthesis. *Psychological Bulletin, 132*(3), 354–380. https://doi.org/10.1037/0033-2909.132.3.354

Delaney, P. F., Verkoeijen, P. P., & Spirgel, A. (2010). Spacing and testing effects: A deeply critical, lengthy, and at times discursive review of the literature. *Psychology of Learning and Motivation, 53*, 63–147. https://doi.org/10.1016/S0079-7421(10)53003-2

Doctorow, M., Wittrock, M. C., & Marks, C. (1978). Generative processes in reading comprehension. *Journal of Educational Psychology, 70*(2), 109–118. https://doi.org/10.1037/0022-0663.70.2.109

Dunlosky, J., Rawson, K. A., Marsh, E. J., Nathan, M. J., & Willingham, D. T. (2013). Improving students' learning with effective learning techniques: Promising directions from cognitive and educational psychology. *Psychological Science in the Public Interest, 14*(1), 4–58. https://doi.org/10.1177/1529100612453266

Fritz, C. O., Morris, P. E., Acton, M., Voelkel, A. R., & Etkind, R. (2007). Comparing and combining retrieval practice and the keyword mnemonic for foreign vocabulary learning. *Applied Cognitive Psychology, 21*(4), 499–526. https://doi.org/10.1002/acp.1287

Hartley, J., Bartlett, S., & Branthwaite, A. (1980). Underlining can make a difference—Sometimes. *The Journal of Educational Research, 73*(4), 218–224. https://www.jstor.org/stable/27539753

Jamieson, J. P., Mendes, W. B., & Nock, M. K. (2013). Improving acute stress responses: The power of reappraisal. *Current Directions in Psychological Science, 22*(1), 51–56. https://doi.org/10.1177/0963721412461500

Johnson, L. L. (1988). Effects of underlining textbook sentences on passage and sentence retention. *Literacy Research and Instruction, 28*(1), 18–32. https://doi.org/10.1080/19388078809557955

Kang, S. H., & Pashler, H. (2012). Learning painting styles: Spacing is advantageous when it promotes discriminative contrast. *Applied Cognitive Psychology, 26*(1), 97–103. https://doi.org/10.1002/acp.1801

Kiewra, K. A., Mayer, R. E., Christensen, M., Kim, S. I., & Risch, N. (1991). Effects of repetition on recall and note-taking: Strategies for learning from lectures. *Journal of Educational Psychology, 83*(1), 120–123. https://doi.org/10.1037/0022-0663.83.1.120

Leutner, D., Leopold, C., & Sumfleth, E. (2009). Cognitive load and science text comprehension: Effects of drawing and mentally imagining text content. *Computers in Human Behavior, 25*(2), 284–289. https://doi.org/10.1016/j.chb.2008.12.010

Lorch, R. F. (1989). Text-signaling devices and their effects on reading and memory processes. *Educational Psychology Review, 1*, 209–234. https://doi.org/10.1007/BF01320135

McDade, C. E., Austin, D. M., & Olander, C. P. (1985). Technological advances in precision teaching: A comparison between computer testing and SAFMEDS. *Journal of Precision Teaching, 6*(3), 49-53.

Potts, L., Eshleman, J. W., & Cooper, J. O. (1993). Ogden R. Lindsley and the historical development of precision teaching. *The Behavior Analyst, 16*(2), 177–189. https://doi.org/10.1007/BF03392622

Ramirez, G., & Beilock, S. L. (2011). Writing about testing worries boosts exam performance in the classroom. *Science, 331*(6014), 211–213. https://doi.org/10.1126/science.1199427

Rawson, K. A., & Dunlosky, J. (2011). Optimizing schedules of retrieval practice for durable and efficient learning: How much is enough? *Journal of Experimental Psychology: General, 140*(3), 283–302. https://doi.org/10.1037/a0023956

Rawson, K. A., & Kintsch, W. (2005). Rereading effects depend on time of test. *Journal of Educational Psychology, 97*(1), 70–80. https://doi.org/10.1037/0022-0663.97.1.70

Roediger, H. L., III, & Butler, A. C. (2011). The critical role of retrieval practice in long-term retention. *Trends in Cognitive Sciences, 15*(1), 20–27. https://doi.org/10.1016/j.tics.2010.09.003

Roediger, H. L., III, Putnam, A. L., & Smith, M. A. (2011). Ten benefits of testing and their applications to educational practice. *Psychology of Learning and Motivation, 55*, 1–36. https://doi.org/10.1016/B978-0-12-387691-1.00001-6

Rothkopf, E. Z. (1968). Textual constraint as function of repeated inspection. *Journal of Educational Psychology, 59*(1, Pt 1), 20–25. https://doi.org/10.1037/h0025378

Rozek, C. S., Ramirez, G., Fine, R. D., & Beilock, S. L. (2019). Reducing socioeconomic disparities in the STEM pipeline through student emotion regulation. *Proceedings of the National Academy of Sciences, 116*(5), 1553–1558. https://doi.org/10.1073/pnas.1808589116

Shapiro, A. M., & Waters, D. L. (2005). An investigation of the cognitive processes underlying the keyword method of foreign vocabulary learning. *Language Teaching Research, 9*(2), 129–146. https://doi.org/10.1191/1362168805lr151oa

Taylor, K., & Rohrer, D. (2010). The effects of interleaved practice. *Applied Cognitive Psychology, 24*(6), 837–848. https://doi.org/10.1002/acp.1598

Thompson, S. V. (1990). Visual imagery: A discussion. *Educational Psychology, 10*(2), 141–182.

Verkoeijen, P. P., Rikers, R. M., & Özsoy, B. (2008). Distributed rereading can hurt the spacing effect in text memory. *Applied Cognitive Psychology, 22*(5), 685–695. https://doi.org/10.1002/acp.1388

3

Behaviorism and Philosophical Foundations

LEARNING OBJECTIVES

The following Test Content Outline (TCO) Tasks (Behavior Analyst Certification Board®, 2024, p. 1) related to behaviorism and the philosophical foundations of behavior analysis (A.1 through A.5) will serve as the learning objectives of this chapter:

- A.1 Identify the goals of behavior analysis as a science (i.e., description, prediction, control).
- A.2 Explain the philosophical assumptions underlying the science of behavior analysis (e.g., selectionism, determinism, empiricism, parsimony, pragmatism).
- A.3 Explain behavior from the perspective of radical behaviorism.
- A.4 Distinguish among behaviorism, the experimental analysis of behavior, applied behavior analysis, and professional practice guided by the science of behavior analysis.
- A.5 Identify and describe dimensions of applied behavior analysis.

TASK A.1

Identify the goals of behavior analysis as a science (i.e., description, prediction, control). The goal of our science is to achieve a thorough understanding of socially important behaviors. The knowledge learned from science allows for one or more of three levels of understanding: (a) description, (b) prediction, and (c) control.

DESCRIPTION

Systematic observations enable us to describe events in quantifiable terms that can be examined for possible interactions with other known facts. These descriptions often suggest hypotheses or questions for further research.

- **Example:** Rate of verbal praise statements used by a classroom teacher.

PREDICTION

This level of understanding (also known as *covariation* or *correlation*) occurs when repeated observations demonstrate that two events systematically covary (i.e., correlate). While correlations do not provide evidence of a causal relationship between variables, they can be used to predict with a certain degree of confidence the relative probability that one event will occur based on the presence or absence of another event.

- **Example:** When repeated observations demonstrate that there are fewer incidents of problem behavior among students on days when teachers use more praise statements, we can predict with some degree of confidence that one will occur based on the presence or absence of the other.

CONTROL

This level of understanding (also known as *causation*) results from the discovery of functional relations in controlled experiments that demonstrate that a specific change to one event (independent variable [IV]) reliably produces a specific change in another event (dependent variable [DV]). This is considered the highest level of scientific understanding.

- **Example:** A controlled experiment demonstrates that fewer incidents of problem behavior are observed on days when teachers use praise statements in the classroom.

MNEMONIC AID

Please (for Prediction) **C**lean (for Control) the **D**ishes (for Description). Please clean the dishes when asked about the goals of behavior analysis as a science!

TASK A.2

Explain the philosophical assumptions underlying the science of behavior analysis (e.g., selectionism, determinism, empiricism, parsimony, pragmatism). We employ the scientific method to understand and intervene in human behavior. As an applied science, applied behavior analysis (ABA) adheres to the six attitudes of science; this set of presuppositions and values informs a scientific approach to understanding reality. These shared assumptions are foundational for the development of scientific knowledge.

DETERMINISM

This refers to the assumption that the universe is rational, governed by discoverable laws, and that events are completely determined by previously existing causes. As a result, all behavior possesses an identifiable cause and is thus predictable and to some degree determinable.

REPLICATION

The validity, reliability, and usefulness of scientific findings are increased when experiments are reproduced, and the basic pattern of results is replicated numerous times. This attitude of science requires the replication of findings for results to be included in the knowledge base of any field.

PARSIMONY

This is the principle that an explanation of a thing or event ought to be based on the fewest possible assumptions or unobservable constructs. This attitude of science encourages scientists to prefer the simplest, logical explanation supported by experiments or reason.

EMPIRICISM

This refers to the practice of objective observation of an event of interest. Systematic measurement and accurate quantification are empirical methods used to develop scientific knowledge.

EXPERIMENTATION

This is the chief strategy used to develop scientific knowledge. It is performed to investigate whether a functional relation exists between events. In an experiment, the IV is systematically controlled and manipulated to clarify its effects on the DV. The aim is to determine whether a functional relation exists between the two variables or events, such that one event plays a causal role in the other event.

PHILOSOPHIC DOUBT

This refers to the attitude of viewing scientific knowledge as tentative and continually developing. Consequently, scientists remain skeptical about the validity and truthfulness of all scientific knowledge and open to modifying their beliefs based on new knowledge and discoveries.

SELECTIONISM

This concept was employed by B. F. Skinner to explain the origin and extinction of behavior. Selectionistic explanations of behavior posit that behavior is selected to continue or to be extinguished based on an individual's experiences and the consequences of their behavior. The environment affects living things through selectionism at the individual level (ontogeny) and the species level (phylogeny).

MNEMONIC AID

The great philosophy professor, DR. PEEPS, can help you remember the philosophical assumptions underlying the science of behavior analysis: **D**eterminism, **R**eplication, **P**arsimony, **E**mpiricism, **E**xperimentation, **P**hilosophic Doubt, **S**electionism.

▶ PRACTICE QUESTION

The part of the human brain that processes visual information has evolved over millions of years, from perceiving engraved markings to recognizing repeating patterns and ultimately making sense of letters, which has become known as reading. Daniel has been interested in books since he was a young toddler. His parents read to him frequently and many books were available in his environment. Daniel's development is accelerated, and he is reading three grade levels above his peers.

Choose the pair of assumptions that best represent the example in the previous scenario.

A. Determinism and empiricism
B. Replication and experimentation
C. Philosophic doubt and parsimony
D. Phylogeny and ontogeny

Before moving on to the section that follows for the solution, we recommend that you provide a brief explanation for the answer option you selected here:

____

____

When you're ready, move on to the next section for the solution!

Practice Question Breakdown

Step 1: Examine the question

The question calls for the identification of the philosophical assumptions underlying ABA that best describe the evolution of human reading ability over time, and particularly Daniel's individual reading development since toddlerhood.

Step 2: Analyze the answer options

A. This is a distractor. Determinism refers to the assumption that all behavior is predictable, while empiricism is the objective observation of an event. While these two terms are included among the six philosophical assumptions underlying ABA, they are not directly related to the scenario at hand, which is about factors influencing the development of reading ability over time.

B. This is a distractor. Replication refers to the repetition of an experiment under exact or similar conditions, and experimentation is a controlled study performed to determine whether a functional relation exists between variables. The scenario does not mention replication and experimentation, but rather the evolution of reading ability in humans and Daniel's individual reading trajectory.

C. This is a distractor. Philosophic doubt considers scientific knowledge as tentative, with some skepticism about its absolute validity. Parsimony refers to the simplest scientific explanation. These philosophical assumptions are not directly related to the scenario.

D. As behavior analysts, we must always consider how the environment impacts human beings and other living things. Explanations of behavior that are based on the experiences of the organism refer to selectionism. One type of selectionism, phylogeny, is defined as how a group of organisms evolve over time (i.e., humans learning to read was shaped by millions of years of evolution), while ontogeny is focused on the development of an individual organism (environmental variables related to reading behaviors shaped Daniel's reading ability).

Step 3: Select the best answer

Among the four answer options presented, answer D (phylogeny and ontogeny) appears to be the best answer.

▸ TASK A.3

Explain behavior from the perspective of radical behaviorism. The conceptual system of radical behaviorism was developed by B. F. Skinner. Radical behaviorism seeks to understand behavior in all its forms and collapses the distinction between private events (i.e., thoughts and feelings) and public events (i.e., behavior that is observable and measurable).

It is *radical* in the sense that it includes all behavior, both public and private, and assumes they are influenced by the same kinds of variables and result from an individual's experiences and environments. From the perspective of radical behaviorism, thoughts and feelings do not cause behavior—thoughts and feelings *are* behavior. As such, thoughts and feelings conform to the laws of behavior and can be addressed utilizing the principles of behavior.

From the perspective of radical behaviorism, all human behavior is understandable in terms of how an individual's behavior develops over its lifetime based on their experiences with the environment (ontogeny) and how a species' behavior has evolved over evolutionary time as it slowly makes changes necessary for survival (phylogeny). See Table 3.1.

Table 3.1 The Difference Between Ontogeny and Phylogeny

ONTOGENY	PHYLOGENY
Recounts the developmental history of an individual within its own lifetime	Recounts the evolutionary history of a species
Focuses on the degree to which the behavior can be changed through learning	Describes the history of the behavior and its shaping through past selective pressures

TASK A.4

Distinguish among behaviorism, the experimental analysis of behavior, applied behavior analysis, and professional practice guided by the science of behavior analysis.

BEHAVIORISM

This is the philosophy of the science of behavior and its various forms. It assumes that a science of behavior is possible, and that behavior can be studied and changed in a manner similar to other sciences (e.g., biology). Behaviorism primarily looks to causes in the external environment for explanations of behavior. As an intervention, behaviorism holds that it is often most effective to organize the environment in such a way that certain behaviors are more or less likely.

EXPERIMENTAL ANALYSIS OF BEHAVIOR

Experimental analysis of behavior (EAB) is a natural science approach to research that defines and clarifies the basic processes and principles of behavior. It was founded by B. F. Skinner with the publication of *The Behavior of Organisms* in 1938. Skinner articulated two types of behavior: (a) *respondent behaviors* that are reflexive and elicited by stimuli immediately preceding them, and (b) *operant behaviors* that are elicited by the effects of consequences of past behaviors. The operant three-term contingency is the primary unit of analysis. EAB is primarily a laboratory-based experimental approach that established the foundational principles of operant behavior.

APPLIED BEHAVIOR ANALYSIS

This is the science in which behavior analysts apply techniques derived from the principles of behavior to change behavior (e.g., increase behavior, teach and maintain behavior, reduce problem behavior, etc.) and positively enhance socially significant areas (e.g., classroom management, generalization and maintenance of learning, communication, etc.). ABA utilizes experimentation to clearly identify the variables driving changes in behavior, then applies principles derived from EAB to change behavior.

PROFESSIONAL PRACTICE

This domain of behavior analysis is guided by the science of behavior analysis and involves delivering behavior analytic services to human subjects in diverse settings and environments. It is grounded in the principles of behaviorism, research from the EAB, and ABA. The professional practice of behavior analysis is a hybrid discipline informed by various mental health fields, education, communication disorders, physical therapy, and criminal justice.

TASK A.5

Identify and describe dimensions of applied behavior analysis. ABA is defined by seven core dimensions: (a) applied, (b) behavioral, (c) analytic, (d) technologic, (e) conceptually systematic, (f) effective, and (g) generality (Baer et al., 1968).

APPLIED

This means that the variable of interest is important to an individual and/or society; that is, changes that improve an individual's quality of life (i.e., socially significant behaviors) are targeted.

BEHAVIORAL

This term means that a study or intervention analyzes observable and measurable behavior in a precise and objective manner.

ANALYTIC

This means that control over a target behavior can be demonstrated (i.e., can be turned on and off), evidencing the existence of a functional relationship between the manipulated event and occurrence/nonoccurrence of the target behavior.

TECHNOLOGIC

This means that all procedures of an intervention are clearly detailed and described and that data and results of an experiment or study are clearly presented in an understandable and replicable manner.

CONCEPTUALLY SYSTEMATIC

This means that all of the interventions or procedures are grounded in the basic behavioral principles of behavior analysis in a manner that fosters integration and systematic expansion of the procedures.

EFFECTIVE

An intervention is considered effective if it has altered the target behavior to a significant degree, is meaningful or socially important, and promotes long-term positive changes in the client.

GENERALITY

A change in behavior is considered to have generality when it holds over time, across different settings, and/or spreads to other relevant and related behaviors.

MNEMONIC AID

GET A CAB (**G**enerality, **E**ffective, **T**echnologic, **A**pplied, **C**onceptually systematic, **A**nalytic, **B**ehavioral). You can also use BAT CAGE or BEG A CAT, whichever you fancy.

CONCLUSION

In this chapter, we reviewed ABA's conceptual foundations, scientific framework, defining dimensions, and overall aims. This included the goals of behavior analysis and its philosophical assumptions. We also described and explained the perspective of radical behaviorism and what distinguishes it from other approaches to understanding behavior. Having a firm grasp of these key concepts will inform how you approach your practice as a BCBA®, so this chapter covered ABA's manifestations as both a science and a practice and delved into how to distinguish among behaviorism, EAB, ABA, and practice guided by the science of behavior analysis. To support your acquisition and retention of the content covered in this chapter, we added several mnemonic aids.

REFERENCES

Baer, D. M., Wolf, M. M., & Risley, T. R. (1968). Some current dimensions of applied behavior analysis. *Journal of Applied Behavior Analysis, 1*(1), 91–97. https://doi.org/10.1901/jaba.1968.1-91

Behavior Analyst Certification Board. (2024, September). *BCBA test content outline* (6th ed.). https://www.bacb.com/wp-content/uploads/2022/01/BCBA-6th-Edition-Test-Content-Outline-240903-a.pdf (Original work published in 2022).

BIBLIOGRAPHY

Cooper, J. O., Heron, T. E., & Heward, W. L. (2020). *Applied behavior analysis* (3rd ed.). Pearson Education.

Morris, E. K., Altus, D. E., & Smith, N. G. (2013). A study in the founding of applied behavior analysis through its publications. *The Behavior Analyst, 36*(1), 73–107. https://doi.org/10.1007/BF03392293

KNOWLEDGE CHECK

1. The knowledge learned from science allows for one or more of three levels of understanding. These are:
   - **A.** Correlation, control, and definition
   - **B.** Control, description, and prediction
   - **C.** Covariance, prediction, and selectionism
   - **D.** Description, probability, and replication

2. Which level of scientific understanding occurs when controlled experiments demonstrate that a specific change to an independent variable (IV) reliably produces a specific change in a dependent variable (DV)?
   - **A.** Control
   - **B.** Definition
   - **C.** Prediction
   - **D.** Replication

3. A behavior analyst is reviewing data from an intervention aimed at reducing a child's disruptive behavior in the classroom. They believe that every instance of disruptive behavior is caused by identifiable factors, such as teacher responses or peer interactions, and that by controlling these factors, they can predict and change future occurrences of the behavior. Which philosophical assumption is the behavior analyst applying by assuming that all instances of disruptive behavior are caused by specific environmental factors and can be modified?
   - **A.** Determinism
   - **B.** Empiricism
   - **C.** Experimentation
   - **D.** Parsimony

4. A behavior analyst is working with a client to reduce aggressive outbursts. The analyst initially implements a token economy system, but it does not seem to reduce the aggressive behavior. After trying a different intervention focused on teaching functional communication skills, the aggressive behavior decreases significantly. Which philosophical concept from behavior analysis does this situation best illustrate?
   - **A.** Behavior should be understood in terms of hypothetical constructs.
   - **B.** Only innate behaviors should be considered in analysis.
   - **C.** Theoretical knowledge is valued over practical application.
   - **D.** Truth is determined by how well a concept or procedure works in achieving desired outcomes.

(*See answers on the next page.*)

1. **B) Control, description, and prediction**
   The goal of science in any field of study is to develop a greater understanding of its subject. The goal of our science is to understand socially important behaviors through varying levels of description, prediction, and control. Thus, efforts are made to describe behavior in measurable terms, demonstrate correlation between events, and identify variables that reliably predict the occurrence of a behavior or event.

2. **A) Control**
   Control, as a level of scientific understanding, is said to occur when controlled experiments demonstrate that a specific change to an IV reliably produces a specific change in a DV. Prediction, which refers to another level of scientific understanding, along with definition and replication function as distractors.

3. **A) Determinism**
   Determinism assumes that all behavior is caused by identifiable factors and can be predicted. In the scenario, the behavior analyst believes disruptive behavior is caused by specific environmental factors and can be modified by controlling these causes, which reflects determinism. The other answer options refer to other philosophical assumptions that do not capture the concept of behavior as the result of preceding causes.

4. **D) Truth is determined by how well a concept or procedure works in achieving desired outcomes.**
   Pragmatism focuses on the effectiveness of interventions in achieving practical results, as seen in the scenario where the behavior analyst switches from an ineffective token economy to a successful intervention focused on teaching communication skills. The other answer options either emphasize hypothetical constructs, restrict analysis to innate behaviors, or prioritize theory over practical application, all of which contrast with the pragmatic focus of behavior analysis on effective, real-world outcomes.

5. ________________ is a natural science approach to research founded by B. F. Skinner that defines and clarifies the basic processes and principles of behavior.

   A. Applied behavior analysis (ABA)

   B. Experimental analysis of behavior (EAB)

   C. Radical behaviorism

   D. Positive behavior support (PBS)

6. A behavior analyst is developing an intervention to help a student with autism spectrum disorder improve their social skills. The intervention focuses on behaviors that are socially significant, clearly defined, and measurable. The analyst ensures that the procedures are replicable by others and are grounded in established behavior-analytic principles. The analyst demonstrates a functional relationship between the intervention and improved social behavior and plans for generalization by teaching the skills in various settings. How many dimensions of applied behavior analysis (ABA) are demonstrated in this scenario?

   A. Three

   B. Five

   C. Seven

   D. Nine

7. Radical behaviorism, as proposed by B. F. Skinner, includes which of the following beliefs?

   A. Behavior is primarily shaped by unconscious drives and conflicts.

   B. Human behavior cannot be predicted or controlled.

   C. Internal events such as thoughts and feelings are considered behavior and should be analyzed.

   D. Only observable behavior should be studied, excluding thoughts and feelings.

8. Which of the following is the core dimension of applied behavior analysis (ABA) that is concerned with the extent to which procedures are described in a manner consistent with basic behavioral principles?

   A. Applied

   B. Conceptually systematic

   C. Effective

   D. Generality

9. A behavior analyst works with a child to increase communication skills. Initially, the intervention is implemented in the classroom, where the child shows a significant increase in appropriate communication. Later, the child begins using these communication skills at home, and the improved behavior remains stable even after the intervention is discontinued. The child also starts using the skills in other social settings, such as during extracurricular activities, without the need for further prompting or reinforcement from adults. Which dimension of applied behavior analysis is being demonstrated in this situation?

   A. Applied

   B. Behavioral

   C. Effective

   D. Generality

(*See answers on the next page.*)

5. **B) Experimental analysis of behavior (EAB)**
   EAB is the natural science approach to research founded by B. F. Skinner that defines and clarifies the basic processes and principles of behavior. ABA, which is the science in which behavior analysts apply techniques derived from the principles of behavior, along with radical behaviorism and PBS, function as distractors.

6. **C) Seven**
   In this scenario, the behavior analyst addresses all seven core dimensions of ABA. The intervention targets socially significant behaviors (applied), ensures the behaviors are observable and measurable (behavioral), and demonstrates a functional relationship between the intervention and the behavior change (analytic). The procedures are described clearly so that they can be replicated by others (technologic), and the intervention is designed according to behavior-analytic principles (conceptually systematic). The intervention is effective in producing meaningful behavior change (effective), and the plan includes strategies to ensure the behavior generalizes across various settings (generality).

7. **C) Internal events such as thoughts and feelings are considered behavior and should be analyzed.**
   Radical behaviorism, developed by B. F. Skinner, extends the study of behavior to include internal events like thoughts and feelings, viewing them as behaviors that follow the same principles as observable actions. This approach maintains that all behaviors, whether internal or external, are subject to analysis and influence.

8. **B) Conceptually systematic**
   ABA is conceptually systematic. That is, all of the interventions or procedures are grounded in the basic behavioral principles. Applied, effective, and generality refer to other core principles.

9. **D) Generality**
   Generality refers to the persistence of behavior change across time, settings, and related behaviors. In the scenario, the child applies communication skills not only in the classroom but also at home and in other settings, and the improvements are maintained over time without further intervention. This demonstrates generalization. The other answer options refer to other core principles that do not fully capture the spread and maintenance of behavior as generality does.

4

Concepts and Principles

LEARNING OBJECTIVES

The following Test Content Outline (TCO) Tasks (Behavior Analyst Certification Board®, 2024, p. 1) related to concepts and principles of applied behavior analysis (ABA) (B.1 through B.24) will serve as the learning objectives of this chapter:

- B.1 Identify and distinguish among behavior, response, and response class.
- B.2 Identify and distinguish between stimulus and stimulus class.
- B.3 Identify and distinguish between respondent and operant conditioning.
- B.4 Identify and distinguish between positive and negative reinforcement contingencies.
- B.5 Identify and distinguish between positive and negative punishment contingencies.
- B.6 Identify and distinguish between automatic and socially mediated contingencies.
- B.7 Identify and distinguish among unconditioned, conditioned, and generalized reinforcers.
- B.8 Identify and distinguish among unconditioned, conditioned, and generalized punishers.
- B.9 Identify and distinguish among simple schedules of reinforcement.
- B.10 Identify and distinguish among concurrent, multiple, mixed, and chained schedules of reinforcement.
- B.11 Identify and distinguish between operant and respondent extinction as operations and processes.
- B.12 Identify examples of stimulus control.
- B.13 Identify examples of stimulus discrimination.
- B.14 Identify and distinguish between stimulus and response generalization.
- B.15 Identify examples of response maintenance.
- B.16 Identify examples of motivating operations.
- B.17 Distinguish between motivating operations and stimulus control.
- B.18 Identify and distinguish between rule-governed and contingency-shaped behavior.
- B.19 Identify and distinguish among verbal operants.
- B.20 Identify the role of multiple control in verbal behavior.
- B.21 Identify examples of processes that promote emergent relations and generative performance.

B.22 Identify ways behavioral momentum can be used to understand response persistence.
B.23 Identify ways the matching law can be used to interpret response allocation.
B.24 Identify and distinguish between imitation and observational learning.

TASK B.1

Identify and distinguish among behavior, response, and response class. This is the "activity of living organisms" (Cooper et al., 2020, p. 25) and includes all manner of human actions (e.g., eating, walking, speaking, breathing, crying). More technically, behavior is an organism's activity that results in a measurable change in its environment. The "dead man's test" for behavior is a rather crude but memorable way of clarifying what is and what is not behavior; if a dead person can do it, it is not considered behavior—unless, of course, the dead person is a zombie.

RESPONSE

This refers to a specific instance (i.e., occurrence) of behavior.

- **Example (reading):** When you read the previous sentence (i.e., definition of a response); that was a response.
- **Example (passing the guac):** You pass the guacamole after a friend asks you for it.

RESPONSE CLASS

This is a group of responses defined by (a) form or (b) function.

TOPOGRAPHICAL RESPONSE CLASS

This defines members of its class in terms of their form (i.e., what they look like; Table 4.1).

Table 4.1 The Difference Between Functional and Topographical Response Classes

FUNCTIONAL RESPONSE CLASS	TOPOGRAPHICAL RESPONSE CLASS
Form of the response may vary	Specifies the form
Includes responses whose occurrence depends on particular antecedent and/or consequence stimuli	May include responses that make up only a subset of those from a functional response class

- **Example:** The diagnostic criteria for autism spectrum disorders is an example of a topographical response class system. A set of symptoms (i.e., behaviors) forms the class that results in the diagnosis, but they don't tell you anything about why they occur (i.e., function).

FUNCTIONAL RESPONSE CLASS

This is a group of responses that share a common function. In other words, this refers to two or more behaviors that produce the same outcome in the environment.

- **Example:** A child may receive attention as a result of several responses that vary in form—yelling, crying, smiling, speaking, and so on.

TASK B.2

Identify and distinguish between stimulus and stimulus class. This is an event that affects the behavior of an individual. It involves a change in energy that affects a living organism through one or more of its sense organs. All living organisms monitor and respond to changes in their environment and inside their body. Our five senses are examples of *exteroceptors.* Humans also have sense organs that detect changes inside the body (*interoceptors*) and that foster movement and balance (*proprioceptors*).

- **Example:** The sound (stimulus) of the postal delivery truck stopping at your residence may serve as a stimulus that leads you to walk to the door to see if a package is being delivered.

STIMULUS CLASS

This is a cluster of stimuli with elements in common across one or more of the following dimensions: (a) formal, (b) temporal, and (c) functional.

Formal
This refers to the stimulus class's shared physical feature(s). They either look or sound alike.

- **Example:** A stimulus class that consists of things that are blue in color

Temporal
This refers to the timing of a stimulus class's occurrence in relation to a behavior of interest. They are antecedents or consequences for a particular response.

- **Example:** A stimulus class that consists of things that happen right before you check your mobile phone

Functional
This refers to a stimulus class's common effect on behavior. They serve as discriminative stimuli for a particular response.

- **Example:** A stimulus class that consists of things that prompt you to check your mobile phone

ADDITIONAL NOTE(S)

You may also encounter the terms *arbitrary stimulus class* (which are antecedent stimuli that are dissimilar but bring about the same response) and *feature stimulus class* (which are stimuli that have shared physical features or relative relationships).

TASK B.3

Identify and distinguish between respondent and operant conditioning. This is a type of learning (also known as *classical, Pavlovian,* or *stimulus-response conditioning*) whereby new stimuli develop the capacity to elicit responses through the pairing process. Respondent conditioning focuses on responses that are inborn, automatic, and involuntary. Pavlov, with whom this type of learning is most associated, focused on the connections between stimuli and responses, which are known as *reflexes.* Unconditioned reflexes are involuntary (i.e., not learned) and involve an unconditioned stimulus (US) evoking an unconditioned response (UR).

In short, respondent conditioning (Figure 4.1) pairs a US with a neutral stimulus (NS) until the NS becomes a conditioned stimulus (CS) that elicits a conditioned response (CR). Thus, antecedents elicit respondent behavior.

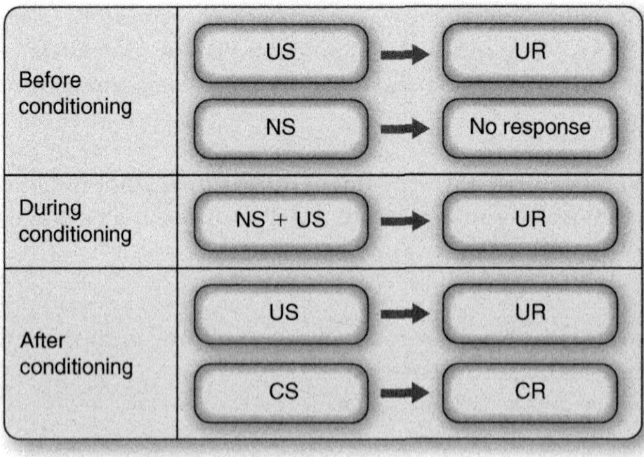

Figure 4.1 Respondent Conditioning

CR, conditioned response; CS, conditioned stimulus; NS, neutral stimulus; UR, unconditioned response; US, unconditioned stimulus.

- **Example:** Pavlov's famous experiments with dogs demonstrated how meat powder (US), which naturally caused dogs to salivate (UR), was repeatedly paired with a tone (NS) until the tone elicited salivation (UR). In this well-known example, the tone was transformed from an NS to a CS, thus establishing a CR (Figure 4.2).

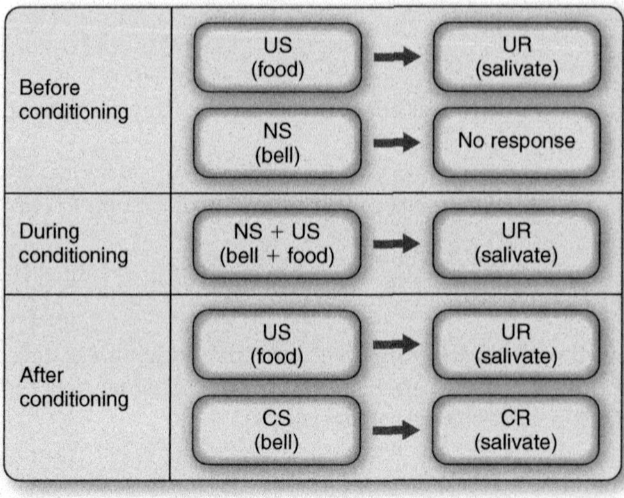

Figure 4.2 Example of Respondent Conditioning: Pavlov's Experiment

CR, conditioned response; CS, conditioned stimulus; NS, neutral stimulus; UR, unconditioned response; US, unconditioned stimulus.

OPERANT CONDITIONING

This is a type of learning (also known as *instrumental* or *Skinnerian conditioning*) that occurs as a result of rewards and punishments. This concerns operant behavior, which is behavior we have control over. Operant behavior is modified by its history of consequences (i.e., stimulus changes that immediately follow a response). Consequences can be (a) reinforcing, thereby increasing the frequency of a behavior, or (b) punishing, thereby decreasing the frequency of a behavior.

- **Example (reinforcing consequence):** A client is learning to ask for water (the operant behavior) when he is thirsty. When he demonstrates the behavior, water (the reinforcer) is delivered, thereby increasing the future frequency of asking for water when he is thirsty.
- **Example (punishing consequence):** A client is learning to ask for water (the operant behavior) when he is thirsty. When he demonstrates the behavior, a vocal reprimand (an aversive stimulus) is delivered, thereby decreasing the future frequency of the behavior (asking for water).

TASK B.4

Identify and distinguish between positive and negative reinforcement contingencies. Reinforcement is a basic principle that describes a functional relationship in which a behavior immediately followed by a stimulus change (i.e., consequence) increases the future frequency of the behavior.

Reinforcement can be (a) positive or (b) negative.

POSITIVE REINFORCEMENT

This refers to the presentation (or increase in intensity) of a stimulus immediately subsequent to a behavior that serves to increase the future frequency of the behavior (Table 4.2).

Table 4.2 Example of Positive Reinforcement

R	S^{R+}	FUTURE FREQUENCY OF R
Student raises hand	Teacher praise	Increases

R, response; S^{R+}, unconditioned positive reinforcer.

NEGATIVE REINFORCEMENT

This refers to the removal (or reduction in intensity) of a stimulus immediately subsequent to a behavior that serves to increase the future frequency of the behavior (Table 4.3). This stimulus is often referred to as an aversive stimulus whose removal results in relief.

Table 4.3 Example of Negative Reinforcement

R	S^{R-}	FUTURE FREQUENCY OF R
Closes door when there are loud noises outside	Removal (or reduction) of loud noises	Increases

R, response; S^{R-}, unconditioned negative reinforcer.

MNEMONIC AID

It can be helpful to think of the words *positive* and *negative* in the mathematical sense, where positive = addition (+) and negative = subtraction (−). Positive reinforcement involves the addition of a stimulus, and negative reinforcement involves the subtraction of a stimulus.

TASK B.5

Identify and distinguish between positive and negative punishment contingencies. Punishment is a basic principle that describes a functional relationship in which a behavior immediately followed by a stimulus change (i.e., consequence) decreases the future frequency of the behavior. Punishment can be (a) positive or (b) negative.

POSITIVE PUNISHMENT

This refers to the presentation (or increase in intensity) of a stimulus immediately following a behavior, which decreases the future frequency of the behavior (Table 4.4).

Table 4.4 Example of Positive Punishment

R	S^{P+}	FUTURE FREQUENCY OF R
Student yells	Teacher reprimand	Decreases

R, response; S^{P+}, unconditioned positive punisher.

NEGATIVE PUNISHMENT

This refers to the removal (or reduction in intensity) of a stimulus immediately following a behavior, which decreases the future frequency of the behavior (Table 4.5).

Table 4.5 Example of Negative Punishment

R	S^{P-}	FUTURE FREQUENCY OF R
Student yells	Reduction in length of recess time	Decreases

R, response; S^{P-}, conditioned negative punisher.

MNEMONIC AID

It can be helpful to think of the words *positive* and *negative* in the mathematical sense, where *positive* = addition (+) and *negative* = subtraction (–). Positive punishment involves the addition of a stimulus, and negative punishment involves the subtraction of a stimulus.

TASK B.6

Identify and distinguish between automatic and socially mediated contingencies.

AUTOMATIC CONTINGENCIES

Also referred to as *direct contingencies*, these refer to environmental contingencies that can affect behavior without the mediation or deliberate actions of another person. As such, these contingencies are considered *nonsocial*. While there are many types of automatic contingencies (e.g., automatic punishment, automatic motivating operation (MO) control, automatic stimulus control), behavior analysts have primarily focused on automatic reinforcement.

Automatic Reinforcement

This occurs when reinforcement is (a) a response product of a behavior (Table 4.6) or (b) a product of the physical environment resulting from a behavior (Table 4.7).

Table 4.6 Example of Automatic Reinforcement as a Response Product of a Behavior

R	S^{R+}
Singing	Desirable stimulation

R, response; S^{R+}, unconditioned positive reinforcer.

Table 4.7 Example of Automatic Reinforcement as a Product of the Physical Environment Resulting from a Behavior

R	S^{R+}
Turning on the radio	Desirable stimulation

R, response; S^{R+}, unconditioned positive reinforcer.

SOCIALLY MEDIATED CONTINGENCIES

Also referred to as *indirect contingencies*, these refer to environmental contingencies that can affect behavior with the mediation or deliberate actions of another person. Behavior analysts have primarily focused on socially mediated reinforcement.

Socially Mediated Reinforcement

This occurs when reinforcement is a product of the actions of another person resulting from a behavior (Table 4.8).

Table 4.8 Example of Socially Mediated Reinforcement

R	S^{R+}
Asking for "cookie"	Someone delivers a cookie

R, response; S^{R+}, unconditioned positive reinforcer.

TASK B.7

Identify and distinguish among unconditioned, conditioned, and generalized reinforcers.

REINFORCER

This is a stimulus change that increases the future frequency of the behavior that it immediately follows. Reinforcers can be (a) unconditioned, (b) conditioned, or (c) generalized.

Unconditioned Reinforcer

Also known as a *natural* or *primary reinforcer*, this is a stimulus change that increases the future frequency of the behavior that it immediately follows independent of the individual's learning history. It is the product of phylogeny and satisfies the basic life needs of an organism.

- **Examples:** water, food, oxygen, warmth, sex

Conditioned Reinforcer

Also known as a *learned* or *secondary reinforcer*, this is a stimulus change that increases the future frequency of the behavior that it immediately follows as a result of its previous pairing with one or more other reinforcers. It is the product of ontogeny, varies across individuals, and changes throughout the individual's life span.

- **Examples:** money, grades, praise, tokens

GENERALIZED REINFORCER

This is a conditioned reinforcer that has been paired with many other reinforcers.

- **Example:** money (because it can be used to gain access to many reinforcing stimuli)

TASK B.8

Identify and distinguish among unconditioned, conditioned, and generalized punishers.

PUNISHER

This is a stimulus change that decreases the future frequency of the behavior that it immediately follows. Punishers can be (a) unconditioned, (b) conditioned, or (c) generalized.

Unconditioned Punisher

Also known as an *unlearned* or *primary punisher*, this is a stimulus change that decreases the future frequency of any behavior that it immediately follows independent of the individual's learning history. It is the product of phylogeny and is naturally undesirable.

- **Examples:** extreme temperatures, painful stimulation

Conditioned Punisher

Also known as a *learned* or *secondary punisher*, this is a stimulus change that decreases the future frequency of the behavior that it immediately follows as a result of its previous pairing with one or more other punishers. It is the product of ontogeny.

- **Example:** sight of blood (because it has been previously paired with painful stimulation)

Generalized Punisher

This is a conditioned punisher that has been paired with many other punishers.

- **Example:** verbal reprimands (because they have been consistently paired with other forms of social disapproval and unconditioned/conditioned punishers)

TASK B.9

Identify and distinguish among simple schedules of reinforcement. Simple schedules of reinforcement are rules that specify the requirements for reinforcement. There are two main types: (a) a continuous schedule of reinforcement and (b) intermittent schedules of reinforcement (INT).

CONTINUOUS REINFORCEMENT SCHEDULE

A continuous reinforcement schedule (CRF or FR1) is a schedule that requires the delivery of reinforcement after every occurrence of a target behavior (Table 4.9).

Table 4.9 Example of Using a Continuous Reinforcement Schedule; Target Behavior = Raising Hand

TRIAL	S^D	R	S^{R+}
1	Teacher asks question	Raises hand	Delivered
2	Teacher asks question	Raises hand	Delivered
3	Teacher asks question	Raises hand	Delivered

R, response; S^D, discriminative stimulus; S^{R+}, unconditioned positive reinforcer.

INTERMITTENT SCHEDULE OF REINFORCEMENT

This schedule does not involve reinforcing every occurrence of a target behavior. Basic intermittent schedules include (a) fixed ratio (FR) schedules (with the exception of FR1), (b) fixed interval (FI) schedules, (c) variable ratio (VR) schedules, and (d) variable interval (VI) schedules.

Fixed Ratio

This schedule specifies the number of times a target behavior must occur to receive reinforcement. An FR2 schedule means reinforcement is delivered after every two occurrences of the target response, whereas an FR3 means reinforcement is delivered after every three occurrences (Table 4.10), and so forth.

Table 4.10 Example of Using an FR3 Schedule; Target Behavior = Raising Hand

TRIAL	S^D	R	S^{R+}
1	Teacher asks question	Raises hand	Not delivered
2	Teacher asks question	Raises hand	Not delivered
3	Teacher asks question	Raises hand	Delivered

R, response; S^D, discriminative stimulus; S^{R+}, unconditioned positive reinforcer.

Fixed Interval

This schedule specifies the duration that must pass before the first occurrence of a target response will be reinforced (Table 4.11). An FI2 (minutes) schedule means reinforcement is delivered for the first occurrence of a target behavior after 2 minutes have elapsed. Once reinforcement is delivered, the time is reset and another 2 minutes must elapse before the next delivery of reinforcement can occur.

Table 4.11 Example of Using an FI5 (Minutes) Schedule; Target Behavior = Raising Hand

TRIAL	TIME THAT MUST ELAPSE BEFORE S^{R+} IS AVAILABLE	R	S^{R+}
1	5 minutes	First raising hand response	Delivered
2	5 minutes	First raising hand response	Delivered
3	5 minutes	First raising hand response	Delivered

R, response; S^{R+}, unconditioned positive reinforcer.

Variable Ratio

This schedule specifies the average number of times a target behavior must occur to receive reinforcement. Thus, the occurrence of reinforcement is less predictable. A VR2 schedule means reinforcement is delivered after an average of every two occurrences of the target response, a VR3 means reinforcement is delivered after an average of every three occurrences, and so forth.

In the example in Table 4.12, reinforcement was delivered three out of six times, which is essentially an average of every two occurrences of the target behavior.

Table 4.12 Example of Using a VR2 Schedule; Target Behavior = Raising Hand

TRIAL	S^D	R	S^{R+}
1	Teacher asks question	Raises hand	Delivered
2	Teacher asks question	Raises hand	Not delivered
3	Teacher asks question	Raises hand	Delivered
4	Teacher asks question	Raises hand	Not delivered
5	Teacher asks question	Raises hand	Not delivered
6	Teacher asks question	Raises hand	Delivered

R, response; S^D, discriminative stimulus; S^{R+}, unconditioned positive reinforcer.

Variable Interval

This schedule specifies the average duration that must pass before the first occurrence of a target response will be reinforced. Thus, the time interval that must elapse before reinforcement is made available is less predictable. A VI2 (minutes) schedule means reinforcement is delivered for the first occurrence of a target behavior after a variable (average) duration of 2 minutes have elapsed. Once reinforcement is delivered, the time is reset and another variable duration of 2 minutes must elapse before the next delivery of reinforcement can occur.

In the example in Table 4.13, the average of the time elapsed before reinforcement was made available for the first occurrence of the target response is 5 minutes.

Table 4.13 Example of Using a VI5 (Minutes) Schedule; Target Behavior = Raising Hand

TRIAL	TIME THAT ELAPSES BEFORE S^{R+} IS AVAILABLE	R	S^{R+}
1	3 minutes	First raising hand response	Delivered
2	5 minutes	First raising hand response	Delivered
3	7 minutes	First raising hand response	Delivered
4	4 minutes	First raising hand response	Delivered
5	5 minutes	First raising hand response	Delivered
6	6 minutes	First raising hand response	Delivered

R, response; S^{R+}, unconditioned positive reinforcer.

A number of variations of the basic schedules have been presented. These include (a) schedules of differential reinforcement, (b) progressive schedules, and (c) compound schedules.

ADDITIONAL NOTE(S)

The effects of the four basic schedules (i.e., FR, VR, FI, and VI) derived from basic research are well-documented. FR schedules produce a break-and-run pattern of responding (i.e., pause [little to no responding] after reinforcement, followed by a transition to a high and constant rate of responding). VR schedules produce a high and constant rate of responding. FI schedules produce a scalloped pattern of responding (i.e., slow at the start, but accelerates toward the end of the interval and typically reaches the highest rate immediately before reinforcement). Lastly, VI schedules produce a constant, low-to-moderate rate of responding.

TASK B.10

Identify and distinguish among concurrent, multiple, mixed, and chained schedules of reinforcement. Concurrent, multiple, mixed, and chained schedules of reinforcement are considered compound schedules; they are more complex schedules that build upon the simple schedules to better understand and influence behavior.

CONCURRENT SCHEDULES OF REINFORCEMENT

This is a schedule in which two or more separate schedules of reinforcement (e.g., FI and VR), each associated with an independent response (i.e., target behavior), are implemented at the same time. A concurrent schedule of reinforcement is identifiable by the following criteria: It involves two or more contingencies in effect simultaneously or independently for two or more behaviors.

- **Example:** A client can choose between two tasks, each with its own reinforcement schedule. Task A is on an FI2 (minutes) schedule, and Task B is on a VR5 schedule.

MULTIPLE SCHEDULES OF REINFORCEMENT

The multiple schedules of reinforcement (MULT) a schedule where two or more basic schedules of reinforcement are implemented in an alternating and, typically, random order. Only one schedule operates at a time.

- **Example:** A client might work on Task A under an FR5 schedule when a green light is on, and then switch to Task B under an FI3 (minutes) schedule when a red light is on. The different colored lights signal which schedule is in effect.

MIXED SCHEDULES OF REINFORCEMENT

The mixed schedules of reinforcement (MIX) uses a procedure identical to MULT with the exception that no discriminative stimuli are correlated with the independent schedules. As such, a MIX implements two or more schedules of reinforcement in a random/alternating order without correlated discriminative stimuli. Thus, the individual experiences different schedules in an unpredictable sequence.

- **Example:** A client receives reinforcement after an FR5 schedule for a period, then switches to a VI2 (minutes) without any signal indicating the change.

CHAINED SCHEDULES OF REINFORCEMENT

The chained schedules of reinforcement (CHAIN) is similar to MULT and typically used to investigate conditioned reinforcement. In a CHAIN, at least two schedules, each accompanied by a distinctive stimulus, must be completed before primary reinforcement occurs. Thus, it makes reinforcement contingent on the client's successful completion of all components in the proper order.

- **Example:** A client must complete an FR1 schedule (e.g., brush teeth when instructed, "Brush your teeth"), then an FI5 (minutes) schedule (e.g., gather clothes and get dressed within 5 minutes when instructed, "Get changed"), followed by a VR3 schedule (e.g., pack a backpack with three specific school items when instructed, "Get your backpack"). Only after completing all these steps in sequence does the client receive reinforcement.

TASK B.11

Identify and distinguish between operant and respondent extinction as operations and processes. Operant and respondent extinction are both processes used to change behavior, but they apply to different types of responses and involve different underlying mechanisms.

OPERANT EXTINCTION

This refers to a reduction in behavior resulting from the discontinuation of reinforcement for it. Operant extinction (EXT) procedures involve withholding reinforcers that maintain undesirable behavior. In other words, the problem behavior no longer results in reinforcement. As a result, the frequency of its occurrence will decrease in the future.

- **Example:** A client's yelling behavior is maintained by access to toys (Table 4.14)

Table 4.14 Problem Behavior and Resulting Consequence (Positive Reinforcer)

R	S^{R+}
Yell	Adult delivers toy

R, response; S^{R+}, unconditioned positive reinforcer.

Implementation of an EXT procedure will involve withholding toys from the client when they yell, resulting in less yelling in the future (Table 4.15).

Table 4.15 Example of Using an Extinction Procedure to Address Problem Behavior

R	S^{R+}	FUTURE FREQUENCY
Yell	Adult does not deliver toy	↓

R, response; S^{R+}, unconditioned positive reinforcer.

RESPONDENT EXTINCTION

This involves reducing the strength or frequency of a CR by presenting the CS without the US (Figure 4.3).

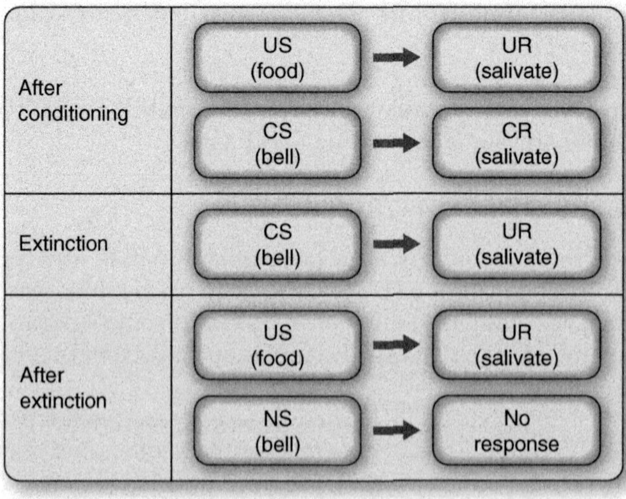

Figure 4.3 Example of Respondent Extinction (For a Dog That Has Been Conditioned to Salivate in Response to Hearing a Bell)

CR, conditioned response; CS, conditioned stimulus; NS, neutral stimulus; UR, unconditioned response; US, unconditioned stimulus.

In short, operant extinction targets operant (i.e., voluntary) responses influenced by their consequences, whereas respondent extinction focuses on reflexive or involuntary responses that are elicited by specific stimuli.

▸ TASK B.12

Identify examples of stimulus control. Stimulus control refers to the alteration of the frequency, duration, latency, or magnitude of behavior by the presence or absence of an antecedent stimulus. In other words, behavior changes based on whether or not some stimulus is present.

Stimulus control is established when a response is (a) only reinforced when a specific stimulus (discriminative stimulus or S^D) is present, and (b) not reinforced when other stimuli (S^Δ) are present.

- **Example:** The doorbell chime acquires stimulus control when opening the door is only reinforced after the doorbell chimes (and not other stimulus events; Table 4.16).

Table 4.16 Contingencies for Doorbell Chime to Acquire Stimulus Control

S^D	R	S^{R+}
Doorbell chimes	Open door	See friend on doorstep
S^D	R	S^Δ
Cell phone chimes	Open door	No friend on doorstep
Alarm clock chimes	Open door	No friend on doorstep
Dog barks	Open door	No friend on doorstep

R, response; S^D, discriminative stimulus; S^Δ, stimulus delta; S^{R+}, unconditioned positive reinforcer.

TASK B.13

Identify examples of stimulus discrimination. Stimulus discrimination refers to the emission of a differential response when presented with two or more stimuli.

SIMPLE DISCRIMINATION

This occurs when the client emits a response that is controlled by a single stimulus.

- **Example:** A client sees a friend at school, Cara, and greets her with, "Hey, Cara!" (Table 4.17)

Table 4.17 Simple Discrimination

S^D	R
Cara	"Hey, Cara!"

R, response; S^D, discriminative stimulus.

CONDITIONAL DISCRIMINATION

This occurs when the client emits a response that is controlled by a single stimulus when it is in the presence of another stimulus.

- **Example:** A client sees a friend at school, Cara, and greets her with, "Hey, Cara!" only when it is recess time (Table 4.18).

Table 4.18 Conditional Discrimination

CONDITIONAL STIMULUS	S^D	S^{R+}
Recess time	Cara	"Hey, Cara!"

S^D, discriminative stimulus; S^{R+}, unconditioned positive reinforcer.

TASK B.14

Identify and distinguish between stimulus and response generalization. Generalization refers to the spreading of the effects of some operation (e.g., reinforcement, punishment, or extinction) on one stimulus to other, different stimuli. When responding is similar in the presence of two different stimuli, the client has generalized between them.

STIMULUS GENERALIZATION

This occurs when the client emits a trained response in the presence of a stimulus that is physically similar to the stimulus that was used to train it.

- **Example:** A client learns to say "Bunny" in the presence of a bunny rabbit (Table 4.19).

Table 4.19 Trained Response in Presence of a Specific Stimulus

S^D	R
Bunny	"Bunny"

R, response; S^D, discriminative stimulus.

Then, in the presence of other small, furry animals, the client says, "Bunny" (Table 4.20).

Table 4.20 Stimulus Generalization

S^D	R
Ferret	"Bunny"
Guinea Pig	"Bunny"
Squirrel	"Bunny"

R, response; S^D, discriminative stimulus.

RESPONSE GENERALIZATION

This occurs when the client emits an untrained response that serves the same function as the trained target behavior. The focus is on function, not form.

- **Example:** A client learns to greet a friend with "Hello" (Table 4.21)

Table 4.21 Learned Response

S^D	R
Friend	"Hello"

R, response; S^D, discriminative stimulus.

Then, in the presence of familiar people, the client uses different, untrained responses that serve the same function as "hello" (Table 4.22).

Table 4.22 Response Generalization

S^D	R
Friend	"Hey"
Another friend	"Good morning"
Therapist	Waves hand

R, response; S^D, discriminative stimulus.

ADDITIONAL NOTE(S)

It may be helpful to think of discrimination and generalization as two ends of the same spectrum related to stimulus function.

▶ TASK B.15

Identify examples of response maintenance. Maintenance refers to the extent to which a client continues to perform a behavior when some or all of an intervention that evokes it has been removed.

- **Example:** An intervention is implemented to teach a client to independently put on their backpack in the morning before leaving home for school, 5 days of the week. After the intervention has been withdrawn, the client has "maintained" the skill by continuing to put on their backpack in the morning before leaving home for school, 5 days of the week.

▶ TASK B.16

Identify examples of motivating operations. MOs are environmental variables that alter the value of the reinforcer and the likelihood of a behavior occurring. They produce two different effects: (a) value-altering and (b) behavior-altering.

The value-altering effect is a momentary increase or decrease in the reinforcing effects of a stimulus. If the MO increases the reinforcing effects of a stimulus, it is said to have produced a reinforcer-establishing effect. This type of MO is referred to as an establishing operation (EO). If the MO decreases the reinforcing effects of a stimulus, it is said to have produced a reinforcer-abolishing effect. This type of MO is referred to as an abolishing operation (AO).

The behavior-altering effect is a momentary increase or decrease in the frequency of a behavior that has been reinforced or punished by the stimulus whose value has been changed by the MO. If the MO increases the frequency of a behavior that has been reinforced by some stimulus, it is said to have produced an evocative effect. If the MO decreases the frequency of a behavior that has been reinforced by some stimulus, it is said to have produced an abative effect.

- **Example:** Food deprivation increases the effectiveness of food as a reinforcer (value-altering; reinforcer-establishing effect) and food-seeking behaviors (behavior-altering; evocative effect; Figure 4.4).

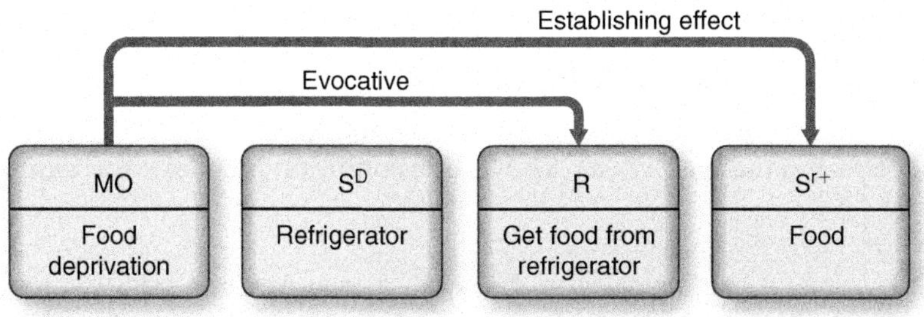

Figure 4.4 Example of Value-Altering and Behavior-Altering Effects of Food Deprivation
MO, motivating operation; R, response; S^D, discriminative stimulus; S^{r+}, conditioned positive reinforcer.

If the MO was food ingestion instead of deprivation, we would see a decrease in the effectiveness of food as a reinforcer (value-altering; reinforcer-abolishing effect) and food-seeking behaviors (behavior-altering; abative effect).

MOs can be (a) conditioned or (b) unconditioned.

UNCONDITIONED MOTIVATING OPERATION

An unconditioned motivating operation (UMO) is an MO that does not require learning to produce value-altering and behavior-altering effects.

UMOs that have reinforcer-establishing and evocative effects include:

- deprivation of food, water, sleep, activity, oxygen, sex
- being too hot or cold
- onset/increase in painful stimulation

UMOs that have reinforcer-abolishing and abative effects include ingestion and engaging in specific activities (e.g., sleep, activity, breathing, sex).

CONDITIONED MOTIVATING OPERATION

Like UMOs, conditioned motivating operations (CMOs) produce value-altering and behavior-altering effects. But unlike UMOs, the value-altering effect of CMOs depends on a learning history. There are three types of CMOs: (a) surrogate, (b) reflexive, and (c) transitive.

SURROGATE CONDITIONED MOTIVATING OPERATION

A surrogate conditioned motivating operation (CMO-S) is a stimulus that has acquired its effects as an MO as a result of being paired with a UMO.

- **Example:** A person might go to the kitchen where food is kept when they haven't eaten for a period of time. After multiple pairings of food deprivation (UMO) with the kitchen, the kitchen may become a CMO-S that establishes food as a reinforcer and evokes food-seeking behaviors.

REFLEXIVE CONDITIONED MOTIVATING OPERATION

A reflexive conditioned motivating operation (CMO-R) is a stimulus that has acquired its effects as an MO as a result of it preceding the onset of unpleasant/painful stimulation. Its own offset functions as a reinforcer.

TRANSITIVE CONDITIONED MOTIVATING OPERATION

A transitive conditioned motivating operation (CMO-T) is a stimulus that establishes or abolishes the reinforcing or punishing value of another stimulus.

- **Example:** Your head hurts. As a CMO-R, this condition (i.e., your head hurting) is only getting worse, which establishes its own offset as a reinforcer and evokes behavior that has resulted in its offset in the past. As a CMO-T, this condition increases the reinforcing value of aspirin (Figure 4.5).

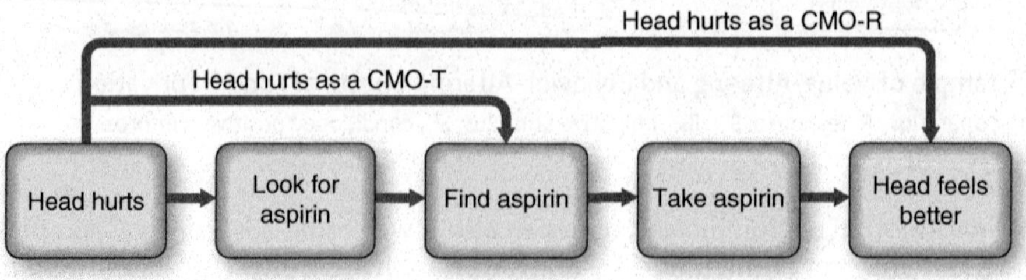

Figure 4.5 Example of Painful Stimulus (Head Hurts) as a CMO-R and CMO-T
CMO-R, reflexive conditioned motivating operation; CMO-T, transitive conditioned motivating operation

▶ TASK B.17

Distinguish between motivating operations and stimulus control. As described previously (see Tasks B.12 and B.17), MOs are environmental variables that alter the value of a reinforcer and the likelihood of a behavior occurring, and stimulus control refers to the degree to which a behavior is emitted in the presence of specific antecedent stimuli but not in their absence. They can be distinguished in terms of their (a) function and (b) focus.

DIFFERENT FUNCTION

MOs alter the value of reinforcers and the likelihood of behavior, while stimulus control involves the antecedent stimuli signaling when a behavior will be reinforced.

DIFFERENT FOCUS

MOs focus on the effect of environmental variables on the reinforcing effectiveness of stimuli, while stimulus control focuses on the discriminative stimuli that occasion or evoke specific behaviors.

TASK B.18

Identify and distinguish between rule-governed and contingency-shaped behavior.

RULE-GOVERNED BEHAVIOR

This refers to behavior that is under the control of verbal antecedents that are considered rules. There are two types of rules: (a) those in the form of a simple request or instruction, and (b) those that describe a behavioral contingency.

Rule-governed behavior is generated through exposure to rules and enables organisms to respond effectively without directly contacting contingencies that would be harmful or inefficient to contact.

For example, a commonly understood rule is that if you touch a stove when it is on you will get burned. This represents an "if-then" rule; if you touch a stove when it is on, then you get burned. An if-then statement is a simple rule that specifies both the antecedent and the behavior(s) that should occur in its presence.

- **Example (simple request or instruction):** "Do not touch that stove when it is on."

- **Example (describing a contingency):** "If you touch that stove when it is on, you will burn your hand."

CONTINGENCY-SHAPED BEHAVIOR

This refers to behavior that is learned through experience with contingencies.

- **Example:** You avoid touching the stove when it is on because you have learned from experience that doing so will burn your hand.

TASK B.19

Identify and distinguish among verbal operants. Verbal operants are types of expressive language (i.e., verbal behavior), which include the (a) duplic, (b) mand, (c) tact, (d) intraverbal, and (e) codic types. Each verbal operant is identified by its source of antecedent control and history of resultant consequence.

DUPLIC

This type is under the control of a verbal stimulus with point-to-point correspondence (i.e., stimulus parts correspond with response parts), formal similarity (i.e., stimulus and response physically resemble each other), and has a history of generalized reinforcement. There are three types of duplics: the (a) echoic, (b) mimetic (i.e., motor imitation), and (c) copying text.

- **Example (echoic):** A client hears "Hi" and then says, "Hi" (Table 4.23).

Table 4.23 Echoic

VERBAL S^D	R	CONSEQUENCE
Hears "Hi"	Says "Hi"	Generalized S^r (e.g., smile, praise)

R, response; S^D, discriminative stimulus; S^r, conditioned reinforcer.

- **Example (mimetic):** A client sees an adult wave a hand and then waves a hand (Table 4.24).

Table 4.24 Mimetic

VERBAL S^D	R	CONSEQUENCE
Sees a hand wave	Waves hand	Generalized S^r

R, response; S^D, discriminative stimulus; S^r, conditioned reinforcer.

- **Example (copying text):** A client sees "hi" written on the whiteboard and then writes the word "hi" on a piece of paper (Table 4.25).

Table 4.25 Copying Text

VERBAL S^D	R	CONSEQUENCE
Sees "hi" written on board	Writes "hi" on paper	Generalized S^r

R, response; S^D, discriminative stimulus; S^r, conditioned reinforcer.

MAND

This type is under the control of an MO and has a history of specific reinforcement.

- **Example:** A client is thirsty and signs "water" (Table 4.26).

Table 4.26 Mand

MOTIVATING OPERATION	R	SPECIFIC CONSEQUENCE
Deprived of water for a period of time (value of water is high)	Signs "water"	Water

R, response.

TACT

This type is under the control of a nonverbal stimulus and has a history of specific reinforcement.

- **Example:** A client sees a glass of water and then says, "Water" (Table 4.27).

Table 4.27 Tact

NONVERBAL S^D	R	CONSEQUENCE
Sees a glass of water	"Water"	Generalized S^r

R, response; S^D, discriminative stimulus; S^r, conditioned reinforcer.

INTRAVERBAL

This type is under the control of a verbal stimulus without point-to-point correspondence and has a history of generalized reinforcement.

- **Example:** A client hears "How are you?" and responds, "I'm fine," (Table 4.28).

Table 4.28 Intraverbal

VERBAL S^D	R	CONSEQUENCE
Hears "How are you?"	"I'm fine"	Generalized S^r

R, response; S^D, discriminative stimulus; S^r, conditioned reinforcer.

CODIC

This type is under the control of a verbal stimulus with point-to-point correspondence but without formal similarity and has a history of generalized reinforcement. There are two types of codics: (a) textual and (b) dictation.

- **Example (textual):** A client sees the written word "fine" in a book and then says, "Fine," (Table 4.29).

Table 4.29 Textual Verbal Operant

VERBAL S^D	R	CONSEQUENCE
Sees "fine" in a book	Says "Fine"	Generalized S^r

R, response; S^D, discriminative stimulus; S^r, conditioned reinforcer.

- **Example (dictation):** A client hears the word "Fine" and then write the word "Fine" on a piece of paper (Table 4.30).

Table 4.30 Taking Dictation Verbal Operant

VERBAL S^D	R	CONSEQUENCE
Hears "Fine"	Writes "Fine" on paper	Generalized S^r

TASK B.20

Identify the role of multiple control in verbal behavior. Multiple control in verbal behavior is a concept that underscores the complexity of human communication. It refers to situations where a single verbal response is influenced by multiple antecedent variables. This influence can take two forms: (a) convergent multiple control and (b) divergent multiple control.

CONVERGENT MULTIPLE CONTROL

This occurs when a single response is controlled by more than one antecedent variable.

- **Example:** A request (i.e., mand) may be prompted by both an MO (e.g., the desire for social attention) and a specific S^D (e.g., the presence of another person).

Convergent control involving multiple MOs demonstrates how various motivational factors can synergize or compete in prompting behavior. For instance, the desire for food and social interaction may either reinforce or counteract each other in evoking a response.

Additionally, convergent control involving MOs and S^Ds highlights the joint influence of environmental cues and motivational factors on behavior. Combining MOs with S^Ds can amplify or attenuate the evocative effect. For example, combining prompts with MOs and salient nonverbal cues can aid in early mand training for nonverbal individuals.

DIVERGENT MULTIPLE CONTROL

This occurs when a single antecedent variable prompts multiple responses.

- **Example:** An ambiguous statement like "What's that?" may elicit different responses depending on context, such as "It's a book" or "It's a cat."

MAND CONTROL

Lastly, mand control underscores that an MO alone may not suffice to prompt behavior. However, when combined with other variables, it can effectively evoke responses. This supplementary form of control underscores the complex interaction of multiple variables in shaping verbal behavior.

Understanding multiple control in verbal behavior is crucial for deciphering the nuanced dynamics of human communication and language usage and sheds light on how motivational factors, environmental cues, and other variables converge to shape our verbal responses across various contexts.

TASK B.21

Identify examples of processes that promote emergent relations and generative performance.

EMERGENT RELATIONS

These refer to the spontaneous emergence of new behaviors, skills, or relations that aren't explicitly taught or trained. They arise from learning experiences, guided by principles like (a) reflexivity, (b) symmetry, and (c) transitivity, which underpin stimulus equivalence.

Reflexivity

This type of stimulus-stimulus relation is indicated in the selection of a comparison stimulus that matches the sample stimulus (e.g., A = A) without training to do so.

- **Example:** A client is given the following sample stimulus (i.e., picture; Figure 4.6):

Figure 4.6 Sample Stimulus

And the following comparison stimuli (i.e., pictures; Figure 4.7):

Figure 4.7 Comparison Stimuli

Without training, the client makes the following sample stimulus to comparison stimulus match (Figure 4.8).

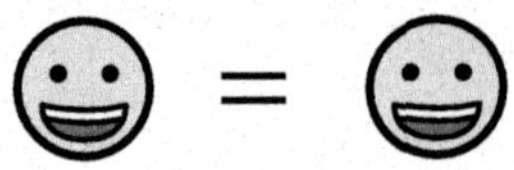

Figure 4.8 Demonstration of Reflexivity

Symmetry

This type of stimulus-stimulus relation is indicated in the demonstration of reversibility of a sample stimulus and comparison stimulus (e.g., if A = B, then B = A) without training to do so.

- **Example:** A client is taught the following sample stimulus (i.e., picture) to comparison stimulus (i.e., spoken word) relation (Figure 4.9):

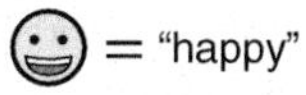

Figure 4.9 Sample Stimulus (Picture) to Comparison Stimulus (Spoken Word)

Without training, the client selects the picture of the happy face when presented with the spoken word "happy" (Figure 4.10).

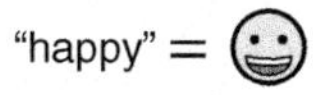

Figure 4.10 Demonstration of Symmetry

Transitivity

This type of stimulus-stimulus relation is indicated in the demonstration of a derived stimulus-stimulus relation following the training of two other stimulus-stimulus relations (e.g., if A = B and B = C, then A = C and C = A).

- **Example:** A client is taught the following relations (Figure 4.11):

Figure 4.11 A (Spoken Word) = B (Picture), and B = C (Written Word)

Without training, the following relation emerges (Figure 4.12):

Spoken word		Written word
"happy"	=	"happy"

Figure 4.12 Demonstration of Transitivity

While these principles primarily relate to stimulus equivalence, other types of emergent relations exist. For instance, derived stimulus relations involve the emergence of new relations between stimuli based on established relations.

GENERATIVE PERFORMANCE

This refers to the ability to demonstrate novel behaviors, responses, or relations beyond explicitly taught or learned ones. It includes the spontaneous application of learned skills in new contexts and emerging new behaviors based on existing repertoires.

ADDITIONAL NOTE(S)

Processes that promote emergent relations and generative performance can include behavioral skills training (BST); the teaching of relational framing skills, such as matching, opposition, comparison, and distinction; and stimulus equivalence training.

TASK B.22

Identify ways behavioral momentum can be used to understand response persistence.

BEHAVIORAL MOMENTUM

This is a concept derived from Newtonian physics, referring to the resistance to change in a behavior's rate once it has been established. Like the physical momentum of an object, behaviors that have been consistently reinforced tend to persist even in the face of disruptors or changes in the environment. This concept is instrumental in understanding why certain behaviors are more resistant to change than others.

HIGH-PROBABILITY REQUEST SEQUENCE

One practical application of behavioral momentum is the high-probability (high-*p*) request sequence, which is a contingency-independent antecedent intervention that involves (a) presenting a series of easy-to-follow requests for which the client has a history of compliance (i.e., high-probability or high-*p* requests), and (b) presenting the target request (i.e., low-probability or low-*p* request) after the client has complied with the high-*p* requests. Typically, two to five high-*p* requests precede the presentation of a low-*p* request. The compliance with high-probability requests builds behavioral momentum, increasing the likelihood that the individual will comply with the subsequent low-*p* request.

To effectively implement this procedure, the following guidelines should be followed: (a) present high-*p* requests that the client is currently able to comply with, (b) present requests in rapid succession, (c) acknowledge compliance with each request, and (d) use high-quality reinforcers.

- **Example:** A client throws tantrums when they are asked to wash their hands. Their teacher uses a high-*p* to increase the likelihood of compliance with the request without the tantrum.

  Teacher: "Give me five!" (high-*p* request)

  Client complies.

  Teacher: "Awesome!" (acknowledgment of compliance) "Now touch your nose." (high-*p* request)

  Client complies.

  Teacher: "That's great!" (acknowledgment of compliance) "Now make a silly face!" (high-*p* request)

  Client complies.

  Teacher: "Okay, nice job!" (acknowledgment of compliance) "Now please go wash your hands." (low-*p* request)

  Client complies.

  Teacher delivers high-quality reinforcer for compliance.

BEHAVIORAL MOMENTUM AND RESPONSE PERSISTENCE

Behavioral momentum can be used to explain response persistence in various ways, including (a) how reinforcement history strengthens behavior, (b) how behaviors resist extinction, and (c) how behaviors persist despite disruptive contexts.

Reinforcement History

Behaviors with a strong history of reinforcement are more likely to persist. For example, a client's on-task behavior that has been frequently reinforced with praise and rewards will be more resistant to disruption.

Resistance to Extinction

Behaviors that have been consistently reinforced are less likely to undergo extinction quickly. For instance, a behavior such as completing homework, which has been reinforced over time, will persist longer even if reinforcement is temporarily withdrawn.

Disruptive Contexts

Behavioral momentum helps understand why certain behaviors persist despite challenges or disruptors. For example, in a classroom setting, if a client has built momentum in completing tasks, they are more likely to continue working despite minor disruptions.

ADDITIONAL NOTE(S)

To leverage behavioral momentum in practice, you can build momentum with high-*p* requests and reinforce desirable behaviors to enhance their persistence.

TASK B.23

Identify ways the matching law can be used to interpret response allocation. The matching law describes how responses are distributed among available alternatives based on the relative rates of reinforcement associated with each alternative. It can be used to interpret response allocation in several ways.

PROPORTIONAL ALLOCATION

Proportional allocation predicts that organisms distribute their responses among available options in proportion to the relative rates of reinforcement associated with each option.

BIAS ANALYSIS

By examining deviations from proportional allocation, researchers can identify biases toward certain options, which may provide insights into individual preferences or environmental influences.

SENSITIVITY TO REINFORCEMENT CHANGES

The matching law helps researchers understand how organisms adjust their response allocation in response to changes in reinforcement rates, providing insights into behavioral flexibility and adaptability.

PREDICTING BEHAVIOR IN COMPLEX ENVIRONMENTS

By applying the principles of the matching law, researchers can predict how organisms will allocate their responses in complex environments with multiple competing options and varying reinforcement rates.

TASK B.24

Identify and distinguish between imitation and observational learning. Imitation and observational learning are both processes through which individuals acquire new behaviors by observing others. However, they diverge notably in terms of the immediacy of the replication of behavior, the depth of understanding of observed actions and their consequences, and the degree of reliance on the observed model as a guiding influence.

IMITATION

This refers to the direct replication of an observed behavior without necessarily understanding its purpose or underlying mechanisms. The criteria for imitation are: (a) it is prompted by a behavioral model, (b) the imitation is similar in form to the model, (c) it happens promptly following the modeled behavior, and (d) the model serves as the main controlling variable.

OBSERVATIONAL LEARNING

This is considered a more complex form of learning when compared to imitation. Observational learning involves observing the behavior of others and their consequences, then using that information to determine whether or not to imitate the behavior. Unlike imitation, it involves understanding the context and consequences of observed behaviors, thereby allowing the learner to make informed decisions about whether to replicate the behavior.

▸ PRACTICE QUESTION

For practice, examine the following question and answer options. After carefully reading the question and answer options through and conducting your analysis, select the best answer option.

A client, Milo, eats with his hands. After mealtime, his hands are covered with pieces of food. Milo doesn't like this and, in response, wipes his hands on his shirt. Wiping his hands on his shirt effectively removes the pieces of food that were sticking to his hands, which makes Milo more likely to wipe his hands on his shirt in the future. Which of the following provides the best explanation for Milo's increased likelihood of engaging in this behavior (wiping his hands on his shirt) in the future?

A. Negative punishment
B. Negative reinforcement
C. Positive reinforcement
D. Positive punishment

Before moving on to the following section for the solution, we recommend that you provide a brief explanation for the answer option you selected here:

____

____

When you're ready, move on to the next section for the solution!

Practice Question Breakdown

Step 1: Examine the question

The question calls for the identification of the behavior principle that explains Milo's increased likelihood of engaging in a behavior in the future. In the scenario presented, Milo's behavior (wiping his hands on his shirt) resulted in the effective removal of an aversive condition (having his hands covered with pieces of food).

Step 2: Analyze the answer options

A. Negative punishment involves the removal of a stimulus to decrease the likelihood of engaging in a behavior in the future. The question asks for the principle that explains an *increased* likelihood of engaging in a behavior in the future. This answer option is a distractor.

B. Negative reinforcement involves the removal of a stimulus to increase the likelihood of engaging in a behavior in the future. The scenario describes removal of an aversive stimulus condition *and* increased likelihood of engaging in a behavior in the future. This appears to be a promising option!
C. Positive reinforcement involves the presentation of a stimulus to increase the likelihood of engaging in a behavior in the future. However, the scenario involves the *removal* of an aversive stimulus condition. This answer option is a distractor.
D. Positive punishment involves the presentation of a stimulus to decrease the likelihood of engaging in a behavior in the future. The scenario describes the *removal* of an aversive stimulus condition and *increased* likelihood of engaging in a behavior in the future. This answer option is a distractor.

Step 3: Select the best answer

Among the four answer options presented, answer B (Negative reinforcement) appears to be the best answer.

CONCLUSION

In this chapter, we reviewed key content for TCO Tasks related to concepts and principles of ABA, including core elements constituting a scientific analysis of behavior and the core principles produced by this analysis. Since the scientific analysis of behavior focuses on controlling variables in the environment, this chapter defined and explicated foundational concepts like behavior, response, response class, stimulus, and stimulus class. The chapter also defined respondent and operant behavior and explained how these two types of behavior are influenced by the environment in respondent and operant conditioning. Building on this foundation, the chapter defined and provided examples of many of the most important concepts and principles in ABA, including reinforcement and punishment; concepts related to the all-important three-term contingency, such as stimulus control; and operant extinction, generalization, maintenance, contingency-shaped behavior, and more.

REFERENCES

Behavior Analyst Certification Board. (2024). *BCBA test content outline* (6th ed.). Author. https://www.bacb.com/wp-content/bcba-outline-6thEd
Cooper, J. O., Heron, T. E., & Heward, W. L. (2020). *Applied behavior analysis* (3rd ed.). Pearson Education.

BIBLIOGRAPHY

Behavior Analyst Certification Board. (2022). *BACB fact sheet*. Author.
Edwards, T. L., Lotfizadeh, A. D., & Poling, A. (2019). Motivating operations and stimulus control. *Journal of the Experimental Analysis of Behavior, 112*(1), 1–9. https://doi.org/10.1002/jeab.516
Johnston, J. M., & Pennypacker, H. S. (1993). *Readings for strategies and tactics of behavioral research*. Lawrence Erlbaum Associates, Inc.
Michael, J. L. (2004). *Concepts and principles of behavior analysis*. Western Michigan University, Association for Behavior Analysis International.
Miltenberger, R. (2008). *Behaviour modification*. Wadsworth Publishing.
Schlinger, H. D., Derenne, A., & Baron, A. (2008). What 50 years of research tell us about pausing under ratio schedules of reinforcement. *The Behavior Analyst, 31*(1), 39–60. https://doi.org/10.1007/BF03392160
Sidman, M. (1994). *Equivalence relations and behavior: A research story*. Authors Cooperative.
Skinner, B. F. (1957). *Verbal behavior*. Appleton-Century-Crofts.
Skinner, B. F. (1974). *About behaviorism*. Vintage.

KNOWLEDGE CHECK

1. A topographical response class defines members of its class in terms of their:

A. Form

B. Function

C. Rate

D. Time or place of occurrence

2. A behavior analyst observes that a client in class uses different methods to gain the teacher's attention. Sometimes the client raises their hand, other times they call out loudly, or they tap the teacher on the shoulder. All these behaviors result in the same outcome: the teacher giving attention. Which type of response group is the client demonstrating?

A. Behavioral cluster

B. Functional response class

C. Response hierarchy

D. Topographical response class

3. A behavior technician is teaching a client to recognize different fruits. The client is taught that fruits like apples, oranges, and bananas can be grouped based on their physical characteristics (shape and color), their purpose (as food), and when they are typically consumed (during meals or as snacks). Which of the following dimensions is NOT typically a factor in grouping fruits into a stimulus class?

A. Formal

B. Functional

C. Spatial

D. Temporal

4. Respondent conditioning is a type of learning whereby new stimuli develop the capacity to ________________ responses through the ________________ process.

A. Elicit, pairing

B. Elicit, conditioning

C. Evoke, pairing

D. Evoke, conditioning

5. Pavlov's famous experiments with dogs demonstrated how meat powder, which naturally caused dogs to salivate, was repeatedly paired with a tone until the tone elicited salivation. In this example, the meat powder served as:

A. A conditioned stimulus (CS)

B. A neutral stimulus (NS)

C. An unconditioned stimulus (US)

D. An unconditioned response (UR)

(*See answers on the next page.*)

1. **A) Form**
   A topographical response class defines members of its class in terms of their form, not function. The other answer options (function, rate, time or place of occurrence) serve as distractors.

2. **B) Functional response class**
   In this scenario, the client engages in different behaviors (raising their hand, calling out, and tapping the teacher) that all result in the same effect of gaining the teacher's attention. This describes a functional response class, where various behaviors produce the same effect on the environment. The other answer options, including the topographical response class that groups behaviors based on physical form, function as distractors.

3. **C) Spatial**
   In a stimulus class, stimuli are grouped based on shared characteristics across three common dimensions: formal (physical features like shape and color), temporal (when the stimulus occurs in time), and functional (the purpose or use of the stimulus). In this scenario, the client is learning to group fruits based on these dimensions. Spatial properties are not typically a factor in grouping stimuli into a class, whereas the other answer options (formal, temporal, and functional) are commonly used to group stimuli into classes.

4. **A) Elicit, pairing**
   Respondent conditioning is a type of learning whereby new stimuli develop the capacity to elicit responses through the pairing process. The other answer options (elicit, conditioning; evoke, pairing; evoke, conditioning) do not fit into this definition.

5. **C) An unconditioned stimulus (US)**
   In the example presented, the meat powder served as a US that naturally caused Pavlov's dogs to salivate (UR). The tone is the NS that, after pairing with the meat powder, becomes the CS.

6. A researcher is studying a rat in a lab setting where the rat can press a lever to receive food. After several trials, the rat presses the lever more frequently to obtain food. The researcher notes that the rat's behavior of pressing the lever is under the rat's control and is influenced by the consequence of receiving food. Which aspect of the rat's behavior indicates that operant conditioning is at work?

   A. The rat's lever-pressing is an automatic response.

   B. The rat's lever-pressing is voluntary and influenced by consequences.

   C. The rat's behavior of pressing the lever is involuntary.

   D. The rat is habituating to the lever-pressing behavior.

7. Which of the following refers to the removal of a stimulus immediately subsequent to a behavior that serves to increase the future frequency of the behavior?

   A. Negative punishment

   B. Negative reinforcement

   C. Positive punishment

   D. Positive reinforcement

8. A behavior analyst is working with a client to increase the frequency of polite requests during social interactions. Each time the client makes a polite request, the analyst immediately provides positive reinforcement in the form of verbal praise. Over time, the client starts making polite requests more frequently, as they consistently receive praise after each polite request. This is an example of which of the following?

   A. Fixed interval

   B. Continuous reinforcement

   C. Variable interval

   D. Intermittent reinforcement

9. A behavior analyst is teaching a client to stay on task during training sessions. Reinforcement is provided in the form of a token, but the time between each reinforcement varies. Sometimes the client is reinforced after 5 minutes, other times after 12 or 8 minutes, but on average, reinforcement is provided every 10 minutes as long as the client stays on task. Which schedule of reinforcement is the behavior analyst using?

   A. Fixed interval (FI)

   B. Fixed ratio (FR)

   C. Variable interval (VI)

   D. Variable ratio (VR)

(See answers on the next page.)

6. **B) The rat's lever-pressing is voluntary and influenced by consequences.**
Operant conditioning involves voluntary behaviors that are shaped by consequences, such as receiving food after pressing the lever. In this scenario, the rat presses the lever (voluntary behavior) more frequently because the behavior is reinforced by food (consequence). The other answer options either refer to involuntary, automatic behaviors or habituation.

7. **B) Negative reinforcement**
Negative reinforcement refers to the removal of a stimulus immediately subsequent to a behavior that serves to increase the future frequency of the behavior. The other response options (negative punishment, positive punishment, positive reinforcement) function as distractors.

8. **B) Continuous reinforcement**
A continuous schedule of reinforcement requires the delivery of reinforcement after each occurrence of a target behavior. The other response options refer to other schedules that provide reinforcement after a set time period regardless of behavior, after varying time intervals, or only for some occurrences of the target behavior.

9. **C) Variable interval (VI)**
The VI schedule of reinforcement specifies the average duration that must pass before the first occurrence of a target response will be reinforced. The other answer options (FI, FR, VR) refer to other schedules of reinforcement and function as distractors.

10. A client with autism repeatedly rubs their hands together throughout the day, even when they are alone. The behavior analyst hypothesizes that the client engages in this behavior because the tactile sensation of hand-rubbing itself is reinforcing, rather than any external consequence or social attention. What type of reinforcement is the hand-rubbing behavior MOST likely being maintained by?

A. Automatic

B. Positive

C. Negative

D. Socially mediated

11. A client engages in tantrum behavior when they want a toy. In response, the parent often gives the child the toy to stop the tantrum. Over time, the behavior analyst notices that the tantrums increase because the child learns that the tantrum will result in getting the toy from the parent. What type of reinforcement is at play when the child's tantrum is reinforced by the parent giving the toy?

A. Automatic reinforcement

B. Positive reinforcement

C. Socially mediated reinforcement

D. Negative reinforcement

12. Water and food are examples of:

A. Arbitrary reinforcers

B. Conditioned reinforcers

C. Generalized reinforcers

D. Unconditioned reinforcers

13. A behavior analyst is working with a client to increase several behaviors, such as following instructions and engaging in social interactions. The analyst uses social praise (e.g., "Good job!" or "Well done!") after the client performs these behaviors. The client responds positively because, in the past, social praise has been consistently paired with access to other reinforcers like attention, privileges, and tangible rewards. What type of reinforcer is social praise in this scenario?

A. A conditioned reinforcer

B. A generalized reinforcer

C. An arbitrary reinforcer

D. An unconditioned reinforcer

14. Operant extinction refers to ________________ in behavior resulting from the ________________ of reinforcement for it.

A. A reduction; delivery

B. A reduction; discontinuation

C. An increase; delivery

D. An increase; discontinuation

(*See answers on the next page.*)

10. **A) Automatic**
    In the scenario, the client's hand-rubbing behavior is reinforced by the tactile sensation it produces, which occurs without external or social input. This is an example of automatic reinforcement, where the behavior itself produces the reinforcing consequence. The other answer options refer to external consequences (adding or removing stimuli) or reinforcement that comes from others, which is not the case here.

11. **C) Socially mediated reinforcement**
    In this scenario, the child's tantrum behavior is reinforced by the parent's action of giving the toy, which increases the likelihood of future tantrums. This is an example of socially mediated reinforcement, where the behavior is strengthened by the actions of another person. Positive reinforcement refers to adding a stimulus to increase behavior but doesn't specify that the reinforcement comes from another person. The other answer options refer to reinforcement produced by the behavior itself or the removal of an aversive stimulus, which is not the case here.

12. **D) Unconditioned reinforcers**
    Unconditioned reinforcers are the product of phylogeny and satisfy basic life needs, such as water and food. The other answer options (arbitrary reinforcers, conditioned reinforcers, generalized reinforcers) refer to other types of reinforcers and function as distractors.

13. **B) A generalized reinforcer**
    In the scenario, social praise functions as a generalized reinforcer because it has been paired with access to various reinforcers like attention, privileges, and rewards in the past. This pairing allows social praise to reinforce multiple behaviors across different situations, as the client has learned that praise is associated with positive outcomes. The other answer options refer to reinforcers that are typically associated with a specific reinforcing consequence, lack the broad reinforcing power of generalized reinforcers, or are inherently reinforcing without prior pairing.

14. **B) A reduction; discontinuation**
    Operant extinction refers to a reduction in behavior resulting from the delivery of reinforcement for it. The other answer options (a reduction, delivery; an increase, delivery; an increase, discontinuation) do not fit this definition and function as distractors.

15. Which of the following is established when a response is only reinforced when a specific stimulus is present but NOT reinforced when other stimuli are present?

A. Discrimination

B. Response class

C. Stimulus class

D. Stimulus control

16. What type of discrimination occurs when a client emits a response that is controlled by a single stimulus when it is in the presence of another stimulus?

A. Conditional discrimination

B. Relational discrimination

C. Simple discrimination

D. Successive discrimination

17. An intervention is implemented to teach a client to perform a skill. After the intervention has been withdrawn, the client continues to perform the skill. This is an example of:

A. Maintenance

B. Persistence

C. Response generalization

D. Stimulus generalization

18. If a motivating operation (MO) momentarily increases the reinforcing effects of a stimulus, it is said to have produced a ________________ effect.

A. Behavior-altering

B. Reinforcer-abolishing

C. Reinforcer-establishing

D. Second-order

19. A client has not had water for several hours and is very thirsty. The client begins asking for water more frequently. The behavior analyst notes that the client's thirst has increased the frequency of behaviors that lead to obtaining water. What type of effect does the client's thirst produce?

A. Evocative

B. Abative

C. Primacy

D. Reinforcer-establishing

(*See answers on the next page.*)

15. **D) Stimulus control**
    Stimulus control is established when a response is only reinforced when a specific stimulus is present but not reinforced when other stimuli are present. The other answer options (discrimination, response class, stimulus class) refer to other concepts and function as distractors.

16. **A) Conditional discrimination**
    Conditional discrimination occurs when a client emits a response that is controlled by a single stimulus when it is in the presence of another stimulus. The other answer options (relational discrimination, simple discrimination, successive discrimination) refer to other types of discrimination and function as distractors.

17. **A) Maintenance**
    When an intervention has been implemented to teach a skill and is subsequently withdrawn but the client continues to perform it, the skill is said to have been maintained. This is an example of maintenance. Persistence is not the correct technical term for this concept. The other answer options (persistence, response generalization, stimulus generalization) function as distractors.

18. **C) Reinforcer-establishing**
    An MO produces value-altering and behavior-altering effects. If it momentarily increases the reinforcing effects of a stimulus, it is said to have produced a reinforcer-establishing effect. The other answer options (behavior-altering, reinforcer-abolishing, second-order) serve as distractors.

19. **A) Evocative**
    In this scenario, the client's thirst increases the frequency of behaviors (asking for water) that lead to obtaining water, which demonstrates an evocative effect. An evocative effect occurs when a motivating operation (MO) increases the likelihood of behaviors that have been previously reinforced. The other answer options refer to effects that are either unrelated to MOs, decrease the frequency of behavior, or increase the value of a reinforcer without directly describing an increase in behavior frequency.

20. A behavior analyst observes a client during lunchtime at school. The client has not eaten since breakfast, and as lunchtime approaches, the client's food-seeking behavior increases. The behavior analyst explains that the client's hunger increases the value of food as a reinforcer and directly affects the client's behavior of looking for food, without the need for prior learning. Which type of motivating operation (MO) is this an example of?

A. AO

B. CMO-R

C. CMO-S

D. UMO

21. A person experiences a stomachache, which is gradually worsening. As a ________________, the condition establishes its own offset as a reinforcer and evokes medicine-seeking behavior that has resulted in relieving stomach pain in the past.

A. CMO-R

B. CMO-S

C. CMO-T

D. UMO

22. ________________ refers to behavior that is under the control of verbal antecedents that are considered rules, whereas ________________ refers to behavior that is learned through experience with contingencies.

A. Contingency-governed; conditioned response

B. Contingency-shaped behavior; rule-governed behavior

C. Discrete; discriminated

D. Rule-governed behavior; contingency-shaped behavior

23. A behavior analyst presents a toy car to a client and asks, "What is this?" The client responds by saying "Car." The behavior analyst provides praise, reinforcing the correct response. This type of interaction has occurred multiple times, with the client consistently labeling objects based on what they see, and receiving specific reinforcement each time. Which verbal operant has the client demonstrated?

A. Duplic

B. Mand

C. Intraverbal

D. Tact

24. Which of the following verbal operants is under the control of a verbal stimulus without point-to-point correspondence and has a history of generalized reinforcement?

A. Duplic

B. Mand

C. Intraverbal

D. Tact

(*See answers on the next page.*)

20. D) UMO
The scenario describes hunger, which is an example of a UMO (unconditioned motivating operation). UMOs do not require any prior learning to affect the value of a reinforcer or to influence behavior. In this case, the client's hunger increases the value of food as a reinforcer and leads to food-seeking behavior. The other answer options (AO [abolishing operation], CMO-R [reflexive conditioned motivating operation], CMO-S [surrogate conditioned motivating operation]) refer to other types of MOs and function as distractors.

21. A) CMO-R
A CMO-R (reflexive conditioned motivating operation) is a stimulus that acquires its effects as a result of it preceding the onset of unpleasant/painful stimulation. In the example provided, the stomach pain is a CMO-R and its own offset functions as a reinforcer. The other answer options (CMO-S [surrogate conditioned motivating operation], CMO-T [transitive conditioned motivating operation], UMO [unconditioned motivating operation]) are distractors.

22. D) Rule-governed behavior; contingency-shaped behavior
Rule-governed behavior refers to behavior that is under the control of verbal antecedents that are considered rules, whereas contingency-shaped behavior refers to behavior that is learned through experience with contingencies. The other answer options (contingency-governed, conditioned response; contingency-shaped behavior, rule-governed behavior; discrete, discriminated) do not accurately fit into this statement and function as distractors.

23. D) Tact
The tact, often referred to as labeling, is under the control of a nonverbal stimulus and has a history of specific reinforcement. In this scenario, the client labeled the object they saw (the toy car) by saying "Car," which was reinforced by praise. The other answer options refer to other types of verbal operants and function as distractors.

24. C) Intraverbal
The intraverbal is under the control of a verbal stimulus without point-to-point correspondence and has a history of generalized reinforcement. The other answer options (duplic, mand, tact) are other types of verbal operants and function as distractors.

25. Identify the type of stimulus-stimulus relation that is indicated when a response demonstrates a derived stimulus-stimulus relation following the training of two other stimulus-stimulus relations.

A. Connectedness

B. Reflexivity

C. Symmetry

D. Transitivity

26. Identify the type of stimulus-stimulus relation that is indicated when a response demonstrates reversibility of a sample stimulus and comparison stimulus without training to do so.

A. Connectedness

B. Reflexivity

C. Symmetry

D. Transitivity

(*See answers on the next page.*)

25. **D) Transitivity**
Transitivity is a type of stimulus-stimulus relation that is indicated when a client's response demonstrates a derived stimulus-stimulus relation following the training of two other stimulus-stimulus relations (if A = B and B = C, then A = C and C = A). The other answer options (connectedness, reflexivity, symmetry) function as distractors.

26. **C) Symmetry**
Symmetry is a type of stimulus-stimulus relation that is indicated when a client's response demonstrates reversibility of a sample stimulus and comparison stimulus without having been trained to do so (if A = B, then B = A). The other answer options (connectedness, reflexivity, transitivity) function as distractors.

5

Measurement, Data Display, and Interpretation

LEARNING OBJECTIVES

The following Test Content Outline (TCO) Tasks (Behavior Analyst Certification Board®, 2024, p. 2) related to measurement, data display, and interpretation (C.1 through C.12) will serve as the learning objectives of this chapter:

- C.1 Create operational definitions of behavior.
- C.2 Distinguish among direct, indirect, and product measures of behavior.
- C.3 Measure occurrence.
- C.4 Measure temporal dimensions of behavior (e.g., duration, latency, interresponse time).
- C.5 Distinguish between continuous and discontinuous measurement procedures.
- C.6 Design and apply discontinuous measurement procedures (e.g., interval recording, time sampling).
- C.7 Measure efficiency (e.g., trials to criterion, cost-benefit analysis, training duration).
- C.8 Evaluate the validity and reliability of measurement procedures.
- C.9 Select a measurement procedure to obtain representative data that accounts for the critical dimension of the behavior and environmental constraints.
- C.10 Graph data to communicate relevant quantitative relations (e.g., equal-interval graphs, bar graphs, cumulative records).
- C.11 Interpret graphed data.
- C.12 Select a measurement procedure to obtain representative procedural integrity data that accounts for relevant dimensions (e.g., accuracy, dosage) and environmental constraints.

TASK C.1

Create operational definitions of behavior. Behavior must be defined before it can be measured. Well-written operational definitions of target behaviors allow behavior analysts to gather complete information about its occurrence and nonoccurrence (i.e., measure behavior), precisely apply procedures in a timely manner, and produce an accurate evaluation of intervention effectiveness. For researchers, employing operational definitions allows for others to replicate their work.

OPERATIONAL DEFINITION

This is an objective, clear, and complete description of an observable and measurable target behavior.

Observable

This means the behavior can be seen or heard.

- **Examples (observable behaviors):** asking, hitting, speaking, sitting, touching

Measurable

This means the behaviors can be quantified (i.e., counted or timed).

Write definitions that are (a) objective, (b) clear, and (c) complete.

Objective

This describes the behavior in observable terms.

Clear

This means unambiguous. Observers should be able to read it and then accurately paraphrase it.

Complete

This establishes which response(s) will count as an instance of the target behavior, and which response(s) do not.

- **Example (definition of "on task"):** This includes looking at the teacher/board/seatwork, contributing to the assigned task, and being quiet when expected to work independently.
- **Example (definition of "talking out"):** This includes any vocalizations that are not initiated by the teacher, are out of turn, and/or are unrelated to academic content.
- **Example (definition of "tantrum"):** This includes laying on the floor, crying, yelling, throwing objects, and/or pounding fists on the desk. The episode is counted if it lasts 10 seconds or more and is counted as a new incident if separated by 5 minutes or more.

ADDITIONAL NOTE(S)

Operational definitions can include examples and nonexamples that further clarify what is to be counted as an occurrence and what is not, thereby reducing ambiguity and increasing the odds of reliable measurement.

▶ PRACTICE QUESTION

Calvin is a third-grade student in a general education classroom. He is often asked to leave the classroom due to off-task behaviors that interfere with instruction and work completion, as well as instances of disruptive or disrespectful behavior toward his teacher and peers. Calvin's teacher requests a behavior support specialist, who is a contracted BCBA®, to observe Calvin during his literacy block. Prior to observing Calvin, the behavior support specialist meets with the teacher to narrow down a definition of his problem behavior. Which of the following is an example of an operational definition of Calvin's behavior?

A. The behavior is "disruption," which includes behaviors that interfere with instruction and make the teacher/staff angry and irritated.

B. The behavior is "disrespect," which includes vocalizing or gesturing obscenities at staff, screaming (vocalizations above normal conversational volume) at peers, and screaming "No" when asked by the teacher to begin work.

C. The behavior is "off task," which includes not completing assignments he is asked to.

D. None of the above.

Before moving on to the following section for the solution, we recommend that you provide a brief explanation for the answer option you selected here:

____

____

When you're ready, move on to the next section for the solution!

Practice Question Breakdown

Step 1: Examine the question

The question calls for an example of an operational definition of Calvin's off-task and/or disruptive/disrespectful behavior that interferes with his learning. Remember that an operational definition of behavior must be observable, measurable, objective, clear, and complete. Be sure to review the statements presented and evaluate whether they meet all the necessary characteristics of an operational definition.

Step 2: Analyze the answer options

A. This answer does not include specific examples of disruption, which makes it unclear, incomplete, and impossible to measure. It also describes the outcome of a behavior.

B. This definition appears to meet the criteria for an operational definition. It is observable (you can hear vocalizations/screams and observe gestures), measurable (you can tally frequency or document the duration of the behaviors), objective (based on observable behaviors such as vocalizing or gesturing obscenities, screaming = vocalizations above normal conversational volume; screaming "No"), clear and complete (includes information about who the behavior is directed at [staff, peers, teacher], the level of behavior that necessitates an occurrence [screaming = vocalizations above normal conversational volume], and under what conditions the behavior occurs [when asked by the teacher to begin work]).

C. This answer does not describe the behavior in observable terms such as walking around the room without permission, and so on, but describes a broad category of possible behavior with no specificity. This is a distractor.

D. There appears to be at least one response that meets the criteria for an operational definition. This is a distractor.

Step 3: Select the best answer

Among the four answer options presented, answer B (The behavior is "disrespect," ...) appears to be the best answer.

TASK C.2

Distinguish among direct, indirect, and product measures of behavior. Behavioral assessment involves a variety of measures. These include (a) direct measures, (b) indirect measures, and (c) product measures.

DIRECT MEASURES

This refers to measures that involve the observer recording the target behavior as it occurs.

INDIRECT MEASURES

This refers to measures that do not involve direct observation but require the client or others (e.g., parent, teachers, staff) to recall and report information about the target behavior. These measures include interviews, checklists, and rating scales.

PRODUCT MEASURES

This refers to measures of behavior through examination of its effects produced on the environment (i.e., permanent product). Measurement takes place after the occurrence of the behavior.

- **Example:** Number of toys placed inside a bin.

MNEMONIC AID

Direct, **I**ndirect, and **P**roduct measures. Use DIP in your assessments. It just tastes better.

TASK C.3

Measure occurrence. The occurrence of behavior can be measured in terms of (a) frequency, (b) rate, and (c) percentage. Frequency and rate are measures of the fundamental dimensional quantity of *repeatability*. Percentage is a derivative measure that combines the same dimensional quantities (e.g., count/count).

FREQUENCY

This refers to a count of a behavior or behavior class, which is calculated by simply adding up the number of occurrences.

- **Example:** A target behavior occurred three times.

RATE

This refers to a count of behavior or behavior class *per unit of time* (e.g., per minute/hour/day). This is calculated by dividing the number of occurrences by the unit of time in which observations were conducted.

- **Example:** A target behavior occurred three times per hour.

PERCENTAGE

This refers to a ratio expressed as a fraction of 100, which is calculated by multiplying the numeric value (e.g., count of a response divided by the total number of responses or opportunities/intervals in which it could have occurred) by 100.

- **Example:** A target behavior occurred during 60% of intervals recorded during the observation.

MNEMONIC AID

Please (for Percentage) **R**emember (for Rate) to **F**loss (for Frequency). When measuring occurrence of behavior, please remember to floss!

DESCRIPTIVE PROPERTIES OF BEHAVIOR

Although topography and magnitude are not fundamental dimensional quantities, they provide useful information about behavior that allows us to define it and determine its occurrence versus nonoccurrence.

Topography

This refers to the physical form of the behavior; in other words, what it looks (or sounds) like. Behaviors with different topographies may or may not serve the same function.

- **Example:** Pointing to a ball and vocally requesting a ball are two different topographical responses that may serve the same function (i.e., obtaining access to a ball).

Magnitude

This refers to the intensity of the behavior; in other words, the strength/severity of it. Behaviors must typically meet or surpass some designated threshold in magnitude to be counted.

- **Example:** Talking with a soft voice and talking with a loud voice are two vocalization responses with different magnitudes. In order for talking to be counted as yelling, it must reach or surpass 75 decibels.

TASK C.4

Measure temporal dimensions of behavior (e.g., duration, latency, interresponse time). The temporal dimensions of behavior can be measured in terms of (a) duration, (b) latency, and (c) interresponse time (IRT). Duration is a measure of the fundamental dimensional quantity of *temporal extent*, while latency and IRT are measures of *temporal locus*.

DURATION

This refers to the length of time that behavior occupies; in other words, the time elapsed between the onset and offset of the behavior.

- **Example:** The student was seated at his desk for 10 minutes.

LATENCY

This refers to the length of time from the onset of a stimulus (e.g., verbal instruction, cue) to the initiation of a behavior.

- **Example:** The student sat down 10 seconds after the teacher verbally instructed them to.

INTERRESPONSE TIME

This refers to the length of time between two responses; in other words, the time elapsed between the onset of one response and the onset of the next response.

- **Example:** From the time the student first left their assigned seat to the start of the second time they left their seat, 10 minutes had passed.

TASK C.5

Distinguish between continuous and discontinuous measurement procedures. Accurately measuring and recording behavior is important for effective assessment and intervention. Measurement procedures can be broadly categorized into two types: (a) continuous and (b) discontinuous.

CONTINUOUS MEASUREMENT PROCEDURES

These involve the ongoing, real-time recording of every instance of a target behavior as it occurs. The primary advantage of continuous measurement procedures, which include (a) frequency recording, (b) duration recording, (c) latency recording, and (d) IRT, is its accuracy and detail. See Tasks C.3 and C.4 for a review of the procedures for measuring frequency, duration, latency, and IRT.

DISCONTINUOUS MEASUREMENTS PROCEDURES

These involve sampling behavior periodically rather than continuously. These methods provide a more practical and less time-consuming way to measure behavior, especially when continuous observation is not feasible. Common types of discontinuous measurement include: (a) partial interval recording, (b) whole interval recording, (c) momentary time sampling, and (d) planned activity check (PLACHECK). See Task C.6 for a review of the procedures for partial and whole interval recording, momentary time sampling, and PLACHECK.

ADDITIONAL NOTE(S)

The choice between continuous and discontinuous measurement procedures depends on several factors, including the nature of the behavior, the setting, available resources, and the goals of the assessment. Continuous measurement is ideal for obtaining detailed and precise data, making it suitable for behaviors that are infrequent but highly significant or for intensive interventions. Discontinuous measurement, on the other hand, is more practical for behaviors that occur frequently or when observation resources (i.e., available personnel and time) are limited.

▸ TASK C.6

Design and apply discontinuous measurement procedures (e.g., interval recording, time sampling). Interval recording and time sampling refer to a collection of procedures for observing and recording behavior. These include (a) whole interval recording, (b) partial interval recording, and (c) momentary time sampling. For each of these recording procedures, divide the observation period into smaller intervals of equal length. Data obtained from all three procedures are typically *reported as percentages* of the total interval in which the behavior was recorded as having occurred.

WHOLE INTERVAL RECORDING

At the end of each interval, the target behavior is recorded as having occurred if it occurred *throughout the entire interval.* This method usually underestimates the occurrence of the behavior; the longer the interval, the greater the underestimation.

This method is often used to target behaviors that are (a) continuous, (b) high-frequency, and (c) to be increased.

PARTIAL INTERVAL RECORDING

At the end of each interval, the target behavior is recorded as having occurred if it occurred at *any time during the interval.* This method usually overestimates the total duration of the behavior; however, the rate of high-frequency behaviors may be underestimated.

This method can be used to target multiple behaviors at the same time. It is often used to target behaviors that are to be decreased.

MOMENTARY TIME SAMPLING

At the end of each interval, the target behavior is recorded as having occurred if it occurred *only at the end of the interval.* This method may over- or underestimate the occurrence of the behavior when intervals exceed 2 minutes.

Unlike whole or partial interval recording, this method does not require the observer's undivided attention to measurement; however, much behavior will be missed as a result. The PLACHECK method is a variation of momentary time sampling that involves recording the count of individuals in a group that are engaged in the target behavior only at the end of the interval.

TASK C.7

Measure efficiency (e.g., trials to criterion, cost-benefit analysis, training duration). Measuring efficiency (e.g., cost per unit of improvement, time saved, or productivity gains) provides valuable insights into the effectiveness and cost-effectiveness of interventions and training programs. Efficient interventions and programs optimize resource utilization, maximize outcomes, and ultimately contribute to the success of behavioral interventions. Key measures of efficiency can include (a) trials to criterion, (b) cost-benefit analysis, and (c) training duration.

TRIALS TO CRITERION

This is a measure of the number of response opportunities (i.e., trials) required to achieve a predetermined level of performance (i.e., mastery criterion). What the trials look like depend on the target behavior and desired level of performance. Trials to criterion data can be reported in terms of count, rate, duration, or latency.

- **Example:** The student required 25 trials of adding two single-digit numbers to master the skill.

Trials to criterion can be used to evaluate efficiency of learning and skill acquisition, with fewer trials indicating higher efficiency.

COST-BENEFIT ANALYSIS

This evaluates the efficiency of an intervention by comparing the costs and benefits of implementation. It involves quantifying both costs (e.g., time, resources, personnel) and benefits (e.g., improvements in behavior, performance, quality of life), and helps decision-makers prioritize interventions in a manner that optimizes resource allocation.

Before Implementation

Cost-benefit analyses can be conducted before or after the implementation of an intervention, with each serving distinct purposes. When conducted before implementation, the analysis provides insights into the potential costs and benefits of different intervention options, helping stakeholders to select the best approach.

After Implementation

When conducted postintervention, the analysis evaluates actual costs and benefits, allowing for assessment of the intervention's effectiveness and efficiency in achieving its objectives. This retrospective analysis can be used to inform future decision-making and program refinement, contributing to continuous improvement in resource allocation and intervention strategies.

TRAINING DURATION

This is a measure of the amount of time required to learn new skills, behaviors, or competencies through intervention or training programs. Training duration provides insights into the efficiency of training protocols, with shorter durations indicating higher efficiency.

TASK C.8

Evaluate the validity and reliability of measurement procedures. Measurements should be valid, accurate, and reliable (Table 5.1).

VALIDITY

This refers to the degree to which *we are measuring what we intend to measure.* Valid measurement requires that (a) a socially significant behavior is directly measured, (b) its relevant dimension (e.g., rate, duration) for answering the question is measured, and (c) the data represents its occurrence under relevant conditions (e.g., time, place) for answering the question.

- **Example:** To measure the weight of an object, it is placed on a properly tuned weight scale.

RELIABILITY

This refers to the degree to which the measure will *produce consistent results.*

- **Example:** A properly tuned scale repeatedly reports that an object weighs 10 lbs.

You cannot have a valid measure that lacks reliability. However, it is possible to have a reliable measure that is not valid (e.g., an improperly tuned weight scale may reliably report that a banana weighs 50 lbs, but the measurement would clearly be invalid).

Measurement should also be accurate. *Accuracy* refers to the degree to which the observed value approximates the true value.

Table 5.1 Data Outcomes by Measurement Characteristics

MEASUREMENT THAT IS...	RESULTS IN DATA THAT ARE...
Valid, accurate, and reliable	Most useful for guiding practice
Accurate and reliable, but not valid	Not helpful for answering the question
Valid and reliable, but not accurate	Wrong
Valid and accurate, but not reliable	At least sometimes wrong

TASK C.9

Select a measurement procedure to obtain representative data that accounts for the critical dimension of the behavior and environmental constraints. There are different features of behavior that can be measured. These are referred to as dimensional quantities, which include: (a) repeatability, (b) temporal extent, and (c) temporal locus.

REPEATABILITY

This refers to the trait in which behavior can be counted as it repeats across time. Measures based on repeatability include: (a) count, (b) rate, and (c) celeration.

Count

This refers to the number of occurrences.

Rate

This refers to the number of occurrences over a certain period of time.

Celeration

This refers to the rate over a certain period of time. This is a measure of how the rate of a behavior can increase (i.e., accelerate) or decrease (i.e., decelerate) over time.

TEMPORAL EXTENT

Behavior can be timed as it occurs during some amount of time. The measure of duration is based on temporal extent.

Duration

This refers to the amount of time that elapses between the onset and offset of a behavior.

TEMPORAL LOCUS

The point when a behavior happens can be measured as it occurs at a certain point in time with respect to other events. Measures based on temporal locus include: (a) latency and (b) IRT.

Latency

This refers to the amount of time that elapses between the onset of a stimulus and a response that follows it.

Interresponse Time

This refers to the amount of time that elapses between two consecutive occurrences of a behavior.

Methods for measuring behavior include: (a) event recording, (b) timing, and (c) various time sampling procedures.

EVENT RECORDING

This involves recording the number of times that a behavior occurs.

TIMING

This involves recording the passage of time with the use of a timing device (e.g., stopwatch).

TIME SAMPLING

This involves recording the occurrence or nonoccurrence of behavior during intervals of time or at specific points in time. See Task C.6 for a summary of time sampling (i.e., interval recording [DV]) methods used by behavior analysts (Table 5.2).

Table 5.2 Measurement Procedure Selection

IF YOU WANT TO MEASURE...	THEN...
The number of times a behavior occurs, and the behavior can be sufficiently counted	Use event recording.
The number of times a behavior occurs, but the behavior is difficult to count	Use time sampling.
How long a behavior lasts	Use duration recording.
How long before the behavior occurs	Use latency recording.

ADDITIONAL NOTE(S)

Consider the following recommendations:

- If the behavior is not observable but produces a physical change in the environment, *permanent product recording* may be used. See Task C.2 for a review of product measures.
- Schedule observation sessions to obtain data that are generally representative of the behavior.

- If recording data to determine the effects of an intervention, schedule observations when the behavior is most likely to occur if it is targeted for reduction, but schedule observation when the behavior is least likely to occur if it is targeted for increase.
- Ensure that observers are sufficiently trained. Ongoing training can help to minimize unwanted changes to the way data is collected (i.e., observer drift).
- Monitor observers in the most discreet way possible to minimize measurement errors resulting from their awareness that you are watching them (i.e., observer reactivity).

TASK C.10

Graph data to communicate relevant quantitative relations (e.g., equal-interval graphs, bar graphs, cumulative records). Data is gathered throughout a behavior change program to inform important decisions regarding treatment, including whether to continue or change an intervention. To interpret the data gathered and communicate these results to others, behavior analysts use *graphs* which are visual displays of data. Different types of graphs are used, including (a) equal-interval graphs and (b) semilogarithmic charts.

EQUAL-INTERVAL GRAPH

This is a graph with both the vertical and horizontal axes divided into equal distances between marks to indicate the addition or subtraction of constant amounts. Equal-interval graphs include: (a) line graphs, (b) bar graphs, (c) cumulative records, and (d) scatter plots.

LINE GRAPH

This type of graph, based on the Cartesian plane (i.e., two perpendicular number lines), is used to display change over time as a series of connected data points (Figure 5.1). Each data point represents a relationship between some dimensional quantity of behavior (i.e., dependent variable [DV]) and time and/or environmental condition (i.e., independent variable).

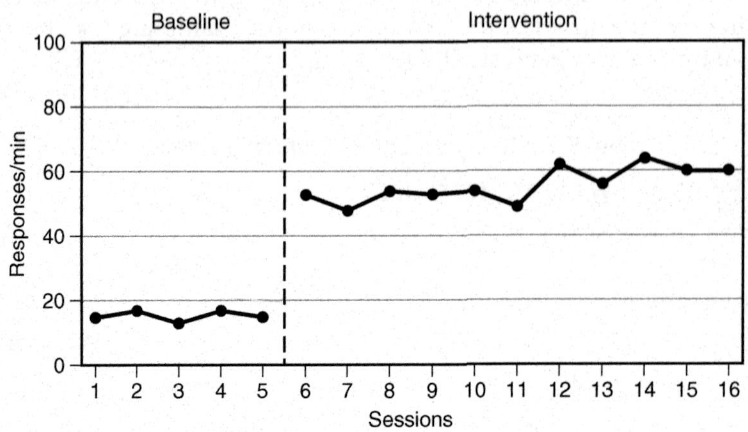

Figure 5.1 Example of a Line Graph

BAR GRAPH

This type of graph, also referred to as a histogram, is used to display discrete sets of data (e.g., performance of an individual or group of subjects during different conditions). Unlike the line graph, there are no data points plotted to represent responses over time (Figure 5.2).

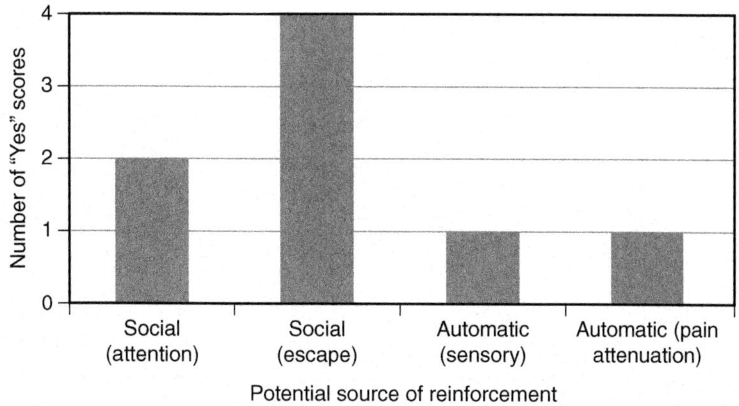

Figure 5.2 Example of a Bar Graph Summarizing the Results of a Questionnaire

CUMULATIVE RECORD

This type of graph is used to display the running total of responses over time. The cumulative total is represented on the vertical axis. The data path never descends. A steeper data path indicates a higher response rate (Figure 5.3).

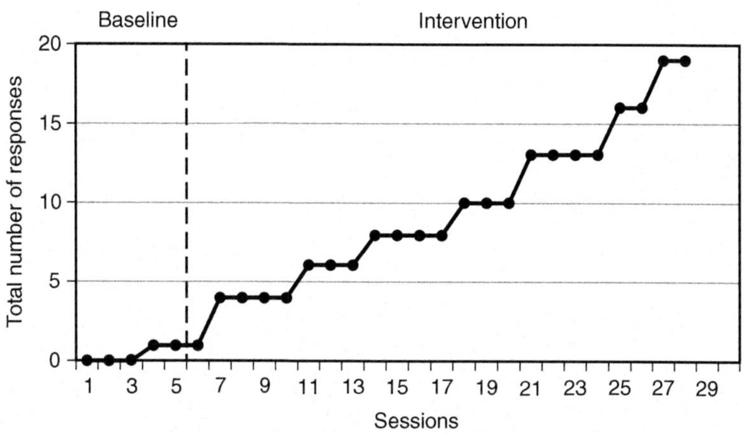

Figure 5.3 Example of a Cumulative Record

SCATTER PLOT

This type of graph is used to display the relationship between the variables depicted by the horizontal *x* and vertical *y* axes. The data points do not form a data path, but they can form patterns on the plane that suggest certain relationships (Figures 5.4–5.6).

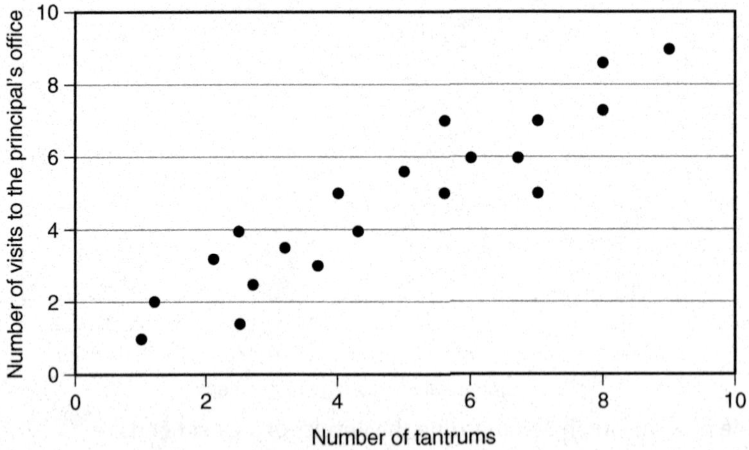

Figure 5.4 Example Scatter Plot: As *x* (# of Tantrums) Increases, *y* (# of Visits to the Principal's Office) Increases (i.e., Positive Correlation)

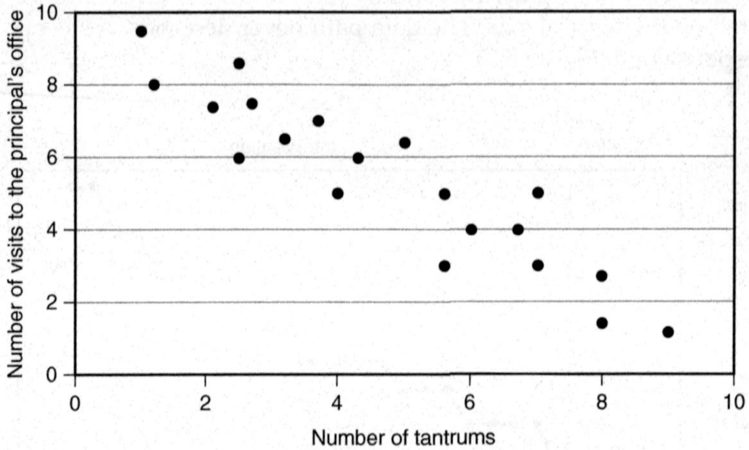

Figure 5.5 Example Scatter Plot: As *x* Increases, *y* Decreases (i.e., Negative Correlation)

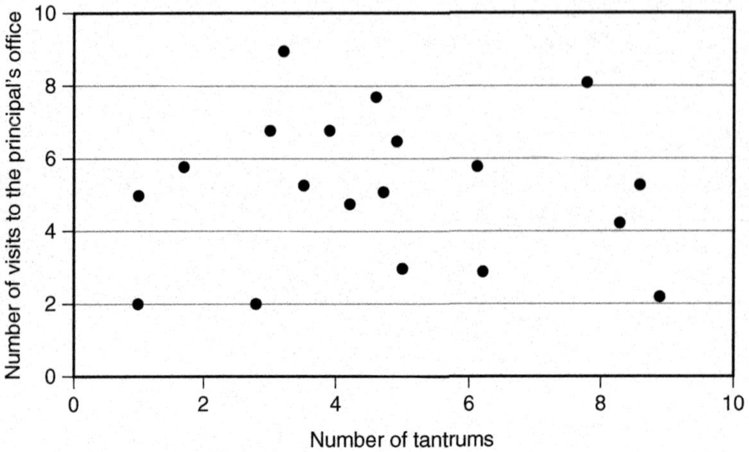

Figure 5.6 Example Scatter Plot: No Clear Indication of Relationship Between *x* and *y* (i.e., No Correlation)

Behavior analysts also use scatter plots to show when a target behavior occurs and whether it is associated with certain times.

- **Example (scatter plot for timing of behavior):** The graph in Figure 5.7 shows that the behavior is occurring only in the mornings between 9:00 a.m and 10:00 a.m.

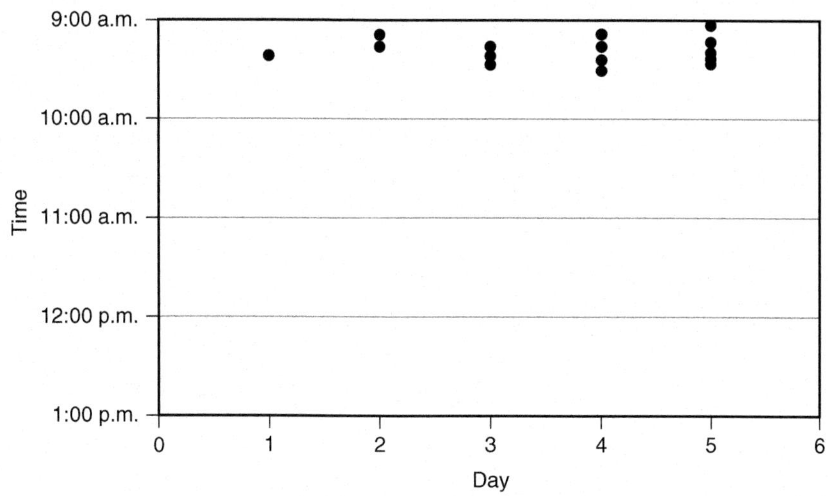

Figure 5.7 Scatter Plot for Timing of Behavior

SEMILOGARITHMIC CHART

This type of graph, also referred to as a ratio chart, has a horizontal *x* axis that is divided into equal distances between marks, but the vertical *y* axis uses a logarithmic scale (Figure 5.8). The standard celeration chart (SCC) is a semilogarithmic chart.

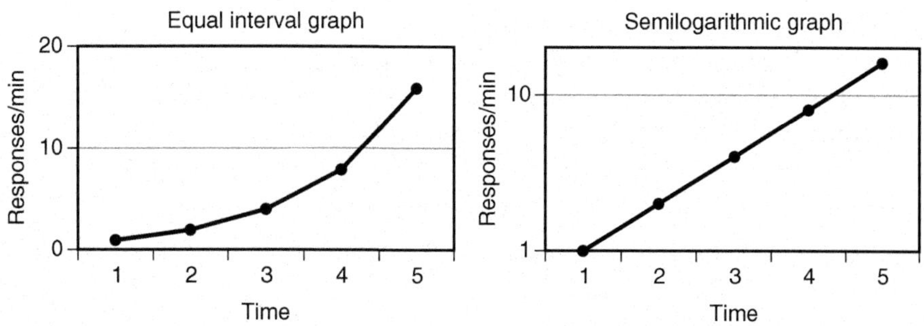

Figure 5.8 The Same Sample Data Plotted on an Equal Interval Scale Versus a Logarithmic Scale

STANDARD CELERATION CHART

This type of graph is primarily used to display the fluency and accuracy of a target behavior. The vertical *y* axis uses a logarithmic scale that allows us to record data points representing 0.001 to 1,000 times per minute.

ADDITIONAL NOTE(S)

For those who are interested in learning more about SCCs and how to use them, consider reviewing Calkin's (2005) article on SCCs, Cancio and Maloney's (1994) article on teaching students how to utilize SCCs, and/or White and Neely's (2012) graphic overview of SCC conventions and practices.

TASK C.11

Interpret graphed data. The three basic properties of behavior change over time that are effectively communicated through graphs are (a) level, (b) variability, and (c) trend.

LEVEL

This relates to the position along the vertical *y* axis where a series of data points converge.

- **Example:** In Figure 5.9, the data representing the frequency of a particular response occurs at a low level in Condition A and at a high level in Condition B.

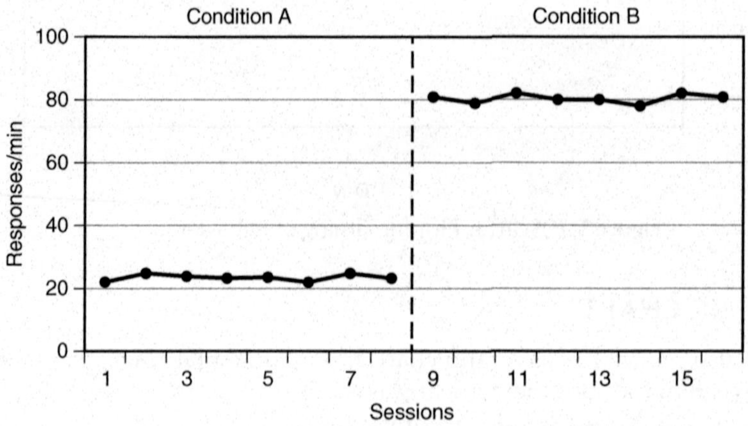

Figure 5.9 Low Level of Responding in A, High Level of Responding in B

A horizontal mean level line can be drawn to summarize the overall level of behavior in a condition if the data points remain fairly stable (i.e., low variability) data paths. If the data points are fairly stable but there are several outliers (i.e., data points that are significantly higher or lower than the others in a series of data points), a median level line can be used instead.

VARIABILITY

This relates to the amount of discrepancy between the values of a series of data points.

- **Example:** In Figure 5.10, the data representing the frequency of a particular response occurs with a low degree of variability in Condition A and with a high degree of variability in Condition B.

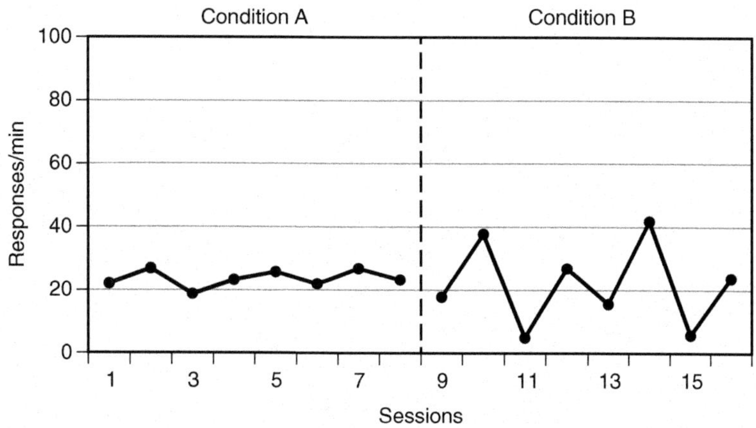

Figure 5.10 Low Variability in Responding in A, High Variability in Responding in B

Greater variability observed within a condition requires a higher number of data points to establish a predictable pattern in the data, whereas lower variability observed within a condition requires fewer data points to establish a predictable pattern in the data.

TREND

This relates to the direction of a series of data points. The trend is described in terms of direction (i.e., increasing, decreasing, or zero), magnitude, and degree of variability of data points along the data path.

- **Example:** In Figure 5.11, the data representing the frequency of a particular response occurs with an increasing trend in Condition A, decreasing trend in Condition B, and zero trend in Condition C.

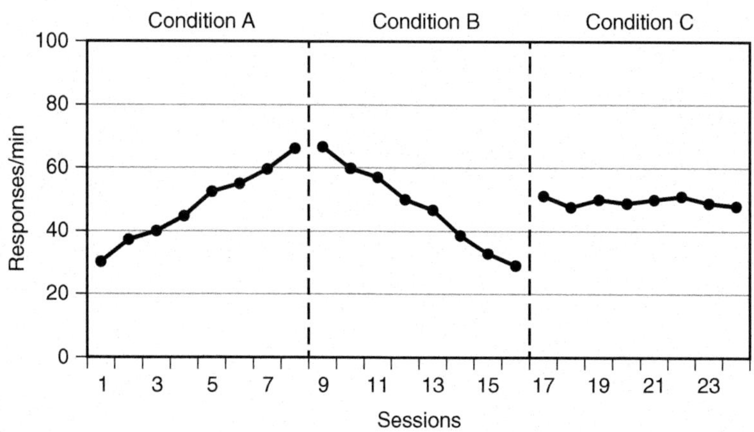

Figure 5.11 Increasing Trend in A, Decreasing Trend in B, Zero Trend in C

- In Figure 5.12, the magnitude of the increasing trendline is greater in Condition A than it is in Condition B.

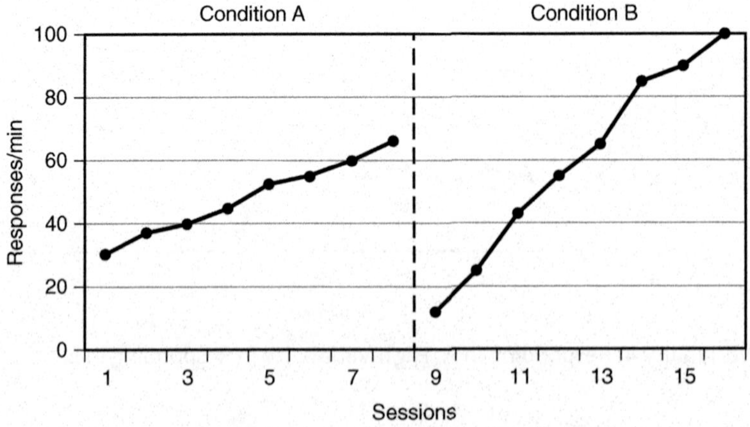

Figure 5.12 Greater Magnitude of Trendline in A Than B

- In Figure 5.13, the variability of the data points along the data path is greater in Condition B than it is in Condition A.

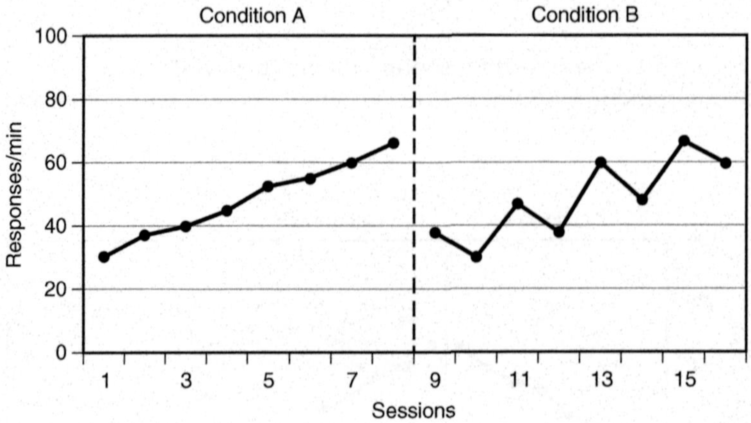

Figure 5.13 Greater Variability of Responding in B Than A

▶ PRACTICE QUESTION

You are collecting data on an intervention to increase the number of social initiations with a young child having difficulty appropriately interacting with peers. Your single subject data show the following BASELINE pattern (upward trend with moderate variability; Figure 5.14)

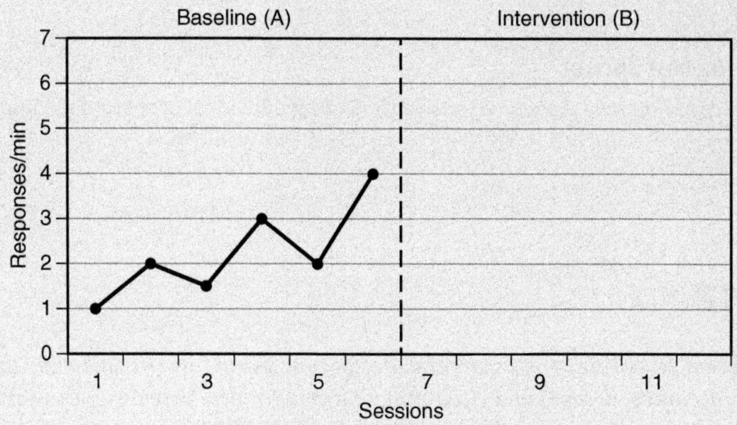

Figure 5.14 Graph of Baseline Data

Your next step should be to...

A. Introduce the intervention (IV) to see if it has a positive impact.

B. Choose another target behavior.

C. Collect additional baseline data to see if stability is achieved.

D. None of the above.

Before moving on to the following section for the solution, we recommend that you provide a brief explanation for the answer option you selected here:

____

____

When you're ready, move on to the next section for the solution!

Practice Question Breakdown

Step 1: Examine the question

The question asks you to examine the baseline data phase of a graph measuring the number of social initiations for a young child having difficulty appropriately interacting with peers. In the baseline data, you observe an upward trend in baseline, with moderate variability.

Step 2: Analyze the answer options

A. This answer is incorrect as baseline data is already increasing in the absence of intervention implementation, so something else is associated with the increase. Despite the behavior increasing (improving in the case of this targeted DV), this is a commonly misunderstood data pattern and one that is not ideal in that it provides little stability and predictability.

B. This step is not advised; because you do not know why the increase is occurring in the number of social initiations, why introduce or try to measure a different behavior?

C. The best option is to continue to collect baseline data to determine if the behavior stabilizes or becomes more predictable. Remember, greater variability (and/or unexplained trend) observed within a condition requires a higher number of data points to establish a predictable pattern in the data.

D. This answer cannot be correct, because answer C offers a reasonable course of action given there is an unexplained trend in the baseline data in the absence of intervention implementation.

Step 3: Select the best answer

Among the four answer options presented, answer C (Collect additional baseline data) appears to be the best answer.

TASK C.12

Select a measurement procedure to obtain representative procedural integrity data that accounts for relevant dimensions (e.g., accuracy, dosage) and environmental constraints. Selecting an appropriate measurement procedure to obtain representative procedural integrity data is essential for evaluating the effectiveness and fidelity of an intervention. Procedural integrity (also known as *treatment integrity* or *treatment fidelity*) refers to the degree to which an intervention is implemented as intended.

DIMENSIONS OF PROCEDURAL INTEGRITY

These include (a) accuracy, (b) dosage, and (c) environmental constraints.

Accuracy

This involves the precise implementation of each component of the intervention according to the prescribed protocol. To measure accuracy, use detailed checklists or direct observation to ensure each step is carried out correctly.

Dosage

This refers to the quantity and frequency of the intervention delivered, including the number of sessions, their duration (i.e., length of time an intervention session lasts), and the intensity of the intervention (i.e., level of effort, engagement, or resources involved in the intervention activities). To measure duration, track the total time of each intervention session. To measure intensity, assess the level of effort, engagement, or resources involved in the intervention activities. This can be accomplished with the use of detailed protocols, checklists, or observational checks to ensure that the activities meet the intended intensity.

Environmental Constraints

This refers to the contextual factors that might impact the implementation of an intervention. To evaluate environmental constraints, document any contextual limitations (e.g., resource availability, physical space constraints, or logistical challenges). Surveys, interviews, or observations can be used to gather data on these constraints. Also, consider the impact of external factors (e.g., organizational policies or cultural norms) on intervention delivery.

SELECTING A MEASUREMENT PROCEDURE

This process involves (a) identifying the critical components of the intervention, (b) selecting an appropriate measurement procedure, (c) ensuring measurement consistency, and (d) accounting for environmental constraints.

Identify the Critical Components of the Intervention

Clearly define the key elements of the intervention that need to be measured. This should include aspects of the intervention that are most relevant for assessing fidelity and effectiveness (i.e., specific actions, sequences, and conditions essential for successful implementation).

Select an Appropriate Measurement Procedure

Evaluate the available measurement options and consider factors such as the accuracy, reliability, and feasibility of each. It's important to select a procedure that can effectively capture the intended aspects of the intervention while being practical to implement in the given context.

Ensuring Measurement Consistency

This involves establishing clear protocols, providing training, and conducting regular monitoring to maintain uniformity in data collection.

Accounting for Environmental Constraints

This involves ensuring that the selected procedure aligns with the context's limitations, optimizing the effectiveness of the assessment.

- **Example (intervention designed to improve reading skills in children):** The intervention protocol includes specific steps such as phonemic awareness activities, guided reading sessions, and comprehension questions. To measure procedural integrity, the following will be measured: (a) accuracy, using a checklist to ensure each phonemic exercise activity is conducted as specified; (b) dosage, by tracking the number of sessions per week and the duration of each session using session logs; and (c) environmental constraints, by recording any deviations due to classroom disruptions or limited access to reading materials and conducting interviews with teachers to identify challenges faced during implementation.

ADDITIONAL NOTE(S)

The selected measurement procedure can be pilot tested to ensure its feasibility and reliability in practice. This involves implementing the procedure on a small scale and collecting data to assess its effectiveness and identify any potential challenges or modifications needed before full-scale implementation.

CONCLUSION

In this chapter, we covered the TCO Tasks related to measurement, data display, and interpretation in ABA. This included establishing operational definitions of behavior and practices related to the measurement of behavior, such as different approaches to measuring behavior, measurement variables, and different features of behavior that can be measured (e.g., temporal extent, repeatability). In this chapter we also delved into measurement system selection for obtaining representative data, effectively graphing data using different types of graphs to clearly communicate results to others, and interpreting data according to the three basic properties of behavior change over time. Given behavior analysts' commitment to data-based decision-making and practice, the content covered in this chapter is of paramount importance.

REFERENCES

Behavior Analyst Certification Board. (2024). *BCBA test content outline* (6th ed.). Author. https://www.bacb.com/wp-content/bcba-outline-6thEd

Calkin, A. B. (2005). Precision teaching: The standard celeration charts. *The Behavior Analyst Today, 6*(4), 207–215. https://doi.org/10.1037/h0100073

Cancio, E. J., & Maloney, M. (1994). Teaching students how to proficiently utilize the standard celeration chart. *Journal of Precision Teaching, 12*(1), 15–45.
White, O. R., & Neely, M. D. (2012). *The chart book. An overview of standard celeration chart conventions and practices*. Behavior Research Company.

BIBLIOGRAPHY

Cooper, J. O., Heron, T. E., & Heward, W. L. (2020). *Applied behavior analysis* (3rd ed.). Pearson Education.
Hawkins, R. P., & Dobes, R. W. (1977). Behavioral definitions in applied behavior analysis: Explicit or implicit. In B. C. Etzel, J. M. LeBlanc, & D. M. Baer (Eds.), *New developments in behavioral research: Theory, method, and application* (pp. 167–188). Lawrence Erlbaum.
LeBlanc, L. A., Raetz, P. B., Sellers, T. P., & Carr, J. E. (2016). A proposed model for selecting measurement procedures for the assessment and treatment of problem behavior. *Behavior Analysis in Practice, 9*(1), 77–83. https://doi.org/10.1007/s40617-015-0063-2
Pennypacker, H. S., Gutierrez, A., & Lidsley, O. R. (1992). *Handbook of the standard celeration chart* (deluxe ed.). Cambridge Center for Behavioral Studies.

KNOWLEDGE CHECK

1. A behavior analyst is creating an operational definition for a client's disruptive behavior. The definition specifies that disruptive behavior includes instances of yelling, standing up from the desk without permission, and throwing objects. The behavior analyst ensures that each behavior can be easily identified, counted, and recorded by different observers in various settings. Which of the following characteristics is NOT required for the definition?
   - **A.** Adaptable
   - **B.** Clear
   - **C.** Measurable
   - **D.** Observable

2. A well-written operational definition of a target behavior allows the behavior analyst to do all of the following, EXCEPT:
   - **A.** Gather complete information about its occurrence and nonoccurrence
   - **B.** Establish the reliability of measurement data
   - **C.** Precisely apply procedures in a timely manner
   - **D.** Produce an accurate evaluation of intervention effectiveness

3. A behavior analyst is observing a child in the classroom and records each instance of the child raising their hand during the lesson. The analyst tracks the behavior in real-time, noting every occurrence as it happens to analyze how frequently the child raises their hand. Which type of measurement is the behavior analyst using?
   - **A.** Direct
   - **B.** Indirect
   - **C.** Product
   - **D.** Scatter plot

4. A behavior analyst is evaluating the success of a cleaning routine for a client. Instead of observing the client while they clean, the analyst inspects the room afterward to assess how many tasks were completed (e.g., bed made, floor swept, trash emptied). The behavior analyst reviews the results to determine whether the behavior occurred. What type of measurement did the behavior analyst use to assess the completed tasks?
   - **A.** Direct
   - **B.** Indirect
   - **C.** Product
   - **D.** Scatter plot

(*See answers on the next page.*)

1. **A) Adaptable**
   Operational definitions are observable, measurable, and clear. They are also objective and complete. While adaptability may be useful in some cases, it is not a required characteristic of an operational definition.

2. **B) Establish the reliability of measurement data**
   A well-written operational definition of a target behavior does not allow behavior analysts to establish the reliability of measurement data. A well-written operation definition does, however, assist behavior analysts in the gathering of information about the occurrence and nonoccurrence of behavior, precisely apply procedures in a timely manner, and produce an accurate evaluation of intervention effectiveness.

3. **A) Direct**
   In this scenario, the behavior analyst is using direct measurement because they are observing and recording the target behavior (raising a hand) in real time as it occurs. Direct measurement involves tracking behaviors as they happen, thereby allowing for immediate and accurate data collection. The other answer options refer to other types of measures. Direct measurement involves an observer recording the target behavior as it occurs. The other answer options refer to other types of measurement methods or a type of graph.

4. **C) Product**
   In this scenario, the behavior analyst is using permanent product measurement because they are assessing the outcome or effect of the behavior (cleaning) by inspecting the completed tasks after the fact, without directly observing the behavior as it occurred. The use of product measures involves the examination of the effects produced on the environment by a behavior. The other answer options refer to other types of measurement methods or a type of graph.

5. A behavior analyst is assessing a child's tantrum behaviors in a classroom. Instead of directly observing the child, the analyst asks the teacher to complete a daily behavior checklist based on their recollection of how often the tantrums occurred and what preceded them. The teacher's report is used to evaluate the frequency of the tantrum behavior. This is an example of what type of measurement?

A. Direct

B. Indirect

C. Product

D. Scatter plot

6. A behavior analyst is tracking how often a child raises their hand during a class session. The behavior analyst counts each instance of hand-raising and calculates the number of hand-raises per hour. Which measures of repeatability is the behavior analyst using?

A. Duration and frequency

B. Frequency and rate

C. Interresponse time and latency

D. Percentage and duration

7. What derivative measure is calculated by multiplying the numeric value (e.g., count of a response divided by the total number of responses or opportunities/intervals in which it could have occurred) by 100?

A. Frequency

B. Latency

C. Percentage

D. Rate

8. A behavior analyst is tracking the number of times a client engages in a specific behavior during therapy sessions. The analyst counts each occurrence of the behavior and divides it by the total time spent observing the client to calculate how often the behavior occurs per hour. Which type of measurement is the behavior analyst using?

A. Duration

B. Frequency

C. Latency

D. Rate

9. Which of the following is a measure of the length of time from the onset of a stimulus to the initiation of a behavior?

A. Celeration

B. Duration

C. Interresponse time (IRT)

D. Latency

(*See answers on the next page.*)

5. **B) Indirect**
   In the scenario, the behavior analyst relies on the teacher's recollection and report of the child's tantrum behavior, which is an example of indirect measurement. Indirect measurement involves gathering information from others based on their memory of the behavior, rather than observing it directly. The other answer options refer to other types of measurement methods or a type of graph.

6. **B) Frequency and rate**
   In the scenario, the behavior analyst is using frequency by counting the number of interruptions and rate by calculating how often these interruptions occur per minute. Both frequency (the total number of occurrences) and rate (the frequency of occurrences over a specific time period) are measures based on the dimensional quantity of repeatability, which tracks how often a behavior happens. The other answer options refer to measures based on other fundamental dimensional quantities and serve as distractors.

7. **C) Percentage**
   Percentage is a derivative measure that is calculated by multiplying the numeric value (e.g., count of a response divided by the total number of responses or opportunities/intervals in which it could have occurred) by 100. Frequency, latency, and rate are not derivative measures and function as distractors.

8. **D) Rate**
   Rate involves counting of the behavior or behavior class over the unit of time in which observations were conducted, whether that is by X amount of minutes, hours, and so on. The other answer options measure how long a behavior lasts, the total occurrences of the behavior without considering time, or the time between a stimulus and the onset of a behavior, none of which calculate behavior occurrences per unit of time as rate does.

9. **D) Latency**
   Latency is the length of time from the onset of a stimulus to the initiation of a behavior. Celeration, duration, and IRT refer to other dimensional quantities and function as distractors.

10. A behavior analyst is working with a client who engages in repetitive tapping behavior. The analyst records the time from the end of one tapping instance to the beginning of the next to measure how much time passes between behaviors and to track how frequently the tapping occurs over time. What type of measurement is the behavior analyst recording?

A. Celeration

B. Duration

C. Interresponse time (IRT)

D. Latency

11. Which of the following BEST describes the magnitude of a behavior?

A. Duration of the behavior

B. Intensity of the behavior

C. Physical form of the behavior

D. Rate of the behavior

12. A behavior technician is working with a client to teach them how to use a communication device. The technician records how many practice opportunities are needed before the client can use the device independently to request items correctly five times in a row. The technician uses this measure to determine when the client has mastered the skill. This is an example of what type of measure?

A. Count

B. Event recording

C. Percentage

D. Trials to criterion

13. A behavior analyst is using event recording to measure a client's out-of-seat behavior. Given the target behavior, which of the following is a limitation of the measurement procedure used?

A. It is not suitable for high-frequency behaviors.

B. It requires continuous observation.

C. It may not accurately capture the duration of the behavior.

D. It is only useful for behaviors with a clear beginning and end.

14. A behavior technician is working with a client to teach them to independently brush their teeth. The technician tracks the number of trials it takes for the client to master brushing without prompts. In addition to counting the number of trials, the technician also measures how quickly the client starts brushing after a prompt, how long it takes to complete the brushing, and how frequently the client brushes during the session. Which of the following measures can the behavior technician use to report trials to criterion data?

A. Count, rate, duration, or latency

B. Count, rate, latency, interresponse time (IRT)

C. Duration, rate, IRT, magnitude

D. Frequency, rate, percentage, or latency

(*See answers on the next page.*)

10. **C) Interresponse time (IRT)**
In this scenario, the behavior analyst is measuring the time between the end of one tapping behavior and the beginning of the next, which is an example of IRT. IRT specifically refers to the length of time between the completion of one response and the onset of the next. The other answer options refer to measures of rate changes (celeration), how long a behavior lasts (duration), or the time between a stimulus and response (latency).

11. **B) Intensity of the behavior**
Magnitude refers to the intensity of the behavior. The other answer options (duration of the behavior, physical form of the behavior, rate of the behavior) do not accurately describe magnitude and serve as distractors.

12. **D) Trials to criterion**
In this scenario, the behavior technician is using trials to criterion, which measures the number of practice opportunities required for the client to reach a predetermined level of performance (in this case, using the communication device independently and correctly five times in a row). The other answer options refer to other measures that track total occurrences (count), record individual instances of behavior (event recording), or calculate accuracy (percentage), none of which measure the number of trials needed to reach mastery.

13. **C) It may not accurately capture the duration of the behavior.**
Event recording counts the number of times a behavior occurs but does not provide information about the duration of each instance. For behaviors where duration is important (e.g., out-of-seat behavior), other measures like duration recording would be more appropriate.

14. **A) Count, rate, duration, or latency**
Trials to criterion data can be reported in terms of count, rate, duration, or latency. These are standard measures used to evaluate performance in a trials-to-criterion framework. The other answer options include measurement terms that trials to criterion data are not reported in (e.g., latency, IRT, frequency, magnitude, percentage) and function as distractors.

15. In which type of sampling procedure is the target behavior recorded as having occurred at the end of an interval only if it occurred throughout the entire interval?

A. Momentary time sampling

B. Partial interval recording

C. Planned activity check (PLACHECK)

D. Whole interval recording

16. A teacher wants to track how many students in her classroom are on-task during group work. Every 5 minutes, she looks around the room and counts how many students are engaged in their assigned activity at that exact moment. She uses this data to evaluate the overall engagement levels of the class during group work. Which sampling procedure is the teacher using?

A. Momentary time sampling

B. Partial interval recording

C. Planned activity check (PLACHECK)

D. Whole interval recording

17. Which sampling procedure usually overestimates the total duration of a targeted behavior, but may underestimate the rate of high-frequency behaviors?

A. Momentary time sampling

B. Partial interval recording

C. Planned activity check (PLACHECK)

D. Whole interval recording

18. _________________ refers to the degree to which we are measuring what we intend to measure, whereas _________________ refers to the degree to which the measure will produce consistent results.

A. Accuracy; repeatability

B. Accuracy; reliability

C. Reliability; validity

D. Validity; reliability

19. A behavior technician is working with a client to improve their response time during a learning task. The technician records the amount of time it takes for the client to start responding after a prompt is given and also tracks the time between the client's responses. These measures help the technician assess how quickly the client responds to prompts and how much time passes between responses. Which measures of temporal locus is the behavior analyst using?

A. Count and rate

B. Duration and latency

C. Latency and interresponse time (IRT)

D. IRT and count

(*See answers on the next page.*)

15. **D. Whole interval recording**
When implementing whole interval recording, the target behavior is recorded as having occurred at the end of an interval only if it occurred throughout the entire interval. The other answer options (momentary time sampling, partial interval recording, PLACHECK) refer to other sampling procedures and function as distractors.

16. **C) Planned activity check (PLACHECK)**
In this scenario, the teacher is using PLACHECK, a sampling procedure where the number of students engaged in the target behavior (on-task) is recorded at the end of each interval. This method is used to assess the proportion of individuals in a group who are engaged in the behavior at specific points in time. The other answer options refer to other sampling procedures and function as distractors.

17. **B) Partial interval recording**
Partial interval recording has been identified as a sampling procedure that usually overestimates the total duration of a targeted behavior but may underestimate the rate of high-frequency behaviors. The other answer options (momentary time sampling, PLACHECK, whole interval recording) are measures that have not been found to share these exact same characteristics and function as distractors.

18. **D) Validity, reliability**
Validity refers to the degree to which we are measuring what we intend to measure, whereas reliability refers to the degree to which the measure will produce consistent results. The other answer options (accuracy, repeatability; accuracy, reliability; reliability, validity) do not accurately fit into the statement and serve as distractors.

19. **C) Latency and interresponse time (IRT)**
Latency measures the time between a stimulus and the initiation of a response, whereas IRT measures the time between two successive responses. These measures are based on the concept of temporal locus, which deals with the timing of behaviors in relation to other events. The other answer options are measures based on other fundamental dimensional quantities and function as distractors.

20. A behavior analyst is collecting data on a client's performance across different skill areas, such as communication, social interaction, and motor skills. The analyst wants to present the data to show how the client performed in each skill area, but there is no need to track progress over time. The goal is to compare the performance levels across these discrete categories. Which type of graph should the behavior analyst use?

A. Bar graph

B. Equal-interval graph

C. Line graph

D. Scatter plot

21. The ________________ is a type of graph that is used to display the running total of responses over time. The data path never descends, and a steeper data path indicates a higher response rate.

A. Bar graph

B. Cumulative record

C. Equal-interval graph

D. Scatter plot

22. A behavior analyst is reviewing a client's progress in a behavior intervention. The graph shows how the client's behavior changed over time, including how consistent the behavior has been (variability), the overall increase or decrease in the behavior (trend), and the average level of behavior during each phase (level). The analyst notes that the graph does not provide information about how large the behavior change is in comparison to other behaviors or baseline levels. Which of the following properties of behavior change is NOT communicated by the graph?

A. Effect size

B. Level

C. Trend

D. Variability

(*See answers on the next page.*)

20. **A) Bar graph**
Bar graphs are specifically designed to display discrete sets of data, where each bar represents a distinct category (e.g., different skill areas). The other answer options are better suited for tracking changes in behavior over time or examining relationships between two variables, rather than comparing discrete categories.

21. **B) Cumulative record**
The cumulative record is a type of graph that is used to display the running total of responses over time, with a data path that never descends. The other answer options (bar graph, equal-interval graph, scatter plot) are other types of graphs and function as distractors.

22. **A) Effect size**
In the scenario, the behavior analyst is reviewing key features of the graph: level (the average rate of behavior during a phase), trend (the direction of change over time), and variability (the degree of fluctuation in the data). These are the three basic properties of behavior change that graphs effectively communicate. However, effect size, which measures the magnitude or significance of change relative to a baseline or other behaviors, is not typically represented in standard graphs.

6

Experimental Design

LEARNING OBJECTIVES

The following Test Content Outline (TCO) Tasks (Behavior Analyst Certification Board®, 2024, p. 2) related to experimental design (D.1 through D.9) will serve as the learning objectives of this chapter:

- D.1 Distinguish between dependent and independent variables.
- D.2 Distinguish between internal and external validity.
- D.3 Identify threats to internal validity (e.g., history, maturation).
- D.4 Identify the defining features of single-case experimental designs (e.g., individuals serve as their own controls, repeated measures, prediction, verification, replication).
- D.5 Identify the relative strengths of single-case experimental designs and group designs.
- D.6 Critique and interpret data from single-case experimental designs.
- D.7 Distinguish among reversal, multiple-baseline, multielement, and changing-criterion designs.
- D.8 Identify rationales for conducting comparative, component, and parametric analyses.
- D.9 Apply single-case experimental designs.

TASK D.1

Distinguish between dependent and independent variables.

DEPENDENT VARIABLE

The dependent variable (DV) is the target behavior; thus, the DV represents some measure of socially significant behavior that an intervention is designed to change. In an experiment, this is measured to ascertain whether systematic manipulations of the independent variable (IV) alter it.

- **Example:** DV = student's aggressive behavior

INDEPENDENT VARIABLE

The IV is the intervention; thus, the IV represents some treatment variable that is used to intervene on the phenomenon of interest (i.e., target behavior). In an experiment, this is systematically manipulated to determine if alterations to it will produce reliable alterations in the DV.

- **Example:** IV = differential reinforcement procedure

ADDITIONAL NOTE(S)

Any investigation of the "causes" of behavior represents a search for the particular IVs of which behavior is a function.

TASK D.2

Distinguish between internal and external validity. Behavior analysts implementing interventions are concerned with internal and external validity, which are concepts that communicate how trustworthy and meaningful results are.

INTERNAL VALIDITY

This refers to the degree that the changes in the DV (i.e., target behavior) can be attributed to the manipulation of the IV (i.e., intervention) and not the result of uncontrolled/extraneous factors. Experiments that reliably demonstrate a cause-and-effect relationship between the IV and DV are said to have a high degree of internal validity.

Internal validity is threatened when there is the possibility that results are affected by uncontrolled/extraneous factors.

EXTERNAL VALIDITY

This refers to the degree the results of the intervention (i.e., functional relationship demonstrated in an experiment) can be generalized to other behaviors, environments, and individuals/populations.

External validity is threatened when conditions inherent in the experimental design may limit the generalizability of the results.

Threats to internal and external validity can be reduced through replication. Major threats to internal validity are addressed by behavior analysts using baseline logic (see Task D.4) and steady state strategy (i.e., measuring a target behavior repeatedly under each condition and obtaining a stable pattern of responding prior to a condition change).

TASK D.3

Identify threats to internal validity (e.g., history, maturation). Threats to internal validity pose challenges to the accuracy and reliability of research findings, and can include (a) subject confounds, (b) setting confounds, (c) measurement confounds, and (d) IV confounds.

SUBJECT CONFOUNDS

A range of subject variables can confound study results, including (a) history and (b) maturation.

History

This refers to external events or changes in the environment (e.g., a significant life event, such as moving to a new home or experiencing a family crisis) that can impact the outcomes of interventions implemented in practice settings.

Maturation

This refers to changes in subjects/clients over time that can affect the outcomes of interventions (e.g., physical growth or acquisition of skills) particularly in long-term interventions or treatments.

SETTING CONFOUNDS

These include (a) natural setting variables and (b) *bootleg* reinforcement.

Natural Setting Variables

Studies conducted in natural settings face numerous uncontrollable variables (e.g., changes in daily routine or social dynamics) that can confound results.

Bootleg Reinforcement

Subjects accessing the same reinforcers outside the study can diminish their effectiveness within the experiment, introducing confounding variables.

MEASUREMENT CONFOUNDS

These include (a) observer bias and drift and (b) reactivity to measurement.

Observer Bias and Drift

Observer bias, where expectations influence recordings, and drift, where criteria change over time, can confound data.

Reactivity to Measurement

Subjects may alter their behavior simply due to their awareness of being observed.

INDEPENDENT VARIABLE CONFOUNDS

These include (a) multifaceted IVs and (b) control procedures.

Multifaceted Independent Variables

These variables have multiple components that can confound results (e.g., a treatment program [i.e., the IV] that combines behavior management strategies with social skills training).

Control Procedures

These are systematic methods used in research to regulate variables and are essential for ensuring reliability and validity of research findings; however, they can also become a threat to internal validity when they inadvertently influence the outcomes of the study.

ADDITIONAL NOTE(S)

It's important to consider and address threats to internal validity throughout the research or intervention process. By identifying potential threats and implementing appropriate controls or strategies, researchers and practitioners can enhance the validity of their findings and ensure that observed changes in behavior are indeed attributable to the intended interventions rather than extraneous factors.

TASK D.4

Identify the defining features of single-case experimental designs (e.g., individuals serve as their own controls, repeated measures, prediction, verification, replication). Behavior analysts use single-subject experimental designs (also referred to as *single-case, within-subject, intrasubject*, and *repeated-measures designs*) to provide experimental evaluations of intervention effects. In other words, these experimental designs are used to determine whether changes in the IV are driving changes in the DV. See Task D.7 for a review of the types of single-subject experimental designs used by behavior analysts.

The defining features of single-subject experimental designs include: (a) the subject is the unit of intervention and data analysis, (b) the subject provides its own control for comparison, and (c) the target behavior is measured repeatedly across different levels or conditions of the intervention.

Note that the subject (sometimes referred to as "the case") may be an individual client or cluster of individuals (e.g., class or school).

SUBJECT SERVES AS ITS OWN CONTROL

This means that measurements of the DV between conditions are compared for each subject. In single-subject experimental designs, precise control is maintained of the IV. Thus, the intervention (i.e., IV) is presented, withdrawn, or its value is varied to demonstrate the effect it has on the target behavior (i.e., DV) when compared to the subject's own data. To achieve experimental control, a predictable change in the target behavior is demonstrated to be reliable and repeatedly produced by the systematic manipulation of the intervention.

TARGET BEHAVIOR IS MEASURED REPEATEDLY

The target behavior is repeatedly measured. Single-case experimental designs arrange comparisons between control and experimental conditions so that the target behavior is measured multiple times in a condition before contacting the next condition.

Additionally, baseline logic is used.

BASELINE LOGIC

This is a powerful form of experimental reasoning that calls for three elements: (a) prediction, (b) verification, and (c) replication, each of which depends on *steady state strategy*.

Prediction

This is the anticipated outcome of an unknown/future measurement. Sufficient baseline data is needed to allow for a behavior analyst to confidently predict a future measurement of the target behavior.

It is recommended that measurement continues until the behavior pattern is clearly stable. If the behavior analyst is unsure about the stability of responding in the baseline condition, then it probably isn't stable enough and additional data should be collected before the intervention is introduced.

Verification

This is the demonstration of a functional relationship between the intervention and target behavior. This would require observing changes in the target behavior associated with the introduction and withdrawal of the intervention and is accomplished when data convincingly shows that baseline responding would remain as-is without introduction of the intervention.

Replication

This is the repeating of IV manipulations and obtaining outcomes similar to those of a previous study. Replication provides additional evidence that a particular IV is responsible for change in a DV, and that the behavior change can be reliably made to occur again.

ADDITIONAL NOTE(S)

In single-case experimental studies, basic features also include the following: (a) details of subject(s)/setting(s) are sufficient to allow for others to replicate them, (b) DVs are operationally defined, (c) implementation fidelity (i.e., whether the IV was presented as intended) is documented, and (d) social significance is established.

TASK D.5

Identify the relative strengths of single-case experimental designs and group designs. Behavior analysts focus on the direct and repeated measurement of individuals' behavior. Thus, they use single-subject experimental designs rather than group experimental designs that have historically predominated the social sciences.

GROUP DESIGNS

This type of experimental design, also known as between-groups experimental designs, include the following features:

- Subjects are randomly selected from a population of interest.
- Subjects are randomly assigned to two or more groups and organized.
- Groups are organized into a minimum of one treatment group and one control group.
- Subjects in the treatment group (but not the control group) are exposed to the intervention.
- Measurements of the DV are conducted for each group; results for each group are combined.
- Analysis is conducted at the level of the group, not the individual.
- Conclusions are drawn at the level of the group, not the individual.

SINGLE-SUBJECT EXPERIMENTAL DESIGN

See Task D.4 for a review of the features of single-subject experimental designs. The advantages of this type of experimental design are as follows:

- Subjects serve as their own control.
- It reveals the performance of individual subjects.
- Data for subjects are not combined/averaged, which helps to prevent distortion/masking of variability in the data.
- It enables the demonstration of behavior-environment relations at the level of the individual.
- It allows for replication of effects within and across individual subjects.

TASK D.6

Critique and interpret data from single-case experimental designs. Single-case experimental designs offer valuable insights into the effectiveness of behavioral interventions for individuals. However, interpreting and critiquing data from such designs require careful consideration of various factors to ensure valid and meaningful conclusions. These include the (a) clarity and precision of operational definitions, (b) robustness of experimental control, (c) effectiveness of the intervention, and (f) potential threats to validity. In addition, behavior analysts must conduct visual analyses of graphical displays of data.

CLARITY AND PRECISION OF OPERATIONAL DEFINITIONS

See Task C.1 (Chapter 5) for a review of operational definitions. Assess their clarity and precision by examining how well they define and measure target behaviors. Also, ensure that definitions are consistently applied across all phases of a study to maintain reliability and validity of measurement.

ROBUSTNESS OF EXPERIMENTAL CONTROL

This is essential for demonstrating that the changes in the DV are directly attributable to the manipulation of the IV. To evaluate the robustness of experimental control, examine the (a) implementation of reliable measurement procedures, (b) adequacy of baseline stability, and (c) efforts to minimize confounding variables.

Measurement Reliability

Evaluate the reliability of measurement procedures by examining their consistency and accuracy. Look for evidence of interobserver agreement and test-retest reliability to ensure the consistency of data collection methods. Reliable measurement procedures yield consistent and trustworthy data.

Baseline Stability

Evaluate the adequacy of baseline stability by examining the consistency of baseline measures. Stable baseline trends with minimal variability indicate a solid foundation for assessing intervention effects. Consider the duration of the baseline phase and the number of data points collected to ensure sufficient stability before implementing the intervention. This can be accomplished through visual analysis of data graphs; however, statistical analyses such as trend analysis and stability metrics like the percentage of nonoverlapping data points (PND) can be conducted to provide quantitative measures of baseline stability.

Confounding Variables

These can obscure the relationship between the IVs and DVs. Look for control procedures designed to minimize the influence of extraneous variables. Effective experimental control isolates the effects of the intervention from other factors that could influence study outcomes.

Control Procedures for Subject Confounds

- Employing experimental designs that introduce and withdraw the IV multiple times or with rapidly changing conditions to effectively control for maturation effects
- Ensuring participants remain unaware of the experimental conditions and expected outcomes to minimize potential biases
- Using intrasubject experimental designs where each participant serves as their own control, thereby eliminating confounding by individual differences

Control Procedures for Setting Confounds

- Maintaining consistent environmental conditions throughout the study to mitigate the influence of external factors on participant behavior
- Holding all aspects of the experiment constant when unexpected events occur, and treating these events as IVs if necessary for experimental manipulation

Control Procedures for Measurement Confounds

- Implementing standardized measurement protocols and providing rigorous observer training to ensure accurate and consistent data collection
- Keeping observers naive to the conditions and expected outcomes of the experiment to reduce potential biases
- Randomizing the scoring of papers from baseline and treatment conditions to control for observer drift or bias

Control Procedures for Independent Variable Confounds

- Applying counterbalancing techniques or matched control conditions to mitigate potential biases arising from variations in the IV
- Employing placebo controls in experiments to separate effects produced by subjects' expectations from the actual effects of the IV
- Implementing double-blind control procedures where neither the subjects nor the observers know whether the IV is present or absent, thereby eliminating confounding by subject and observer biases

INTERVENTION EFFECTIVENESS

Evaluate the effectiveness of the intervention by examining the degree to which the intervention produces the desired changes in behavior. This can be accomplished through visual analysis of data graphs; the extent to which the intervention has achieved its intended outcomes can be determined by comparing the level, trend, and variability of behavior before and after the intervention (see Task C.11 [Chapter 5] for a review of interpreting graphed data). In addition, statistical analyses such as effect size calculations or comparative analyses between baseline and intervention phases can provide quantitative measures of intervention effectiveness.

THREATS TO VALIDITY

Look for potential threats to internal and external validity that may impact the findings and determine whether they have been identified and sufficiently addressed (e.g., minimized through careful use of control procedures and systematic replication) in the study (see Tasks D.2 and D.3 for a review of internal/external validity and potential threats to internal validity, respectively).

TASK D.7

Distinguish among reversal, multiple-baseline, multielement, and changing-criterion designs.

AB DESIGN

This is the most basic single-subject design. It involves repeated measures taken during a preintervention baseline condition (A) and then again during an intervention condition (B; Figure 6.1). It is generally only used when other, more powerful designs are untenable.

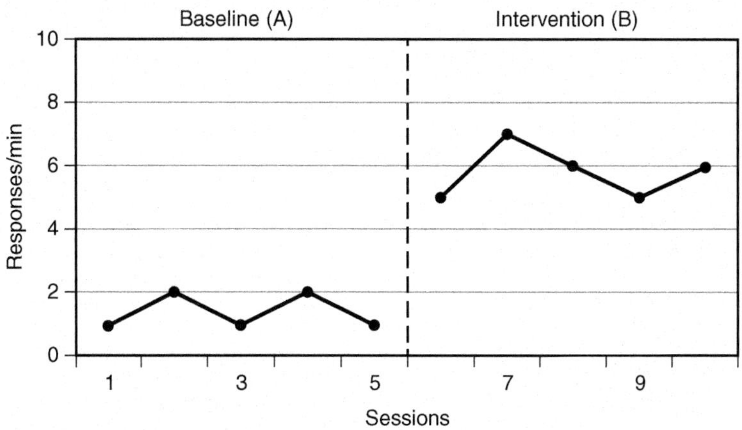

Figure 6.1 Example of a Graph of Data Using an AB Design

ABC DESIGN

This is a variant of the AB design in which a second intervention phase (C) is added following the first intervention phase (B; Figure 6.2). Consider this an exploratory design.

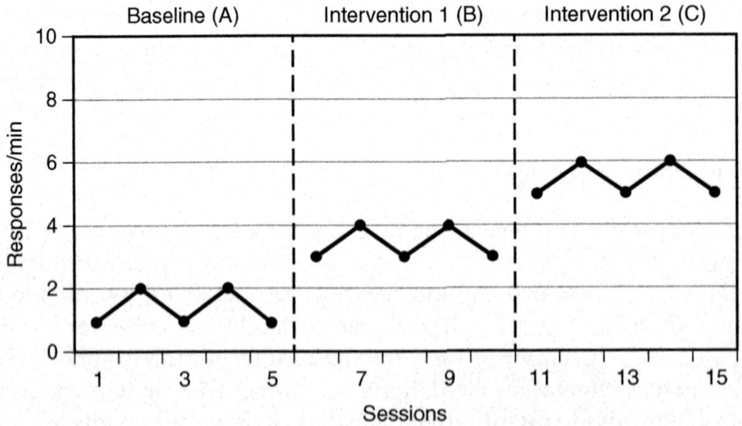

Figure 6.2 Example of a Graph of Data Using an ABC Design

This is an additive design. It doesn't have to end after C. You can also have ABCD, ABCDE, and so on.

REVERSAL DESIGNS

These are designs that demonstrate the effect of an intervention by alternating its presentation and removal over time. Use these when (a) the target behavior is reversible; (b) removal of treatment does not present a concern; and (c) stability, order, and time do not present a concern.

ABA Design

This is the most basic reversal design. It involves repeated measures taken during an initial baseline condition (A), then an intervention condition (B), and again after returning to the baseline condition (A; Figure 6.3).

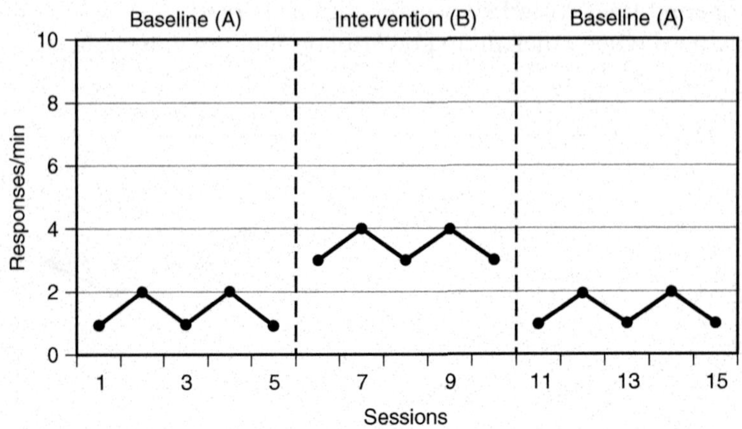

Figure 6.3 Example of a Graph of Data Using an ABA Design

The condition in which there is a return to baseline is also referred to as the *withdrawal phase*.

ABAB Design

This is a type of reversal design that involves an initial baseline phase (A), followed by an intervention phase (B), followed by a withdrawal phase (A), followed by a final intervention phase (B; Figure 6.4).

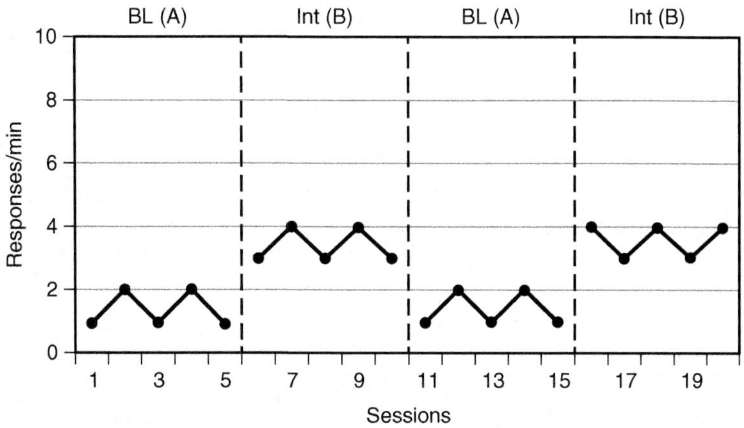

Figure 6.4 Example of a Graph of Data Using an ABAB Design
BL, baseline; Int, intervention.

This is a powerful design that is preferred over the basic ABA design. It is also possible to extend this fundamental reversal design (e.g., ABABA).

Other types of reversal designs include: (a) repeated reversals (e.g., ABABAB), (b) BAB reversal, (c) multiple treatment reversal (e.g., ABCBC), (d) noncontingent reinforcement (NCR) reversal (e.g., A [NCR on fixed ratio or variable ratio schedule] B [contingent reinforcement] A [return to NCR]), and (e) differential reinforcement of other (DRO)/differential reinforcement of incompatible (DRI)/differential reinforcement of alternative (DRA) behavior reversal (e.g., A [DRO] B [contingent reinforcement] A [return to DRO]).

MULTIPLE BASELINE DESIGN

This type of design is commonly used when a reversal is determined to be impractical or unethical. This involves (a) establishing two or more independent baselines, and (b) introducing the intervention in a staggered fashion for each baseline. When the behavior for the first baseline is stable, the intervention is then introduced to the second baseline, and so forth (Figure 6.5). This design can be used to compare responding across different behaviors for a client, a behavior across different clients, or a behavior across different settings.

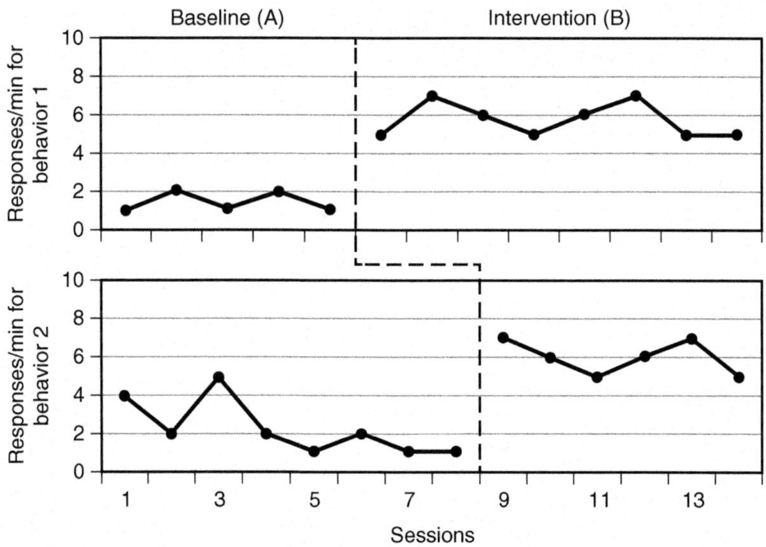

Figure 6.5 Example of a Graph of Data Using Multiple Baseline Design (Two Baselines Representing Two Different Behaviors)

The more baselines you include in a multiple baseline design, the more convincing your results will be.

MULTIELEMENT DESIGN

Also commonly referred to as an alternating treatments design, this type of design involves delivering and measuring effects of two or more interventions in a rapid, alternating fashion (Figure 6.6). This allows behavior analysts to compare the effects of different interventions. It can also be used to compare the effects of an intervention with no intervention (i.e., baseline).

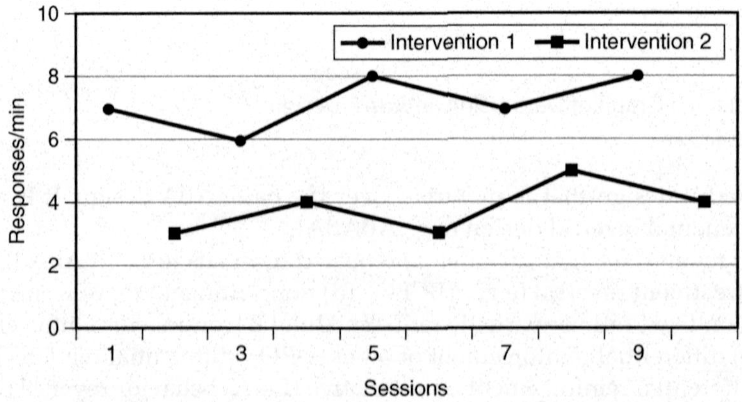

Figure 6.6 Example of a Graph of Data Using a Multielement Design (Two Interventions)

CHANGING CRITERION DESIGN

This is a design in which the initial baseline phase is followed by a series of intervention phases with successive/gradual criteria for change. See Task C.7 (Chapter 5) for a review of measuring trials to criterion.

- **Example (changing criterion design):** In Figure 6.7, a behavior was targeted for decrease. After the initial baseline phase, an intervention phase was introduced with the goal of decreasing the behavior to six times per hour. Once reached, the next intervention phase followed with a goal of three times per hour.

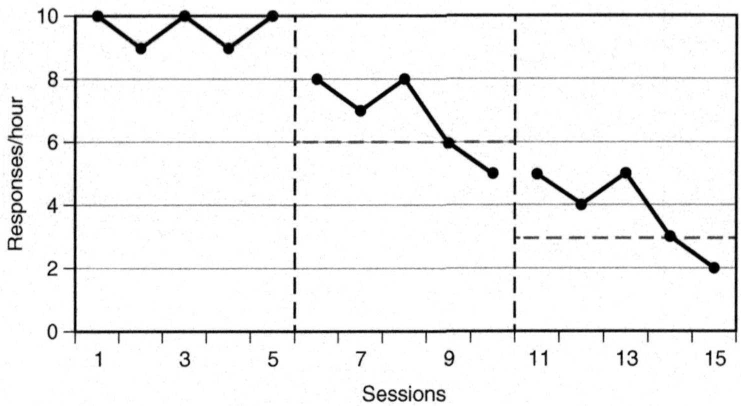

Figure 6.7 Graph of Data Using a Changing Criterion Design

TASK D.8

Identify rationales for conducting comparative, component, and parametric analyses.

COMPARATIVE ANALYSIS

This type of analysis compares two or more distinct interventions (e.g., multielement experimental designs). Rationales for its use include:

- to evaluate the effects of two or more interventions
- to answer the question, "Which intervention was most effective?"

COMPONENT ANALYSIS

This type of analysis evaluates the relative contributions of the parts of an intervention. There are two types: (a) *drop-out*, which involves implementing an intervention and then systematically removing parts of it; and (b) *add-in*, which involves systematically assessing parts individually or together before implementing the intervention. Rationales for its use include:

- to evaluate the effects of the individual parts of an intervention
- to answer the question, "Which part of the intervention was most effective?"

PARAMETRIC ANALYSIS

This type of analysis compares different levels of an intervention. It involves examining the effects generated by manipulating one or more dimensions/levels of the intervention. Rationales for its use include:

- to evaluate the differential effects of a range of values of an intervention on behavior
- to answer the question, "How much intervention is required to be effective?"
- to answer the question, "How much intervention is most effective?"

▶ PRACTICE QUESTION

A first-grade teacher wants to know how much time is optimal for the instruction of a reading fluency intervention within the scheduled literacy block. They currently instruct this skill for 5 minutes each day. They are investigating the following research question: What effect will incremental increases (5, 10, 15 min) in the IV (fluency intervention) have on the DV (fluency probes)? What type of analysis is described?

A. Comparative analysis
B. Competitive analysis
C. Component analysis
D. Parametric analysis

Before moving on to the following section for the solution, we recommend that you provide a brief explanation for the answer option you selected here:

___

___

When you're ready, move on to the next section for the solution!

Practice Question Breakdown

Step 1: Examine the question

The question calls for the identification of the type of analysis used to assess how different durations of a fluency intervention affect a student's reading fluency. The scenario involves manipulating the amount of time spent on the fluency intervention (the IV) and observing the resulting changes in fluency probe performance (the DV).

Step 2: Analyze the answer options

A. Comparative analysis investigates two or more distinct interventions in relation to a DV. There are not two distinct interventions in the previous scenario. This answer option is a distractor.
B. This is a type of analysis used in business and does not apply here. This answer option is a distractor.
C. Component analysis examines the individual elements or "parts" from a multicomponent intervention on the DV. There was not mention of multiple components in the fluency intervention. This answer option is a distractor.
D. Parametric analysis examines how behavior changes in relation to variation in the level (or number of minutes) of a reading fluency intervention. This looks like the one!

Step 3: Select the best answer

Among the four answer options presented, answer D (Parametric analysis) appears to be the best answer.

TASK D.9

Apply single-case experimental designs. The key steps to applying single-case experimental designs include (a) defining operational terms, (b) selecting an appropriate design, (c) establishing baseline stability, (d) implementing the intervention, (e) utilizing continuous and reliable measurement, (f) performing visual analysis (and statistical analysis, if applicable), and (g) addressing and mitigating confounding variables.

DEFINING OPERATIONAL TERMS

Applying single-case experimental designs begins with clear and precise operational definitions of the target behavior and the intervention. These definitions ensure that all observers and researchers have a consistent understanding of what is being measured and manipulated, which is crucial for reliable data collection and analysis. See Task C.1 (Chapter 5) for a review of operational definitions.

SELECTING AN APPROPRIATE DESIGN

There are multiple design types that can be applied, including reversal, multiple-baseline, changing criterion, and alternating treatments designs. See Task D.7 for a review of single-case experimental designs. The choice of design depends on the research question, the nature of the behavior, and ethical considerations.

ESTABLISHING BASELINE STABILITY

A stable baseline is important in many single-case experimental designs as it provides a point of comparison for assessing the impact of the intervention. For reversal and multiple-baseline designs, they are essential. For changing criterion and alternating treatments designs, they are less critical but can still be beneficial for demonstrating the initial level of behavior before performance criteria are changed or interventions are applied. Baseline data should be collected until the behavior shows a stable pattern, minimizing variability that could obscure the effects of the intervention.

IMPLEMENTING THE INTERVENTION

Once baseline stability is achieved, the intervention is systematically introduced. The intervention phase should be clearly defined and consistently applied. Also, incorporate strategies to support procedural integrity such as (a) providing detailed protocols to implementers, (b) monitoring implementation and providing feedback to implementers, and (c) using fidelity checklists or logs.

Detailed Protocols

Provide detailed, step-by-step instructions for implementing the intervention to the implementers.

Monitoring and Feedback

Regularly monitor the implementation process and provide feedback to implementers to correct any deviations from the protocol.

Fidelity Checklists or Logs

Use fidelity checklists or logs to document the consistency and accuracy of implementation.

See Tasks C.12 (Chapter 5) and H.6 (Chapter 10) for a review of the measurement and monitoring of procedural integrity, respectively.

CONTINUOUS AND RELIABLE MEASUREMENT

Data should be collected consistently across all phases of the study, ensuring that any observed changes can be accurately attributed to the intervention. Techniques such as interobserver agreement (IOA) checks can enhance the reliability of the data.

VISUAL AND STATISTICAL ANALYSIS

Data analysis typically involves visual inspection of graphs, focusing on changes in level, trend, and variability between phases (see Task C.11 [Chapter 5] for a review of interpretation of graphed data). Look for clear patterns that indicate the intervention's effects. In some cases, statistical analysis can supplement visual inspection to provide additional evidence of intervention effectiveness.

ADDRESSING AND MITIGATING CONFOUNDING VARIABLES

Control procedures are essential to mitigate confounding variables that could threaten the validity of the study. See Task D.6 for a review of control procedures for subject, setting, measurement, and IV confounds.

CONCLUSION

In this chapter, we reviewed key content for TCO Tasks related to experimental design for behavior analysts. This included the features and advantages of single-subject designs, as well as the various types of experimental configurations that allow the behavior analyst to attribute changes in a DV (i.e., behavior of interest) to the actions of an IV (i.e., intervention). In other words, experimentation allows behavior analysts to demonstrate evidence of functional relations. It is through this process that we can evaluate how effective our treatments are in affecting change in behavior. Whether you go on to become a behavior analyst conducting research or delivering behavior analytic services to clients, this content is both relevant and necessary for you.

REFERENCE

Behavior Analyst Certification Board. (2024). *BCBA test content outline* (6th ed.). Author. https://www.bacb.com/wp-content/bcba-outline-6thEd

BIBLIOGRAPHY

Cooper, J. O., Heron, T. E., & Heward, W. L. (2020). *Applied behavior analysis* (3rd ed.). Pearson Education.

Hayes, S. C., Rincover, A., & Solnick, J. V. (1980). The technical drift of applied behavior analysis. *Journal of Applied Behavior Analysis, 13*(2), 275–285. https://doi.org/10.1901/jaba.1980.13-275

Horner, R. H., Carr, E. G., Halle, J., McGee, G., Odom, S., & Wolery, M. (2005). The use of single-subject research to identify evidence-based practice in special education. *Exceptional Children, 71*(2), 165–179. https://doi.org/10.1177/001440290507100203

Kennedy, C. H. (2005). *Single-case designs for educational research*. Prentice Hall.

Kratochwill, T. R., Hitchcock, J., Horner, R. H., Levin, J. R., Odom, S. L., Rindskopf, D. M., & Shadish, W. R. (2010). *Single-case designs technical documentation*. What Works Clearinghouse.

Pennypacker, H. S., & Johnston, J. M. (1980). *Strategies and tactics of human behavioral research*. Erlbaum.

Poling, A., & Grossett, D. (1986). Basic research designs in applied behavior analysis. In A. Poling & R. W. Fuqua (Eds.), *Research methods in applied behavior analysis* (pp. 7–27). Springer.

Ward-Horner, J., & Sturmey, P. (2010). Component analyses using single-subject experimental designs: A review. *Journal of Applied Behavior Analysis, 43*(4), 685–704. https://doi.org/10.1901/jaba.2010.43-685

KNOWLEDGE CHECK

1. The ________________ is the target behavior, whereas the ________________ represents some treatment variable.
   A. Dependent variable (DV): independent variable (IV)
   B. Discrete variable; nominal variable
   C. IV; DV
   D. Intervening variable; control variable

2. A researcher is studying the effects of a new social skills program on students' interactions with their peers. The researcher implements the social skills program in one group and uses traditional instruction in another group. The researcher then measures the number of positive peer interactions each student has during recess to determine if the social skills program leads to improvements in social behavior. What is the researcher measuring?
   A. Control variable
   B. Dependent variable (DV)
   C. Independent variable (IV)
   D. Intervening variable

3. A behavior analyst is working with a child on a self-monitoring intervention to reduce disruptive classroom behaviors. After a successful intervention in one classroom, the behavior analyst wants to determine whether the intervention will work in other settings. They plan to implement the same self-monitoring strategy during recess, lunch, and in a different classroom setting. What is the behavior analyst assessing in this scenario?
   A. Accuracy
   B. External validity
   C. Internal validity
   D. Reliability

4. A researcher is working with a child to reduce tantrum behaviors using a differential reinforcement procedure. During the intervention, the researcher ensures that all other variables, such as the child's sleep schedule, diet, and daily routine, remain consistent to isolate the effect of the reinforcement. By doing so, what is the researcher focusing on?
   A. Accuracy
   B. External validity
   C. Internal validity
   D. Reliability

(*See answers on the next page.*)

1. **A) Dependent variable (DV), independent variable (IV)**
The DV is the target behavior, whereas the IV represents some treatment variable. The other answer options (discrete variable, nominal variable; IV, DV; intervening variable, control variable) do not accurately fit into the statement and instead function as distractors.

2. **B) Dependent variable (DV)**
In an experiment, the DV is measured to ascertain whether systematic manipulations of the IV alter it. In this scenario, the researcher is measuring the number of positive peer interactions (DV) to determine if changes occur as a result of the social skills program (IV). The other answer options refer to other types of variables and serve as distractors.

3. **B) External validity**
External validity refers to the extent to which the results of an intervention or study can be generalized to other behaviors, environments, individuals, or populations. In this scenario, the behavior analyst is applying the self-monitoring strategy in different settings (recess, lunch, and another classroom) to see if the results of the intervention can be generalized beyond the original classroom. This is a direct assessment of external validity. The other answer options refer to other measurement-related concepts and function as distractors.

4. **C) Internal validity**
Internal validity refers to the degree to which changes in the dependent variable (tantrum behaviors) can be attributed directly to the manipulation of the independent variable (differential reinforcement procedure) and not to uncontrolled or extraneous factors. In this scenario, the behavior analyst controls variables such as the child's sleep schedule, diet, and daily routine to ensure that no other factors are influencing the child's behavior, thus protecting internal validity. The other answer options refer to other concepts and function as distractors.

5. The defining features of single-subject experimental designs include all of the following, EXCEPT:

A. The internal validity of results is accomplished through replication of treatment effects.

B. The subject serves as the unit of intervention and data analysis.

C. The subject provides its own control for comparison.

D. The target behavior is measured repeatedly across different levels or conditions of the intervention.

6. A researcher is conducting a study to increase physical activity among students during gym class. During the study, the local sports team wins a major championship, which generates excitement among students and leads to increased participation in gym activities. The researcher is unsure if the intervention or the excitement surrounding the championship is responsible for the change in physical activity levels. Which threat to internal validity might explain the increase in physical activity?

A. History effect

B. Maturation

C. Regression to the mean

D. Selection bias

7. A behavior analyst is using an ABAB design to assess the impact of a differential reinforcement procedure on a client's disruptive behavior. During the second baseline phase, the behavior analyst observes that the client's disruptive behavior returns to the same level as during the initial baseline, providing evidence that the behavior is influenced by the presence or absence of the differential reinforcement procedure. What term refers to the process of confirming that the target behavior is influenced by the intervention?

A. Prediction

B. Replication

C. Validation

D. Verification

8. A researcher is studying the impact of two different reinforcement strategies on increasing the social interactions of a group of students. The researcher alternates between using praise and using tokens as reinforcement, sometimes switching the reinforcement strategy multiple times in the same session. By comparing the effects of each reinforcement strategy, the researcher aims to determine which one has a greater impact on the students' social interactions. Which type of single-subject experimental design is the researcher using?

A. ABC

B. Changing criterion

C. Multielement

D. Multiple baseline

(*See answers on the next page.*)

5. **A) The internal validity of results is accomplished through replication of treatment effects.**
   In single-subject experimental designs, the subject serves as the unit of intervention and data analysis; the subject provides its own control for comparison, and the target behavior is measured repeatedly across different levels or conditions of the intervention. It is not the case, however, that the internal validity of results in single-subject designs is accomplished through replication of treatment effects.

6. **A) History effect**
   In this scenario, the history effect is the most likely threat to internal validity. The increase in physical activity could be influenced by an external event (the local sports team winning a championship) that occurred at the same time as the intervention. The history effect refers to changes in the dependent variable caused by external events happening concurrently with the intervention. The other answer options refer to other types of threats to internal validity and function as distractors.

7. **D) Verification**
   Verification involves the demonstration of a functional relationship between the intervention and the target behavior in baseline logic. In this scenario, the behavior analysis is confirming that the target behavior (disruptive behavior) is influenced by the intervention (differential reinforcement procedure) by showing that the behavior returns to baseline levels when the intervention is removed. The other answer options refer to anticipating behavior trends (prediction), repeating the intervention to assess consistency (replication), or a term not commonly used in baseline logic (validation).

8. **C) Multielement**
   In this scenario, the researcher is using a multielement design because they are rapidly alternating between two reinforcement strategies (praise and tokens) and measuring their effects on social interactions. Multielement designs are used to compare the effects of two or more interventions by alternating them quickly. The other answer options refer to other types of single-subject experimental designs and function as distractors.

9. A teacher is implementing a new classroom management strategy to increase on-task behavior. The teacher first records students' on-task behavior without the strategy for 2 weeks, then introduces the new strategy and continues recording the behavior. The teacher wants to compare student behavior before and during the use of the strategy. This is an example of what type of single-subject experimental design?

   A. AB

   B. ABC

   C. Multiple baseline

   D. Reversal

10. Which of the following single-subject experimental designs involves establishing two or more independent baselines and introducing the intervention in a staggered fashion for each baseline?

   A. ABAB

   B. Changing criterion

   C. Multielement

   D. Multiple baseline

11. A behavior analyst is using an ABAB design to measure the effects of a reinforcement procedure on a client's on-task behavior. During the first phase, the behavior analyst collects baseline data. Then, the reinforcement procedure is implemented to observe changes in behavior. After some time, the behavior analyst removes the reinforcement procedure to see if the student's behavior returns to baseline levels. In this ABAB design, during which phase is the reinforcement procedure removed?

   A. The first A condition

   B. The first B condition

   C. The second A condition

   D. The second B condition

12. A researcher is investigating the effects of a new behavior intervention by testing its effectiveness at different intensities. First, the researcher implements the intervention with low-intensity support and then gradually increases the intensity to see how different levels impact the behavior. The goal is to determine the optimal intensity of the intervention that leads to the best outcomes. Which of the following types of analyses is the researcher conducting?

   A. Comparative analysis

   B. Component analysis

   C. Functional analysis

   D. Parametric analysis

13. Which of the following types of analyses evaluates the relative contributions of the parts of an intervention?

   A. Comparative analysis

   B. Component analysis

   C. Functional analysis

   D. Parametric analysis

(*See answers on the next page.*)

9. **A) AB**
In this scenario, the teacher is using an AB design because they are taking repeated measures during the baseline phase (before the classroom management strategy is implemented) and again during the intervention phase (after the strategy is implemented). This allows for a comparison of behavior before and during the intervention. The other answer options refer to other types of single-subject experimental designs and function as distractors.

10. **D) Multiple baseline**
The multiple baseline design involves establishing two or more independent baselines and introducing the intervention in a staggered fashion for each baseline. The other answer options (ABAB, changing criterion, multielement) refer to other types of single-subject experimental designs and function as distractors.

11. **C) The second A condition**
In an ABAB design (A = baseline; B = intervention), the withdrawal phase occurs during the second A condition, when the intervention (in this case, the reinforcement procedure) is removed to see if the behavior returns to baseline levels. This phase helps determine whether the behavior was maintained by the intervention. The other answer options refer to other phases of the ABAB design, none of which represent the withdrawal phase.

12. **D) Parametric analysis**
In this scenario, the researcher is using a parametric analysis because they are comparing different levels of the intervention's intensity to determine which level produces the best outcomes. Parametric analysis is specifically used to test the effects of varying levels of an intervention. The other answer options refer to analyses that compare different interventions, break down an intervention to assess the effects of each part, or identify the function of a behavior.

13. **B) Component analysis**
Component analysis can be used to evaluate the relative contributions of the parts of an intervention. The other answer options (comparative analysis, functional analysis, parametric analysis) refer to other types of analyses and serve as distractors.

7

Ethics

LEARNING OBJECTIVES

The following Test Content Outline (TCO) Tasks (Behavior Analyst Certification Board® [BACB®], 2024a, p. 2) related to ethics (E.1 through E.12) will serve as the learning objectives of this chapter:

- E.1 Identify and apply core principles underlying the ethics codes for BACB certificants (e.g., benefit others; treat others with compassion, dignity, and respect; behave with integrity).
- E.2 Identify the risks to oneself, others, and the profession as a result of engaging in unethical behavior.
- E.3 Develop and maintain competence by engaging in professional development activities (e.g., read literature, seek consultation, establish mentors).
- E.4 Identify and comply with requirements for collecting, using, protecting, and disclosing confidential information.
- E.5 Identify and comply with requirements for making public statements about professional activities (e.g., social media activity; misrepresentation of professional credentials, behavior analysis, and service outcomes).
- E.6 Identify the conditions under which services or supervision should be discontinued and apply steps that should be taken when transitioning clients and supervisees to another professional.
- E.7 Identify types of and risks associated with multiple relationships, and how to mitigate those risks when they are unavoidable.
- E.8 Identify and apply interpersonal and other skills (e.g., accepting feedback, listening actively, seeking input, collaborating) to establish and maintain professional relationships.
- E.9 Engage in cultural humility in service delivery and professional relationships.
- E.10 Apply culturally responsive and inclusive service and supervision activities.
- E.11 Identify personal biases and how they might interfere with professional activity.
- E.12 Identify and apply the legal, regulatory, and practice requirements (e.g., licensure, jurisprudence, funding, certification) relevant to the delivery of behavior-analytic services.

In this chapter, please note that "client" refers to someone who receives services directly from a behavior analyst, and "stakeholder" refers to someone who does not receive services directly from a behavior analyst but is nevertheless impacted by those services.

Please note that this chapter does not provide a comprehensive review of the standards in the Ethics Code, as the focus is limited to the TCO Tasks. We strongly advise that you carefully review the complete Code (available at www.bacb.com/ethics-information/ethics-codes) and familiarize yourself with the standards therein. As you review the Code, focus on the meaning of each standard and what it requires of behavior analysts in practice. You do not need to remember labels (i.e., standard numbers)—no one will ask you, "What exactly does standard 1.06 refer to?" It should be noted that although the standards may seem reasonably straightforward, it is still an imperfect set of rules that can present problems for behavior analysts in practice. This is evident when strict adherence seems contraindicated or even impossible in situations where (a) the context of the dilemma conflicts with the Code, (b) two or more standards conflict with each other, or (c) cultural considerations conflict with the Code. To address some of the most common ethical "dilemmas" or "tensions," extra practice questions will be presented to engage you further in the work of applying the standards to various situations that BCBAs® may encounter in the field. To learn more about how behavior analysts can address ethical problems, we encourage readers to seek out additional readings about this highly important topic.

TASK E.1

Identify and apply core principles underlying the ethics codes for BACB certificants (e.g., benefit others; treat others with compassion, dignity, and respect; behave with integrity). The introduction section of the Ethics Code describes the core principles that underlie the standards of the Code and how behavior analysts are to apply it.

CORE PRINCIPLES

The four core principles that serve as the framework for standards are: (a) benefit others; (b) treat others with compassion, dignity, and respect; (c) behave with integrity; and (d) ensure their competence.

Benefit Others

Engage in behaviors that do no harm and increase benefit to those we serve, including those that:

- Protect the welfare and rights of clients (i.e., your priority) and others you work with.
- Consider both short- and long-term impact of your professional activities.
- Identify and address any conflicts of interest or factors that may negatively impact your ability to do your work as a behavior analyst.
- Collaborate with others in the best interest of clients.

Treat Others With Compassion, Dignity, and Respect

Engage in behaviors that treat others with compassion, dignity, and respect, including those that:

- Treat others equitably, regardless of their demographic attributes (e.g., age, ethnicity, religion).
- Respect others' privacy/confidentiality.
- Promote clients' self-determination (i.e., ability to make choices that pertain to their lives).
- Provide clients and stakeholders with the information necessary to make informed choices about services.

Behave With Integrity

Engage in behaviors that satisfy your responsibility to society, the professional/scientific communities of which you are a part, and the communities you serve. This includes those behaviors that:

- Are honest and dependable.
- Accurately present your work (or that of others).
- Fulfill professional obligations.
- Ensure your accountability as a supervisor who is responsible for the work of their supervisees.
- Meet BACB and other regulatory requirements.
- Create professional environments that uphold the Code.
- Educate others about the Code and how violations can be addressed.

Ensure Their Competence

Engage in behaviors that ensure your professional competence as a behavior analyst. This includes those behaviors that:

- Ensure you practice what is within your scope of practice.
- Regularly evaluate the boundaries of your competence.
- Engage in professional development (PD) activities to increase your knowledge of best practices in the field.
- Ensure you remain current about potentially risky interventions used in the field.
- Develop your cultural competence.

APPLICATION

Behavior analysts must comply with the Code. Claiming lack of awareness or understanding of the Code (e.g., stating "I didn't know" or "I didn't understand") is not defensible and cannot justify violations of the Code. When addressing violations, document all steps taken to address them. When the professional misconduct of others appears resolvable and does not place anyone at undue risk, the behavior analyst should address concerns directly with the subject (i.e., individual alleged to have violated the Code). This section also (a) emphasizes the importance of behavior analysts' compliance with all laws and requirements relevant to their various professional roles and actively upholding the interests of their clients, and (b) recommends following a systematic approach to ethical decision-making.

TASK E.2

Identify the risks to oneself, others, and the profession as a result of engaging in unethical behavior. Engaging in unethical behavior poses significant risks to oneself, others, and the profession of behavior analysis. Understanding these risks is crucial for maintaining the integrity of the field and ensuring the welfare of clients.

RISKS TO ONESELF

These include (a) legal consequences, (b) loss of certification and employment, and (c) emotional and psychologic impact.

Legal Consequences

Engaging in unethical behavior can result in legal action against the behavior analyst. Violations of ethical guidelines may lead to lawsuits, criminal charges, or fines. For example, breaching client confidentiality or engaging in fraudulent billing practices can have severe legal repercussions.

Loss of Certification and Employment

Unethical conduct can lead to the loss of professional certification and job termination. The BACB has the authority to revoke or suspend certification for ethical violations. Without certification, one cannot practice as a behavior analyst, resulting in loss of livelihood and professional reputation.

Emotional and Psychologic Impact

Unethical behavior can also have a profound emotional and psychologic impact on the individual. Guilt, stress, and anxiety stemming from unethical actions can affect personal well-being and mental health. This emotional toll can impair professional performance and personal relationships.

RISKS TO OTHERS

These include (a) harm to clients, (b) breach of trust, and (c) impact on colleagues.

Harm to Clients

Behavior analysts are responsible for protecting the welfare of their clients. Unethical behavior, such as implementing unvalidated interventions or failing to obtain informed consent, can cause significant harm. Clients may experience ineffective or harmful treatment, leading to a deterioration in their condition or overall well-being.

Breach of Trust

Unethical conduct can erode the trust between clients and behavior analysts. Trust is foundational to the therapeutic relationship and, if broken, can be difficult to repair. A lack of trust can negatively impact the effectiveness of interventions and reduce client engagement and cooperation.

Impact on Colleagues

Unethical behavior can also negatively impact colleagues. It can create a hostile or toxic work environment, reducing morale and productivity. Colleagues may feel compelled to report unethical actions, leading to strained professional relationships and division within the workplace.

RISKS TO THE PROFESSION

These include (a) damage to the field, (b) regulatory and policy implications, and (c) impact on quality of services.

Damage to the Field

Unethical behavior by individuals can tarnish the reputation of the entire field of behavior analysis. High-profile cases of ethical violations can lead to public distrust and skepticism about the profession's legitimacy and efficacy. This damage to reputation can decrease public and institutional support for behavior analysis services and research.

Regulatory and Policy Implications

Widespread unethical practices can lead to increased regulatory scrutiny and the imposition of stricter regulations and policies. This can result in more rigorous oversight and potentially burdensome requirements for practice, which can hinder the flexibility and innovation within the field.

Impact on Quality of Services

When unethical behavior becomes prevalent, the overall quality of services within the field may decline. This can lead to poorer outcomes for clients and a reduction in the perceived value of behavior analysis interventions. Ultimately, this can diminish the profession's ability to attract new clients and practitioners.

▶ PRACTICE QUESTION

ATTUNE is a community applied behavior analysis (ABA) provider for children and adolescents with developmental disabilities. At several clinical team meetings, the BCBA seems distracted (e.g., scrolls through phone, reads other documents, completes paperwork during portions of the team discussion). While presenting on the behavioral-change plan, the BCBA is on point and talks with the family and other team members; however, once done speaking, the BCBA goes back to doing other tasks. Which of the following ethical standards BEST addresses this scenario?

A. Consulting with other providers
B. Responsibility to clients
C. Limitations to confidentiality
D. Documenting professional activity

Before moving on to the following section for the solution, we recommend that you provide a brief explanation for the answer option you selected here:

____

____

When you're ready, move on to the next section for the solution!

Practice Question Breakdown

Step 1: Examine the question

The question calls for you to consider the distracted and off-task behavior of the BCBA while in meetings with the client/stakeholders and determine the ethical standard that is most relevant to this scenario.

Step 2: Analyze the answer options

A. It might seem like consulting with other providers is relevant to interactions in this multidisciplinary team meeting; however, the BCBA does discuss the behavior-change plan with other providers at particular times in the meeting. This answer does not BEST address the ethical violation. This answer option is a distractor.
B. Professional responsibility to the client/stakeholders in this meeting seems to be lacking on the part of the BCBA, who is providing direct services. While we are all busy and likely multitasking as part of our job, it is important to act in the best interest of the client/stakeholders and remain engaged and active in all aspects of the clinical team meeting. This appears to be a promising option!
C. The scenario does not involve issues around the limits of confidentiality in the treatment team meeting. It is likely that prior to this meeting, confidentiality limits were already discussed and agreed to. This answer option is a distractor.
D. Detailed and organized documentation of the BCBA's work activities is not at the heart of this particular scenario. Documenting professional activity covers service provision at a broad level and is not simply focused on one meeting. This answer option is a distractor.

Step 3: Select the best answer

Among the four answer options presented, answer B (Responsibility to clients) appears to be the best answer.

TASK E.3

Develop and maintain competence by engaging in professional development activities (e.g., read literature, seek consultation, establish mentors). Maintaining competence as a behavior analyst by actively engaging in PD activities is critical for delivering effective and ethical services. These activities include (a) reading relevant literature; (b) attending conferences and conventions; (c) participating in workshops and other training opportunities; (d) obtaining additional coursework; (e) receiving coaching, consultation, supervision, or mentorship; and (f) obtaining and maintaining appropriate professional credentials.

READING RELEVANT LITERATURE

Behavior analysts must remain informed about the latest research and developments relevant to their practice area. This can be accomplished by making regular contact with the scholarly literature. The BACB provides free resources to members, including access to (a) the ProQuest database, which includes the PsycInfo and ERIC searchable research databases; and (b) numerous refereed journals, such as *The Analysis of Verbal Behavior, Behavior Analysis in Practice, Behavior Modification, Behavior Interventions, Journal of Applied Behavior Analysis, Journal of the Experimental Analysis of Behavior, Journal of Organizational Behavior Management, Journal of Positive Behavior Interventions*, and *Perspectives on Behavior Science*. You can access these through the "Resources" tab in the BACB Certification Gateway (gateway.bacb.com).

ATTENDING CONFERENCES AND CONVENTIONS

Conferences and conventions offer valuable opportunities for professional networking and learning from esteemed experts in the field. These events feature presentations on cutting-edge research, novel intervention techniques, and innovative approaches to behavior analysis. Attendance at such events enables behavior analysts to enhance their skills and knowledge, bringing new insights and strategies to their practice. Additionally, conferences often provide opportunities to earn continuing education (CE) credit required for maintaining certification. Plan ahead for major conferences and, when you're there, actively participate to get the most out of your experience.

PARTICIPATING IN WORKSHOPS AND OTHER TRAINING OPPORTUNITIES

Workshops and training sessions (available at conferences and conventions as well as a range of other venues) offer hands-on learning experiences and opportunities to practice new skills in a structured environment. These training opportunities typically focus on specific techniques or methodologies, allowing behavior analysts to deepen their expertise in particular areas of interest. To ensure you maximize gains in the skill areas that are most relevant for your practice, take some time to identify areas where you need further development and then seek out workshops and training opportunities that align with those areas.

OBTAINING ADDITIONAL COURSEWORK

Engaging in additional coursework is instrumental in expanding a behavior analyst's knowledge base and competencies. Whether through formal degree programs, online courses, or specialized training programs, further education helps practitioners remain current with the latest advancements and best practices in behavior analysis. Ongoing education is vital for upholding a high standard of professional practice.

RECEIVING COACHING, CONSULTATION, SUPERVISION, OR MENTORSHIP

Engaging in coaching, consultation, supervision, or mentorship is crucial for sustained professional growth. Experienced colleagues or mentors can offer invaluable guidance, feedback, and support. These relationships assist behavior analysts in navigating complex cases, refining their skills, and ensuring adherence to ethical and effective practice standards. Regular supervision or consultation sessions provide ongoing support and contribute to continuous PD.

OBTAINING AND MAINTAINING APPROPRIATE PROFESSIONAL CREDENTIALS

Maintaining certification and licensure is a fundamental aspect of professional competence. Obtaining and renewing credentials, including the BCBA certification, requires ongoing education and strict adherence to professional standards. Keep track of your certification renewal dates, ensure you meet CE requirements, and stay informed about any changes in certification standards or requirements.

ADDITIONAL NOTE(S)

See Chapter 14 "After the Exam" for additional information related to PD and options for obtaining CE credits.

TASK E.4

Identify and comply with requirements for collecting, using, protecting, and disclosing confidential information. Behavior analysts must adhere to stringent requirements for handling confidential information to ensure the protection of clients' privacy and confidentiality rights while upholding professional standards of practice.

CONFIDENTIAL INFORMATION

This includes all client-related information obtained during the course of assessment, intervention, and consultation. Confidential information encompasses sensitive data such as personal identifiers, behavioral observations, assessment results, treatment plans, progress notes, and any other information disclosed by clients or their legal guardians.

COMPLIANCE WITH REQUIREMENTS

Behavior analysts are obligated to comply with all relevant laws, regulations, and ethical requirements governing the collection, use, protection, and disclosure of confidential information. This includes adhering to the Health Insurance Portability and Accountability Act (HIPAA) Privacy Rule, which sets forth strict standards for safeguarding protected health information (PHI). Additionally, behavior analysts must adhere to the Code (i.e., BACB Ethics Code for Behavior Analysts), which outlines the requirements for maintaining client confidentiality.

COLLECTING AND USING CONFIDENTIAL INFORMATION

Behavior analysts are permitted to collect and use confidential information only for purposes directly related to assessment, intervention, and consultation services. This information should be collected through legally and ethically sound methods, with explicit consent obtained from clients or their legal representatives. When using confidential information, behavior analysts must ensure that it is accurate, relevant, and securely stored to prevent unauthorized access or disclosure.

PROTECTING CONFIDENTIAL INFORMATION

Protecting confidential information is paramount to maintaining client trust and upholding professional integrity. Behavior analysts must implement appropriate safeguards to prevent unauthorized access, use, or disclosure of confidential information. This includes implementing secure data storage systems, restricting access to confidential information on a need-to-know basis, and using encryption or other secure methods when transmitting sensitive data.

DISCLOSING CONFIDENTIAL INFORMATION

Behavior analysts may only disclose confidential information when (a) informed consent is obtained; (b) attempting to protect the client or others from harm; (c) attempting to resolve contractual issues; (d) attempting to prevent a crime that is reasonably likely to cause physical, mental, or financial harm to another; or (e) compelled to do so by law or court order.

TASK E.5

Identify and comply with requirements for making public statements about professional activities (e.g., social media activity; misrepresentation of professional credentials, behavior analysis, and service outcomes). Behavior analysts must appropriately represent professional credentials, behavior analysis, and service outcomes in various public forums, including social media. Adherence to these requirements, as outlined in the Code, ensures that public statements made by behavior analysts are truthful, responsible, and reflective of the profession's commitment to scientific rigor and ethical practice.

ETHICAL USE OF SOCIAL MEDIA

Social media has become a prominent platform for professionals to share information and engage with the public. However, behavior analysts must exercise caution when using social media to discuss professional activities. According to the Code, behavior analysts should avoid sharing confidential information or case-specific details on social media. They must also refrain from offering direct advice to individuals who are not their clients, as this can be construed as establishing a professional relationship without proper consent and assessment.

Behavior analysts should also be mindful of the potential for their social media activity to be perceived as professional endorsements or public statements. Posts, comments, and shares should be consistent with the ethical standards of the profession and should not imply any form of professional relationship or guarantee specific outcomes.

ACCURATE REPRESENTATION OF PROFESSIONAL CREDENTIALS

Behavior analysts are required to accurately represent their credentials in all public statements. This includes correctly listing their certification status, degrees, titles, and professional affiliations. Misrepresentation of credentials can lead to misinformation, erosion of public trust, and potential disciplinary action. For instance, a behavior analyst should not claim to have a certification or specialization that they have not officially earned. When presenting themselves to the public, behavior analysts must ensure that all provided information is current, accurate, and verifiable.

TRANSPARENT COMMUNICATION ABOUT BEHAVIOR ANALYSIS

When making public statements about behavior analysis, behavior analysts must provide accurate and scientifically supported information. This includes clearly explaining the nature, purpose, and expected outcomes of behavior-analytic services. Any claims made about the effectiveness of interventions should be based on peer-reviewed research and established scientific principles.

Behavior analysts should avoid making exaggerated or unfounded claims about the success of their services. They must also provide a balanced view of the potential benefits and limitations of behavior-analytic interventions. For example, while promoting a successful intervention, they should acknowledge any existing limitations or the need for further research.

PREVENTING MISREPRESENTATION OF SERVICE OUTCOMES

It is crucial for behavior analysts to avoid misrepresenting service outcomes in public statements. This includes being transparent about the scope and limitations of their interventions. Behavior analysts should present data and results in an accurate and unbiased manner, avoiding any selective reporting or misinterpretation of findings that could mislead the public.

When discussing case studies or success stories, behavior analysts must ensure that all shared information respects client confidentiality and accurately reflects the intervention's outcomes without embellishment. Any public testimonials or endorsements should be obtained with explicit consent from clients and should not imply guaranteed results.

TASK E.6

Identify the conditions under which services or supervision should be discontinued and apply steps that should be taken when transitioning clients and supervisees to another professional. Behavior analysts must adhere to ethical standards for discontinuing services or supervision and ensure a smooth transition for clients and supervisees.

CONDITIONS FOR THE DISCONTINUATION OF SERVICES

These include (a) achievement of behavior-change goals, (b) lack of benefit, (c) exposure to harmful conditions, (d) client or stakeholder request, (e) noncompliance with intervention, and (f) funding termination.

Achievement of Behavior-Change Goals

When a client has successfully met all the behavior-change goals outlined in their plan, services should be concluded. This ensures that services are provided only as long as necessary and appropriate for the client's needs.

Lack of Benefit

If a client is not benefiting from the service despite appropriate modifications and interventions, discontinuation should be considered. This requires a thorough assessment to determine that continued services are unlikely to be effective.

Exposure to Harmful Conditions

Discontinuation is necessary if the behavior analyst or their supervisees or trainees are exposed to potentially harmful conditions that cannot be reasonably resolved. The safety and well-being of both service providers and recipients must be prioritized.

Client or Stakeholder Request

If a client or relevant stakeholder requests discontinuation, their wishes should be respected. It is important to ensure that the decision is informed and voluntary, and that the potential risks and alternatives are discussed.

Noncompliance With Intervention

If relevant stakeholders are not complying with the behavior-change intervention despite appropriate efforts to address barriers, services may need to be discontinued. Effective interventions require active and consistent participation from all parties involved.

Funding Termination

If services are no longer funded, discontinuation may be necessary. The behavior analyst should work to ensure that the client is informed and that a plan is in place to address the cessation of services.

PROCEDURES FOR DISCONTINUING SERVICES

These include (a) the development of a written plan, (b) documentation of acknowledgment, and (c) ongoing review and documentation.

Written Plan for Discontinuation

Behavior analysts must provide the client and/or relevant stakeholders with a written plan for discontinuing services. This plan should outline the reasons for discontinuation, the steps to be taken, and any recommendations for future actions.

Documentation and Acknowledgment

It is essential to document the acknowledgment of the discontinuation plan by the client and/or relevant stakeholders. This ensures that all parties are aware of and agree to the planned discontinuation.

Ongoing Review and Documentation

Behavior analysts should review the discontinuation plan throughout the discharge process and document all steps taken. This helps to ensure transparency and accountability during the transition.

CONDITIONS FOR DISCONTINUING SUPERVISION

When discontinuing supervision or other services that include supervision, behavior analysts must consider (a) the development of a termination plan and (b) documentation of actions taken.

Development of a Termination Plan

Behavior analysts should work with all relevant parties to develop a plan for terminating supervision that minimizes negative impacts on the supervisee or trainee. This plan should address the reasons for termination and outline steps to support the supervisee's continued development.

Documentation of Actions Taken

All actions taken during the termination process must be documented, including the eventual outcomes. This ensures that there is a clear record of the steps taken to support the supervisee or trainee.

TASK E.7

Identify types of and risks associated with multiple relationships, and how to mitigate those risks when they are unavoidable. Multiple relationships occur when a behavior analyst is in a professional role with a client or supervisee and simultaneously in another role with the same person or someone closely associated. These relationships can present significant ethical risks, and it is crucial to understand and mitigate them to uphold the ethical standards of the Code.

TYPES OF MULTIPLE RELATIONSHIPS

These include (a) personal relationships, (b) financial relationships, and (c) dual professional roles.

Personal Relationships

These involve situations where a behavior analyst provides services or supervision to someone with whom they have a personal connection. For example, a behavior analyst might be asked to work with a family member or a close friend. Such personal relationships can complicate professional interactions and lead to conflicts of interest, as personal feelings might interfere with professional judgment.

Financial Relationships

These occur when there are monetary or business connections between the behavior analyst and their client or supervisee. Examples include entering into business deals with clients or their families or accepting goods and services instead of money as payment for professional services. Financial relationships can create biases and conflicts of interest, as financial gain might influence professional decisions.

Dual Professional Roles

In these situations, a behavior analyst might serve the same individual in more than one professional capacity. For instance, a behavior analyst might also be a teacher or coach for the same client. In addition, they might supervise a colleague who also works with the client. Dual professional roles can blur the lines between different professional responsibilities, leading to boundary issues and compromised objectivity.

RISKS ASSOCIATED WITH MULTIPLE RELATIONSHIPS

These include (a) conflict of interest, (b) impaired objectivity, (c) power imbalance, (d) boundary confusion, and (e) loss of trust.

Conflict of Interest

Multiple relationships can create situations where personal interests might conflict with professional responsibilities, leading to biased decision-making.

Impaired Objectivity

Personal connections can affect the objectivity of the behavior analyst, compromising the quality and integrity of the services provided.

Power Imbalance

Dual roles can create power imbalances that might be exploited, intentionally or unintentionally, affecting the client's or supervisee's autonomy.

Boundary Confusion

Multiple relationships can blur professional boundaries, leading to confusion and potentially harmful situations for clients and supervisees.

Loss of Trust

When clients or supervisees perceive a conflict of interest or bias, it can erode their trust in the behavior analyst, undermining the therapeutic or supervisory relationship.

MITIGATING RISKS OF MULTIPLE RELATIONSHIPS

These include (a) avoidance, (b) transparency, (c) seeking consultation, (d) regular monitoring, (e) documentation, and (f) further training.

Avoidance

The primary strategy for managing multiple relationships is to avoid them whenever possible. Clear professional boundaries should be established and maintained to prevent potential conflicts.

Transparency

When multiple relationships are unavoidable, transparency is crucial. Behavior analysts should openly discuss the potential risks with all parties involved, obtain informed consent, and document these discussions thoroughly.

Seeking Consultation

Seeking advice from colleagues, supervisors, or ethics committees can provide additional perspectives and help in making ethically sound decisions. Regular consultation ensures that the behavior analyst remains accountable and that potential conflicts are addressed appropriately.

Regular Monitoring

Continuously monitoring the relationship helps to ensure that professional boundaries are maintained and that the relationship remains beneficial for the client or supervisee. Regular check-ins and assessments can help identify and address any emerging issues.

Documentation

Keeping detailed records of all interactions, decisions, and steps taken to mitigate risks is essential. This documentation serves as a protective measure and can be crucial if ethical concerns arise.

Further Training

Regular participation in ethics training and staying informed about the latest developments in ethical standards can help behavior analysts recognize and appropriately manage potential multiple relationships. Ongoing education ensures that behavior analysts are equipped, to the extent possible, to handle complex ethical situations.

▸ PRACTICE QUESTION

Dr. Dalton, BCBA-D, is a supervisor at Healthline Community Agency. She mentions during a break in the employee lunchroom that she is leaving for a short vacation. Dr. Dalton elaborates that she is in a tough predicament as her previously scheduled pet sitter has fallen ill and cannot watch the house or care for her dog. She then casually asks a newly hired supervisee, Karen (who loves dogs), if she is available to house/pet sit while she is away. Karen feels bad and knows that Dr. Dalton would have a less stressful trip if someone she trusts cares for her pet. She is a bit conflicted about this because she has plans for the weekend, but eventually says "Yes" and rearranges her plans to help Dr. Dalton with her dilemma. Which of the following ethical standards best describes this situation?

A. Practicing within scope of confidence
B. Multiple relationship
C. Coercive/exploitative relationship
D. None of the above

Before moving on to the following section for the solution, we recommend that you provide a brief explanation for the answer option you selected here:

____

____

When you're ready, move on to the next section for the solution!

Practice Question Breakdown

Step 1: Examine the question

The question calls for you to examine a supervisor-supervisee situation in which Karen's supervisor is asking her to perform a personal favor outside the duties and role of her job. You are asked which ethical standards best characterize the situation that Karen finds herself in.

Step 2: Analyze the Answer Options

A. This answer specifically refers to providing professional services that you have been sufficiently trained and supervised to perform. This standard is not directly related to this scenario because Dr. Dalton is asking Karen for a personal favor outside her professional role. This is a distractor.

B. A multiple or dual relationship is when a BCBA has a professional relationship with a client/stakeholder in addition to at least one other form of relationship with that same individual, either before, during, or after the provision of services. Dr. Dalton is neither a client nor a stakeholder in this scenario. A dual relationship has *not yet* occurred between Karen and Dr. Dalton as they have only had a professional relationship thus far. This answer option is a distractor.

C. The scenario seems to be describing the formation of a coercive relationship between Dr. Dalton and Karen. There is a power differential in this supervisor/supervisee relationship, and Karen may feel obligated to assist Dr. Dalton because she has authority over her and evaluates her caseload and work performance. This is the best answer option so far.

D. This is not correct. Answer C offers the best response to the question.

Step 3: Select the best answer

Among the four answer options presented, answer C (Coercive/Exploitative relationship) appears to be the best answer.

TASK E.8

Identify and apply interpersonal and other skills (e.g., accepting feedback, listening actively, seeking input, collaborating) to establish and maintain professional relationships. The ability to establish and maintain professional relationships is crucial for effective behavior analysis practice. Key skills that behavior analysts must cultivate to foster positive interactions with clients, supervisees, colleagues, and other stakeholders include (a) accepting feedback, (b) listening actively, (c) seeking input, and (d) collaborating effectively.

ACCEPTING FEEDBACK

Accepting feedback is essential for continuous professional growth and maintaining high standards of practice. Behavior analysts should cultivate an open attitude toward feedback from clients, supervisees, and colleagues. This involves actively listening to the feedback, reflecting on its content, and implementing necessary changes to improve service delivery. By demonstrating a willingness to accept constructive criticism, behavior analysts can enhance their effectiveness, foster trust, and model a commitment to PD.

LISTENING ACTIVELY

Active listening is a critical skill for understanding and addressing the needs and concerns of clients and colleagues. This involves fully concentrating on what is being said, understanding the message, responding thoughtfully, and remembering the information. For behavior analysts, active listening helps in accurately assessing client needs, developing effective intervention plans, and ensuring clear communication with supervisees and other stakeholders. Active listening also demonstrates respect and empathy, which are foundational for building strong, trust-based relationships.

SEEKING INPUT

Seeking input from others is vital for collaborative and informed decision-making. Behavior analysts should regularly solicit feedback and perspectives from clients, families, colleagues, and other professionals involved in a client's care. This collaborative approach ensures that all relevant information is considered, promoting comprehensive and effective interventions. Seeking input also empowers clients and stakeholders, making them active participants in the therapeutic process, which can enhance engagement and outcomes.

COLLABORATING EFFECTIVELY

Collaboration is at the heart of multidisciplinary and interprofessional practice. Behavior analysts often work with other professionals, such as teachers, speech therapists, occupational therapists, and medical personnel. Effective collaboration requires clear communication, mutual respect, and a shared commitment to the client's goals. Behavior analysts should establish regular communication channels, define roles and responsibilities clearly, and work cooperatively to integrate various services. Successful collaboration enhances the quality and coherence of the support provided to clients and facilitates holistic care.

PRACTICAL STRATEGIES FOR ENHANCING INTERPERSONAL SKILLS

These include (a) regular training and PD, (b) peer mentoring and supervision, (c) self-reflection and self-assessment, (d) role-playing exercises, and (e) feedback systems.

Regular Training and Professional Development

Engage in workshops, seminars, and courses focused on communication skills, conflict resolution, and teamwork to continuously improve interpersonal skills. This includes cultural competence training to better understand and address diverse backgrounds and perspectives, which is essential for effective communication and collaboration.

Peer Mentoring and Supervision

Participate in peer mentoring programs and seek supervision that focuses on developing interpersonal competencies. Feedback from mentors and supervisors can provide valuable insights and guidance.

Self-Reflection and Self-Assessment

Regularly reflect on personal interactions and assess one's communication style and effectiveness. Tools such as journals or self-assessment checklists can help identify areas for improvement.

Role-Playing Exercises

Engage in role-playing exercises to practice and enhance skills such as active listening, giving and receiving feedback, and collaborative problem-solving.

Feedback Systems

Establish formal systems for obtaining feedback from clients, families, and colleagues. This could include surveys, feedback forms, or regular feedback sessions.

TASK E.9

Engage in cultural humility in service delivery and professional relationships. Cultural humility is an essential competency for behavior analysts to effectively serve diverse populations and maintain professional relationships. It involves a lifelong commitment to self-evaluation and self-critique, recognizing and challenging power imbalances, and fostering respectful partnerships. For behavior analysts, engaging in cultural humility is critical to providing equitable and effective services.

CULTURAL HUMILITY

This is distinct from cultural competence. While cultural competence focuses on acquiring knowledge about different cultures, cultural humility emphasizes an ongoing process of self-reflection and personal growth. It requires behavior analysts to acknowledge their own biases, understand the cultural contexts of their clients, and engage in continuous learning and adaptation. Key elements of cultural humility include (a) self-reflection and lifelong learning, (b) recognizing and addressing power imbalances, and (c) building trusting and respectful partnerships.

Self-Reflection and Lifelong Learning

Behavior analysts must continually reflect on their own cultural identities, biases, and assumptions. This involves seeking out education and experiences that broaden their understanding of different cultures and perspectives. Engaging in regular self-assessment and seeking feedback from colleagues and clients can facilitate this ongoing learning process.

Recognizing and Addressing Power Imbalances

Behavior analysts should be aware of the inherent power dynamics in their relationships with clients and colleagues. Cultural humility involves recognizing these imbalances and actively working to mitigate them. This can include involving clients in decision-making processes, being transparent about the roles and responsibilities within the therapeutic relationship, and ensuring that clients' voices are heard and acknowledged.

Building Trusting and Respectful Partnerships

Establishing trust and respect with clients from diverse cultural backgrounds is fundamental to effective service delivery. Behavior analysts should approach each client as an expert in their own cultural experiences and values. By demonstrating genuine interest and respect for clients' cultural contexts, behavior analysts can build stronger, more collaborative relationships.

PRACTICAL STRATEGIES FOR ENGAGING IN CULTURAL HUMILITY

These include (a) cultural competence training, (b) diverse supervision and mentorship, (c) adopting a client-centered approach, (d) community engagement, (e) resource utilization, and (f) advocacy work.

Cultural Competence Training

Participate in ongoing cultural competence training and workshops. These opportunities provide valuable knowledge and skills for understanding and addressing cultural differences and can enhance a behavior analyst's ability to engage in cultural humility.

Diverse Supervision and Mentorship

Seek supervision and mentorship from professionals with diverse cultural backgrounds or those experienced in working with diverse populations. This can provide valuable insights and guidance for navigating cultural issues in practice.

Adopting a Client-Centered Approach

Adopt a client-centered approach that prioritizes the unique cultural needs and preferences of each client. This involves actively listening to clients' cultural narratives, incorporating culturally relevant practices into interventions, and being flexible and adaptive in the delivery of services.

Community Engagement

Engage with the communities you serve outside of the clinical setting to gain a deeper understanding of the cultural contexts and social dynamics that impact the lives of your clients. Community engagement can also build trust and rapport with clients and stakeholders.

Resource Utilization

Leverage resources such as cultural consultants, interpreters, and culturally adapted assessment tools to provide more accurate and culturally responsive services.

Advocacy Work

Advocate for policies and practices that promote cultural humility and equity within the field of behavior analysis. This includes supporting initiatives that address systemic barriers and inequalities affecting diverse populations.

▶ TASK E.10

Apply culturally responsive and inclusive service and supervision activities. Behavior analysts must integrate culturally responsive and inclusive practices into service delivery and supervision activities to ensure clients and supervisees from diverse backgrounds receive appropriate and effective services. To accomplish this, consider and/or apply (a) your understanding of the cultural context, (b) inclusive assessment and intervention, (c) culturally responsive communication, (d) ongoing PD, (e) inclusive supervision practices, (f) ethical considerations, and (g) collaboration with cultural experts.

UNDERSTANDING OF THE CULTURAL CONTEXT

Behavior analysts must first understand the cultural backgrounds, values, and beliefs of their clients and supervisees. This understanding can be achieved through direct communication, cultural competency training, and engaging with culturally relevant literature. By appreciating the unique cultural contexts of individuals, interventions and supervisions strategies can be tailored to align with these contexts, enhancing their effectiveness and relevance.

INCLUSIVE ASSESSMENT AND INTERVENTION

When assessing behavior and planning interventions, use culturally sensitive tools and methods. This includes selecting assessment instruments that have been validated for the specific cultural group and considering cultural norms when interpreting data. Interventions should be designed to respect and incorporate cultural values and practices (e.g., incorporating family and community involvement in behavior-change programs, which may help to increase their acceptance and success in particular cultural contexts).

CULTURALLY RESPONSIVE COMMUNICATION

Effective communication is crucial for culturally responsive practice. Behavior analysts should use language that is respectful and understandable to clients and supervisees, avoiding jargon and ensuring that translations are accurate if needed. Active listening and empathy are key components of effective communication. In addition, behavior analysts should be aware of and respectful toward nonverbal communication cues that may vary across cultures.

ONGOING PROFESSIONAL DEVELOPMENT

Cultural responsiveness is a dynamic competence that requires continuous learning and self-reflection. Behavior analysts should engage in ongoing PD to stay informed about cultural issues and best practices. This can include attending workshops, participating in cultural competency training, and seeking supervision or mentorship from colleagues with expertise in cultural responsiveness.

INCLUSIVE SUPERVISION PRACTICES

In supervision, it is important to create an inclusive environment where supervisees feel valued and respected. Supervisors should encourage open discussions about cultural issues and provide support for supervisees to explore how their cultural backgrounds impact their practice. Additionally, supervisors should model culturally responsive practices and provide feedback on how supervisees can improve their cultural competence.

ETHICAL CONSIDERATIONS

The Code establishes the need for behavior analysts to ensure that their practices do not discriminate against clients or supervisees based on cultural differences and take appropriate steps to mitigate any potential biases.

COLLABORATION WITH CULTURAL EXPERTS

When necessary, behavior analysts should collaborate with cultural experts or community leaders who can provide insights and guidance on culturally appropriate practices. This collaboration can help bridge any cultural gaps and ensure that interventions are effective and culturally appropriate.

▶ PRACTICE QUESTION

You are a new therapist with less than 3 months of experience working in the field, providing in-home services to a 3-year-old client with behavioral challenges. The home environment is less than ideal for providing services—it's crowded, and there appears to be multiple safety hazards. Child welfare is involved with the family. You are confined to a very small space to provide services and feel as though you are merely keeping the child from injuring themselves rather than working on learning new skills (i.e., you feel more like a babysitter than a therapist). You meet with your BCBA supervisor to ask for assistance. You ask them (a) to attend a home session with you to brainstorm ideas on how to better provide therapy, (b) to hold a clinical team meeting with the family to address safety and space concerns, and/or (c) if they should refer this case to another, more skilled therapist. Your supervisor explains that they are incredibly busy, and unable to accompany you to the home. Also, the agency is short staffed, and you are asked to do the best you can in a difficult situation. Which of the following ethical standards are MOST related to this scenario?

A. Accountability in supervision
B. Supervisory volume
C. Delegation of tasks
D. All of the above

Before moving on to the following section for the solution, we recommend that you provide a brief explanation for the answer option you selected here:

___

___

When you're ready, move on to the next section for the solution!

Practice Question Breakdown

Step 1: Examine the question

The question calls for you to consider interaction between a supervisor and a relatively new supervisee, who has requested help with a particularly complex in-home case. The supervisor responds that they are too busy and cannot help because the agency is severely short staffed. You are asked to identify the ethical standard that is most relevant to this scenario.

Step 2: Analyze the answer options

A. This ethical standard is related to the scenario. Ultimately, the BCBA supervisor is responsible for and must be accountable for all work activities of their supervisees.
B. This ethical standard is related to the scenario. In situations where the supervisee feels unsafe and unable to perform job duties, the supervisor should intervene. If unable to do so because of their supervisory volume, then they must address/adjust their caseload such that they are available to provide effective supervision.
C. This ethical standard is related to the scenario. A supervisor must delegate tasks to supervisees that they can competently complete. Ensuring the therapeutic environment is suitable to accomplish this is under the purview of the supervisor.
D. This answer option includes all three relevant and related ethical standards involving accountability in supervision, supervisory volume, and delegation of tasks. Improper and/or inadequate supervision and supervisory delegation is one of the most common ethical violation categories. This is it!

Step 3: Select the best answer

Among the four answer options presented, answer D (All of the above) appears to be the best answer.

TASK E.11

Identify personal biases and how they might interfere with professional activity. Personal biases are inherent to all individuals. Without sufficient efforts to identify and manage them, they can negatively affect decision-making, client interactions, and the overall effectiveness of interventions.

TYPES OF PERSONAL BIASES

These include (a) cultural, (b) confirmation, (c) implicit, and (d) selection biases.

Cultural Biases

These occur when behavior analysts impose their own cultural values and norms on clients, which can manifest in misunderstanding or misinterpretation of a client's behavior based on the behavior analyst's cultural framework rather than the client's.

Confirmation Biases

These refer to the tendency to search for, interpret, and recall information in a way that confirms one's preexisting beliefs, which can lead to the overlooking or dismissing of data that contradicts preconceived notions about a client's behavior or the effectiveness of an intervention.

Implicit Biases

These are unconscious attitudes or stereotypes that affect our understanding, actions, and decisions, which can influence interactions with clients and colleagues in subtle yet impactful ways.

Selection Biases

These occur when the subjects chosen for a study or intervention are not representative of the broader population, which can skew results and lead to the use of ineffective or inappropriate interventions.

IMPACT OF PERSONAL BIASES ON PROFESSIONAL ACTIVITIES

Personal biases can affect (a) interactions with clients, (b) supervision, (c) assessment, (d) intervention planning and implementation, (e) research and data interpretation, and (f) ethical decision-making.

Interactions With Clients

Personal biases can shape the interactions between behavior analysts and their clients and/or clients' families. If a behavior analyst has a bias against a particular cultural group, they may unintentionally communicate less warmth, empathy, or patience, which can undermine the therapeutic relationship. This can result in clients feeling misunderstood or disrespected, potentially reducing their engagement and cooperation in the treatment process.

Supervision

In supervisory roles, personal biases can affect the guidance and feedback provided to supervisees or trainees. A supervising behavior analyst with a bias toward certain educational backgrounds or theoretical orientations may give preferential treatment to some supervisees over others, affecting the quality of supervision and PD opportunities. This can result in an uneven learning experience and may discourage supervisees from exploring diverse approaches and perspectives.

Assessment

Personal biases can affect the accuracy of assessment findings. For example, a bias toward certain behaviors or cultural practices might lead to misinterpretation of a client's behavior and, in turn, result in the use of inappropriate or ineffective intervention plans that do not address the client's actual needs.

Intervention Planning and Implementation

Personal biases can influence the design and implementation of interventions, resulting in the behavior analyst favoring interventions that align with their beliefs rather than those that are most effective for the client. For instance, if a behavior analyst is biased against incorporating family members into treatment sessions due to personal beliefs about family dynamics, they may miss out on valuable support systems that could enhance the client's progress.

Research and Data Interpretation

Personal biases can influence research activities, from the design of studies to the interpretation of data. A behavior analyst with a strong preference for particular outcomes may intentionally or unintentionally design experiments in ways that favor those outcomes. During data interpretation, confirmation bias might lead to overemphasizing findings that support preconceived notions while disregarding data that contradict them. This can compromise the validity and reliability of research findings and their applicability to broader populations.

Ethical Decision-Making

Biases can compromise ethical decision-making. For example, a behavior analyst who holds biases against certain behaviors or lifestyles may impose their personal value on professional decisions, such as determining the appropriateness of interventions. This can result in ethical issues, such as advocating for treatments that align more with personal beliefs than with evidence-based practices or the client's best interests.

ADDITIONAL NOTE(S)

There are self-assessment tools that behavior analysts can use to reflect on their own cultural values and biases, including the *Diversity Self-Assessment* or *Multicultural Sensitivity Scale*.

TASK E.12

Identify and apply the legal, regulatory, and practice requirements (e.g., licensure, jurisprudence, funding, certification) relevant to the delivery of behavior-analytic services. Behavior analysts must navigate a complex landscape of legal, regulatory, and practice requirements to ensure the ethical and effective delivery of services. This includes understanding and adhering to licensure, jurisprudence, funding, and certification requirements.

LICENSURE

This is a state-level requirement that grants behavior analysts the authority to practice within a particular jurisdiction. As of June 2024, there are 38 states in the United States that have passed legislation to license behavior analysts. See www.bacb.com/u-s-licensure-of-behavior-analysts for a full list of each of these states, as well as links to each state's licensure board that details the requirements for obtaining a license.

JURISPRUDENCE

This refers to the legal knowledge and understanding necessary for practicing within a given jurisdiction, which often includes familiarity with state laws, regulations, and ethical guidelines (i.e., BACB Ethics Code) related to the practice of behavior analysis. Behavior analysts are advised to regularly review updates to state laws and regulations. Joining professional organizations or subscribing to legal updates can help you stay informed.

FUNDING

This refers to the financial support available for the provision of behavior analytic services. This includes understanding how to secure and manage funds from various sources, such as private insurance, government programs (e.g., Medicaid), grants, and client self-pay. Behavior analysts must be knowledgeable about the eligibility criteria, application processes, and compliance requirements associated with each funding source. Additionally, they need to stay updated on changes in funding policies and ensure that their billing practices are ethical and align with regulatory standards. Adequate knowledge of funding mechanisms helps ensure that services are accessible to clients and that the practice remains financially viable.

CERTIFICATION

This refers to the formal recognition provided by a governing body that an individual has met specific educational, training, and professional standards required to practice as a behavior analyst. For behavior analysts, this typically involves obtaining a credential from the BACB. Certification ensures that practitioners have the necessary skills and knowledge to provide effective and ethical services. The process includes meeting educational requirements, completing supervised experience, passing a certification exam, and adhering to the Ethics Code. Behavior analysts must also engage in ongoing PD to maintain their certification, demonstrating their commitment to continuous improvement and adherence to best practices in the field.

▶ PRACTICE QUESTION

You are a BCBA working at a community agency that contracts with a local school district to provide ABA. While supporting a neurodivergent student with focused interests, occasional aggression toward others, and social communication differences, you notice that there are some district/school policies that conflict with your knowledge about evidence-based practice. You observe members of the school multidisciplinary problem-solving team recommend retention as well as use of zero tolerance and exclusionary discipline as a means of addressing behavioral issues and rule violations. Which of the following ethical standards are involved in this situation?

A. Providing effective treatment
B. Selecting, designing, and implementing behavior-change interventions
C. Minimizing risk of behavior-change interventions
D. All of the above

Before moving on to the following section for the solution, we recommend that you provide a brief explanation for the answer option you selected here:

____

____

When you're ready, move on to the next section for the solution!

Practice Question Breakdown

Step 1: Examine the question

The question calls for you to examine the recommended interventions by a multidisciplinary school team that include grade retention as well as use of zero tolerance and exclusionary discipline to address behavioral challenges and rule infractions. In this all-too-common scenario, several ethical standards are intertwined and related to a behavior analyst's responsibility in practice.

Step 2: Analyze the answer options

A. This ethical standard is involved in the scenario. As an ethically minded BCBA, you must provide effective treatment, which includes evidence-based interventions; retention and zero tolerance policies are not currently supported by the empirical literature. Ideally, you want to recommend behavior-change interventions that are consistent with behavioral principles; however, the reality is that schools (and other agencies) sometimes use practices that are not grounded in applied behavioral analysis.
B. This ethical standard is involved in the scenario. As a BCBA, you strive to design, select, and implement behavior-change interventions that facilitate habilitative outcomes, such as inclusion and access to the instructional curriculum, and are responsive to the needs of the clients/stakeholders.
C. This answer is related to the scenario. Chosen interventions must minimize risk that is associated with all interventions, especially those that include restrictive, punitive practices (e.g., retention, zero tolerance policies).
D. The answers refer to standards that all seem to be involved. In choosing the most appropriate intervention for a neurodivergent student (with focused interests, occasional aggression toward others, and social communication differences), you must consider providing effective treatment, carefully select and implement the behavior-change interventions, and minimize the risk of the intervention. As a BCBA, while you may not be able to change prevailing educational policies or practices, continue to advocate for effective treatments and share with colleagues the latest research supporting or discouraging specific practices.

Step 3: Select the best answer

Among the four answer options presented, answer D (All of the above) appears to be the best answer.

CONCLUSION

In this chapter, we provided a review of the TCO Tasks related to ethics for behavior analysts. This included coverage of the core principles underlying the Ethics Code and various aspects of the standards related to responsibilities in practice, to clients and stakeholders, to supervisees and trainees, in public statements, and in research. Behavior analysts encounter ethical dilemmas regularly in the field; thus, a Code is necessary for ensuring that they practice in a manner that protects and benefits consumers. Although the content presented in this chapter provides an overview of key ethical concepts and their applications, it is by no means comprehensive. It must be recognized that the topic of ethics is riddled with complexity and this resource alone is insufficient for interpreting the Code and its application to all events. To expand your knowledge in this content area, we strongly recommend that you review the full BACB Ethics Code for Behavior Analysts (Behavior Analyst Certification Board, 2024b) and seek out additional readings. The bibliography for this chapter may be a good place to start.

REFERENCES

Behavior Analyst Certification Board. (2024a). *BCBA test content outline* (6th ed.). Author. https://www.bacb.com/wp-content/bcba-outline-6thEd

Behavior Analyst Certification Board. (2024b). *Ethics code for behavior analysts*. Author.

BIBLIOGRAPHY

Bailey, J., & Burch, M. (2022). *Ethics for behavior analysts*. Routledge.

Beaulieu, L., & Jimenez-Gomez, C. (2022). Cultural responsiveness in applied behavior analysis: Self-assessment. *Journal of Applied Behavior Analysis, 55*(2), 337–356. https://doi.org/10.1002/jaba.907

Britton, L. N., & Crye, A. A. (2021). Cultivating the ethical repertoires of behavior analysts: Prevention of common violations. *Behavior Analysis in Practice, 14*(2), 534–548. https://doi.org/10.1007/s40617-020-00540-w

Cooper, J. O., Heron, T. E., & Heward, W. L. (2020). *Applied behavior analysis* (3rd ed.). Pearson Education.

Fong, E. H., Catagnus, R. M., Brodhead, M. T., Quigley, S., & Field, S. (2016). Developing the cultural awareness skills of behavior analysts. *Behavior Analysis in Practice, 9*(1), 84–94. https://doi.org/10.1007/s40617-016-0111-6

Rosenberg, N. E., & Schwartz, I. S. (2019). Guidance or compliance: What makes an ethical behavior analyst? *Behavior Analysis in Practice, 12*(2), 473–482. https://doi.org/10.1007/s40617-018-00287-5

Sadavoy, J. A., & Zube, M. L. (Eds.). (2021). *A scientific framework for compassion and social justice: Lessons in applied behavior analysis*. Routledge.

Wright, P. I. (2019). Cultural humility in the practice of applied behavior analysis. *Behavior Analysis in Practice, 12*(4), 805–809. https://doi.org/10.1007/s40617-019-00343-8

KNOWLEDGE CHECK

In addition to reviewing the content in this chapter, please review the Code (available at www.bacb.com/ethics-information/ethics-codes) before attempting the following questions.

1. The four core principles that serve as the framework for the Ethics Code's standards include all of the following, EXCEPT:
   A. Behaving with integrity
   B. Benefiting others
   C. Ensuring competence
   D. Respecting others' privacy

2. A behavior analyst makes a small error in a client's data but decides not to correct it, thinking it is insignificant. Which core principle is being violated?
   A. Behaving with integrity
   B. Benefiting others
   C. Ensuring competence
   D. Treating others with compassion, dignity, and respect

3. A behavior analyst is preparing a treatment plan for a new client and realizes they lack experience with the specific issues presented. What core principles should guide their next steps?
   A. Behaving with integrity
   B. Benefiting others
   C. Demonstrating self-awareness
   D. Ensuring competence

4. Behavior analysts select, design, and use interventions that are all of the following, EXCEPT:
   A. Assessment results–based
   B. Positive and negative reinforcement–focused
   C. Consistent with behavioral principles
   D. Sensitive to the needs and context of the client/stakeholders

5. A behavior analyst is starting a new case with a client and their family. During the initial meeting, the family asks about how their personal information will be kept confidential. The behavior analyst explains the circumstances under which confidential information may need to be shared with others, such as during a legal investigation or when the client's safety is at risk. At what point should the behavior analyst inform the family about the limits of confidentiality?
   A. After assessment, but before implementation of the behavior-change program
   B. After confidential information has been disclosed to a third party
   C. At the outset of the professional relationship
   D. When there is a potential need to disclose confidential information to a third party

(*See answers on the next page.*)

1. **D) Respecting others' privacy**
   The four core principles that serve as the framework for the Ethics Code's standards include: benefit others; treat others with compassion, dignity, and respect; behave with integrity; and ensure their competence. Although respecting others' privacy is required for treating others with compassion, dignity, and respect, it does not function as a core principle for the Ethics Code's standards.

2. **A) Behaving with integrity**
   Behaving with integrity involves honesty and accuracy in all professional activities, including data collection and reporting. Not correcting an error compromises integrity. The other answer options (benefitting others; treating others with compassion, dignity, and respect; ensuring competence) are core principles that do not directly address this behavior and serve as distractors.

3. **D) Ensuring competence**
   Ensuring competence requires the behavior analyst to practice what is within their scope of practice, to evaluate the boundaries of their competence, and to seek additional professional development (e.g., training, supervision) or provide appropriate referral to address the client's needs. The other answer options (behaving with integrity, benefiting others, demonstrating self-awareness), only two of which are core principles, serve as distractors.

4. **B) Positive and negative reinforcement–focused**
   Behavior analysts select, design, and use interventions that are assessment results–based, consistent with behavioral principles, and sensitive to the needs and context of the client/stakeholders. However, the Code does not explicitly communicate that they must be positive and negative reinforcement–focused.

5. **C) At the outset of the professional relationship**
   The Code requires that behavior analysts inform clients and stakeholders of the limits to confidentiality at the outset of the professional relationship. This ensures that clients and stakeholders fully understand the circumstances under which their confidential information might need to be disclosed, such as for legal or safety reasons, before any sensitive information is shared. The other response options do not provide the necessary upfront transparency and serve as distractors.

6. A behavior analyst is considering collaborating on a case with a colleague who is also a family member. Although there are no immediate conflicts of interest, the behavior analyst is concerned that their personal relationship might affect their objectivity when making professional decisions. How should the behavior analyst proceed?

   A. Proceed with the collaboration as long as the relationship does not currently impact decision-making

   B. Report the personal relationship to the BACB before continuing the collaboration

   C. Avoid entering the collaboration to prevent any future ethical issues

   D. Proceed with the collaboration but keep personal and professional issues separate

7. A behavior analyst discovers that one of their clients has recently become close friends with a family member of theirs. The behavior analyst is aware that this situation creates a multiple relationship and wants to handle the situation appropriately. The analyst consults colleagues and reviews the BACB guidelines to assess the risks and determine how to manage the situation. What should the behavior analyst document in response to this multiple relationship?

   A. The personal benefits they might gain

   B. The steps taken to mitigate risks and the outcomes of any consultations

   C. The reasons why the multiple relationship is unavoidable

   D. The client's consent to continue services despite the multiple relationship

8. Which of the following scenarios MOST likely involves a power imbalance in a multiple relationship?

   A. A behavior analyst providing services to a friend's child

   B. A behavior analyst supervising a current client's parent

   C. A behavior analyst renting office space from a client's family

   D. A behavior analyst working with a client's sibling

9. A behavior analyst observes a colleague using outdated intervention methods that are not harmful but are less effective. What should the behavior analyst do first to address this issue?

   A. Discuss the issue with the colleague and offer resources for updated practices

   B. Inform the clients directly about the colleague's practices

   C. Report the colleague to the BACB immediately

   D. Report the colleague to their supervisor immediately

10. A behavior analyst is working with a client whose parent requests access to confidential records to resolve a billing dispute. The behavior analyst considers the request but wants to ensure they adhere to the Ethics Code regarding the disclosure of confidential information. In which condition would the behavior analyst NOT be justified in disclosing confidential client information?

    A. To protect the client or others from harm

    B. When disclosure is required by law

    C. When the request is for resolving a billing issue

    D. When informed consent has been obtained

(*See answers on the next page.*)

6. **C) Avoid entering the collaboration to prevent any future ethical issues**
In this scenario, the behavior analyst should avoid entering into the multiple relationship (professional and personal) to prevent potential conflicts of interest or compromised objectivity in the future. Simply put, behavior analysts are to avoid multiple relationships to maintain professional integrity and avoid ethical dilemmas. The other answer options function as distractors.

7. **B) The steps taken to mitigate risks and the outcomes of any consultations**
In this scenario, the behavior analyst should document the steps taken to minimize risks and the outcomes of any consultations with colleagues or supervisors, as this demonstrates an ethical approach to managing the multiple relationship. The other answer options do not fulfill the requirement to document efforts to provide a clear record of the actions taken to address potential ethical concerns, which is crucial for accountability and transparency.

8. **B) A behavior analyst supervising a current client's parent**
Supervising a current client's parent creates a power imbalance, as the behavior analyst holds authority over someone closely connected to their client, complicating the professional relationship. The other answer options involve other issues (objectivity, financial conflicts, familial conflicts) more than power imbalance.

9. **A) Discuss the issue with the colleague and offer resources for updated practices**
When the professional misconduct of others appears resolvable and does not place anyone at undue risk, the behavior analyst should address concerns directly with the subject. In this scenario, the most constructive approach is to address the issue directly with the colleague and provide resources to help them improve their practices.

10. **C) When the request is for resolving a billing issue**
Confidential information is shared only when you have informed consent, to protect the client or others from harm, to resolve contractual issues, to prevent a crime that can harm someone, or it's required by law. Disclosure is not warranted when it is requested for the purpose of resolving a billing issue.

11. A behavior analyst is working with a client whose progress has plateaued for several months. What is the MOST appropriate next step?

A. Continue the current intervention plan

B. Discontinue services immediately

C. Reassess the intervention plan and consider alternative strategies

D. Reduce the frequency of sessions

12. Restrictive/punishment-based procedures are to be recommended ONLY when:

A. Less restrictive interventions have been ineffective.

B. The risk of harm is greater than the risk associated with the intervention.

C. The risk of harm is lower than the risk associated with the intervention.

D. Both A and B

13. A behavior analyst is working with a client whose parent requests the discontinuation of services due to a change in their family's circumstances. The behavior analyst wants to ensure that this request is handled ethically and that the client's needs are still being addressed during the transition. What should the behavior analyst do next?

A. Continue services until the next scheduled review

B. Discuss the reasons for the request and plan for a transition

C. Immediately comply with the request

D. Seek approval from a supervisor before discontinuing

14. In supervision, how can a behavior analyst foster an inclusive environment for trainees from diverse cultural backgrounds?

A. Adapt supervision strategies to accommodate the cultural needs and preferences of each trainee

B. Apply the same supervision approach to all trainees

C. Avoid discussing cultural differences to maintain a neutral environment

D. Encourage trainees to adapt to the supervisor's cultural norms

15. A behavior analyst is reviewing their records and notices that some supervision documentation from 7 years ago is about to reach the minimum retention period. The analyst is unsure whether they should keep the records longer or if they can now dispose of them in accordance with the Ethics Code. What is the minimum number of years that supervision documentation should be kept?

A. 3

B. 5

C. 7

D. 10

(See answers on the next page.)

11. **C) Reassess the intervention plan and consider alternative strategies**
When a client's progress plateaus, an appropriate next step would be to reassess the intervention plan and explore alternative strategies that may better meet the client's needs. Simply continuing the current plan or reducing the frequency of sessions may not address the lack of progress, and discontinuing without reassessment may leave the client without needed support.

12. **D) Both A and B**
See Standard 2.15 (Minimizing Risk of Behavior-Change Procedures) of the Code. Restrictive/punishment-based procedures are to be recommended only when less restrictive interventions have been tried and found to be ineffective, and the risk of harm is greater than the risk associated with the intervention. It is not the case that they are to be recommended if the risk of harm is lower than the risk associated with the intervention.

13. **B) Discuss the reasons for the request and plan for a transition**
If a client or their legal representative requests discontinuation of services, the behavior analyst should discuss the reasons for the request and collaboratively plan for a transition to ensure the client's needs are met during the discontinuation process. The other answer options disregard the client's or representative's autonomy, could result in harm, or are unnecessary unless required by specific organizational policies.

14. **A) Adapt supervision strategies to accommodate the cultural needs and preferences of each trainee**
Adapting supervision strategies to accommodate the cultural needs and preferences of each trainee ensures that supervision is supportive and inclusive, promoting professional growth. The other answer options (apply the same supervision approach to all, avoid discussing cultural differences, encourage trainees to adapt to the supervisor's cultural norms) do not account for individual cultural differences and misses the opportunity for cultural responsiveness.

15. **C) 7**
According to the Ethics Code, supervision documentation must be retained for a minimum of 7 years. This ensures that records are available for any audits, reviews, or legal needs that may arise within this period.

16. A behavior analyst suspects that personal biases may be influencing their interactions with a client. What is the MOST appropriate action for the behavior analyst to take?

A. Discontinue services immediately

B. Identify the biases and take steps to minimize their impact

C. Ignore the biases and continue with the current approach

D. Refer the client to another qualified provider

17. A client has reached the end of their funding period but has not fully achieved their behavior-change goals. What is the BEST course of action for the behavior analyst?

A. Discontinue services immediately and inform the client that funding has ended

B. Ignore the funding issue and continue services without payment

C. Reduce service intensity without discussing the implications with the client

D. Work with the client and their funding source to seek additional funding and provide a plan for continued services if feasible

18. A service agreement should address all of the following, EXCEPT:

A. The behavior analyst's obligation to the Code

B. The fee schedule

C. The responsibilities of all parties involved

D. The scope of the behavior analyst's services

19. What is an appropriate action for a behavior analyst to take if they recognize a personal bias that might interfere with their professional duties?

A. Discuss the bias openly with clients

B. Only work with clients who do not trigger their biases

C. Seek supervision or consultation to address and mitigate the bias

D. Ignore the bias and continue with their work as usual

20. A behavior analyst is working with a client whose parent and school staff have conflicting opinions about the direction of the client's behavior plan. The parent is pushing for a specific approach, while the school wants to follow a different intervention. The behavior analyst must decide how to proceed while ensuring that they are adhering to the highest ethical standard. Whose welfare should the behavior analyst prioritize in this situation?

A. The parent

B. The school staff

C. The client

D. The funding agency

(*See answers on the next page.*)

16. **B) Identify the biases and take steps to minimize their impact**
Recognizing and addressing personal biases is crucial for behavior analysts to provide unbiased and effective services. Taking steps to minimize bias helps ensure ethical and culturally responsive practice. Discontinuing services immediately or referring to another provider is not necessary if the behavior analyst addresses the biases and their impact. Ignoring the biases and continuing the current approach is unethical.

17. **D) Work with the client and their funding source to seek additional funding and provide a plan for continued services if feasible**
The behavior analyst should work with the client and their funding source to seek additional funding and provide a plan for continued services if feasible. The other answer options (discontinue services immediately, ignore the funding issue, reduce service intensity) fail to seek proper solutions.

18. **B) The fee schedule**
See Standard 3.01 (Service Agreement) of the Code. A service agreement should address responsibilities of all parties, scope of your services, your obligations to the Code, and the procedure for filing a complaint against you. Although financial agreements related to fees and billing practices need to be documented, it is not required that a fee schedule is included as a component of the service agreement.

19. **C) Seek supervision or consultation to address and mitigate the bias**
Seeking supervision or consultation is an appropriate step to address and mitigate personal biases, ensuring that they do not interfere with professional responsibilities. The other answer options (ignore the bias, only work with clients who do not trigger their biases, discuss the bias openly with clients) may not be appropriate or professional and fail to directly address the bias.

20. **C) The client**
In this scenario, the behavior analyst must prioritize the welfare of the client above all other parties, including the parent and school staff, in accordance with the BACB Ethics Code. The behavior analyst's primary obligation is to act in the best interest of the client, ensuring that their needs are met, regardless of external pressures or conflicting opinions from stakeholders. The other options, such as prioritizing the parent, school staff, or funding agency, would conflict with the ethical requirement to place the welfare of the client above all others.

21. Under what circumstances is it permissible for a behavior analyst to publish digital content of their clients on a personal social media account?

    A. A disclaimer is posted to warn against the reusing of any shared content without express permission.

    B. Informed consent has been obtained.

    C. Informed consent has been obtained and the content is published in a way that reduces the potential for sharing.

    D. It is never permissible to publish digital content of clients on a personal social media account.

22. If a behavior analyst was to accept a gift from a client, it cannot be valued at more than ________________.

    A. $5 USD

    B. $10 USD

    C. $25 USD

    D. $50 USD

23. Prior to conducting research, a behavior analyst must receive approval from:

    A. A formal research review committee

    B. Their intended participants

    C. Their supervisor

    D. None of the above

24. Which of the following is NOT considered a risk to the profession due to unethical behavior?

    A. Damage to the field

    B. Harm to clients

    C. Increased regulatory scrutiny

    D. Negative impact on the quality of services

(*See answers on the next page.*)

21. **D) It is never permissible to publish digital content of clients on a personal social media account.**
See Standard 5.10 (Social Media Channels and Websites) of the Code. It is never permissible for behavior analysts to publish digital content of clients on their personal social media accounts, regardless of any consent or disclaimers given.

22. **B) $10 USD**
See Standard 1.12 (Giving and Receiving Gifts) of the Code. If a behavior analyst was to accept a gift from a client, it cannot be valued at more than $10 USD.

23. **A) A formal research review committee**
See Standard 6.02 (Research Review) of the Code. Prior to conducting research, a behavior analyst must receive approval from a formal research review committee.

24. **B) Harm to clients**
While harm to clients is a serious consequence of unethical behavior, it is not a risk to the profession itself, but rather a direct negative impact on individuals receiving services. The other answer options (damage to the field, increased regulatory scrutiny, negative impact on quality of services) are potential risks that may result from unethical behavior.

8

Behavior Assessment

LEARNING OBJECTIVES

The following Test Content Outline (TCO) Tasks (Behavior Analyst Certification Board®, 2024, p. 2) related to behavior assessment (F.1 through F.8) will serve as the learning objectives of this chapter:

- F.1 Identify relevant sources of information in records (e.g., educational, medical, historical) at the outset of the case.
- F.2 Identify and integrate relevant cultural variables in the assessment process.
- F.3 Design and evaluate assessments of relevant skill strengths and areas of need.
- F.4 Design and evaluate preference assessments.
- F.5 Design and evaluate descriptive assessments.
- F.6 Design and evaluate functional analyses.
- F.7 Interpret assessment data to determine the need for behavior-analytic services and/or referral to others.
- F.8 Interpret assessment data to identify and prioritize socially significant, client-informed, and culturally responsive behavior-change procedures and goals.

TASK F.1

Identify relevant sources of information in records (e.g., educational, medical, historical) at the outset of the case. At the outset of a case and prior to assessment, behavior analysts need to consider the available records and data on what has taken place to identify and address the target behavior.

Some clients may have many types of records available for review while others may have very little available. Possible records may include medical reports, psychologic assessment reports, individualized education plans, family service plans, and documents from other allied health providers (e.g., speech therapists, occupational therapists, etc.). At the very minimum, behavior analysts should aim to review the relevant educational data, medical data, and historical data.

RELEVANT EDUCATIONAL DATA

This includes information related to the client's education (e.g., transcripts, academic program, and disciplinary file). Educational records may contain documents that evidence the use of behavioral interventions and include functional assessment reports, behavior intervention plans, and progress monitoring data.

RELEVANT MEDICAL DATA

This includes information related to the client's health (e.g., clinical findings, diagnostic test results, care plans, and medication). It is important to rule out medical reasons for behavior. If a medical reason is found, treatment of the condition may be necessary prior to the implementation of behavioral interventions.

RELEVANT HISTORICAL DATA

This includes a variety of information from the client's history that may be learned through the review of many different possible types of records available. For behavior analysts, information is reviewed with attention to information that informs them of the nature of the target behavior, its development, and the relevant contingencies at work.

MNEMONIC AID

Sometimes, a review of records can be MEH (**M**edical, **E**ducational, **H**istorical).

TASK F.2

Identify and integrate relevant cultural variables in the assessment process. Incorporating cultural variables into the assessment process is essential for behavior analysts to provide effective and individualized support to clients. This approach ensures that assessments are accurate and culturally sensitive, leading to more effective interventions and better client outcomes.

CULTURAL VARIABLES

These include ethnicity, language, religion, socioeconomic status, family dynamics, and cultural norms, which can significantly influence an individual's behavior, interactions, and response to intervention. Understanding and integrating these factors into the assessment process helps avoid misinterpretations and ensures that the services provided are respectful and relevant to the client's cultural background.

STEPS FOR INTEGRATING CULTURAL VARIABLES

These include (a) initial consultation and data gathering, (b) cultural competence training, (c) use of culturally appropriate assessment tools, (d) language considerations, (e) family and community involvement, (f) contextual factors, and (g) ongoing reflection.

Initial Consultation and Data Gathering

Start by collecting detailed background information about the client. This includes understanding their cultural background, language preferences, and any relevant cultural practices. Use culturally sensitive questionnaires and conduct interviews with family members or other relevant stakeholders to gather comprehensive information.

Cultural Competence Training

Engage in ongoing cultural competence training. This involves educating oneself about different cultures, attending workshops, and seeking guidance from cultural experts. Training helps behavior analysts recognize their own biases and understand how cultural factors influence behavior.

Use of Culturally Appropriate Assessment Tools

Ensure that the assessment tools and methods used are culturally relevant and validated for the client's cultural group. Standardized tests and measures may need adjustments or accommodations to accurately assess clients from diverse backgrounds.

Language Considerations

Provide assessment materials in the client's preferred language and consider using interpreters if necessary. Clear communication is vital to avoid misunderstandings and ensure accurate assessments.

Family and Community Involvement

In many cultures, family and community play a significant role in shaping behavior. Involve family members and community representatives in the assessment process to gain a holistic understanding of the client's behavior within their cultural context.

Contextual Factors

Consider the broader social and environmental context in which the client lives. This includes understanding the client's living conditions, access to resources, and any systemic barriers they may face. These contextual factors can greatly influence behavior and should be considered during the assessment.

Ongoing Reflection

Continuously reflect on your own cultural biases and how they may impact the assessment process. Regular reflection helps maintain cultural sensitivity and effectiveness in practice.

TASK F.3

Design and evaluate assessments of relevant skill strengths and areas of need. Methods of assessment to discover the skill strengths and deficits of a client may include (a) indirect and (b) direct assessments.

INDIRECT ASSESSMENT

This includes the use of (a) interviews, (b) checklists, and (c) rating scales.

Interview

This involves meeting with significant others (e.g., caregivers, teachers) to obtain relevant information. Behavior analysts conduct interviews that primarily focus on *what* and *when* questions related to the behavior of interest.

Checklist

This is a list of specific behaviors with a description of the conditions under which each behavior will occur.

Rating Scale

This is a list of items (i.e., specific behaviors or statements/questions related to the behavior of interest) that respondents (i.e., significant others) can rate on a numerical or ordinal scale.

ADDITIONAL NOTE(S)

Checklists and rating scales may be used during interviews. Also, indirect assessment information gathered from interviews, checklists, and rating scales should be examined for patterns of behavior and environmental events. Behavior analysts examine the results and consider a possible hypothesis that states: (a) what antecedent(s) may serve to trigger the target behavior, (b) what the target behavior looks like (i.e., topography), and (c) what consequence(s) may serve to maintain the target behavior.

DIRECT ASSESSMENT

This includes the use of (a) standardized tests, (b) criterion-referenced measures, (c) curriculum-based measures, and (d) direct observations.

Standardized Test

This is an assessment instrument with specific procedures that must be followed for its administration.

Criterion-Referenced Measure

This is an assessment that measures a client's performance against some predetermined standard.

Curriculum-Based Measure

This is a type of criterion-referenced measure that is used to measure performance on tasks the client performs as a part of planned instruction (i.e., curriculum).

Direct Observation

This involves directly observing the behavior of interest.

When a client experiences language delays, assessment can be used to determine what they can and cannot do (e.g., mand, tact, etc.). See Task B.19 (Chapter 4) for a review of verbal operants. Data obtained through the use of assessment can help to (a) identify the cause of the delay, (b) compare the client's performance against that of others, and (c) guide intervention planning.

MAND ASSESSMENT

Assessing the mand repertoire involves identifying the evocative effects of motivating operations (MOs) on verbal responses.

TACT ASSESSMENT

Assessing the tact repertoire involves identifying the evocative effects of nonverbal stimuli on verbal responses.

DUPLIC AND CODIC ASSESSMENT

Assessing the duplic and codic repertoire involves identifying the evocative effects of verbal discriminative stimuli (S^D) on verbal and nonverbal responses.

LISTENER ASSESSMENT

Assessing the listener repertoire involves measurement of the client's (a) verbal discriminations (i.e., simple verbal discriminations, auditory conditional discriminations, compound verbal discriminations, verbal conditional discriminations, and verbal function-altering effect) and (b) parts of speech (e.g., verbs, adjectives, etc.).

INTRAVERBAL ASSESSMENT

Assessing the intraverbal repertoire is arguably the most difficult of the elementary verbal operants. It involves evaluation of verbal discriminations, parts of speech, and evocative effects of MOs and nonverbal S^D.

ADDITIONAL NOTE(S)

Autoclitic verbal behavior (i.e., autoclitic mands and tacts) can also be assessed.

▶ PRACTICE QUESTION

Direct observation is the hallmark of behavioral assessment. As a Board Certified Behavior Analyst® working in a classroom, you are trying to determine how to gather data about the target behavior (aggression toward peers) of a middle school student. As you develop and refine your direct observation protocol, you realize that there are advantages and disadvantages to every behavioral assessment tool (both direct and indirect). Which of the following are disadvantages associated with direct observation of behavior?

A. Direct observation data can confirm information collected during functional behavior assessment (FBA) interviews.
B. Temporally distant antecedent events may not be observable during a scheduled observation session.
C. Observer drift might impact the data you collect.
D. B and C only

Before moving on to the following section for the solution, we recommend that you write a brief explanation for the answer option you selected here:

____

____

When you're ready, move on to the next section for the solution!

Practice Question Breakdown

Step 1: Examine the question

In the scenario, you are choosing a behavioral assessment tool to gather data about the target behavior (aggression toward peers) of a middle school student. Be sure to carefully reread the question whenever you feel an answer does not fit with what you initially read as the question's objective. The question asks you to consider ONLY the disadvantages associated with direct observation of behavior.

Step 2: Analyze the answer options

A. This is actually an advantage of direct observation methods as it is often used to confirm information gathered from other methods (indirect) of behavioral assessment. This answer option is a distractor.
B. This is a disadvantage of direct observation of behavior. Temporally distant antecedent events may not be readily observable during the time you are observing a student, making it harder to determine what sets the occasion for behavior to occur—this is indeed one disadvantage to using direct observation. You must realize that you might miss important information about why a behavior occurs or what is maintaining it if those events do not occur within an observation session.
C. This is a disadvantage of direct observation of behavior. Observer drift, or the tendency for raters to become inconsistent in the application of their observational measurement system, can also be a disadvantage and result in measurement error.
D. This answer includes answers B and C, which are both identified disadvantages of direct observation of behavior. Be sure to remember that all behavioral assessment tools have advantages and disadvantages. To further increase your understanding, try to list three advantages and disadvantages of each method you learn about!

Step 3: Select the best answer

Among the four answer options presented, answer D (B and C only) appears to be the best answer.

TASK F.4

Design and evaluate preference assessments. Preference assessments (also known as *stimulus preference assessments* or *SPAs*) are conducted to determine what stimuli can be used as reinforcers. There are three types of SPAs: (a) asking about preferences, (b) free-operant observation, and (c) trial-based methods.

ASKING ABOUT PREFERENCES

This involves asking the client what they like. There are multiple approaches to asking about preferences, including the use of (a) open-ended questions, (b) presenting questions in a choice format, and (c) asking the client to rank-order items.

Open-Ended Questions

This involves asking the client questions about preferences that cannot simply be answered with a "yes" or "no."

- **Example:** "What do you like to do during recess?"

Choice-Formatted Questions

This involves asking the client questions about preferences that are formatted as a choice.

- **Example:** "Would you rather play hopscotch or tag?"

Rank-Ordering Items

This involves giving the client a list of items or activities and asking them to put the items in order from most to least preferred.

ADDITIONAL NOTE(S)

Questions can be asked orally or in writing, depending on the client's communication abilities and preferences. There are also surveys that have been developed to assess client preferences.

FREE-OPERANT OBSERVATION

This involves observing and recording the length of time (i.e., duration) that a client *approaches*, *contacts*, or *engages* with the stimuli when they are "free" to emit any responses. There are two types of free-operant observation: (a) contrived and (b) naturalistic.

Contrived Free-Operant Observation

This involves prearrangement of the environment to include items/activities that the client may like and can engage with prior to observing.

Naturalistic Free-Operant Observation

This involves no prearrangement of the environment prior to observing. It takes place in the client's natural environment.

ADDITIONAL NOTE(S)

The more a client approaches (i.e., moves toward), contacts (i.e., touches), or engages (i.e., interacts with) a stimulus, the more it is considered a preferred stimulus.

TRIAL-BASED METHODS

This involves presenting a series of trials to the client and recording their responses to determine preferences. There are three types of trial-based methods: (a) single stimulus, (b) paired stimulus, and (c) multiple stimulus.

Single-Stimulus Preference Assessment

This method involves presenting target stimuli one at a time in random order. Each item is presented several times, and the client's response to each item (i.e., whether they approach the item, frequency of contacts, and/or duration of interaction) is recorded.

Paired-Stimulus Preference Assessment

This method involves presenting two target stimuli at a time. Each stimulus is randomly paired with all other stimuli, but every possible pair must be presented. The client's selection between the two target stimuli presented at each trial is recorded.

Multiple-Stimulus Preference Assessment

This method involves presenting an array of three or more stimuli at a time. There are two variations used: (a) multiple stimulus without replacement (MSWO) and (b) multiple stimulus with replacement (MSW).

Multiple Stimulus Without Replacement Preference Assessment

The MSWO method involves removing the item selected by the client from the array, rearranging the remaining unselected items, and then beginning the next trial with a reduced array.

Multiple Stimulus With Replacement Preference Assessment

The MSW method involves keeping the item selected by the client in the array, replacing the remaining unselected items with new items, and then beginning the next trial with the same number of items in the array.

ADDITIONAL NOTE(S)

Trial-based methods, like in free-operant observation, use one or more of the three measures indicative of preference (i.e., approach, contact, and engagement).

TASK F.5

Design and evaluate descriptive assessments. Descriptive assessment involves observation of the target behavior in relation to other events under naturally occurring conditions.

DESCRIPTIVE ASSESSMENTS

These include (a) continuous ABC (Antecedent-Behavior-Consequence) recording, (b) narrative ABC recording, and (c) scatter plot recording. ABC analyses view behavior as a function of the antecedents that precede it and the consequences that follow it.

Continuous ABC Recording

This involves recording the occurrences of the target behavior and environmental events (i.e., specified antecedents and consequences; Table 8.1). Environmental events are recorded when they occur, even when the problem behavior has not.

Table 8.1 Example of a Continuous ABC Recording Form

A	B	C
☐ Teacher instruction ☐ Transition ☐ Unstructured time	☐ Elopement ☐ Tantrum	☐ Access to preferred activity ☐ Peer attention ☐ Task removal ☐ Teacher reprimand
☐ Teacher instruction ☐ Transition ☐ Unstructured time	☐ Elopement ☐ Tantrum	☐ Access to preferred activity ☐ Peer attention ☐ Task removal ☐ Teacher reprimand
☐ Teacher instruction ☐ Transition ☐ Unstructured time	☐ Elopement ☐ Tantrum	☐ Access to preferred activity ☐ Peer attention ☐ Task removal ☐ Teacher reprimand

ABC, antecedent-behavior-consequence.

Narrative Antecedent-Behavior-Consequence Recording

This involves recording data only when the target behavior occurs. Unlike continuous ABC recording, environmental events are not specified and are instead open-ended (Table 8.2). Any events immediately preceding and following the target behavior are recorded.

Table 8.2 Example of a Narrative ABC Recording Form

A	B	C

ABC, antecedent-behavior-consequence.

Scatter Plot Recording

This involves recording when the target behavior occurs. Specifically, time is divided into shorter intervals (e.g., 15 minutes) and different marks are made on the observation form to indicate the extent to which the behavior occurred for each time interval.

- **Example (scatter plot recording form; chart divided into 1-hour intervals;** Figure 8.1):

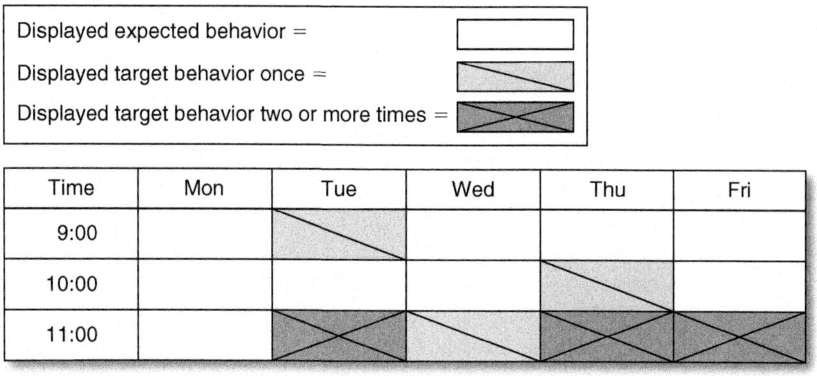

Figure 8.1 Scatter Plot Recording Form (Chart Divided Into 1-Hour Intervals)

INTERPRETING DESCRIPTIVE ASSESSMENT OUTCOMES

Data gathered from ABC recording can be examined for patterns (i.e., specific antecedent and consequence events that occur with the target behavior). Review of ABC recording data may reveal a correlation between specific events and the target behavior, which then allows for the formulation of a possible hypothesis. Behavior analysts may also graph the data obtained from ABC recording for visual inspection.

- **Example:** The graphs in Figures 8.2 and 8.3 show the number of times that specific events (i.e., antecedents and consequences) occurred with a target behavior. They suggest the following hypothesis: The target behavior is motivated by task demands and maintained by their removal (i.e., escape; negative reinforcement).

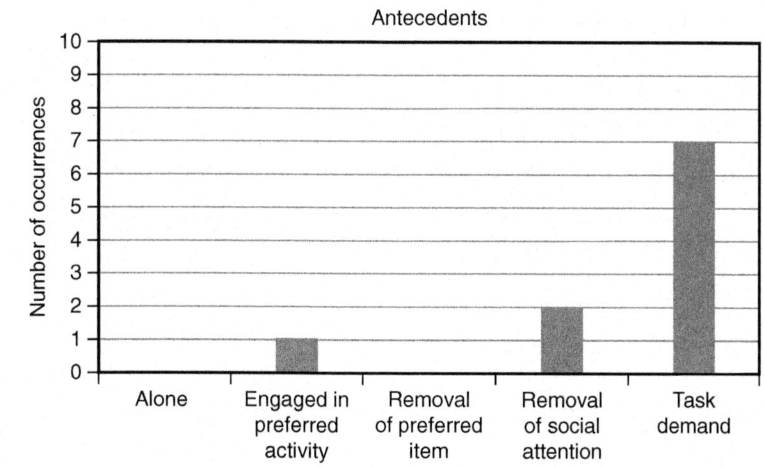

Figure 8.2 Graph of the Number of Times Specific Antecedent Events Occurred With a Target Behavior

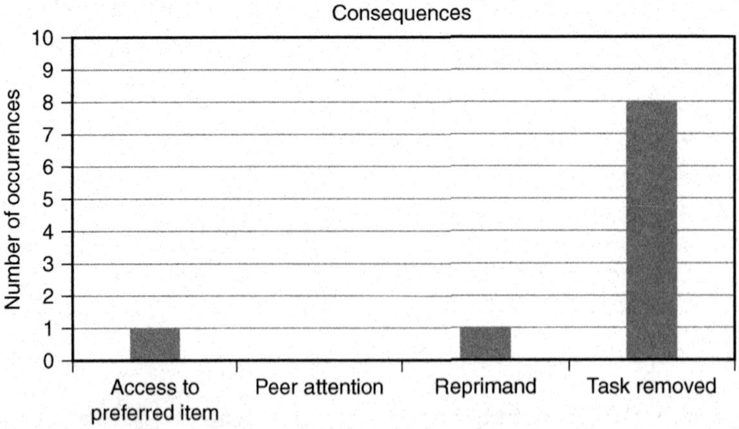

Figure 8.3 Graph of the Number of Times Specific Consequent Events Occurred With a Target Behavior

When interpreting scatter plot recording data, behavior analysts conduct a visual examination of the scatter plot to identify specific times when the target behavior occurs. Recurring patterns in data may also be examined in relation to environmental events.

- **Example (interpretation of scatter plot data):** A target behavior repeatedly occurs across weekdays around noon, a time that is correlated with unstructured time in the lunchroom.

▶ TASK F.6

Design and evaluate functional analyses. A functional analysis (FA) can be conducted to observe and measure the separate effects of antecedents and consequences on problem behavior. When conducting FAs, analog conditions are used to allow for enhanced control of variables hypothesized to be related to the problem behavior.

FUNCTIONAL ANALYSES

The basic FA includes four conditions: (a) contingent attention, (b) contingent escape, (c) alone, and (d) play (i.e., control). The conditions are individually presented and repeated in an alternating sequence. During the presentation of each condition, occurrences of the problem behavior are recorded (Table 8.3).

Table 8.3 Example of an FA Protocol With Four Conditions

CONDITION	ANTECEDENT/EO	CONSEQUENCE FOR PROBLEM BEHAVIOR
Attention	Attention withheld	Attention provided
Escape	Task demands presented	Task demands removed
Alone	Nothing; limited stimulation	Problem behavior ignored or redirected
Play/control	Free social attention & access to preferred activities	Problem behavior ignored or redirected

EO, establishing operation; FA, functional analysis.

In addition to the basic FA, there have been several variants developed. These include: (a) brief functional analysis (BFA), (b) trial-based FA (TBFA), (c) latency-based FA (LBFA), (d) FA of precursor behavior, and (e) interview-informed synthesized contingency analysis (IISCA).

Brief Functional Analysis

This involves presenting each condition only once or twice, with each session lasting 5 to 10 minutes in length.

Trial-Based Functional Analysis

This involves interspersing a series of trials among regular, naturally occurring activities. Each trial consists of a test and control condition, each lasting 1 minute in length. Sessions are terminated when the problem behavior occurs.

Latency-Based Functional Analysis

This involves presenting the establishing operation (EO) and then immediately terminating the session when the problem behavior occurs. Unlike the previously described methods that involve recording occurrences of the problem behavior, the LBFA is conducted by recording the time between the onset of the EO and the first occurrence of the problem behavior.

Functional Analysis of Precursor Behavior

This involves presenting the EO and then immediately terminating the session when a precursor behavior (i.e., a behavior that reliably precedes the problem behavior) occurs. The time between the onset of the EO and first occurrence of the precursor behavior is recorded.

Interview-Informed Synthesized Contingency Analysis

This involves presenting synthesized antecedents and consequences (i.e., multiple contingencies) during the test condition to emulate the natural context in which the problem behavior reportedly occurs. In the control condition, noncontingent access to the reinforcers used in the test condition is provided.

EVALUATING FUNCTIONAL ANALYSES

This involves assessing the validity and reliability of the procedures and data collection methods used, interpreting the results to inform intervention planning, and continuously monitoring and adjusting interventions based on ongoing data collection. This ensures that the assessment accurately identifies the function(s) maintaining the target behavior, informs effective intervention strategies, and promotes meaningful behavior change over time.

Functions of Behavior

The function(s) of a behavior answers the question, "Why is this behavior occurring?" The answer to this question, based on decades of research, is, "To get or get out of something." In other words, a function refers to the source of reinforcement for a behavior. Common functions of problem behavior include sources of positive reinforcement (i.e., social positive, tangible, and automatic) and negative reinforcement (i.e., social negative, automatic negative; Figure 8.4).

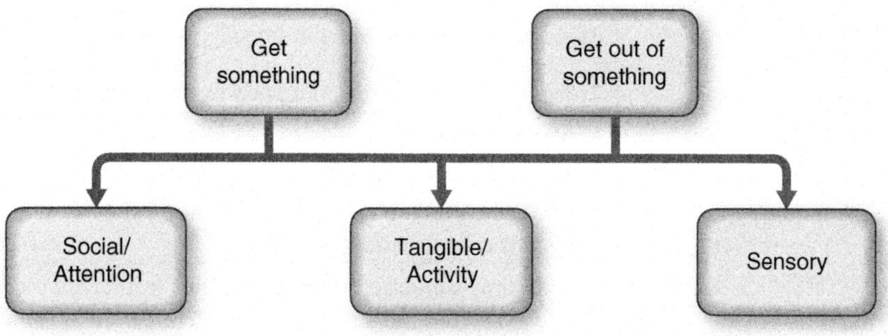

Figure 8.4 The Functions of Behavior

Social Positive Reinforcement
This refers to reinforcing reactions from others (i.e., attention).

- **Example:** A client engages in yelling behavior that results in and is maintained by surprised facial expressions from peers.

Tangible Reinforcement
This refers to reinforcing materials or other stimuli.

- **Example:** A client engages in yelling behavior that results in and is maintained by access to cookies.

Automatic Reinforcement
This refers to reinforcement that is directly produced by the behavior (i.e., sensory stimulation).

- **Example:** A client engages in yelling behavior that results in and is maintained by the physical stimulation it produces in their mouth.

Social Negative Reinforcement
This refers to the termination or postponement (i.e., escape) of unwanted interactions with others as well as unpleasant tasks/activities.

- **Example:** A client engages in yelling behavior that results in and is maintained by the termination of teacher demands to complete unwanted math worksheets.

Automatic Negative Reinforcement
This refers to the termination or postponement (i.e., escape) of aversive stimulation. The behavior directly accomplishes this.

- **Example:** A client engages in eloping behavior that results in and is maintained by the termination of loud noises in the room.

Interpreting Functional Analysis Outcomes
Data gathered from an FA can be plotted on a graph for visual inspection (Table 8.4).

Table 8.4 Interpretation of Data by Pattern of Responding Across Conditions

IF OCCURRENCES OF THE PROBLEM BEHAVIOR ARE...	THEN...
Elevated in the contingent attention condition	The data suggests it is maintained by social positive reinforcement
Elevated in the contingent escape condition	The data suggests it is maintained by negative reinforcement
Elevated in the alone condition	The data suggests it is maintained by automatic reinforcement
Low in the play/control condition	That is to be expected
Frequent across all conditions	Responding is undifferentiated and thus results are inconclusive; however, this can also occur when the behavior is maintained by automatic reinforcement.
Variable across conditions	Responding is undifferentiated and thus results are inconclusive; however, this can also occur when the behavior is maintained by automatic reinforcement.

TASK F.7

Interpret assessment data to determine the need for behavior-analytic services and/or referral to others. Behavior analysts interpret assessment data to guide decisions on whether to provide behavior-analytic services or refer clients to other professions. This process involves (a) collecting and analyzing data, (b) incorporating client and stakeholder input, (c) assessing social significance, and (d) determining whether services are warranted.

COLLECTING AND ANALYZING DATA

Begin by collecting comprehensive data using various assessment tools and methods, such as direct observations, interviews, standardized assessments, and historical data review. This thorough data collection process helps in obtaining a clear picture of the client's behavior within their specific context.

The next step involves analyzing the data to identify patterns in the client's behavior and understanding the contextual factors influencing these behaviors. Examine the

- frequency, intensity, and duration of target behaviors,
- antecedent and consequent events related to the behavior, and
- environmental variables and settings affecting behavior.

INCORPORATING CLIENT AND STAKEHOLDER INPUT

In addition, consider input from the client and relevant stakeholders (e.g., family members, caregivers, teachers) by conducting interviews to gather perspectives and priorities and using person-centered planning tools (i.e., methods and strategies used to ensure that the client's preferences, strengths, and needs are at the forefront of the planning process) to ensure the assessment reflects the client's goals and preferences.

ASSESSING SOCIAL SIGNIFICANCE

The decision to recommend behavior-analytic services or not depends on whether such services may help to improve the client's quality of life (i.e., useful and habilitative to maximize reinforcement and minimize punishment for them and others). At least one socially significant behavior must be identified as a target for change. The identification of potential target behaviors is a product of assessment.

To determine the social significance of a potential target behavior, the following 10 questions are asked. Is the behavior:

- likely to result in reinforcement for the client even after services end?
- required for learning a useful skill?
- something that will increase the client's access to environments where other desirable behaviors can be learned and practiced?
- one that can result in others interacting with the client in a more positive and helpful way?
- a behavioral cusp (i.e., a behavior that can lead to new environments/reinforcers) or pivotal behavior (i.e., a behavior that can lead to new untrained behaviors)?
- age-appropriate?
- a problem behavior that can be replaced with an adaptive behavior?
- directly related to the problem/goal?
- really the behavior of interest?
- an actual behavior?

Each answer of "yes" increases the likelihood that a given target behavior can be considered socially significant.

DETERMINING WHETHER SERVICES ARE WARRANTED

Based on the analysis, behavior analysts determine whether behavior-analytic services are warranted. If social significance is established, behavior-analytic services may be warranted. However, behavior analysts must also recognize when referral to other professionals is necessary. Referral is considered when

- the assessment data indicate issues beyond the scope of behavior analysis (e.g., medical conditions, psychologic disorders);
- the client requires specialized services (e.g., speech therapy, occupational therapy) that behavior analysts are not equipped to provide; and
- collaborative support from multiple disciplines would benefit the client's overall treatment plan.

ADDITIONAL NOTE(S)

When referrals are made, behavior analysts collaborate with other professionals to ensure a coordinated approach to the client's care. This can involve (a) sharing relevant assessment data and insights, (b) participating in multidisciplinary team meetings, and (c) making efforts to ensure continuity and consistency in the client's treatment plan.

TASK F.8

Interpret assessment data to identify and prioritize socially significant, client-informed, and culturally responsive behavior-change procedures and goals. Interpreting assessment data to identify and prioritize behavior-change procedures and goals is a dynamic and collaborative process. By focusing on social significance, client input, and cultural responsiveness, behavior analysts can develop interventions that are not only effective but also meaningful and respectful of the client's unique context.

PRIORITIZING SOCIALLY SIGNIFICANT BEHAVIOR

Behavior analysts interpret assessment data to identify and prioritize socially significant behaviors. These are behaviors that have a meaningful impact on the client's quality of life, daily functioning, and social integration. See Task F.7 for a review of the assessment of social significance.

CLIENT-INFORMED

Behavior analysts ensure that the client's preferences, values, and goals are considered in the process of developing behavior-change procedures and goals. See Task F.7 for a review of the incorporation of client and stakeholder input in the assessment process.

CULTURAL RESPONSIVENESS

Cultural responsiveness is vital in the assessment and intervention process. Behavior analysts are advised to

- acknowledge and respect the client's cultural background, including language, traditions, and beliefs;
- adapt assessment tools and procedures to be culturally appropriate and sensitive; and
- seek input from cultural consultants or community members when necessary to ensure interventions are aligned with cultural norms and values.

Goal-setting, which involves establishing criteria for behavior change, occurs after identification of at least one socially significant target behavior. See Task H.1 (Chapter 10) for a review of developing intervention goals in observable and measurable terms.

If more than one behavior-change goal is identified, the behavior analyst should consider the order in which goals should be addressed (i.e., *prioritize* goals). To assist in this process, it is important to consider the following questions (Table 8.5) in review of the target behavior for each goal.

Table 8.5 Questions to Consider for Prioritizing Target Behaviors

QUESTION	NOTE
Does it pose a danger to the client or others?	More danger = higher priority
How often will the client use it in the natural environment? If it's a problem behavior, how often does it happen?	More often = higher priority
How long has it been a problem?	Longer = higher priority
Will changing it result in the client receiving more reinforcement?	More reinforcement = higher priority
Is it important for the client's future development of other skills or independence?	More important = higher priority
Will changing it result in fewer negative interactions with others?	Fewer negative interactions = higher priority
Will changing it result in the client providing more reinforcement to others?	More reinforcement to others = higher priority
Is its treatment likely to succeed?	More likely to succeed = higher priority
Is its treatment costly?	High financial cost cannot be an excuse for withholding services. However, the cost of the client's time should be considered. In some cases, a behavior-change program's demand of a client's time may be too much and fail to justify treatment.

Note. A ranking matrix can be used to calculate a numerical score for each target behavior.

CONCLUSION

In this chapter, we reviewed key content for TCO Tasks related to behavior assessment. This included setting behavior-change goals and the use of various assessment methods to learn about clients' skill strengths and deficits, preferences, and functions of problem behavior. As a data-based practice, applied behavior analysis requires the gathering of relevant information via assessment prior to the development and implementation of an intervention plan. Although the goal is to treat behavior, doing so in a manner that will most efficiently and effectively yield desirable outcomes requires the use of assessment data. By conducting assessment prior to intervention, behavior analysts can use the information collected from the assessment process to identify the intervention strategies most likely to produce the desired change in behavior.

REFERENCE

Behavior Analyst Certification Board. (2024). *BCBA test content outline* (6th ed.). Author. https://www.bacb.com/wp-content/bcba-outline-6thEd

BIBLIOGRAPHY

Behavior Analyst Certification Board. (2024). *Ethics code for behavior analysts*. Author.

Cooper, J. O., Heron, T. E., & Heward, W. L. (2020). *Applied behavior analysis* (3rd ed.). Pearson Education.

Hanley, G. P., Jin, C. S., Vanselow, N. R., & Hanratty, L. A. (2014). Producing meaningful improvements in problem behavior of children with autism via synthesized analyses and treatments. *Journal of Applied Behavior Analysis*, *47*(1), 16–36. https://doi.org/10.1002/jaba.106

Houten, R. V. (1979). Social validation: The evolution of standards of competency for target behaviors. *Journal of Applied Behavior Analysis*, *12*(4), 581–591. https://doi.org/10.1901/jaba.1979.12-581

Iwata, B. A., Dorsey, M. F., Slifer, K. J., Bauman, K. E., & Richman, G. S. (1982). Toward a functional analysis of self-injury. *Analysis and Intervention in Developmental Disabilities*, 2(1), 3–20. https://doi.org/10.1016/0270-4684(82)90003-9

Northup, J., Wacker, D., Sasso, G., Steege, M., Cigrand, K., Cook, J., & DeRaad, A. (1991). A brief functional analysis of aggressive and alternative behavior in an outclinic setting. *Journal of Applied Behavior Analysis*, *24*(3), 509–522. https://doi.org/10.1901/jaba.1991.24-509

Sigafoos, J., & Meikle, B. (1996). Functional communication training for the treatment of multiply determined challenging behavior in two boys with autism. *Behavior Modification*, *20*(1), 60–84. https://doi.org/10.1177/01454455960201003

Smith, R. G., & Churchill, R. M. (2002). Identification of environmental determinants of behavior disorders through functional analysis of precursor behaviors. *Journal of Applied Behavior Analysis*, *35*(2), 125–136. https://doi.org/10.1901/jaba.2002.35-125

Thomason-Sassi, J. L., Iwata, B. A., Neidert, P. L., & Roscoe, E. M. (2011). Response latency as an index of response strength during functional analyses of problem behavior. *Journal of Applied Behavior Analysis*, *44*(1), 51–67. https://doi.org/10.1901/jaba.2011.44-51

KNOWLEDGE CHECK

1. A behavior analyst is beginning services with a new client who has a history of disruptive behavior in school. To gather the necessary information, the behavior analyst reviews the client's records. At the very minimum, what types of data should the behavior analyst review?

A. Educational, financial, and medical

B. Educational, historical, and medical

C. Personal, correspondence, and medical

D. Legal, financial, and medical

2. To determine the social significance of a potential target behavior, all of the following questions are asked, EXCEPT:

A. Is the behavior age-appropriate?

B. Is the behavior directly related to the problem or goal?

C. Is the behavior likely to generalize across settings?

D. Is the behavior required for learning a useful skill?

3. A behavior analyst is conducting a functional behavior assessment for a student who exhibits disruptive behavior. To gather more information, the behavior analyst interviews the student's teacher and reviews previously completed rating scales. However, the behavior analyst knows they need to include direct observation to accurately assess the behavior. Which of the following assessment methods used by the analyst is NOT an indirect assessment method?

A. Interviews with the teacher

B. Reviewing rating scales

C. Direct observation of the student

D. Reviewing checklists from previous assessments

4. Which of the following is an example of a descriptive assessment?

A. Administering standardized tests to assess the client

B. Conducting interviews with the client's parents

C. Evaluating the products of the target behavior

D. Observing the client and recording behavior, antecedents, and consequences

(See answers on the next page.)

1. **B) Educational, historical, and medical**
   At the outset of a case, behavior analysts should, at the very least, review educational data (such as school records), historical information (such as past behavior patterns or previous interventions), and medical history to fully understand the client's background and needs. This ensures that they have all relevant information to design an effective intervention plan. The other answer options include financial, personal, or legal information that is not typically required for behavior analysts to review.

2. **C) Is the behavior likely to generalize across settings?**
   Whether the behavior is likely to generalize across settings is not one of the 10 questions for determining the social significance of a potential target behavior. Whether the behavior is age-appropriate, directly related to the problem or goal, and required for learning a useful skill are among the 10 questions asked for determining social significance.

3. **C) Direct observation of the student**
   In this scenario, direct observation is the correct answer because it involves observing the behavior firsthand, making it a direct assessment method, not an indirect one. Indirect assessment methods, such as interviews, rating scales, and checklists, gather information through reports from others, rather than directly observing the behavior.

4. **D) Observing the client and recording behavior, antecedents, and consequences**
   Descriptive assessment involves directly observing the client's behavior in their natural environment and recording the occurrences of a target behavior and specified antecedents and consequences. Administering standardized tests, conducting interviews, and evaluating the products do not involve direct observation of the target behavior in natural settings.

5. A behavior analyst is using a tool to assess the progress of a client's social skills. The tool includes a list of specific social behaviors, such as "initiates conversations" and "maintains eye contact." The client's caregiver is asked to rate each behavior on a scale from 1 to 5, where 1 means "never" and 5 means "always." After receiving the completed tool, the behavior analyst uses the caregiver's ratings to analyze the client's behavior and adjust the intervention plan accordingly. Which type of tool is the behavior analyst using?

A. Rating scale

B. Checklist

C. Interview

D. Standardized test

6. A behavior analyst is assessing a client's progress in a social skills program. To determine how well the client has mastered specific skills, the behavior analyst uses an assessment that measures the client's performance against a predetermined set of criteria, such as initiating conversations and maintaining eye contact. What type of assessment is the behavior analyst using?

A. Competency-based measure

B. Criterion-reference measure

C. Rating scale

D. Standardized test

7. Which of the following is a type of criterion-referenced measure that is used to measure performance on tasks the client performs as a part of planned instruction?

A. Curriculum-based measure

B. Direct observation

C. Standardized test

D. Trials to criterion

8. A behavior analyst is working with a child who struggles to request items when they need them. To assess this, the analyst creates situations where the child is motivated (such as being presented with a preferred toy that is out of reach) and observes whether the child uses verbal requests to ask for the toy. The analyst wants to identify how the child's verbal behavior is influenced by their motivation to obtain specific items. What type of assessment is the behavior analyst conducting?

A. Duplic assessment

B. Intraverbal assessment

C. Listener assessment

D. Mand assessment

9. Assessing the listener repertoire involves measurement of:

A. Evocative effects of motivating operations (MOs) and nonverbal discriminative stimuli (S^D)

B. Parts of speech and evocative effects of nonverbal S^D

C. Verbal discriminations and parts of speech

D. None of the above

(See answers on the next page.)

5. **A) Rating scale**
In this scenario, the behavior analyst is using a rating scale because the caregiver is asked to rate the client's behaviors on a numerical scale (1 to 5), indicating how frequently each behavior occurs. A rating scale involves respondents evaluating behaviors or statements by assigning a number or value. The other answer options refer to other forms of assessment.

6. **B) Criterion-referenced measure**
In this scenario, the behavior analyst is using a criterion-referenced measure because the client's performance is being assessed against predetermined criteria, such as initiating conversations and maintaining eye contact. This type of assessment evaluates whether the client meets specific standards rather than comparing their performance to others. The other answer options refer to other types of assessment and function as distractors.

7. **A) Curriculum-based measure**
A curriculum-based measure is a type of criterion-referenced measure that is used to measure performance on tasks the client performs as a part of planned instruction. Direct observation, standardized tests, and trials to criterion refer to other forms of assessment.

8. **D) Mand assessment**
In this scenario, the behavior analyst is conducting a mand assessment because they are evaluating how the child's motivation (such as wanting a toy) evokes verbal requests (mands) for that item. A mand assessment focuses on the relationship between motivating operations (MOs) and verbal behavior, specifically how a client's needs or desires influence their requests. The other answer options refer to other types of assessment and function as distractors.

9. **C) Verbal discriminations and parts of speech**
Assessing the listener repertoire involves understanding how the listener discriminates between different verbal stimuli and responds appropriately. This includes measuring the listener's ability to make verbal discriminations (e.g., understanding different commands or instructions) and their understanding of parts of speech (e.g., nouns, verbs, adjectives) within those instructions. The other answer options that focus more on the evocative effects of MOs and nonverbal S^D are more relevant to assessing the speaker repertoire rather than the listener repertoire.

10. Which of the following preference assessment methods involves observing and recording the length of time that a client approaches, contacts, or engages with the stimuli when they are "free" to emit any responses in an environment that has not been prearranged?

A. Multiple stimulus without replacement (MSWO)

B. Naturalistic free-operant observation

C. Contrived free-operant observation

D. Single-stimulus preference assessment

11. The ________________ preference assessment method involves presenting an array of three or more stimuli at a time. The item selected by the client is removed from the array, the remaining unselected items are rearranged, and the subsequent trial consists of a reduced array.

A. Free operant

B. Paired stimulus

C. Multiple stimulus with replacement (MSW)

D. Multiple stimulus without replacement (MSWO)

12. A behavior technician is working with a client to determine their preferred toys for use as reinforcers. The behavior technician presents several toys to the client in a structured format, where the client is asked to choose between different pairs of toys in multiple trials. The technician also observes the client during a free-play session, where the client is allowed to play with any toy they choose, without any structured prompts or choices. Which of the following methods used by the behavior technician is NOT a trial-based method for assessing the client's preferences?

A. Free-operant observation

B. Paired-stimulus preference assessment

C. Multiple stimulus with replacement preference assessment

D. Multiple stimulus without replacement preference assessment

13. Common functions of problem behavior include sources of ________________.

A. Positive and automatic reinforcement

B. Positive and negative reinforcement

C. Positive reinforcement

D. Negative reinforcement

14. A behavior analyst is working with a client who frequently engages in tantrums during group activities. After observing the behavior, the behavior analyst notices that the client's tantrums consistently result in being removed from the group, effectively avoiding further interaction with peers. Which type of reinforcement is MOST likely maintaining the client's problem behavior during group activities?

A. Automatic negative reinforcement

B. Automatic reinforcement

C. Social negative reinforcement

D. Social positive reinforcement

(*See answers on the next page.*)

10. **B) Naturalistic free-operant observation**
Naturalistic free-operant observation is a preference assessment method that involves observing and recording the length of time that a client approaches, contacts, or engages with the stimuli when they are "free" to emit any responses in an environment that has not been prearranged. Contrived free-operant observation, MSWO, and single-stimulus preference assessment refer to other preference assessment methods.

11. **D) Multiple stimulus without replacement (MSWO)**
The MSWO preference assessment method involves presenting an array of three or more stimuli at a time, removing the item selected by the client from the array, and then rearranging the remaining items in the array. Free operant, paired stimulus, and MSW are other preference assessment methods.

12. **A) Free-operant observation**
In this scenario, the behavior technician is using free-operant observation when allowing the client to freely choose and engage with toys during a play session without any structured prompts or trials. This method is not considered trial-based because the client is not presented with specific choices but instead interacts with items naturally. The other answer options are trial-based methods that involve presenting items systematically and recording the client's choices in a structured format.

13. **B) Positive and negative reinforcement**
Common functions of problem behavior include sources of positive and negative reinforcement. Positive and automatic reinforcement, positive reinforcement, and negative reinforcement function as distractors.

14. **C) Social negative reinforcement**
In this scenario, the client's tantrums are maintained by social negative reinforcement because the behavior leads to the termination or avoidance of unwanted social interactions with peers during group activities. The client is using the tantrums to escape the group setting, which reinforces the behavior by removing the aversive social situation. The other answer options refer to other sources of reinforcement and function as distractors.

15. A client engages in singing behavior that results in, and is maintained by, the auditory stimulation it produces. Which of the following sources of reinforcement best explains the function of the singing behavior?

A. Automatic reinforcement

B. Automatic negative reinforcement

C. Social positive reinforcement

D. Social negative reinforcement

16. A client engages in yelling behavior that results in, and is maintained by, the termination of parent demands to eat broccoli. Which of the following sources of reinforcement best explains the function of the yelling behavior?

A. Automatic reinforcement

B. Automatic negative reinforcement

C. Social positive reinforcement

D. Social negative reinforcement

17. When using ________________, the occurrences of the target behavior and environmental events (i.e., specified antecedents and consequences) are recorded. Environmental events are recorded when they occur, even when the problem behavior has not.

A. Continuous antecedent-behavior-consequence (ABC) recording

B. Narrative ABC recording

C. Scatter plot recording

D. Whole interval recording

18. A behavior analyst is working with a client who exhibits aggressive behavior at various times during the day. The behavior analyst divides the day into 30-minute intervals and records on a chart whether the aggressive behavior occurs in each interval. The behavior analyst uses different marks to track how often the behavior occurs in the morning versus the afternoon, looking for patterns related to time of day. Which type of recording system is the behavior analyst using?

A. Continuous antecedent-behavior-consequence (ABC) recording

B. Narrative ABC recording

C. Scatter plot recording

D. Whole interval recording

(*See answers on the next page.*)

15. **A) Automatic reinforcement**
If a client engages in singing behavior that results in, and is maintained by, the auditory stimulation it produces, automatic reinforcement best explains the function of the singing behavior. Automatic negative reinforcement, social positive reinforcement, and social negative reinforcement refer to other sources of reinforcement.

16. **D) Social negative reinforcement**
In the scenario presented, the client's yelling behavior results in, and is maintained by, the removal of a demand. Social negative reinforcement, which refers to the termination or postponement of unwanted interactions or tasks, best explains the function of the client's yelling behavior. Automatic reinforcement, automatic negative reinforcement, and social positive reinforcement refer to other sources of reinforcement and function as distractors.

17. **A) Continuous antecedent-behavior-consequence (ABC) recording**
When using continuous ABC recording, the occurrences of the target behavior and environmental events (i.e., specified antecedents and consequences) are recorded. Environmental events are recorded when they occur, even when the problem behavior has not. Narrative ABC recording, scatter plot recording, and whole interval recording refer to other recording procedures.

18. **C) Scatter plot recording**
In this scenario, the behavior analyst is using scatter plot recording because the day is divided into 30-minute intervals, and the occurrence of aggressive behavior is recorded for each time period. This method helps identify patterns of behavior based on specific time intervals, such as when the behavior occurs more frequently during certain parts of the day. The other answer options refer to other recording procedures and function as distractors.

19. A 16-year-old client with autism spectrum disorder (ASD) has been referred for social skills deficits. During the assessment, the behavior analyst discovers that the client has a strong interest in video games but struggles with initiating and maintaining conversations with peers. The client's parents are concerned about their child's social isolation and want them to form meaningful friendships. Additionally, the client mentions feeling anxious in large group settings but expresses interest in joining a small, video game–themed club at school. Which of the following would be the MOST appropriate behavior-change goal to establish?

A. Focus on reducing the client's video game playtime to encourage other activities

B. Develop a plan to help the client initiate conversations and join the video game club

C. Implement a social skills training program in a large group setting

D. Encourage the client to join a variety of clubs to increase social exposure

20. A 10-year-old client with a diagnosis of attention deficit hyperactivity disorder (ADHD) and conduct disorder is referred to a behavior analyst for aggressive behaviors at school. During your assessment, the behavior analyst learns that the client has a history of traumatic experiences, including abuse and neglect. The client exhibits signs of severe emotional distress (e.g., frequent crying, withdrawal from social interactions, occasional panic attacks) and the family has not sought any psychologic or psychiatric help for these issues. What should the behavior analyst do next?

A. Develop a behavior intervention plan targeting aggressive behaviors at school

B. Implement social skills training to help the client engage with peers

C. Refer the client to a psychologic services provider

D. Use positive reinforcement to reduce instances of crying and withdrawal

21. A behavior analyst is conducting an assessment to understand the function of a client's aggressive behavior. Due to time constraints, the behavior analyst decides to present each condition (attention, escape, tangible, and alone) only once, with each session lasting 5 to 10 minutes. Which type of functional analysis (FA) is the behavior analyst using?

A. Brief functional analysis (BFA)

B. Trial-based functional analysis (TBFA)

C. Interview-informed synthesized contingency analysis (IISCA)

D. Latency-based functional analysis (LBFA)

22. Which of the following functional analysis (FA) methods involves presenting the establishing operation (EO), immediately terminating the session when the problem behavior occurs, and recording the time between the onset of the EO and the first occurrence of the problem behavior?

A. Brief functional analysis (BFA)

B. FA of precursor behavior

C. Trial-based functional analysis (TBFA)

D. Latency-based functional analysis (LBFA)

(See answers on the next page.)

19. **B) Develop a plan to help the client initiate conversations and join the video game club**
Behavior analysts identify and prioritize socially significant, client-informed, and culturally responsive behavior-change goals. Developing a plan that helps the client to initiate conversations and join the video game club aligns with their strong interest in video games and desire to engage in social activities within a comfortable, small group setting. Reducing video game playtime disregards the client's interests, social skills training in large groups could heighten their anxiety, and encouraging participation in various clubs overlooks the client's specific interests and comfort levels.

20. **C) Refer the client to a psychologic services provider**
The appropriate next step is to refer the client to a psychologic services provider. Although a behavior support plan for aggression and social skills training might help, they do not address the underlying issue. Positive reinforcement to reduce crying and withdrawal also misses the need for specialized care to address the client's history of trauma and signs of emotional distress.

21. **A) Brief functional analysis (BFA)**
In this scenario, the behavior analyst is using a BFA because they are presenting each test condition only once, with sessions lasting 5 to 10 minutes. The BFA is designed to quickly assess the function of problem behavior in a limited amount of time by keeping sessions short and reducing the number of repetitions for each condition. The other answer options (TBFA, IISCA, LBFA refer to other FA methods and function as distractors.

22. **D) Latency-based functional analysis (LBFA)**
LBFA involves presenting the EO, immediately terminating the session when the problem behavior occurs, and recording the time between the onset of the EO and the first occurrence of the problem behavior. It is sometimes confused with FA of precursor behavior, which involves presenting the EO and then immediately terminating the session when a precursor behavior, rather than the target problem behavior, occurs. BFA, FA of precursor behavior, and TBFA refer to other FA methods.

23. A behavior analyst is assessing a child who displays aggressive behavior at home when demands are placed on them while simultaneously attention is withheld. To replicate this natural context, the analyst presents both contingencies together during the test condition to observe how the child's behavior is influenced by these combined factors. This allows the analyst to better understand the conditions under which the problem behavior occurs. Which type of functional analysis (FA) is the behavior analyst using?

A. Brief functional analysis (BFA)

B. Interview-informed synthesized contingency analysis (IISCA)

C. Latency-based functional analysis (LBFA)

D. Trial-based functional analysis (TBFA)

24. A 7-year-old client from a recently immigrated family is referred for assessment due to difficulties in adjusting to a new school environment. During the initial assessment, the behavior analyst notices that the client is often quiet and avoids eye contact. The client's parents mention that in their culture, children are taught to be respectful by not looking directly at adults. How should the behavior analyst proceed with the assessment?

A. Consider the cultural significance of avoiding eye contact and adapt the assessment

B. Encourage the client to maintain eye contact to assess social skills

C. Focus on verbal communication only, disregarding nonverbal cues

D. Ignore the cultural background and proceed with the standard assessment protocol

25. A 9-year-old client with autism spectrum disorder (ASD) engages in multiple challenging behaviors, including self-injurious behavior (SIB), noncompliance with instructions, and repetitive vocalizations. The SIB includes hitting their head with their fists, which occurs several times a day, causing bruising. Noncompliance occurs during academic tasks and daily routines, while repetitive vocalizations occur sporadically throughout the day. Which behavior should be prioritized for intervention?

A. Noncompliance with instructions

B. Repetitive vocalizations

C. SIB

D. All behaviors should be addressed simultaneously.

(*See answers on the next page.*)

23. **B) Interview-informed synthesized contingency analysis (IISCA)**
In this scenario, the behavior analyst is using IISCA because they are presenting multiple contingencies (such as demands and withheld attention) simultaneously during the test condition to simulate the natural context in which the problem behavior occurs. IISCA is specifically designed to replicate real-life environments by combining contingencies that commonly occur together, providing a clearer picture of what triggers the problem behavior. The other answer options refer to other FA methods that do not synthesize multiple contingencies.

24. **A) Consider the cultural significance of avoiding eye contact and adapt the assessment**
Adapting the assessment to consider cultural significance ensures that the client's behavior is understood within their cultural context. Encouraging eye contact may not be appropriate given the cultural context, and encouraging eye contact, focusing only on verbal communication, and ignoring the cultural background fail to provide the most comprehensive assessment possible.

25. **C) SIB**
SIB should be prioritized due to the immediate risk of physical harm to the client. Addressing SIB is critical to ensure their safety before focusing on other less harmful behaviors like noncompliance and repetitive vocalizations.

Behavior-Change Procedures

9

LEARNING OBJECTIVES

The following Test Content Outline (TCO) Tasks (Behavior Analyst Certification Board®, 2024, p. 3) related to behavior-change procedures (G.1 through G.19) will serve as the learning objectives of this chapter:

- G.1 Design and evaluate positive and negative reinforcement procedures.
- G.2 Design and evaluate differential reinforcement (e.g., DRA, DRO, DRL, DRH) procedures with and without extinction.
- G.3 Design and evaluate time-based reinforcement (e.g., fixed-time) schedules.
- G.4 Identify procedures to establish and use conditioned reinforcers (e.g., token economies).
- G.5 Incorporate motivating operations and discriminative stimuli into behavior-change procedures.
- G.6 Design and evaluate procedures to produce simple and conditional discriminations.
- G.7 Select and evaluate stimulus and response prompting procedures (e.g., errorless, most-to-least, least-to-most).
- G.8 Design and implement procedures to fade stimulus and response prompts (e.g., prompt delay, stimulus fading).
- G.9 Design and evaluate modeling procedures.
- G.10 Design and evaluate instructions and rules.
- G.11 Shape dimensions of behavior.
- G.12 Select and implement chaining procedures.
- G.13 Design and evaluate trial-based and free-operant procedures.
- G.14 Design and evaluate group contingencies.
- G.15 Design and evaluate procedures to promote stimulus and response generalization.
- G.16 Design and evaluate procedures to maintain desired behavior change following intervention (e.g., schedule thinning, transferring to naturally occurring reinforcers).
- G.17 Design and evaluate positive and negative punishment (e.g., time-out, response cost, overcorrection).
- G.18 Evaluate emotional and elicited effects of behavior-change procedures.
- G.19 Design and evaluate procedures to promote emergent relations and generative performance.

TASK G.1

Design and evaluate positive and negative reinforcement procedures. See Task B.4 (Chapter 4) for a review of positive and negative reinforcement, and Task B.9 (Chapter 4) for a review of simple schedules of reinforcement which produce different rates of responding. To strengthen a behavior using positive reinforcement, establish a behavior-consequence contingency in which the consequence is a positive reinforcer.

- **Example:** A socially significant behavior (asking for help) is targeted, and a potential reinforcer (vocal praise) has been identified. To implement positive reinforcement to strengthen this behavior, the following contingency (Table 9.1) will be established:

Table 9.1 Example of a Positive Reinforcement Contingency

R	C
Says "Help"	Praise

C, consequence; R, response.

To strengthen a behavior using negative reinforcement, establish a behavior-consequence contingency in which the consequence is a negative reinforcer.

- **Example:** A socially significant behavior (asking for help) is targeted, and a potential reinforcer (escape from the task) has been identified. To implement negative reinforcement to strengthen this behavior, the following contingency (Table 9.2) will be established:

Table 9.2 Example of a Negative Reinforcement Contingency

R	C
Says "Help"	Escape from the task

C, consequence; R, response.

BOOSTING THE EFFECTIVENESS OF POSITIVE REINFORCEMENT PROCEDURES

Recommendations for increasing the effectiveness of positive reinforcement procedures include (a) start with lower criterion for reinforcement, (b) use reinforcers of sufficient magnitude, (c) keep reinforcers fresh, (d) use direct reinforcement contingencies, (e) combine reinforcement with response prompts, (f) reinforce early and often, (g) provide attention and praise, (h) increase the response-to-reinforcement delay, and (i) fake it 'til you make it (i.e., shift from contrived to naturally occurring reinforcers).

Start With Lower Criterion for Reinforcement

Set a readily obtainable beginning criterion for reinforcement. Use assessment to determine the client's current ability level. Ensure the client receives reinforcement on their first response. Then, gradually increase the criterion for reinforcement as the client's competence improves.

Use Reinforcers of Sufficient Magnitude

Use reinforcers of sufficient magnitude that are highly motivating. The quality of the reinforcer may need to be increased to maintain responding on more challenging tasks. Utilize a preference assessment to determine a client's highly preferred stimuli, which may serve as an effective reinforcer.

Keep Reinforcers Fresh

Overusing particular reinforcers can diminish their potency and effectiveness. Reinforcers should be varied to avoid satiation. Making particular reinforcers available less often or available in an unpredictable manner can also increase their effectiveness.

Use Direct Reinforcement Contingencies

Utilize reinforcement contingencies that grant direct access to the reinforcer to optimize client performance. Research suggests direct reinforcement contingencies are more effective than indirect contingencies.

Combine Reinforcement With Response Prompts

One, reinforce; two, supplement it with a response prompt (e.g., verbal instructions, modeling, and physical guidance) to occasion a correct response—this is the ol' one-two combo! Ka-pow!

Reinforce Early and Often

In the early stages of learning a new behavior, give the client reinforcement for each occurrence of the target behavior to strengthen the behavior. Then, as the target behavior becomes established, the rate of reinforcement can be thinned such that reinforcement of the target behavior is provided intermittently.

Provide Attention and Praise

Providing attention contingently and offering descriptive praise will enhance the effectiveness of positive reinforcement to strengthen behavior. Make it a consistent tool in your intervention toolbelt.

Increase the Response-to-Reinforcement Delay

Gradually increase the response-to-reinforcement delay to help your client learn the highly adaptive skill of developing behaviors that yield delayed reinforcement. Delayed consequences promote generalization and maintenance of behavior changes.

Fake It 'Til You Make It

Design interventions that enable your client to gradually move from needing contrived reinforcers (e.g., tokens) to naturally occurring reinforcers (e.g., praise, intrinsic sense of being successful). The goal is to use positive reinforcers that ultimately foster a client's ability to manipulate the environment; it is the ultimate natural reinforcer because it's ubiquitous!

NEGATIVE REINFORCEMENT FOR STRENGTHENING BEHAVIOR

Historically, behavior analysts have placed significantly more emphasis on using positive rather than negative reinforcement to strengthen behavior; however, negative reinforcement can be used to strengthen behavior. In general, the procedures noted earlier for the use of positive reinforcement procedures also apply to effective use of negative reinforcement procedures. To effectively use negative reinforcement to strengthen behavior, ensure:

- The negative reinforcer immediately follows the target behavior.
- The negative reinforcer's magnitude is sufficiently large.
- The target behavior consistently results in escape/postponement of the establishing operation (EO).
- There is no reinforcement available for other competing, nontargeted responses.

TASK G.2

Design and evaluate differential reinforcement (e.g., DRA, DRO, DRL, DRH) procedures with and without extinction. Differential reinforcement (DR) procedures can be used to increase desirable behaviors while decreasing undesirable behaviors. Types of DR procedures include (a) differential reinforcement of alternative behavior (DRA), (b) differential reinforcement of other behavior (DRO), (c) differential reinforcement of low rates of behavior (DRL), and (d) differential reinforcement of high rates of behavior (DRH). Each of these can be used with or without extinction, depending on the specific goals and context of the intervention (see Task B.11 [Chapter 4] for a review of extinction).

DIFFERENTIAL REINFORCEMENT OF ALTERNATIVE BEHAVIOR

This procedure involves reinforcing a targeted functional alternative behavior for the problem behavior.

- **Example:** A client engages in shouting out behavior to gain attention from their teacher. The alternative behavior selected is raising a hand to get the teacher's attention, so the teacher then reinforces the alternative behavior of raising their hand to gain attention.

ADDITIONAL NOTE(S)

If the procedure uses a negative reinforcer, it is referred to as differential negative reinforcement of alternative behavior (DNRA).

Guidelines for Implementation

- Select an alternative behavior that (a) the client can perform, (b) is less effortful than the problem behavior, (c) happens enough to be reinforced, and (d) is likely to be reinforced in the natural environment.
- Identify and then consistently use effective reinforcers.
- Immediately and consistently deliver reinforcement for the alternative behavior until it is well established. Then, gradually thin the schedule of reinforcement.
- Use it with other procedures.

DIFFERENTIAL REINFORCEMENT OF OTHER BEHAVIOR

This procedure involves providing reinforcement when the problem behavior is absent for a predetermined amount of time and withholding reinforcement for the problem behavior. The time interval is reset upon the occurrence of the problem behavior. DRO procedures can use a (a) fixed or (b) variable interval schedule.

- **Example:** A client engages in self-injurious behavior (SIB) when completing independent seatwork assignments, so the teacher delivers reinforcement when the client does not engage in SIB for X amount of time and resets the time interval.

Momentary Differential Reinforcement of Other Behavior

Momentary schedules that are (a) fixed or (b) variable can also be used, which involve delivering reinforcement when the problem behavior is absent at the exact time that the interval ends.

Guidelines for Implementation

- Shorten the interval initially to provide frequent reinforcement.
- Require the absence of the targeted problem behavior *and other problem behaviors* for reinforcement.
- After the problem behavior is brought under control, increase the interval gradually by a constant duration (e.g., 10 seconds), proportionately (e.g., by 10%), or based on the client's performance (e.g., setting the interval as the average interresponse time (IRT) from the last session).
- Introduce this to other activities/times in the day.
- Use it with other procedures.

DIFFERENTIAL REINFORCEMENT OF LOW RATE BEHAVIOR

This procedure involves providing reinforcement when the targeted behavior occurs at or below a predetermined criterion. There are three types of DRL procedures: (a) full session, (b) interval, and (c) spaced-responding.

Full Session

Reinforcement is delivered if the total number of responses across the entire treatment session is at or below a predetermined criterion.

- **Example:** A client appropriately raises their hand in class but does this too many times per hour, so the teacher delivers reinforcement when the client appropriately raises their hand X amount of times or less in an hour.

Interval

Reinforcement is delivered if the number of responses within a specified time interval of a treatment session is at or below a predetermined criterion.

- **Example:** A client raising their hand no more than once per 5-minute interval earns reinforcement.

Spaced-Responding

Reinforcement is delivered only if a response occurs after a minimum amount of time has passed since the previous response (i.e., when the required IRT has been exceeded).

- **Example:** A client who raises their hand every 20 seconds will receive reinforcement only if they wait at least 2 minutes between each hand raise.

ADDITIONAL NOTE(S)

DRL is typically reserved for socially acceptable behaviors that are occurring too often.

DIFFERENTIAL REINFORCEMENT OF HIGH RATES OF BEHAVIOR

This procedure involves providing reinforcement when the targeted behavior occurs at or above a predetermined criterion. Like DRL, there are three types of DRH procedures: (a) full session, (b) interval, and (c) spaced-responding.

Full Session

Reinforcement is delivered if the total number of responses across the entire treatment session meets or exceeds a predetermined criterion.

- **Example:** A client appropriately raises their hand in class but rarely does this, so the teacher delivers reinforcement when the client appropriately raises their hand X amount of times or more in an hour.

Interval

Reinforcement is delivered if the number of responses within each specified time interval meets or exceeds a predetermined criterion.

- **Example:** A client raising their hand at least 3 times per 10-minute interval earns reinforcement.

Spaced-Responding

Reinforcement is delivered only if responses occur within a specified IRT, meaning the time between responses must be brief.

- **Example:** A client receives reinforcement only if they raise their hand again within 5 minutes of their last hand raise.

ADDITIONAL NOTE(S)

When paired with extinction, DR can be more effective by eliminating reinforcement for the undesirable behavior. If extinction is contraindicated (e.g., not feasible or ethical), DR without extinction can still be effective by emphasizing positive reinforcement for alternative behaviors.

▶ PRACTICE QUESTION

DRA is a procedure that involves reinforcing a targeted alternative behavior for the problem behavior and withholding reinforcement for the problem behavior. When selecting an alternative behavior, which of the following is NOT something you want to do?

A. Select a behavior that the client is unable to perform so you can shape it
B. Select a behavior that happens frequently enough to be reinforced
C. Select a behavior that is less effortful than the problem behavior
D. Select a behavior that is likely to be reinforced in the natural environment

Before moving on to the following section for the solution, we recommend that you provide a brief explanation for the answer option you selected here:

____

____

When you're ready, move on to the next section for the solution!

Practice Question Breakdown

Step 1: Examine the question

The question calls for you to examine the guidelines for selecting an alternative behavior within a DRA procedure. More specifically, this question asks which of the posed guidelines is not advisable in a DRA procedure.

Step 2: Analyze the answer options

A. You want to be sure the client can already perform the alternative behavior; otherwise, they will likely revert to the more familiar effective and efficient problem behavior that already exists in their repertoire. This appears to be a promising option!
B. This answer is advisable when planning for a DRA. You want to be sure the alternative behavior happens frequently enough to be reinforced, because reinforcement of a targeted alternative behavior is a significant component of a DRA procedure. This answer option is a distractor.
C. This answer is advisable when planning for a DRA. If possible, you want to select a behavior that is less effortful than the problem behavior, so the likelihood of it increasing with proper reinforcement is high. This answer option is a distractor.
D. This answer is advisable when planning for a DRA. You want to select a behavior that is likely to be reinforced in the natural environment, because natural reinforcement can be more effective at building lasting behaviors. This answer option is a distractor.

Step 3: Select the best answer

Among the four answer options presented, answer A (Select a behavior that the client is unable to perform so you can shape it) appears to be the best answer.

▶ TASK G.3

Design and evaluate time-based reinforcement (e.g., fixed-time) schedules. Unlike contingency-based schedules that deliver reinforcement based on the occurrence of a specific behavior, time-based schedules provide reinforcement at predetermined intervals regardless of the behavior occurring at the time. There are two main types: (a) fixed-time and (b) variable-time schedules.

FIXED-TIME SCHEDULES

These refer to schedules of reinforcement that establish delivery of reinforcement to occur at predetermined, consistent time intervals.

- **Example:** A reinforcer is delivered every 5 minutes, irrespective of the client's behavior.

VARIABLE-TIME SCHEDULES

These refer to schedules of reinforcement that establish delivery of reinforcement to occur at varying intervals of time, with the average time between reinforcements remaining constant.

- **Example:** A reinforcer is delivered every 4 to 6 minutes, with the average interval being 5 minutes, irrespective of the client's behavior.

DESIGNING TIME-BASED REINFORCEMENT SCHEDULES

The steps for designing time-based reinforcement schedules are (a) identify the target behavior, (b) determine the interval length, (c) select and establish the delivery of appropriate reinforcers.

Identifying the Target Behavior

Clearly define the behavior you aim to influence with the time-based reinforcement schedule. This could be reducing problem behavior or maintaining a desirable behavior.

Determining the Interval Length

Decide on the fixed interval at which reinforcement will be provided. The interval length should be based on the baseline data of the target behavior and the overall goals of the intervention.

Selecting and Establishing Delivery of Appropriate Reinforcers

Choose reinforcers that are meaningful and motivating for the client, and ensure they are consistently delivered at the set intervals.

EVALUATING TIME-BASED REINFORCEMENT SCHEDULES

The steps for evaluating time-based reinforcement schedules are (a) collecting baseline data, (b) monitoring and recording data, (c) evaluating behavior change, and (d) adjusting the schedule as needed.

Collecting Baseline Data

Gather data on the target behavior before implementing the time-based reinforcement schedule. This provides a comparison point to evaluate the effectiveness of the intervention.

Monitoring and Recording Data

Continuously monitor the target behavior and the delivery of reinforcement. Keep detailed records to assess the impact of the reinforcement schedule over time.

Evaluating Behavior Change

Evaluate the data to determine if the reinforcement schedule is having the desired effect on the target behavior. Look for reductions in problem behavior or maintenance of desired behavior.

Adjusting the Schedule as Needed

Based on the evaluation, adjust the reinforcement interval or the type of reinforcer to enhance the effectiveness of the intervention.

ADDITIONAL NOTE(S)

Time-based reinforcement schedules are used to establish and maintain behavior patterns, often in conjunction with other reinforcement strategies.

TASK G.4

Identify procedures to establish and use conditioned reinforcers (e.g., token economies). See Task B.7 (Chapter 4) for a review of conditioned reinforcers (S^rs). S^rs, unlike primary reinforcers such as food and water, acquire their reinforcing properties through association with other reinforcers.

ESTABLISHING CONDITIONED REINFORCERS

This involves pairing a neutral stimulus (NS) with one or more unconditioned reinforcers (S^Rs) or S^rs. See examples in Figures 9.1 and 9.2.

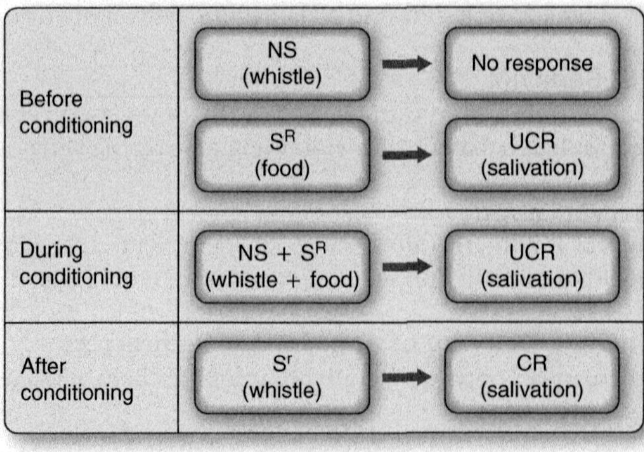

Figure 9.1 Pairing of an NS (Whistle) With an S^R (Food)

CR, conditioned response; NS, neutral stimulus; S^R, unconditioned reinforcer; S^r, conditioned reinforcer; UCR, unconditioned response.

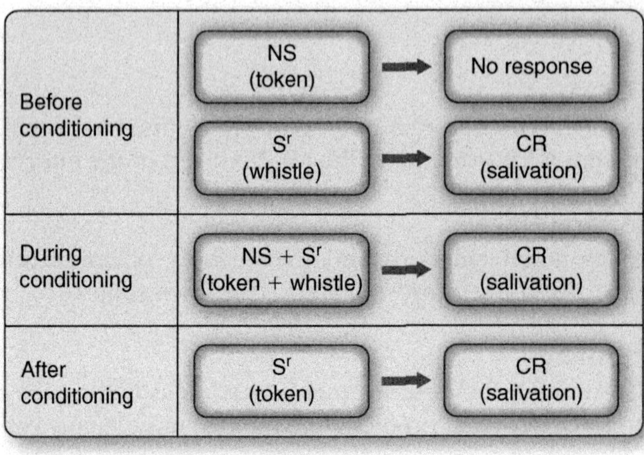

Figure 9.2 Pairing of an NS (Token) With an S^r (Whistle)

CR, conditioned response; NS, neutral stimulus; S^r, conditioned reinforcer.

USING CONDITIONED REINFORCERS

For a review of using positive and negative reinforcers (which also apply to using S^rs), please refer to Task G.1.

ADDITIONAL NOTE(S)

S^rs that are paired with many other reinforcers become generalized S^rs and may become less likely to lose value (i.e., satiate the client).

PROCEDURES TO ESTABLISH AND USE CONDITIONED REINFORCERS

These procedures include (a) token economies, (b) Premack principle, (c) pairing, (d) prompting and fading, (e) modeling, and (f) performance feedback.

Token Economies

These are structured systems where individuals earn tokens for engaging in target behaviors. These tokens can later be exchanged for desired items or privileges (Figure 9.3).

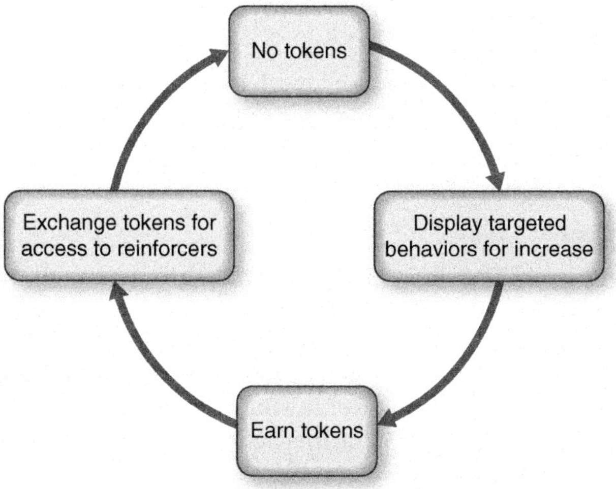

Figure 9.3 Token Economy System

- **Example:** In a classroom setting, students earn tokens (e.g., stickers, points) for completing homework, participating in class, or displaying appropriate behavior. These tokens can be exchanged for rewards such as extra recess time, a small toy, or a special privilege. The tokens themselves become S^rs as they signal the availability of these rewards.

Premack Principle

This involves using a high-probability behavior (a preferred activity) to reinforce a low-probability behavior (a less preferred activity).

- **Example:** A teacher allows students to play a game on the computer (high-probability behavior) after they complete their math assignments (low-probability behavior). The opportunity to play the game becomes an S^r for completing math assignments.

Pairing

This refers to the process of associating an NS with a primary reinforcer until the NS becomes reinforcing on its own.

- **Example:** A therapist pairs the sound of a clicker with the delivery of a small piece of candy (primary reinforcer) to a child with autism. After several pairings, the sound of the clicker alone becomes an S^r, signaling the future availability of the candy.

Prompting and Fading

This involves initially providing prompts to encourage a desired behavior, and then gradually reducing the prompts as the behavior is learned.

- **Example:** A teacher prompts a child to say "Thank you" by providing a verbal prompt and a smile every time the child receives a toy. Over time, the teacher fades the verbal prompt until the child independently says, "Thank you," and receives the smile as an S^r.

Modeling

This procedure uses observation and imitation to teach new behaviors. When the model receives reinforcement for the behavior, observers are more likely to imitate the behavior to receive similar reinforcement.

- **Example:** In a social skills group, a therapist models appropriate conversation skills and receives praise from the group. Other children in the group observe this and are motivated to imitate the conversation skills to receive praise themselves. The praise becomes an S^r for engaging in the modeled behavior.

Performance Feedback

This procedure involves providing information about performance that serves to increase or maintain desired behaviors.

- **Example:** A teacher provides verbal praise to a student who raises their hand before speaking in class. The student's behavior of raising their hand is reinforced by the teacher's positive feedback, which becomes an S^r for this behavior.

TASK G.5

Incorporate motivating operations and discriminative stimuli into behavior-change procedures. For a review of motivating operations (MOs), please refer to Task B.16 (Chapter 4). For a review of discriminative stimuli (S^D), please refer to Task B.12 (Chapter 4). Antecedent interventions based on MOs and S^D are considered *function-based* interventions. Those based on MOs are *contingency-independent* (i.e., do not rely on differential consequences for the target behavior to create evocative or abative effects), whereas those based on stimulus control are *contingency-dependent* (i.e., rely on differential consequences for the target behavior to create evocative or abative effects).

NONCONTINGENT REINFORCEMENT

Noncontingent reinforcement (NCR) is a type of time-based reinforcement schedule and contingency-independent antecedent intervention that involves delivering reinforcement on a fixed or variable interval schedule. The increased contact with reinforcement may function as an abolishing operation (AO) and decrease the motivation to engage in reinforcement-seeking behavior. NCR can be delivered with (a) positive reinforcement, (b) negative reinforcement, or (c) automatic reinforcement.

Noncontingent Reinforcement With Positive Reinforcement

This involves delivering a positive reinforcer on a fixed or variable interval schedule independent of the client's behavior.

Noncontingent Reinforcement With Negative Reinforcement

This involves delivering a negative reinforcer on a fixed or variable interval schedule independent of the client's behavior.

Noncontingent Reinforcement With Automatic Reinforcement

This involves delivering access to highly preferred objects or activities that the client can manipulate on a fixed or variable interval schedule independent of the client's behavior.

Other empirically supported antecedent interventions based on MOs include (a) the high-probability request sequence (high-*p*) procedure and (b) functional communication training (FCT).

High-Probability Request Sequence (High-*p*)

The high-probability request sequence (high-*p*) is a contingency-independent antecedent intervention that may function as an AO and decrease the motivation to escape from requests. It involves (a) presenting a series of easy-to-follow requests for which the client has a history of compliance (i.e., high-*p* requests) and (b) presenting the target request (i.e., low-*p* request) after the client has complied with the high-*p* requests. Typically, two to five high-*p* requests precede the presentation of a low-*p* request.

To effectively implement this procedure, the following guidelines should be followed: (a) present high-*p* requests that the client is currently able to comply with, (b) present requests in rapid succession, (c) acknowledge compliance with each request, and (d) use high-quality reinforcers.

- **Example:** A client throws tantrums when they are asked to wash their hands. Their teacher uses a high-*p* to increase the likelihood of compliance with the request without the tantrum.

  Teacher: "Give me five!" (high-*p* request)

  Client complies.

  Teacher: "Awesome!" (acknowledgment of compliance) "Now touch your nose." (high-*p* request)

  Client complies.

  Teacher: "That's great!" (acknowledgment of compliance) "Now make a silly face!" (high-*p* request)

  Client complies.

  Teacher: "Okay, nice job!" (acknowledgment of compliance) "Now please go wash your hands." (low-*p* request)

  Client complies.

  Teacher delivers high-quality reinforcer for compliance.

Also consider using variant sequences. In other words, do not always present high-*p* requests in the same sequence. There is some evidence that this is more effective than using invariant sequences. The ratio of high-*p* to low-*p* instructions should be gradually faded to 1:1.

Functional Communication Training

This is a contingency-independent antecedent intervention that involves the use of DRA (see Task G.2 for more details) to teach communicative responses that compete with problem behaviors evoked by an MO. Training involves conducting a functional assessment to identify reinforcers maintaining problem behavior, which are then used to teach the communicative behaviors (e.g., vocalizations, signs, etc.).

TASK G.6

Design and evaluate procedures to produce simple and conditional discriminations. Nearly all skills require discrimination among or responding differentially to environmental stimuli (e.g., colors, locations, objects, people, sounds, etc.).

SIMPLE DISCRIMINATIONS

Simple discriminations are established by reinforcing certain responses only in the presence of certain antecedents. Thus, teaching a discriminative response involves (a) presentation of a defined antecedent stimulus and (b) delivery of reinforcement if the response is emitted.

- **Example (naming objects):** In the presence of a cookie, the vocal response "Cookie" is reinforced and "Apple" is not.
- **Example (following instructions):** In the presence of the vocal instruction "Sit down," sitting down is reinforced and standing up is not.

CONDITIONAL DISCRIMINATIONS

Conditional discriminations are established by reinforcing certain responses in the presence of certain antecedents only if they are preceded by certain other stimuli. Thus, teaching a discriminative response involves (a) presentation of a defined antecedent stimulus in the presence of another stimulus and (b) delivery of reinforcement if the response is emitted.

- **Example (naming objects):** In the presence of a cookie, the vocal response "Cookie" is reinforced and "Apple" is not; AND in the presence of an apple, the vocal response "Apple" is reinforced and "Cookie" is not.
- **Example (following instructions):** In the presence of the vocal instruction "Sit down," sitting down is reinforced and standing up is not; AND in the presence of the vocal instruction "Stand up," standing up is reinforced and sitting down is not.

Conditional discriminations can be taught using matching-to-sample (MTS) procedures. See Task G.19 for a review of MTS.

ADDITIONAL NOTE(S)

When evaluating procedures to produce simple and conditional discriminations, ensure the following:

- Data is systematically collected on client performance during training and phases of generalization. Use multiple measures such as accuracy, consistency, and contextual applicability.
- Generalization probes are conducted to assess the client's ability to apply learned discriminations to new, untrained stimuli and contexts.
- Maintenance checks are conducted to evaluate the durability of learned discriminations over time.
- The relevance and importance of learned discriminations from the perspective of clients, caregivers, and other stakeholders are assessed to ensure that outcomes of the intervention are meaningful, socially significant, and practical.

TASK G.7

Select and evaluate stimulus and response prompting procedures (e.g., errorless, most-to-least, least-to-most). Prompting procedures are essential in behavior analysis for teaching new skills and reducing errors. Effective use of prompts can enhance learning by providing guidance that eventually fades as the learner acquires the target behavior independently.

ERRORLESS LEARNING

This is a teaching method designed to prevent or minimize errors during the learning process. It involves providing prompts in a way that ensures the learner responds correctly from the outset, gradually fading these prompts over time.

- **Example:** When teaching a child to identify colors, a behavior analyst might start by presenting the correct color card with a verbal prompt ("This is blue") while ensuring the other color options are not present. As the child consistently identifies "blue" correctly, the analyst gradually introduces other colors and fades the verbal prompt.

Errorless learning is particularly effective for individuals who may become frustrated or discouraged by errors. It helps build confidence and ensures a high rate of reinforcement. However, it requires careful planning to ensure prompts are faded systematically without inducing errors as prompts are removed.

STIMULUS PROMPTS

These are antecedent stimuli that operate directly on the antecedent task stimuli (e.g., movement, positioning, and redundancy) to assist the client in the emission of a target response. Stimulus prompts include: (a) stimulus shaping and (b) stimulus fading.

Stimulus Shaping

This involves gradually altering the form/topography of a stimulus until it eventually resembles the target criterion.

- **Example (target: recognizing the word "cat"):** In the initial trial, the word "cat" is placed among shapes to allow for easy discrimination. Then, in subsequent trials, letters and words are introduced until the client recognizes all the letters in the word "cat" (Table 9.3).

Table 9.3 Stimulus Shaping

TRIAL 1	TRIAL 2	TRIAL 3	TRIAL 4
*** cat *** cat *** *** *** *** cat	L cat a cat S b M s cat	Did cat sit Cat are Tom How dog cat	sat cat tat cat act nat rat can cat

Stimulus Fading

This involves making some feature of a target stimulus (e.g., color, intensity, or size) more salient, and then gradually fading it. Typically, only one feature is altered at a time.

- **Example (target: recognizing the number 1):** In the initial trial, the number 1 is enlarged to allow for easy discrimination. Then, in subsequent trials, the number 1 is gradually made smaller until the client recognizes it among an array of same-sized numbers (Table 9.4).

Table 9.4 Stimulus Fading

TRIAL 1	TRIAL 2	TRIAL 3	TRIAL 4
1 2 5	6 8 1	1 9 7	3 1 4

ADDITIONAL NOTE(S)

Stimulus shaping and fading are considered errorless learning procedures as they involve manipulating tasks to reduce/eliminate the possibility of the client making errors.

RESPONSE PROMPTS

These are antecedent stimuli that operate directly on the response (e.g., modeling, physical guidance, and verbal instructions) to assist the client in the emission of a target response. Response prompts include: (a) prompt delay, (b) least-to-most, (c) most-to-least, and (d) graduated guidance.

Prompt Delay

This is an errorless teaching strategy that involves fading the prompt using increments of time. Ordinarily, a single prompt type (e.g., verbal prompt) is used throughout instruction. There are two types of prompt delays: (a) constant time delay and (b) progressive time delay.

Constant Time Delay

This begins with several rounds of zero-delay instruction (i.e., prompt is delivered at the same time as the S^D). Then, the teacher will add an increment of time (2 to 4 seconds) after the S^D to allow for the client to respond. This increment of time does not change in subsequent rounds. If the client does not emit the desired response within the set amount of time, the prompt is delivered.

Progressive Time Delay

This begins with several rounds of zero-delay instruction (i.e., prompt is delivered at the same time as the S^D). Then, the teacher will add an increment of time (1 to 2 seconds) after the S^D to allow for the client to respond. This increment of time progressively increases by 1 or 2 seconds at a time in subsequent rounds. If the client does not emit the desired response within the set amount of time, the prompt is delivered.

ADDITIONAL NOTE(S)

Simultaneous prompting is another prompting strategy that simply involves the use of zero-delay rounds.

Least-to-Most

This is a prompt system that uses a prompt hierarchy; it starts with the least intrusive prompt and systematically graduates to the most intrusive prompt. Using this prompt system begins with the selection of prompts and establishing a hierarchy of least to most intrusive (e.g., gestural, then model, then physical). Once chosen, the teacher determines an increment of time (3 to 5 seconds) that will occur after the S^D and between prompts to allow for the client to respond with the least intrusive and least amount of prompting possible. If the client does not respond independently within the set amount of time after the S^D is presented, the first prompt in the predetermined prompt hierarchy is used. If the client does not respond within the set amount of time after the first prompt, then the second prompt in the hierarchy is used. This process continues until the client completes the desired response.

- **Example:** An individual teaches a client to tie their shoes by starting with a verbal cue, then providing a visual demonstration if needed, and using physical guidance only if necessary.

Most-to-Least

This is a prompt system that uses a prompt hierarchy that starts with the most intrusive prompt and systematically graduates to the least intrusive prompt as the client responds more independently. The S^D and prompt occur at the same time on each step. A performance criterion must be established for each prompt level; once reached, move to the next (less intrusive) prompt level.

- **Example:** An individual teaches handwashing by providing full physical guidance initially and gradually reducing it to a light touch, then to a verbal prompt, and finally to no prompt.

Graduated Guidance

This involves using highly intrusive prompts until the client begins to demonstrate the target response independently. Prompting is gradually faded as the responding becomes more independent. Prompting can also increase if the client does not participate.

- **Example:** An individual teaches a child to write by initially guiding their hand, then gradually reducing the guidance to a light touch, and finally removing it completely.

ADDITIONAL NOTE(S)

General use guidelines for prompts include: (a) use them judiciously (i.e., fade them quickly but not too quickly), (b) use least-to-most for assessing skills, (c) use most-to-least for teaching new skills, (d) consider returning to a previous prompt level if errors occur, (e) shift from reinforcing prompted to independent responses as soon as possible, and (f) do not assume what works for teaching one skill will also work for another.

To evaluate the effectiveness of prompting procedures, behavior analysts collect and examine data on the client's performance. Key considerations include (a) the accuracy of responses, (b) the level of prompt dependency, and (c) the rate of skill acquisition. The data should be reviewed regularly to determine if the prompts are effective or if adjustments are needed. Ultimately, the goal is to fade prompts and achieve independent, generalized, and maintained performance of the targeted skills.

TASK G.8

Design and implement procedures to fade stimulus and response prompts (e.g., prompt delay, stimulus fading). Procedures designed to fade stimulus and response prompts are essential for promoting independence and reducing prompt dependency in clients.

PROMPT DELAY

See Task G.7 for a review of prompt delay, which involves gradually increasing the time interval between the instruction and the prompt.

- **Example:** When teaching a child to follow a direction such as "Clap your hands," the therapist might initially give the prompt immediately after the instruction. Over time, the therapist increases the delay between the instruction and the prompt, giving the child a chance to respond on their own.

As the client begins to respond correctly, the delay is incrementally increased in small, manageable steps. Throughout this process, continuously monitor the client's responses to ensure that the increasing delay does not become too challenging, and adjust the delay as necessary.

STIMULUS FADING

See Task G.7 for a review and example of stimulus fading, which involves systematically altering a stimulus that prompts a response until the stimulus is no longer needed.

The implementation of stimulus fading starts with using a salient stimulus, such as a highlighted letter or an exaggerated gesture, to prompt the desired response. Gradually, the intensity or prominence of the stimulus is reduced while ensuring that the client continues to respond correctly. The fading continues until the additional stimulus is completely removed, and the client can respond accurately to the natural cue.

ADDITIONAL NOTE(S)

See Task G.7 for a review of least-to-most prompting, most-to-least prompting, and graduated guidance, which are inherently designed to facilitate the fading of prompts and promote independent responses from clients. Least-to-most prompting begins with the least intrusive prompt and progressively intensifies as needed to encourage the client to attempt the task with minimal support before more explicit prompts are introduced. In contrast, most-to-least prompting starts with the most intensive prompt, which is then gradually decreased in intensity, allowing clients to assume greater responsibility for their responses over time. Lastly, graduated guidance begins with full physical assistance, which is systematically reduced as the client demonstrates increased proficiency.

To increase the likelihood of successful fading, (a) gather sufficient data on the client's performance, including the type and level of prompts used, the client's accuracy, and the independence of responses; (b) tailor fading procedures to the client's unique learning history, preferences, and pace of skill acquisition; (c) adjust the rate of fading to balance challenge and success, ensuring that the process does not lead to too many errors; (d) use positive reinforcement to encourage independent responses, with a gradual shift from prompted to independent responses; and (e) incorporate natural cues and reinforcers to facilitate the generalization of skills across different contexts.

TASK G.9

Design and evaluate modeling procedures. The four behavior-environment relations that define modeling and imitation training are: (a) a model stimulus is presented to evoke the imitative response, (b) the imitative response follows immediately (within 3 to 5 seconds), (c) the model and response look/sound alike, and (d) the model serves as the S^D for the imitative response.

Models can be planned or unplanned.

PLANNED MODELS

These are prearranged antecedent stimuli that show the client exactly what to do.

UNPLANNED MODELS

These are antecedent stimuli that occur in everyday social interactions.

PRETRAINING STEPS

Prior to conducting imitation training, behavior analysts should (a) assess and teach any prerequisite skills, (b) select models, (c) pretest, and (d) sequence models for training.

Assess and Teach Any Prerequisite Skills

Imitation requires that the client attends to the model stimulus. Thus, it is important to evaluate and teach, if necessary, basic attending skills (i.e., staying seated, looking at the teacher/objects).

Select Models

Initial imitation training may begin with approximately 25 models. Begin with one model at a time and advance from simple models (e.g., raising hands, touching nose) to more complex models (i.e., sequences of responses or models involving the manipulation of objects).

Pretest

This is conducted to determine if the client already imitates some models. The procedure for pretesting is as follows: (a) have the client get in a "ready position" (e.g., seated with hands in their lap), (b) say the client's name and "Do this," (c) present a model, (d) praise imitative responses, and (e) record the response as correct, incorrect, or approximation to the model.

Sequence Models for Training

This involves using the pretest results to arrange the sequence of models for training. Models should be presented in order of easiest to most difficult. Begin with those that the client correctly imitated, followed by those that were approximated, and ending with those that were incorrectly imitated.

CONDUCTING IMITATION TRAINING

This is a four-step process that involves (a) preassessment, (b) training, (c) postassessment, and (d) probes for imitative behavior.

Preassessment

Assess the client's current performance before the training session by presenting the first three models selected for training. Present them three times each in random order. Remove the models that the client imitates correctly three times.

Training

This involves presenting the model that the client most closely approximates among the three models used in the preassessment repeatedly until the client correctly imitates the model in five consecutive trials (which may require prompting). If prompts are used, gradually fade them as quickly as possible.

Postassessment

Assess the client's ability to perform previously learned imitative responses by presenting five learned models and five in-training models. Present each three times. Learned models that are correctly imitated in 14 out of 15 trials on three consecutive postassessments should be removed from training.

Probes for Imitative Behavior

Assess for generalized imitation by presenting about five untrained models. This can be conducted at the end of the training session or intermixed with trials.

ADDITIONAL NOTE(S)

When conducting imitation training, keep training sessions short (10–15 minutes), differentially reinforce prompted and independent imitative responses, incorporate tangible reinforcers if needed, and fade verbal and physical prompts as quickly as possible.

TASK G.10

Design and evaluate instructions and rules. For a review of rules, please refer to Task B.18 (Chapter 4). Instructions are often viewed as instances of rules, acting as verbal S^D that specify responses and contingencies in rule statements. Alternatively, instructions may function as prompts or controlling verbal stimuli. For this task, we treat instructions simply as verbal stimuli specifying responses, and rules as verbal stimuli specifying both responses and contingencies.

Using an instruction involves: (a) getting the client's attention first, and then (b) delivering a verbal stimulus that specifies what the client is to do. Avoid repeating instructions and using unnecessarily long instructional statements. Target one response at a time.

- **Example:** "*Client's name*" (to get their attention). "Say 'Toy.'"

Using a rule involves the previously noted steps for delivering an instruction and extending it to include a contingency. This can be delivered in the form of an "if/then" statement.

- **Example:** "*Client's name*" (to get their attention). "If you say 'Toy,' then I will give it to you."

Additional recommendations for using instructions and rules include:

- In the event that a client fails to respond to an instruction or rule, use the amount/level of prompting necessary to assist the client in completing the task.
- It is important for clients to receive ample opportunities for practice and reinforcement for following instructions and rules.
- Keep in mind that some clients may require more time to respond than others.
- For some clients, it can be helpful to explain the reasons undergirding particular rules so that the rules do not appear arbitrary.
- Explain the consequences associated with following and not following rules and the reasons behind those consequences.

RELATED STRATEGIES

These strategies include (a) contingency contracting and (b) self-instruction.

Contingency Contracting

This involves the development of a document that clearly identifies the behavior that, when exhibited, grants the client access to or delivery of a specified reward (i.e., a rule). It should be complete and accurate. Contingency contracts can be implemented in a variety of settings, including in the classroom, home, clinic, and workplace.

Contingency contracts should (a) provide a detailed description of the task and all relevant rules, and (b) describe the reward to be provided upon completion of the specific behavior.

Detailed Description of the Task and All Relevant Rules

This should include:

- who will perform the behavior and receive the reinforcer
- what the person must do to receive the reward
- when the behavior will be performed
- how well the task must be performed for the client to gain access to the reward; provide enough detail on the specifics of the task so the client or the behaviorist can use it as a checklist

Detailed Description of the Reward to Be Provided Upon Completion of the Specific Behavior

Specify:

- who will determine completion of the task and release the reward
- what the reward will be
- when the reward will be provided
- how much reward will be given

Document task completion in a task record or chart that provides a record of the behavior. This will serve as a response prompt for the client and aid with motivation, focus, and compliance. Sometimes it is helpful for the client to mark tasks as they are completed, such as with a check mark or sticker.

Contingency contracts can be developed by the person implementing the contracting or in collaboration with the client, student, or students; collaborative contracting tends to be more effective. For example, teachers often develop behavioral contracts or classroom norms with their students. The class discusses and decides on norms for classroom behavior, reasons for those behaviors, rewards for exhibiting the behaviors, and consequences for not exhibiting the behavior. Once the contract is finalized, all students and the teacher sign the contract, display it prominently in the classroom, and periodically review it.

Self-Instruction

Clients may also be taught how to use self-instruction, which involves using self-statements as controlling responses that guide them through tasks. The following steps are used to teach self-instruction:

- Behavior analyst models the task while talking aloud to themselves.
- Client performs the task while the behavior analyst provides verbal instructions and praise.
- Client performs the task while talking aloud to themselves, and the behavior analyst quietly gives instructions.
- Client performs the task while quietly speaking the instructions to themselves and the behavior analyst moves their lips but makes no sound.
- Client performs the task while mouthing instructions without sound.
- Client performs the task while coaching their performance with covert instructions.

Evaluating instructions and rules involves assessing their clarity, effectiveness, and adherence by those targeted. This requires observing and measuring behavior before and after implementing the instructions to determine their impact. Clarity is evaluated by ensuring instructions are understandable and specific, often by soliciting feedback from recipients. Effectiveness is measured by tracking behavior changes and outcomes associated with the instructions. Additionally, adherence is monitored through regular check-ins and observations to ensure compliance. Adjustments are made based on data analysis to improve instruction delivery and effectiveness.

TASK G.11

Shape dimensions of behavior. Shaping is a procedure in which differential reinforcement is systematically applied to successive approximations of a target behavior, progressively refining responses until the terminal behavior is achieved.

SHAPING ACROSS RESPONSE TOPOGRAPHIES

Once a target response has been identified, DR is used to (a) reinforce responses that are successively closer to the terminal behavior, and (b) not reinforce those responses that are not closer to the terminal behavior. This leads to *response differentiation*.

- **Example (shaping of getting food from the refrigerator behavior; Tables 9.5 and 9.6):**

Table 9.5 What Occurred Before Implementation

EO	S^D	R	S^{R+}
Deprived of food	Refrigerator	Walk to refrigerator	Food given

EO, establishing operation; R, response; S^D, discriminative stimuli; S^{R+}, unconditioned positive reinforcer.

Table 9.6 Step 1

EO	S^D	R	S^{R+}
Deprived of food	Refrigerator	Point to refrigerator	Food given

EO, establishing operation; R, response; S^D, discriminative stimuli; S^{R+}, unconditioned positive reinforcer.

Simply walking to the refrigerator and looking at it is no longer reinforced (Table 9.7).

Table 9.7 Step 2

EO	S^D	R	S^{R+}
Deprived of food	Refrigerator	Touch refrigerator	Food given

EO, establishing operation; R, response; S^D, discriminative stimuli; S^{R+}, unconditioned positive reinforcer.

Simply pointing to the refrigerator is no longer reinforced (Table 9.8).

Table 9.8 Step 3

EO	S^D	R	S^{R+}
Deprived of food	Refrigerator	Open refrigerator door	Food given

EO, establishing operation; R, response; S^D, discriminative stimuli; S^{R+}, unconditioned positive reinforcer.

Simply touching the refrigerator is no longer reinforced.
This process continues until the terminal behavior (getting food from the refrigerator) is reached.

SHAPING WITHIN RESPONSE TOPOGRAPHIES

When shaping within response topographies, the topography of behavior remains constant but some other measurable dimension is changed. These other shapeable dimensions include: (a) frequency, (b) latency, (c) duration, and (d) magnitude.

TASK G.12

Select and implement chaining procedures. A behavior chain is a sequence of behaviors that results in a terminal outcome. Chaining refers to several methods used to link specific sequences of stimuli and behaviors. Before behaviors can be linked in a chain, behavior analysts must develop a task analysis (TA) that breaks down a complex task into a series of smaller, teachable steps (Table 9.9).

Table 9.9 Example of a TA for Morning Routine in the Classroom

STEP	R
1	Take off backpack
2	Open backpack
3	Take out homework
4	Close backpack
5	Place backpack in designated space
6	Give homework to the teacher
7	Sit in designated seat

R, response; TA, task analysis.

ADDITIONAL NOTE(S)

Develop and validate a TA using one of the following methods: (a) observe someone competently performing the task, (b) perform the task yourself, (c) ask for input from an expert, or (d) use a systematic trial-and-error procedure. When determining the number of steps, consider the complexity of each step on the basis of what is manageable for the client.

Chaining methods include: (a) forward chaining, (b) total-task chaining, (c) backward chaining, and (d) backward chaining with leap aheads.

FORWARD CHAINING

Teach the client the behaviors identified in the TA in their naturally occurring sequence. Prompt and then fade your prompting to teach the first behavior in the chain. When the first behavior is performed independently, use prompting and prompt fading to teach the second behavior in the chain. Continue this process in a forward fashion until the client is able to independently perform the entire chain of behaviors identified in the TA.

■ **Example (TA for sitting on toilet using forward chaining; Table 9.10):**

Table 9.10 Example of a TA for Sitting on Toilet Using Forward Chaining

STEP	R
1	Grab waist of pants and pull down
2	Grab waist of underwear and pull down
3	Sit down on toilet seat

R, response; TA, task analysis.

The teaching procedure begins with a focus on step 1. Use prompting and prompt fading to teach step 1 (Table 9.11). After step 1 is completed, assist the client in completing the remaining steps.

Table 9.11 Working on Step 1

STEP	R	STATUS
1	Grab waist of pants and pull down	Working on it (use prompting + prompt fading); reinforcement provided for this step
2	Grab waist of underwear and pull down	Not mastered; assist client
3	Sit down on toilet seat	Not mastered; assist client

R, response.

After step 1 is mastered (i.e., completed by the client independently), shift the focus to step 2 (Table 9.12).

Table 9.12 Working on Step 2

STEP	R	STATUS
1	Grab waist of pants and pull down	Mastered
2	Grab waist of underwear and pull down	Working on it (use prompting + prompt fading); reinforcement provided for this step
3	Sit down on toilet seat	Not mastered; assist client

R, response.

After both steps 1 and 2 are mastered, shift the focus to step 3 (Table 9.13).

Table 9.13 Working on Step 3

STEP	R	STATUS
1	Grab waist of pants and pull down	Mastered
2	Grab waist of underwear and pull down	Mastered
3	Sit down on toilet seat	Working on it (use prompting + prompt fading); reinforcement provided for this step

R, response.

TOTAL-TASK CHAINING

This is a variation of forward chaining that calls for the provision of training on each behavior in the TA during every training session. Provide the client with assistance using response prompts on any step the client struggles to perform independently. Continue this process until the client competently performs all steps of the TA.

BACKWARD CHAINING

Teach the client the behaviors identified in the TA beginning with the last behavior in the chain. In other words, teach the sequence of behaviors in reverse order. To do so, perform all the behaviors for or with the client *except for the last behavior in the chain*. Prompt and then fade your prompting to teach the final behavior. When the last behavior is performed independently, use prompting and prompt fading to teach the second to last behavior in the chain. Continue this process in a backward fashion until the client is able to independently perform the entire chain of behaviors identified in the TA (Table 9.14).

Table 9.14 Example of a TA for Blowing Nose

STEP	R
1	Remove one tissue from box
2	Raise tissue to nose
3	Blow into tissue

R, response, TA, task analysis.

The teaching procedure begins with a focus on step 3. Use prompting and prompt fading to teach step 3. After step 3 is completed, assist the client in completing the remaining steps (Table 9.15).

Table 9.15 Working on Step 3

STEP	R	STATUS
1	Remove one tissue from box	Not mastered; assist client
2	Raise tissue to nose	Not mastered; assist client
3	Blow into tissue	Working on it (prompting + prompt fading); reinforcement provided for this step

R, response.

After step 3 is mastered (i.e., completed by the client independently), shift the focus to step 2 (Table 9.16).

Table 9.16 Working on Step 2

STEP	R	STATUS
1	Remove one tissue from box	Not mastered; assist client
2	Raise tissue to nose	Working on it (prompting + prompt fading); reinforcement provided for this step
3	Blow into tissue	Mastered

R, response.

After both steps 3 and 2 are mastered, shift the focus to step 1 (Table 9.17).

Table 9.17 Working on Step 1

STEP	R	STATUS
1	Remove one tissue from box	Working on it (prompting + prompt fading); reinforcement provided for this step
2	Raise tissue to nose	Mastered
3	Blow into tissue	Mastered

R, response.

BACKWARD CHAINING WITH LEAP AHEADS

Follow the same procedures as backward chaining without the requirement that every behavior in the TA is trained. Use of this approach enables the behavior analyst to probe or assess untrained behaviors in the sequence, which can accelerate training of the behavior chain. Backward chaining with leap aheads is helpful when the client already has the prerequisite steps for a final behavior in their behavior chain. For instance, a client may need to learn how to strap the velcro on his shoes (final step). However, he already knows how to sit down (prior step), put his foot in the shoe (prior step), and take hold of the velcro with his hand (prior step), so these steps do not require teaching.

BEHAVIOR CHAINS WITH A LIMITED HOLD

This involves requiring the client to perform the entire behavior chain or steps within the chain in a given period of time to receive reinforcement.

ADDITIONAL NOTE(S)

The previously described chaining methods have each been demonstrated to be effective for a wide range of behaviors. To date, there is no clear indication from the research that any one method is more effective than another.

TASK G.13

Design and evaluate trial-based and free-operant procedures.

TRIAL-BASED PROCEDURES

These are structured, discrete events where a clear beginning and end are defined. These procedures are often used in controlled environments to teach specific skills or assess particular behaviors. Each trial consists of a prompt or cue, a client response, and a consequence or feedback. One common trial-based method is discrete trial training (DTT).

DISCRETE TRIAL TRAINING

This is an instructional procedure that breaks down behavior into discrete steps (i.e., learning trials) with a clear beginning, middle, and end. Trials are repeated with the client receiving reinforcement for correct responding (see Tables 9.18 and 9.19 for examples of correct and incorrect responding). The components of DTT include the (a) antecedent (i.e., S^D), (b) behavior, and (c) consequence.

Antecedent

This is a brief, clear instruction that alerts the client to the task and fosters the client's ability to connect a specific direction with an appropriate response.

Behavior

This is the client's response to the S^D. The client may respond correctly or incorrectly. Establish clear criteria for a correct response beforehand and provide prompting as needed. Prompts used should be faded over time.

Consequence

Deliver reinforcement immediately for a correct response. Provide corrective feedback for an incorrect response in a neutral manner.

There is a brief pause between trials referred to as the *intertrial interval* that lets the client know that the trial has ended and another is beginning.

Table 9.18 Example of Correct Responding in a Discrete Trial

S^D	R	C
Teacher points to a chair as a signal to sit.	Client sits.	Teacher delivers reinforcer.

C, consequence; R, response; S^D, discriminative stimuli.

Table 9.19 Example of Incorrect Responding in a Discrete Trial

S^D	R	C
Teacher points to a chair as a signal to sit.	Client remains standing.	Teacher delivers corrective feedback (i.e., a prompt).

C, consequence; R, response; S^D, discriminative stimuli.

Designing trial-based procedures involves clearly defining the target behavior, creating specific prompts and cues, and planning the reinforcement schedule.

FREE-OPERANT ARRANGEMENT

The free-operant (FO) arrangement is an instructional arrangement that allows for the client to freely emit one or more responses. An S^D is not required but is sometimes present. Reinforcement is not specifically programmed but the client may engage in responses that produce reinforcement continuously or intermittently. Using an FO arrangement involves allowing the client to interact with the environment with naturally occurring MOs. Access to objects may be contingent upon performance of a specific behavior (e.g., saying the name of the object). Interactions with the client around something of interest to them can also serve as teaching moments.

Designing free-operant procedures requires identifying the natural opportunities for the target behavior to occur and determining appropriate intervals or conditions for reinforcement.

Evaluating both trial-based and free-operant procedures involves continuous data collection and analysis. For trial-based procedures, data on the accuracy and speed of responses during each trial help determine the effectiveness of the intervention. For free-operant procedures, data on the frequency, duration, and natural occurrence of the target behavior are essential. Analysts compare baseline data with intervention data to assess the overall impact of the procedures.

TASK G.14

Design and evaluate group contingencies. Group contingencies are often used in schools, classrooms, playgrounds, businesses, and the military. Implementation of group contingencies involves making reinforcement for all members dependent on an individual, a set of members drawn from the larger group, or each member of the whole group achieving a performance criterion. This corresponds to one of three types of group contingencies: (a) dependent, (b) independent, or (c) interdependent.

DEPENDENT GROUP CONTINGENCY

This involves providing reinforcement for all members of a group based on the behavior of one member of the group (or a small group within a larger group; Table 9.20).

Table 9.20 Illustration of a Dependent Group Contingency Resulting in Reinforcement

S^D	R	C
Criterion stated for one client (or small group)	Client (or small group) meets criterion	Reinforcement for the whole group

C, consequence; R, response; S^D, discriminative stimuli.

INDEPENDENT GROUP CONTINGENCY

This involves providing reinforcement for each member of the group based on that member's achievement of a performance criterion that is in place for all members of the group (Table 9.21).

Table 9.21 Illustration of an Independent Group Contingency Resulting in Reinforcement

S^D	R	C
Criterion stated for the whole group	Some or all members meet criterion	Reinforcement only for members that met criterion

C, consequence; R, response; S^D, discriminative stimuli.

INTERDEPENDENT GROUP CONTINGENCY

This involves providing reinforcement for all members of a group based on each member of the group achieving a performance criterion that is in place for all members of the group (Table 9.22).

Table 9.22 Illustration of an Interdependent Group Contingency Resulting in Reinforcement:

S^D	R	C
Criterion stated for the whole group	All members meet criterion	Reinforcement for the whole group

C, consequence; R, response; S^D, discriminative stimuli.

ADDITIONAL NOTE(S)

Group contingencies save time during administration by applying a single consequence to all members. They can also leverage peer influence to achieve the aims of the intervention and foster positive social behaviors within a group. General recommendations for implementation of group contingencies are as follows:

- Identify the behavior to change and possible collateral behaviors.
- Select the type of group contingency based on programmatic goals and clients whenever possible.
- Use generalized S^rs or reinforcer menus whenever possible.
- Ensure that the performance criteria are achievable for clients.
- Monitor the performance of both the group and its individual members.
- Consider combining the group contingency with other procedures (e.g., DRL).

Evaluating group contingencies involves assessing their effectiveness, fairness, and impact on group and individual behavior. This requires collecting data on targeted behaviors before, during, and after implementation to measure their effectiveness. Fairness is evaluated by ensuring the contingency benefits all group members equally, using direct observation and feedback. The overall impact is assessed by examining the social validity, or the acceptability and perceived effectiveness, of the intervention. Additionally, monitoring for unintended effects, such as increased competition or peer pressure, is essential. Continuous data analysis allows for necessary adjustments to optimize the intervention.

▶ TASK G.15

Design and evaluate procedures to promote stimulus and response generalization. When a client generalizes a skill, they (a) exhibit it under different circumstances, settings, or situations (stimulus generalization); and/or (b) use it in an alternative manner that was not trained but is nevertheless functionally equivalent to the target behavior that was trained (response generalization). Thus, behavior analysts strive to promote clients' generalized behavior change across three aspects:

- consistency over time
- appearance across diverse and numerous settings
- diffusion to various other behaviors

ADDITIONAL NOTE(S)

Keep in mind that, while stimulus generalization and response generalization are distinct and can appear in isolation—in practice, they often co-occur.

As a crucial first step, behavior analysts do not simply expect stimulus and response generalization to occur; they systematically plan for it. This planning process involves (a) focusing on target behaviors that will be naturally reinforced by the client's environment; and (b) considering, planning for, and teaching the myriad forms of the target behavior and the varied contexts in which the client is to exhibit it.

General recommendations for teaching relevant stimulus conditions and response requirements include:

- Teach loosely and provide the client with plenty of examples of both stimulus and response.
- Enable the client to experience many different examples in the instructional setting.
- Conduct generalization probes to assess the degree to which the client responds to untaught stimulus and response examples. Discontinue instruction on a class of examples when a probe indicates the client has mastered it.

It may also be helpful to explicitly teach the client in which conditions it would be inappropriate to engage in the target behavior, using negative teaching examples.

PROCEDURES FOR PROMOTING STIMULUS GENERALIZATION

Creating an Instructional Setting That Resembles the Generalization Setting

- Teach the client to perform the target behavior in the instructional setting in a manner that will enable the client to receive reinforcement in the generalization setting.
- Mix it up when you're teaching so that the client experiences a wide range of possible scenarios in the instructional setting that could occur in the generalization setting. For instance, change the organization of the environment, individuals involved, and materials.
- Once the client is proficiently performing a skill in response to a particular instruction, start varying that instruction to reflect the diverse ways the natural environment may prompt the client to perform the behavior.

Providing Instruction on Enough Stimulus Examples

- Provide the client with instructional examples across four dimensions: what is taught (i.e., the item), the stimulus context, the setting, and the teacher.

Ensuring That the Client Receives Ample Reinforcement in the Generalization Setting

- Use intermittent schedules of reinforcement, delayed rewards, and behavior traps.
- Involve caregivers and significant others in the delivery of reinforcement.

Setting Up a Person or Object to Help Facilitate the Generalization of Skills

- In other words, devise a mediating stimulus.
- Teach the client how to use self-management skills to prompt and maintain targeted behavior changes.

PROCEDURES FOR PROMOTING RESPONSE GENERALIZATION

Providing Instruction on Enough Response Examples

- Provide the client with instruction on a wide variety of examples to assist them in acquiring a "feel" for how the target behavior appears in natural settings and promote response generalization.

Proactively Instruct Clients on the Utility of Generalizing Skills

- Teach the client that it works well to generalize a target behavior to other settings and then ask/tell them to do it.

Teach Clients to Try Different Approaches and to Use a Trial-and-Error Approach to Problem-Solving

- Reinforce the client when they exhibit response variability and engage in problem-solving.

Also remember to provide praise and show interest and enthusiasm when the client exhibits new or different forms of the target behavior in the same response class.

TASK G.16

Design and evaluate procedures to maintain desired behavior change following intervention (e.g., schedule thinning, transferring to naturally occurring reinforcers). Maintaining desired behavior change following an intervention is important for ensuring the long-term success and practical impact of treatment. Procedures for maintaining behavior change after some or all of a treatment program has been terminated include (a) schedule thinning, (b) transferring to naturally occurring reinforcers, (c) generalization training, (d) behavior traps, (e) booster sessions, (f) self-management training, and (g) peer-mediated interventions.

SCHEDULE THINNING

This involves gradually increasing the interval or ratio at which reinforcement is provided, thereby reducing the frequency of reinforcement over time. The goal is to move from a dense schedule of reinforcement, where the desired behavior is frequently reinforced, to a leaner schedule, where reinforcement is less frequent.

- **Example:** If a client is initially reinforced with a token every time they complete a household chore, schedule thinning might involve reinforcing them every three chores, then every five chores, and so on.

TRANSFERRING TO NATURALLY OCCURRING REINFORCERS

This involves shifting from contrived, artificial reinforcers to those already present in the individual's natural environment.

- **Example:** If a client is receiving tokens for complete chores, transference might involve gradually transitioning to praise from caregivers as the primary reinforcer.

GENERALIZATION TRAINING

This involves systematically varying the training conditions and incorporating multiple exemplars during the intervention to ensure the behavior changes persist across different settings, situations, and individuals.

- **Example:** A client is not only taught to request help in school, but also at home and in community settings to ensure that the behavior is maintained across various contexts.

BEHAVIOR TRAPS

This involves leveraging naturally occurring reinforcers within an individual's environment to maintain desired behaviors. They are effective because they use the powerful, naturally occurring contingencies already present in the environment.

- **Example:** A client who is taught to initiate and engage in conversation with peers finds their enjoyment in social interactions is "trapped" by the natural reinforcers that result from these experiences (e.g., praise and inclusion) that help to sustain the behavior.

BOOSTER SESSIONS

This involves conducting periodic follow-up sessions after the initial intervention to reinforce the learned behavior and address any emerging issues. Booster sessions provide an opportunity to review and reinforce the desired behaviors, ensuring they persist over time.

- **Example:** A behavior analyst schedules monthly check-ins with a client to review their progress, reinforce successful behaviors, and make necessary adjustments.

SELF-MANAGEMENT TRAINING

This involves teaching clients to monitor and manage their own behavior, thereby reinforcing their ability to maintain behavior changes independently.

- **Example:** A client is taught to use a checklist to track homework completion and reward themselves with a break after meeting their goals.

PEER-MEDIATED INTERVENTIONS

These interventions leverage the influence of peers to support and maintain behavior change. Peers are trained to prompt, reinforce, and model desired behaviors for the client.

- **Example:** In a classroom setting, peers are encouraged to praise a client for following classroom rules, thereby reinforcing the target behavior.

Evaluating procedures to maintain desired behavior change following intervention involves systematically collecting and analyzing data to assess the longevity and consistency of the behavior. By monitoring data, behavior analysts can determine whether the desired behavior persists in the absence of intervention. This data reveals the effectiveness of maintenance strategies. If the data indicate that the behavior is not being maintained, adjustments can be made to maintenance procedures. This could involve reintroducing supports temporarily, modifying reinforcement schedules, or identifying new natural reinforcers to ensure the desired behavior is sustainable in the long term.

TASK G.17

Design and evaluate positive and negative punishment (e.g., time-out, response cost, overcorrection). To weaken/decrease a behavior using positive punishment (also known as Type I punishment), establish a behavior-consequence contingency in which the consequence is a positive punisher.

- **Example:** A problem behavior (yelling) is targeted, and a potential punisher (vocal reprimand) has been identified. To implement a positive punisher to weaken/decrease this behavior, the contingency in Table 9.23 will be established:

Table 9.23 Behavior Followed by Positive Punisher

R	C
Yells	Vocal reprimand

C, consequence; R, response.

Procedures based on positive punishment include: (a) reprimands, (b) response blocking, (c) response interruption and redirection, (d) contingent exercise, and (e) overcorrection.

REPRIMAND

This involves the use of a verbal expression of disapproval following a target behavior.

RESPONSE BLOCKING

This is a physical intervention that is used to interrupt a target behavior at its onset to prevent its completion.

RESPONSE INTERRUPTION AND REDIRECTION (RIRD)

This involves response blocking of stereotypic behavior, followed by redirection to engage in high probability behaviors.

CONTINGENT EXERCISE

This involves requiring a client to perform an aversive activity following a target behavior.

OVERCORRECTION

This involves requiring the client to perform behavior that is clearly connected to remediating the harm or damage stemming from the target behavior. There are two types: (a) positive practice and (b) restitutional overcorrection.

Positive Practice

This involves requiring the client to repeatedly perform a correct form of the target behavior or a behavior that contradicts or impedes the target behavior.

Restitutional Overcorrection

This involves requiring the client to fix any damage caused by their behavior and then to guide the client on how to perform actions that further improve the environment.

To weaken/decrease a behavior using negative punishment (also known as Type II punishment), establish a behavior-consequence contingency in which the consequence is a negative punisher.

- **Example:** A problem behavior (yelling) is targeted, and a potential reinforcer (removal of toy) has been identified. To implement negative punishment to weaken/decrease this behavior, the contingency in Table 9.24 will be established:

Table 9.24 Behavior Followed by Negative Punisher

R	C
Yells	Removal of toy

C, consequence; R, response.

Procedures based on negative punishment include: (a) response cost and (b) time-out.

RESPONSE COST

There are four key methods for implementing response cost.

Directly Fine the Client a Specific Amount of Reinforcers

- **Example:** An individual may take away a specified number of minutes of a preferred activity for each occurrence of a target behavior.

Fine the Client a Specific Amount of Available Bonus Reinforcers

- **Example:** An individual may provide a certain amount of time with a preferred activity that cannot be taken away, along with the possibility of additional "bonus" minutes.

Combine Response Cost With Reinforcement

- **Example:** An individual may offer tokens for on-task behavior in conjunction with removing tokens for off-task behavior.

Combine Response Cost With Group Consequences

- **Example:** An individual may take away a specific amount of reinforcement from a group when one member of the group engages in a target behavior.

ADDITIONAL NOTE(S)

To implement the response cost effectively, (a) implement fines as soon as possible after the occurrence of a target behavior, (b) consider what variation of response cost is best to use (i.e., is less aversive, more socially acceptable, and recommended for the type of behavior targeted), (c) make sure you have enough of the reinforcers you will be using, (d) plan for unexpected outcomes (e.g., aggressive or avoidant behavior), (e) save response cost as a last resort, and (f) take data on the effects of response cost.

TIME-OUT

This involves withdrawing opportunities to access positive reinforcement for a certain amount of time and/or contingent on the performance of a particular behavior. There are two types: (a) nonexclusion and (b) exclusion time-out.

Nonexclusion

This type of time-out does not completely remove the client from the physical time-in environment and can take several forms, including: (a) planned ignoring (i.e., withholding social reinforcement) when the client performs the target behavior, (b) removing access to reinforcement when the client performs the target behavior, (c) contingent observation (i.e., repositioning the client so that they can be monitored; access to reinforcement is removed), and (d) placement in select space time-out (i.e., repositioning the client to a space in the time-in setting that is partitioned off; access to reinforcement is removed).

Exclusion

This type of time-out completely removes the client from the physical time-in environment. It involves placing the client in a separate, safe, secure, and supervised time-out space. It is preferred that this space is minimally furnished and located near the time-in setting.

ADDITIONAL NOTE(S)

To implement time-out effectively, (a) create a reinforcing time-in environment, (b) define the behaviors that lead to time-out for all relevant parties, (c) consider nonexclusion procedures first and determine what can be implemented based on physical factors, (d) get permission before using any time-out procedure from the relevant parties, (e) explain the procedure to clients, (f) use time-out each time a target behavior occurs, (g) determine exit criteria (i.e., how a client can be released from time-out), (h) follow legal and ethical requirements regarding the use of time-out, and (i) collect data to evaluate the effectiveness of time-out.

Recommendations for increasing the effectiveness of positive and negative punishment procedures are as follows:

- Prior to implementation, assess and determine the client's punishers.
- Use a variety of punishers in a consistent and safe manner.
- Apply the punisher as early in the behavior chain as possible.
- Deliver the punisher immediately (or as soon as possible) following each occurrence of the target behavior.
- Calibrate the intensity of the punisher such that it is sufficiently intense to be effective, but not unnecessarily intense.
- Initially implement a continuous schedule of punishment but aim to thin the schedule.
- Utilize mediation with a response-to-punishment delay that more closely approximates how consequences are delivered in the natural environment.
- Implement punishment in conjunction with complementary interventions, such as antecedent interventions, extinction, and DR.
- Be on the lookout for and prepared to address unwanted effects of punishment.
- Collect/review data regularly and make data-based decisions regarding treatment.

TASK G.18

Evaluate emotional and elicited effects of behavior-change procedures. Evaluating the emotional and elicited effects of behavior-change procedures is important for ensuring that treatments are both effective and humane. Behavior analysts must consider not only the direct outcomes of their interventions, but also the broader emotional and psychologic impacts on their clients. This evaluation involves assessing whether the procedures produce any unintended negative emotional responses (e.g., anxiety, frustration) and whether they elicit any other nontargeted behaviors (e.g., reflexive aggression, escape behaviors).

METHODS OF EVALUATION

Direct Observation

Regular and systematic observation of the client's behavior can help identify signs of distress or adverse emotional reactions. This includes recording instances of crying, avoidance, or other indicators of negative emotional states, as well as noting any aggressive behaviors that may be elicited.

- **Example:** If a client shows signs of increased agitation during a new intervention, it might indicate that the procedure is too aversive or stressful. For instance, a client might begin to cry or attempt to flee during the implementation of a new task demand, suggesting that the intervention may need adjustment to reduce its aversiveness.

Behavior Rating Scales

These scales, which can be administered to and completed by caregivers, teachers, or clients themselves, provide a means for behavior analysts to collect data on changes in mood, anxiety levels, and other emotional factors to provide a broader picture of the client's emotional state over time.

- **Example:** A teacher filling out a weekly rating scale might report an increase in a client's anxiety and withdrawal behaviors since the introduction of a new classroom management strategy. This feedback indicates a need to reevaluate the approach to better support the client's well-being.

Self-Report Measures

Gathering insights into clients' emotional experiences through self-report questionnaires or interviews is another effective method. This approach can be particularly valuable for understanding how clients feel in response to specific interventions.

- **Example:** A client participating in a social skills training program might report feeling more anxious and less confident during group activities. This feedback is crucial for tailoring the intervention to better support the client's comfort and engagement.

Physiologic Measures

These measures include devices that monitor physiologic indicators such as heart rate, skin conductance, and cortisol levels. While less common compared to the other methods described, physiologic measures can offer valuable insights into clients' emotional and physiologic responses to interventions.

- Monitoring a client's heart rate during an intervention can reveal increases in physiologic stress, prompting the behavior analyst to modify the procedure to make it less stressful.

TASK G.19

Design and evaluate procedures to promote emergent relations and generative performance. See Task B.21 (Chapter 4) for a review of emergent relations and generative performance, which are important for promoting learning and adaptability in clients. Emergent relations refer to the development of new, untaught relations among stimuli following direct training. Generative performance, on the other hand, involves the spontaneous generation of novel responses or behaviors that have not been explicitly trained. Various procedures can be employed to foster these outcomes, including (a) stimulus equivalence training, (b) relational frame theory (RFT), (c) MTS, (d) multiple exemplar training (MET), (e) common bidirectional naming (C-BiN), (f) joint control, and (g) matrix training.

STIMULUS EQUIVALENCE TRAINING

This involves teaching specific relations to promote the emergence of untaught relations. See Task B.21 (Chapter 4) for a review of reflexivity, symmetry, and transitivity, which are the key principles that underlie stimulus equivalence training. To start, identify stimulus sets to be included in the equivalence classes and then train the client on multiple conditional discriminations (e.g., matching spoken words to pictures and pictures to written words). Gradually introduce new stimuli and reinforce correct responses to strengthen equivalence relations.

- **Example (if A = B and B = C, then A = C):** A client is taught to match the spoken word "cat" (A) to a picture of a cat (B), and to match the picture of a cat (B) to the written word "cat" (C). Through repeated training and reinforcement, these direct relations are learned. Subsequently, the client demonstrates the ability to match the spoken word "cat" (A) with the written word "cat" (C), an emergent relation resulting from transitivity.

Relational Frame Theory

This extends the concept of stimulus equivalence by emphasizing the arbitrary and flexible nature of relational responding. RFT involves teaching clients to respond to stimuli in various relational contexts (e.g., same, different, larger than, and smaller than) to promote generative performance based on learned relational frames. To start, establish a target relational response (e.g., same/different) and reinforce accurate responses consistently. Progress by introducing new relational frames and providing reinforcement for correct responses to develop complex verbal behavior based on relational frames.

Matching-to-Sample

This is a discrete-trial procedure that is foundational in both stimulus equivalence training and RFT. It starts with the client making a response (referred to as the observing response) to the sample stimulus (which is the *conditional sample*). The sample stimulus may or may not be removed before presenting the comparison stimuli (which are the *discriminative events*), one of which matches with the conditional sample. When the client selects the comparison stimulus that matches with the sample stimulus, reinforcement is delivered.

- **Example (teach A = B):** A trial begins with a client making an observing response to the sample stimulus (i.e., listens to the teacher say, "Bird"). Then, the following comparison stimuli are presented (Figure 9.4):

Figure 9.4 Comparison Stimuli

If the client correctly matches the comparison stimulus to the sample stimulus (i.e., selects the second stimulus in the array of three comparison stimuli), reinforcement is provided (Table 9.25).

Table 9.25 Three-Phase MTS Procedure for EBI

PHASE 1	PHASE 2	PHASE 3
Teach A = B	Teach B = C	Test for A = C

EBI, equivalence-based instruction; MTS, matching-to-sample.

To start, use simple stimuli and gradually increase the complexity. Provide reinforcement for correct matches and fade prompts as the individual learns the task, ensuring the task aligns with the learner's abilities and goals.

MULTIPLE EXEMPLAR TRAINING

This involves teaching a range of examples representing a target concept until generalization occurs. To start, identify multiple contexts, stimuli, or situations where the skill needs to be applied. Use a variety of materials, settings, and conditions to teach the skill. Provide systematic reinforcement for correct responses across different exemplars, gradually reducing support as proficiency increases to promote generalization of the skill.

- **Example:** To teach the concept of "circle," a client is shown circles of different sizes, colors, and materials until the client identifies new circles independently.

Common Bidirectional Naming

This involves teaching clients to name stimuli in both directions (e.g., A to B and B to A). To start, establish the bidirectional relationship by pairing stimuli in both directions. Provide systematic reinforcement for correct responses and use error correction procedures as needed. Gradually increase the complexity and diversity of stimuli while reinforcing accurate bidirectional naming.

- **Example:** A client is taught to name a "car" when presented with it, and to identify the object when someone else says "car."

JOINT CONTROL

This involves structuring interactions where multiple individuals respond to stimuli together, fostering shared stimulus control and promoting cooperative behavior. Steps include selecting participants, defining target behaviors (e.g., turn-taking), arranging stimuli, prompting joint responses, gradually reducing prompts, and ensuring generalization and maintenance.

MATRIX TRAINING

This planning process is sometimes referred to as a procedure for promoting generalization and the emergence of novel responses. It involves organizing skills or behaviors into a grid format that combines elements from two dimensions, such as stimuli or responses. To start, identify the target skills to be taught and create a matrix with two dimensions representing the related stimuli or responses. Once the matrix has been populated with combinations from each dimension, select a subset of these combinations for explicit training.

- **Example (teaching action-object combinations; Table 9.26):**

Table 9.26 Example of a Matrix for Teaching Action-Object Combinations

	CAR	BALL	BOOK
Push	Push car	Push ball	Push book
Throw	Throw car	Throw ball	Throw book
Read	Read car	Read ball	Read book

To teach a client to perform specific actions with objects, training begins with "push car," "throw ball," and "read book." These combinations ensure that each action (push, throw, read) and each object (car, ball, book) is included at least once in the training set.

ADDITIONAL NOTE(S)

When evaluating procedures to promote emergent relations, ensure the following:

- Data is systematically collected on client performance during training and phases of generalization. Use multiple measures such as accuracy, consistency, and contextual applicability.
- Generalization probes are conducted to assess the client's ability to apply learned skills to new, untrained stimuli and contexts.
- Maintenance checks are conducted to evaluate the durability of learned behaviors over time.
- The relevance and importance of learned skills from the perspective of clients, caregivers, and other stakeholders are assessed to ensure that outcomes of the intervention are meaningful, socially significant, and practical.

CONCLUSION

This chapter covered key content for TCO Tasks related to behavior-change procedures. It is an important chapter because it delineates how behavior analysts competently employ the most frequently used tools in their "intervention toolbox." As such, this chapter offers clear and practical guidance on how to use behavior-change procedures like positive and negative reinforcement to strengthen behavior; establish and use S^rs; use stimulus and response prompts and fading; use modeling and imitation training; use shaping and chaining; use a variety of teaching arrangements and approaches to instruction; use procedures to promote stimulus and response generalization and maintenance; and more.

REFERENCE

Behavior Analyst Certification Board. (2024). *BCBA test content outline* (6th ed.). Author. https://www.bacb.com/wp-content/bcba-outline-6thEd

BIBLIOGRAPHY

Baer, D. M., Peterson, R. F., & Sherman, J. A. (1967). The development of imitation by reinforcing behavioral similarity to a model. *Journal of the Experimental Analysis of Behavior*, *10*(5), 405–416. https://doi.org/10.1901/jeab.1967.10-405

Baer, D. M., Wolf, M. M., & Risley, T. R. (1968). Some current dimensions of applied behavior analysis. *Journal of Applied Behavior Analysis*, *1*(1), 91–97. https://doi.org/10.1901/jaba.1968.1-91

Cooper, J. O., Heron, T. E., & Heward, W. L. (2020). *Applied behavior analysis* (3rd ed.). Pearson Education.

Davis, C. A., & Reichle, J. (1996). Variant and invariant high-probability requests: Increasing appropriate behaviors in children with emotional-behavioral disorders. *Journal of Applied Behavior Analysis*, *29*(4), 471–481. https://doi.org/10.1901/jaba.1996.29-471

Deitz, S. M. (1977). An analysis of programming DRL schedules in educational settings. *Behaviour Research and Therapy*, *15*(1), 103–111. https://doi.org/10.1016/0005-7967(77)90093-6

Eikeseth, S., & Smith, D. P. (2013). An analysis of verbal stimulus control in intraverbal behavior: Implications for practice and applied research. *The Analysis of Verbal Behavior*, *29*(1), 125–135. https://doi.org/10.1007/bf03393130

Etzel, B. C., & LeBlanc, J. M. (1979). The simplest treatment alternative: The law of parsimony applied to choosing appropriate instructional control and errorless-learning procedures for the difficult-to-teach child. *Journal of Autism and Developmental Disorders*, *9*(4), 361–382. https://doi.org/10.1007/BF01531445

Frampton, S. E., & Axe, J. B. (2023). A tutorial for implementing matrix training in practice. *Behavior Analysis in Practice*, *16*(1), 334–345. https://doi.org/10.1007/s40617-022-00733-5

Green, G. (2001). Behavior analytic instruction for learners with autism: Advances in stimulus control technology. *Focus on Autism and Other Developmental Disabilities*, *16*(2), 72–85. https://doi.org/10.1177/108835760101600203

Hart, B., & Risley, T. R. (1975). Incidental teaching of language in the preschool. *Journal of Applied Behavior Analysis*, *8*(4), 411–420. https://doi.org/10.1901/jaba.1975.8-411

Holth, P. (2003). Generalized imitation and generalized matching to sample. *The Behavior Analyst*, *26*(1), 155–158. https://doi.org/10.1007/BF03392073

LeBlanc, L. A., Esch, J., Sidener, T. M., & Firth, A. M. (2006). Behavioral language interventions for children with autism: Comparing applied verbal behavior and naturalistic teaching approaches. *The Analysis of Verbal Behavior*, *22*(1), 49–60. https://doi.org/10.1007/BF03393026

MacDuff, G. S., Krantz, P. J., & McClannahan, L. E. (2001). Prompts and prompt-fading strategies for people with autism. In C. E. Maurice, G. E. Green, & R. M. Foxx (Eds.), *Making a difference: Behavioral intervention for autism* (pp. 37–50). Pro-Ed.

Meichenbaum, D. H., & Goodman, J. (1971). Training impulsive children to talk to themselves: A means of developing self-control. *Journal of Abnormal Psychology*, *77*(2), 115–126. https://doi.org/10.1037/h0030773

Michael, J. (1993). Establishing operations. *The Behavior Analyst*, *16*(2), 191–206. https://doi.org/10.1007/BF03392623

Miltenberger, R. (2015). *Behavior modification: Principles and procedures*. Cengage Learning.

Ribes-Inesta, E. (2000). Instructions, rules, and abstraction: A misconstrued relation. *Behavior and Philosophy, 28*(1–2), 41–55. https://www.jstor.org/stable/27759403

Sidman, M., Willson-Morris, M., & Kirk, B. (1986). Matching-to-sample procedures and the development of equivalence relations: The role of naming. *Analysis and Intervention in Developmental Disabilities, 6*(1–2), 1–19. https://doi.org/10.1016/0270-4684(86)90003-0

Skinner, B. F. (1957). *Verbal behavior*. Appleton-Century-Crofts.

Smith, T. (2001). Discrete trial training in the treatment of autism. *Focus on Autism and Other Developmental Disabilities, 16*(2), 86–92. https://doi.org/10.1177/108835760101600204

Stokes, T. F., & Baer, D. M. (1977). An implicit technology of generalization. *Journal of Applied Behavior Analysis, 10*, 349–367. https://doi.org/10.1901/jaba.1977.10-349

Stokes, T. F., & Osnes, P. G. (1989). An operant pursuit of generalization. *Behavior Therapy, 20*(3), 337–355. https://doi.org/10.1016/S0005-7894(89)80054-1

Striefel, S. (1974). *Behavior modification: Teaching a child to imitate.* Pro-Ed.

Tarbox, J., Zuckerman, C. K., Bishop, M. R., Olive, M. L., & O'Hora, D. P. (2011). Rule-governed behavior: Teaching a preliminary repertoire of rule-following to children with autism. *The Analysis of Verbal Behavior. 27*(1), 125–139. https://doi.org/10.1007/BF03393096

Terrace, H. S. (1963). Errorless discrimination learning in the pigeon: Effects of chlorpromazine and imipramine. *Science, 140*(3564), 318–319. https://doi.org/10.1126/science.140.3564.318

Wolery, M., & Gast, D. L. (1984). Effective and efficient procedures for the transfer of stimulus control. *Topics in Early Childhood Special Education, 4*(3), 52–77. https://doi.org/10.1177/027112148400400305

KNOWLEDGE CHECK

1. Recommendations for increasing the effectiveness of positive reinforcement procedures include all of the following, EXCEPT:

A. Avoid varying reinforcers to ensure the most effective reinforcers are consistently used

B. Design interventions that enable the client to gradually move from needing contrived reinforcers to naturally occurring reinforcers

C. Set a readily obtainable beginning criterion for reinforcement

D. Use reinforcers of sufficient magnitude that are highly motivating

2. A teacher notices that a student frequently engages in disruptive behavior during long periods of work. To prevent the disruptive behavior, the teacher arranges a system where the student is given a preferred activity at scheduled intervals, regardless of the student's behavior at the time. This intervention is designed to reduce the likelihood of the disruptive behavior by addressing the student's motivation to escape long work periods. Which term best describes this intervention?

A. Consequence-based

B. Contingency-dependent

C. Contingency-independent

D. None of the above

3. A behavior technician is working with a client who frequently engages in disruptive behaviors to gain attention. To reduce the need for attention-seeking behaviors, the technician provides the client with attention every 5 minutes, regardless of the client's behavior during that time. The goal is to deliver reinforcement (attention) in regular intervals without requiring the client to engage in any specific behavior. What type of intervention is the behavior technician conducting?

A. Differential reinforcement of other behavior (DRO)

B. Functional communication training (FCT)

C. High probability request sequence (high-*p*)

D. Noncontingent reinforcement (NCR)

4. A behavior analyst is working with a client who frequently engages in repetitive hand-flapping behaviors when they do not have access to sensory toys. To reduce the hand-flapping, the behavior analyst implements an intervention where the client is provided with a sensory toy (e.g., a toy that lights up or vibrates) every 10 minutes, regardless of the client's behavior. The toy provides sensory stimulation that reinforces the client's behavior without any social interaction. Which type of noncontingent reinforcement (NCR) procedure is the behavior analyst using?

A. NCR with automatic reinforcement

B. NCR with negative reinforcement

C. NCR with positive reinforcement

D. None of the above

(*See answers on the next page.*)

1. **A) Avoid varying reinforcers to ensure the most effective reinforcers are consistently used**
   It is recommended that reinforcers are varied, not held constant. Designing interventions that enable the client to gradually move from needing contrived reinforcers to naturally occurring reinforcers, setting a readily obtainable beginning criterion for reinforcement, and using reinforcers of sufficient magnitude that are highly motivating are recommended practices for increasing the effectiveness of positive reinforcement procedures.

2. **C) Contingency-independent**
   In this scenario, the teacher is using a contingency-independent intervention because the strategy (providing a preferred activity at scheduled intervals) modifies the student's motivation without being contingent on the student's behavior. This intervention focuses on altering the motivating operation to prevent problem behavior from occurring, regardless of the student's actions at the time. Consequence-based interventions refer to those that are applied after the behavior, and contingency-dependent interventions involve changing antecedents based on the presence of a specific behavior.

3. **D) Noncontingent reinforcement (NCR)**
   In this scenario, the behavior technician is using NCR because they are delivering attention to the client on a fixed interval schedule (every 5 minutes) regardless of the client's behavior. NCR involves providing reinforcement on a fixed or variable schedule without requiring the client to engage in a specific behavior. The other answer options refer to other procedures, two of which are also contingency-independent antecedent interventions, but don't involve delivering reinforcement on a fixed or variable interval schedule independent of behavior.

4. **A) NCR with automatic reinforcement**
   In this scenario, the behavior analyst is using NCR with automatic reinforcement because the client is provided with a sensory toy (which lights up or vibrates) that provides sensory stimulation, independent of any social interaction. This is an example of automatic reinforcement because the reinforcement (sensory feedback from the toy) occurs directly from the object itself, without any involvement from another person. The other response options (NCR with negative reinforcement, NCR with positive reinforcement) refer to other NCR procedures that involve other sources of reinforcement.

5. A teacher is trying to establish a sticker as a reinforcer for a student who does not initially find stickers rewarding. The teacher pairs the stickers with the student's favorite snack every time the student completes a task. Eventually, the student begins to work harder to earn stickers, even when the snack is not immediately provided. Before being paired with the snack, what type of stimulus are the stickers considered?

A. A conditioned stimulus

B. A discriminative stimulus

C. A neutral stimulus

D. An unconditioned stimulus

6. A teacher implements a point system in the classroom where students earn points for good behavior. These points can be traded for a variety of rewards, including extra recess, snacks, or small toys. Over time, the students become highly motivated to earn points because they can be exchanged for many different types of reinforcers. What type of reinforcer have the points become due to their pairing with a wide range of available rewards?

A. Generalized conditioned

B. Generalized unconditioned

C. Primary

D. Secondary

7. A teacher is helping a student learn to distinguish the letter "A" from other letters. Initially, the letter "A" is presented in bold, large print to make it stand out. Over time, the teacher gradually reduces the boldness and size of the "A" until the student can identify the letter in regular-sized text. Which procedure is the teacher using?

A. Stimulus fading

B. Shaping

C. Stimulus control

D. Stimulus superimposition

8. What errorless teaching strategy begins with several rounds of zero-delay instruction and is followed by the addition of an increment of time after the discriminative stimulus (S^D) that does not change in subsequent rounds?

A. Assisted time delay

B. Constant time delay

C. Intermittent time delay

D. Progressive time delay

(*See answers on the next page.*)

5. **C) A neutral stimulus**
   In this scenario, the stickers are initially considered a neutral stimulus because they do not have any inherent reinforcing properties for the student. By pairing the stickers with the student's favorite snack (an unconditioned reinforcer), the stickers eventually take on reinforcing properties and become a conditioned reinforcer. The other answer options refer to other types of stimuli and function as distractors.

6. **A) Generalized conditioned**
   In this scenario, the points have become a generalized conditioned reinforcer because they can be exchanged for many different types of rewards, such as extra recess, snacks, or toys. A generalized conditioned reinforcer is effective across many situations due to its association with multiple reinforcing stimuli. The other answer options refer to other types of reinforcers and function as distractors.

7. **A) Stimulus fading**
   In this scenario, the teacher is using stimulus fading because they are initially making the letter "A" more prominent (by making it bold and large) and then gradually reducing its intensity until the student can recognize the letter in a more typical form. Stimulus fading involves enhancing a feature of the target stimulus to make it more noticeable and then fading that feature over time. The other answer options refer to different concepts or procedures that do not involve making a stimulus more salient and gradually fading it.

8. **B) Constant time delay**
   Constant time delay is an errorless teaching strategy that begins with several rounds of zero-delay instruction and is followed by the addition of an increment of time after the S^D that does not change in subsequent rounds. Assisted time delay, intermittent time delay, and progressive time delay, only one of which is an errorless teaching strategy described in the professional literature, function as distractors.

9. A behavior technician is teaching a client how to tie their shoes. Initially, the technician provides physical guidance to help the client manipulate the laces. As the client begins to show some success with tying the shoes, the technician gradually reduces the level of physical guidance, allowing the client to tie the laces with less help. The technician continues to guide as needed but fades the prompts in a gradual manner based on the client's performance. Which prompting procedure is the behavior technician using?

A. Graduated guidance

B. Least-to-most prompting

C. Most-to-least prompting

D. Prompt delay

10. General use guidelines for response prompts include each of the following, EXCEPT:

A. Consider returning to a previous prompt level if errors occur

B. Shift from reinforcing prompted to independent responses as soon as possible

C. Use most-to-least for assessing skills

D. Use response prompts judiciously

11. Prior to conducting imitation training, behavior analysts should:

A. Assess and teach any prerequisite skills, select models, and sequence models for training

B. Assess and teach any prerequisite skills, select models, pretest, and sequence models for training

C. Conduct a functional analysis, pretest, probe for imitative behavior, and select models

D. Probe for imitative behavior, select models, and sequence models for training

12. A teacher has just completed imitation training with a student, where the student successfully learned to imitate several actions such as raising their hand and tapping their desk. As a next step, the teacher presents new actions the student hasn't been directly taught, like stomping their feet, to see if the student can imitate these novel actions. Why is the teacher presenting new actions that were not previously taught during training?

A. To assess the client's ability to perform previously learned imitative responses

B. To assess for generalized imitation

C. To identify additional imitative responses to target

D. To identify models for use in the next set of trials

13. A behavior analyst gradually increases the amount of time a client is to remain seated in a chair before they are allowed to get up from it. This is an example of:

A. Behavior chaining

B. Progressive time delay

C. Shaping across response topographies

D. Shaping within response topography

(*See answers on the next page.*)

9. **A) Graduated guidance**
   In this scenario, the behavior technician is using graduated guidance because they are providing physical guidance to help the client tie their shoes and gradually reducing the level of assistance based on the client's performance. Graduated guidance involves adjusting the physical prompts as needed and fading them over time as the client gains independence. The other answer options refer to other prompt systems and function as distractors.

10. **C) Use most-to-least for assessing skills**
    When using response prompts, behavior analysts should consider returning to a previous prompt level if errors occur, shift from reinforcing prompted to independent responses as soon as possible, and use response prompts judiciously. Using the most-to-least prompt system for assessing skills, however, is not a general use guideline for response prompts.

11. **B) Assess and teach any prerequisite skills, select models, pretest, and sequence models for training**
    Prior to conducting imitation training, behavior analysts should assess and teach any prerequisite skills, select models, pretest, and sequence models for training. The other answer options (assess and teach any prerequisite skills, select models, and sequence models for training; conduct a functional analysis, pretest, probe for imitative behavior, and select models; probe for imitative behavior, select models, and sequence models for training) do not accurately include the pretraining steps for imitation training.

12. **B) To assess for generalized imitation**
    In this scenario, the teacher is using the last step of imitation training, which involves probing for generalized imitation. By presenting new, untaught actions and assessing whether the student can imitate them, the teacher is determining whether the student has generalized the ability to imitate novel behaviors without specific instruction. The other answer options do not serve to probe for generalized imitation and function as distractors.

13. **D) Shaping within response topography**
    This is an example of shaping within response topography. In the scenario presented, the behavior being shaped (remaining seated in a chair) remains constant, but some other measurable dimension (duration) is changed. Behavior chaining, progressive time delay, and shaping across response topographies refer to other procedures.

14. A behavior analyst is teaching a client how to wash their hands. To ensure that the client learns the skill correctly, the behavior analyst breaks down the entire handwashing process into smaller steps, such as turning on the faucet, applying soap, rubbing hands together, and rinsing. Each step will be taught individually before linking them together into a complete sequence. What process has the behavior analyst used to break down the handwashing task into smaller, teachable steps?

A. Item analysis

B. Pretest

C. Task analysis (TA)

D. Task description

15. A behavior technician is teaching a client how to put on a jacket. The behavior technician starts by helping the client with the entire process but focuses on having the client independently zip the jacket at the end. Once the client can consistently zip the jacket on their own, the behavior technician works backward, teaching the client to insert their arms into the sleeves and then eventually to pick up the jacket. Which chaining method is the behavior technician using?

A. Backward chaining

B. Forward chaining

C. Total-task chaining

D. None of the above

16. A behavior technician is teaching a client how to make a sandwich. During each training session, the behavior technician helps the client with every step of the process, from taking out the bread to placing the sandwich on a plate. The behavior technician provides assistance as needed for each step and practices the entire sequence of making the sandwich during every session. Which chaining method is the behavior technician using?

A. Backward chaining

B. Forward chaining

C. Total-task chaining

D. None of the above

17. The brief pause between trials in discrete-trial teaching is referred to as the:

A. Between-trial interval

B. Intertrial interval

C. Postreinforcement pause

D. Posttrial pause

(*See answers on the next page.*)

14. C) Task analysis (TA)
In this scenario, the behavior analyst is using a TA to break down the complex behavior of handwashing into smaller, teachable steps, such as turning on the faucet, applying soap, and rinsing hands. A TA is necessary before behaviors can be linked in a chain to ensure each step is taught correctly. The other answer options focus on evaluating components or describing tasks, but do not involve breaking down complex behaviors into step-by-step teachable actions.

15. A) Backward chaining
In this scenario, the behavior technician is using backward chaining because they start by teaching the client the last step in the sequence (zipping the jacket) and gradually work backward to teach the earlier steps. Backward chaining is useful when the client can experience the completion of the task from the beginning, which can be reinforcing. The other answer options refer to different chaining methods or approaches that do not involve starting with the last behavior in the sequence.

16. C) Total-task chaining
In this scenario, the behavior technician is using total-task chaining because they guide the client through the entire sequence of making a sandwich during every session, providing assistance for each step as needed. Total-task chaining involves teaching all the steps of a task during each training session, rather than focusing on just one step at a time. Backward chaining focuses on teaching the last behavior in the chain first and then working backward, and forward chaining starts by teaching the first step in the sequence and gradually adding subsequent steps, neither of which involve training on all behaviors in the sequence during each session.

17. B) Intertrial interval
The brief pause between trials in discrete-trial teaching is referred to as the intertrial interval, which allows time to reset before the next trial begins. The other answer options refer to terms that are either incorrect or unrelated to the specific pause between discrete trials.

18. A behavior analyst is teaching a client to respond differently to the same instruction depending on the context. For example, when presented with the instruction "Touch red," the client is only reinforced for touching the red item if a blue item is also present. What type of discrimination is the behavior analyst teaching the client?

A. Complex

B. Conditional

C. Contingent

D. Simple

19. A teacher is helping a student learn to recognize shapes. The teacher shows the student a square and a circle, but only reinforces the student when they correctly point to the square. The student's response depends solely on the presence of the square. Which type of discrimination is the teacher establishing?

A. Complex

B. Conditional

C. Contingent

D. Simple

20. Guidelines for the effective implementation of a high-probability request sequence include all of the following, EXCEPT:

A. Present high-*p* requests that the client is currently able to comply with

B. Present each request slowly

C. Acknowledge compliance with each request

D. Use high-quality reinforcers

21. A behavior technician is working with a client who frequently engages in disruptive behaviors during class. The behavior technician implements a procedure where the client receives praise and a token for every 10 minutes they go without engaging in the disruptive behavior. However, if the disruptive behavior occurs, the behavior technician withholds reinforcement until the next interval passes without the behavior. Which reinforcement procedure is the behavior technician using?

A. DRA

B. DRD

C. DRO

D. DRL

22. A teacher is working with a student who raises their hand excessively during class. To reduce the frequency of this behavior, the teacher sets a limit where the student will earn extra recess time if they raise their hand no more than five times during a class period. If the student raises their hand more than five times, they do not receive the extra recess. Which procedure is the teacher using?

A. DRA

B. DRO

C. DRH

D. DRL

(*See answers on the next page.*)

18. **B) Conditional**
In this scenario, the behavior analyst is teaching a conditional discrimination because the client's response (touching the red item) is reinforced only when it is preceded by the presence of specific other stimuli (the blue item). This type of discrimination is conditional upon the presence of additional stimuli beyond the primary antecedent. The other answer options refer to other types of discriminations or concepts that do not involve the need for additional stimuli to influence the response.

19. **D) Simple**
In this scenario, the teacher is using simple discrimination because the student's response (pointing to the square) is reinforced based solely on the presence of a single antecedent (the square). There are no additional conditions or stimuli influencing the reinforcement. The other answer options involve more complex or conditional relationships that require additional stimuli or factors beyond the primary antecedent.

20. **B) Present each request slowly**
Requests are to be presented rapidly, not slowly. Presenting high-*p* requests that the client is currently able to comply with, acknowledging compliance with each request, and using high-quality reinforcers are guidelines to be followed for effectively implementing a high-probability request sequence.

21. **C) DRO**
In this scenario, the behavior technician is using DRO (differential reinforcement of other behavior) because the client receives reinforcement (praise and a token) for the absence of disruptive behavior for a predetermined time interval (10 minutes). Reinforcement is withheld if the problem behavior occurs during the interval. The other answer options (DRA [differential reinforcement of alternative behavior], DRD [differential reinforcement defined], DRL [differential reinforcement of low rates of behavior]) refer to other DR procedures and function as distractors.

22. **D) DRL**
In this scenario, the teacher is using DRL (differential reinforcement of low rates of behavior) because the student is reinforced (with extra recess time) only when the behavior of raising their hand occurs below a predetermined criterion (no more than five times during a class period). The other answer options (DRA [differential reinforcement of alternative behavior], DRO [differential reinforcement of other behavior], DRH [differential reinforcement of high rates of behavior]) refer to other DR procedures and function as distractors.

23. A behavior technician is working with a client who frequently engages in hitting others. As part of the behavior intervention plan, after each instance of hitting, the client is required to complete a series of jumping jacks as a consequence for the behavior. This physical exercise is not related to the behavior of hitting but is intended to reduce its occurrence. Which procedure is the behavior technician implementing?

A. Contingent exercise

B. Overcorrection

C. Response blocking

D. Response interruption and redirection

24. _______________ is a procedure that involves response blocking of stereotypic behavior, followed by redirection to engage in high probability behaviors.

A. Contingent exercise

B. Overcorrection

C. Response blocking

D. Response interruption and redirection (RIRD)

25. A teacher is implementing a behavior plan where each student can earn extra free time if they complete their homework for the week. The same homework completion criterion is set for all students, but only those who meet the criterion will receive the extra free time, regardless of how other students perform. Which type of group contingency is the teacher using?

A. Dependent

B. Independent

C. Interdependent

D. Whole

26. What type of group contingency calls for the delivery of reinforcement to all members of a group based on each member of the group achieving a performance criterion that is in place for all members of the group?

A. Dependent

B. Independent

C. Interdependent

D. Whole

(*See answers on the next page.*)

23. **A) Contingent exercise**
In this scenario, the behavior technician is using contingent exercise because the client is required to perform an unrelated physical activity (jumping jacks) after engaging in the target behavior (hitting). Contingent exercise involves making the client perform an aversive activity that is not functionally related to the problem behavior in order to reduce its occurrence. The other answer options refer to other punishment-based procedures and function as distractors.

24. **D) Response interruption and redirection (RIRD)**
RIRD is a procedure that involves response blocking of stereotypic behavior, followed by redirection to engage in high probability behaviors. Contingent exercise, overcorrection, and response blocking are other punishment-based procedures.

25. **B) Independent**
In this scenario, the teacher is using an independent group contingency because each student's reward (extra free time) is based solely on their individual achievement of the homework completion criterion, even though the same criterion is applied to the entire group. Only students who meet the criterion will receive the reinforcement, regardless of others' performance. The other answer options, two of which refer to other group contingencies, function as distractors.

26. **C) Interdependent**
An interdependent group contingency calls for the delivery of reinforcement to all members of a group based on each member of the group achieving a performance criterion that is in place for all members of the group. Dependent, independent, and whole, two of which refer to other group contingencies, function as distractors.

Selecting and Implementing Interventions

10

LEARNING OBJECTIVES

The following Test Content Outline (TCO) Tasks (Behavior Analyst Certification Board® [BACB®], 2024, p. 3) related to selecting and implementing interventions (H.1 through H.8) will serve as the learning objectives of this chapter:

- H.1 Develop intervention goals in observable and measurable terms.
- H.2 Identify and recommend interventions based on assessment results, scientific evidence, client preferences, and contextual fit (e.g., expertise required for implementation, cultural variables, environmental resources).
- H.3 Select socially valid alternative behavior to be established or increased when a target behavior is to be decreased.
- H.4 Plan for and attempt to mitigate possible unwanted effects when using reinforcement, extinction, and punishment procedures.
- H.5 Plan for and attempt to mitigate possible relapse of the target behavior.
- H.6 Make data-based decisions about procedural integrity.
- H.7 Make data-based decisions about the effectiveness of the intervention and the need for modification.
- H.8 Collaborate with others to support and enhance client services.

TASK H.1

Develop intervention goals in observable and measurable terms. Intervention goals must be stated in observable and measurable terms to allow for the accurate measurement of behavior change. To do this, behavior analysts must be able to (a) define target behaviors and (b) set criteria for behavior change.

DEFINING TARGET BEHAVIORS

An intervention goal may target a behavior that is functionally or topographically defined. The definitions should be (a) objective, (b) clear, and (c) complete.

Objective

This means the definition refers to observable aspects of the behavior (and environment, when applicable).

Clear

This means the definition presents with sufficient detail, leaving no room for confusion or doubt.

Complete

This means the definition accurately and concisely describes the target behavior, allowing for discrimination between occurrences and nonoccurrences.

ADDITIONAL NOTE(S)

Function-based definitions describe responses in terms of their effect on the environment (e.g., "any behavior that results in X") whereas topography-based definitions describe responses in terms of their form. Develop function-based definitions whenever possible.

SETTING CRITERIA FOR CHANGE

After a target behavior has been defined, there are two basic approaches to setting socially significant goals: (a) evaluate the performance of those who are highly competent in the behavior of interest and then use the normative data to set performance goals for those who are less competent; and (b) manipulate the behavior of interest so that different performance levels are observed and then determine which specific level produces the best results.

The format of a goal statement can include the following components: (a) condition, (b) name of client, (c) behavior to be increased or decreased, (d) criterion, (e) indication of how it will be measured, and (f) date by which it will be achieved.

- **Example (goal statement):** After recess, when asked to complete independent writing tasks (condition), Sam (name of client) will remain seated at his desk (behavior to be increased) at least 80% of the time (criterion) as measured by interval recording data (indication of how it will be measured) by 1/1/2026 (date by which it will be achieved).

TASK H.2

Identify and recommend interventions based on assessment results, scientific evidence, client preferences, and contextual fit (e.g., expertise required for implementation, cultural variables, environmental resources). The assessment process can provide an individualized client profile that informs intervention planning, including the selection of specific intervention strategies.

ASSESSMENT RESULTS

This refers to information about (a) the client's level of functioning (e.g., performance in communication skills), (b) the client's response to stimuli (i.e., preferences, reinforcers, and punishers), and (c) environmental variables maintaining behavior learned from indirect and/or direct assessment methods used. See Task C.2 (Chapter 5) for a review of direct and indirect measures of behavior. With assessment results in hand, consider antecedent and consequent intervention strategies when the goal is to (a) strengthen, maintain, or teach a new behavior; or (b) weaken a behavior.

When the Goal Is to Strengthen, Maintain, or Teach a New Behavior

Various strategies are employed to strengthen, maintain, or teach a new behavior. See Tasks under *Behavior-Change Procedures* (G.1 to G.15, and G.19 [Chapter 9]) for a review of relevant strategies.

When the Goal Is to Weaken Behavior

Use extinction to decrease the target behavior. This should be combined with reinforcement to strengthen desired/alternative behavior. Instructions/rules and punishment procedures may also be employed. See Tasks under *Behavior-Change Procedures* (G.2, G.5, G.10, and G.17 [Chapter 9]) for a review of relevant strategies.

ADDITIONAL NOTE(S)

Selected procedures must be conceptually consistent with behavioral principles.

BEST AVAILABLE SCIENTIFIC EVIDENCE

Refer to the scientific literature and consider its relevance and certainty.

Relevance

This refers to the extent to which the evidence corresponds to the problem in terms of (a) client characteristics, (b) the assessments and procedures used, (c) functions of behavior and expected outcomes, and (d) the context in which intervention is delivered.

Certainty

This refers to the extent to which the evidence supports the use of a procedure and rules out alternative explanations. It is based on two factors: (a) the methodological rigor of the evidence, and (b) consistency in replication of outcomes.

Strategies for identifying evidence to guide intervention selection decisions include searching for and reviewing (a) systematic reviews, (b) narrative reviews, (c) best practice guides, and (d) empirically supported practice guides of potential interventions.

ADDITIONAL NOTE(S)

Sometimes, the available scientific evidence lacks relevance and/or certainty, and behavior analysts will need to make selection decisions based on limited evidence. If this is the case, there will be an increased reliance on progress monitoring to determine whether any intervention is effective for a client. Behavior analysts must also aim to minimize risk of harm to the client, prioritize reinforcement procedures, and consider other relevant factors (e.g., risks, benefits, client preferences, feasibility, cost effectiveness) when identifying potential interventions.

Behavior analysts also consider client preferences, supporting environments, risks, constraints, and social validity when recommending intervention goals and procedures.

CLIENT PREFERENCES

When appropriate, collaborate with the client and/or caregivers on the selection of intervention goals and procedures. If the procedures are to be delivered by caregivers, take care to recommend those that caregivers can actually implement. In the event a client is unable or unwilling to clarify their preferences, maintain sensitivity to what may be the client's preference and adjust accordingly as indications of their preferences become known.

SUPPORTING ENVIRONMENTS

Select goals and procedures that are appropriate for the level of support available in the environment where treatment is to occur. There are a wide variety of environmental variables to consider, including physical space, materials, staffing, and abilities of individuals implementing the procedures.

RISKS

Take care in selecting goals and procedures that maximize benefits to the client and minimize, if not entirely eliminate, undesirable outcomes.

CONSTRAINTS

When developing intervention goals and procedures, consider factors that may inhibit successful implementation of a treatment program.

SOCIAL VALIDITY

Develop goals and procedures that target socially significant behaviors and are acceptable to clients. Also consider the social value of behavior change.

▶ TASK H.3

Select socially valid alternative behavior to be established or increased when a target behavior is to be decreased. When a problem behavior is targeted for reduction, consider supplementing reduction contingencies with reinforcement contingencies designed to support its decrease.

Select an acceptable alternative behavior that is (a) already in the client's behavioral repertoire, (b) within their current abilities, and (c) less effortful than the problem behavior.

It is also important to consider the maintaining consequences (i.e., function) of the problem behavior. If the function is acceptable as a reinforcer, then an alternative replacement behavior that produces the same consequences may be selected. If the function is unacceptable as a reinforcer, then an alternative behavior that does not serve as a "replacement" (i.e., does not produce the same consequences) may be selected.

- **Example (function that is typically acceptable as a reinforcer):** This could be social attention from caregivers.
- **Example (function that is unacceptable as a reinforcer):** This could be the effects of fire on flammable materials.

ADDITIONAL NOTE(S)

If the problem behavior is severe, occurs constantly or frequently, and has a significant impact on the environment, consider an alternative behavior that is incompatible with the problem behavior.

▶ TASK H.4

Plan for and attempt to mitigate possible unwanted effects when using reinforcement, extinction, and punishment procedures. When using reinforcement, extinction, and punishment procedures, behavior analysts must consider and plan for the possibility of unwanted effects.

REINFORCEMENT

Possible unwanted effects resulting from reinforcement-based procedures include:

- suppression of the desired response
- lack of feasibility for a client with little to no learning history with the reinforcement contingency

- an increase in problem behavior and a decrease in other desirable behaviors
- evoking aggression in others
- a lower-than-baseline response rate once reinforcement is removed
- excessive occurrence of the desired behavior

EXTINCTION

Possible unwanted effects resulting from extinction procedures include:

- emotional/aggressive reactions
- initial increase in the rate of the problem behavior (i.e., produce an extinction burst)
- initial increase in the magnitude of the problem behavior
- the reappearance of the problem behavior after it has been reduced/eliminated (i.e., spontaneous recovery)
- the reappearance of a previously extinguished problem behavior that was replaced by the targeted problem behavior

PUNISHMENT

Possible unwanted effects resulting from punishment-based procedures include:

- emotional/aggressive reactions
- desire for escape/avoidance
- behavioral contrast effects (i.e., change to the response rate of the problem behavior that may increase in other contexts)
- modeling of undesirable behavior
- overuse of punishment as it produces negative reinforcement for the individual using it

PLANNING FOR UNWANTED EFFECTS

General recommendations for planning for the possibility of unwanted effects include:

- Consider the possibility of unwanted effects that may interfere with an individual client's treatment.
- Monitor the target behavior(s) across contexts. If unwanted effects emerge, take appropriate actions to address them.
- Provide relevant individuals across contexts with necessary information/training to support the client's treatment.
- Monitor progress and adjust treatment as needed to minimize/eliminate risk and maximize benefit for the client.

TASK H.5

Plan for and attempt to mitigate possible relapse of the target behavior. Behavior analysts can plan for and mitigate possible relapse of target behaviors by (a) identifying high-risk situations, (b) reinforcing alternative behaviors, (c) using booster sessions, (d) developing a relapse prevention plan, (e) modifying the environment, (f) monitoring progress, and (g) involving stakeholders.

IDENTIFYING HIGH-RISK SITUATIONS

This involves recognizing specific contexts where the target behavior is most likely to reoccur, such as specific times, social settings, or environmental conditions. By anticipating these situations, tailored interventions can be developed to preemptively manage and mitigate potential triggers.

REINFORCING ALTERNATIVE BEHAVIORS

Reinforce desirable, alternative behaviors that provide clients with appropriate and effective ways to meet their needs. Strengthening alternative behaviors can help to reduce the likelihood of possible relapse of the target behavior.

USING BOOSTER SESSIONS

Conduct periodic review sessions that provide opportunities to revisit and reinforce learned behaviors, address new challenges, and adjust strategies as needed.

DEVELOPING A RELAPSE PREVENTION PLAN

Create a structured plan outlining specific steps to manage potential setbacks. The plan includes identifying early warning signs of relapse and strategies to address them effectively.

MODIFYING THE ENVIRONMENT

This involves altering the physical or social environment to reduce triggers that may lead to relapse. Environmental modifications create a more supportive and conducive environment for maintaining behavior changes.

MONITORING PROGRESS

Regular monitoring and data collection are vital because they provide objective information on the client's progress and early signs of relapse. Continuous data tracking allows for timely interventions and adjustments to the treatment plan.

INVOLVING STAKEHOLDERS

Engaging family members, teachers, and other significant individuals in the client's life and training them to implement and support the treatment plan helps to establish a unified approach to behavior management and maintain support across different environments, such as home, school, or community settings.

ADDITIONAL NOTE(S)

Effectively planning for and mitigating the relapse of target behaviors involves a multifaceted approach. Each strategy, from identifying high-risk situations to involving stakeholders, plays a crucial role in ensuring long-term behavior change. These components work together to create a robust framework for maintaining progress and preventing relapse, ultimately supporting clients in achieving sustained improvements in their behavior.

TASK H.6

Make data-based decisions about procedural integrity. Behavior analysts make data-based decisions about procedural integrity, which is essential for maintaining the fidelity of interventions and ensuring that the outcomes are valid and reliable.

MONITORING CLIENT PROGRESS

Behavior analysts monitor client progress to track and evaluate responsiveness to intervention as evidenced by behavior change over time. To do this, we can follow an eight-step process that involves (a) clearly operationalizing the behavior; (b) developing a progress monitoring plan; (c) selecting/creating data collection tools (i.e., measurement system); (d) collecting baseline data and defining goals; (e) setting intervention goals; (f) collecting progress monitoring data; (g) analyzing, summarizing, and visually presenting the data; and (h) evaluating and utilizing data for decision-making.

Clearly Operationalize the Behavior

Describe the client's target behavior in observable and measurable terms (e.g., frequency rate, duration, latency, topography), and write definitions that are objective, clear, and complete. Develop an operational definition that enables complete information about the behavior's occurrence and nonoccurrence to be gathered and intervention effectiveness to be accurately evaluated. See Task C.1 (Chapter 5) for a review of establishing operational definitions of behavior.

Develop a Progress Monitoring Plan

Prior to initiating the intervention, decide how client progress in the intervention will be evaluated and make a plan for data collection. Determine the type of data (e.g., frequency or rate, percentage, duration, latency) that will be collected, who will collect it, when and where it will be collected, how often it will be collected, and how often the data will be reviewed. Recall that behavior can be measured in terms of occurrence, time, and form and strength. See Tasks C.3 to C.5 (Chapter 5) for a review of measuring behavior in terms of occurrence and temporal dimensions.

Select or Create Data Collection Tools

Behavior analysts employ a variety of evidence-based methods for sampling procedures and collecting progress monitoring data, including direct measures, indirect measures, and product measures. See Task C.2 (Chapter 5) for a review of the distinction between these measures, and C.6 for a review of sampling procedures. Select a progress monitoring tool that is F.R.E.D.

- Flexible; it should be able to assess the behavior across all contexts in which it is exhibited.
- Repeatable; it should be able to be administered repeatedly within a brief time span.
- Efficient; it should be efficient for interventionists to use.
- Defensible; it should provide a reliable and valid measure of the client's behavior and be sensitive to client responsiveness to intervention.

Collect Baseline Data and Define Goals

Collect baseline data to determine the client's current level of functioning vis-a-vis the target behavior (i.e., rate/frequency or severity of behavior) prior to intervention. Conduct observations of the target behavior at a time and in a setting when the behavior is likely to occur. Observe the client for a minimum of 15 to 20 minutes on, at minimum, three to five instances to ensure the behavioral trend observed is stable. If the data from three observations is similar, use those three data points to describe the level of current performance. Adhere to any guidelines on the number of times baseline data should be collected that are provided by the particular assessment tool. Graph the client's baseline data to compare it with data from subsequent observations.

Set Intervention Goals or Benchmarks

Use baseline data to determine appropriate and measurable goals or benchmarks (e.g., rate of increase or decrease in behavior) for the client. Intervention goals should be based on the client's present level of performance, the targeted level of performance for the client, and the date by which the client is expected to achieve the targeted level of performance. See Task H.1 for a review of developing intervention goals in observable and measurable terms; and Task H.2 for a review of recommendations based on assessment results, scientific evidence, client preferences, and contextual fit.

Collect Progress Monitoring Data

Wait to initiate data collection until after the intervention is being fully implemented. Collect progress monitoring data during the intervention phase using the predetermined progress monitoring tool to repeatedly administer probes. Again, observation of behavior should be conducted at a time and in a setting when the behavior is likely to occur. Ensure sufficient progress monitoring data is collected to develop an accurate and reliable representation of the behavior and the degree to which change is evident. Collect progress monitoring data as frequently as needed to detect and document behavior change.

Analyze, Summarize, and Visually Represent the Data

Securely store client progress monitoring data (e.g., in a password-protected spreadsheet) and generate graphs to document and analyze progress monitoring data collection. Visually inspect summarized data and graphs and evaluate the results against the client's rate of progress toward achieving the predetermined goal. See Task C.10 (Chapter 5) for a review of graphing data, and Task C.11 (Chapter 5) for a review of interpreting data.

Evaluate and Utilize Data for Decision-Making

First, assess fidelity of implementation of the intervention; if the intervention was not implemented with fidelity, refrain from altering the intervention until intervention is implemented with fidelity. Based on the progress monitoring data collected, determine whether the client is responding to the intervention and adequate progress toward the goal(s) is being made.

- If progress is being made and the gap between the trend line and the goal line is closing, then continue the intervention. Determine how long the client must consistently exhibit the target behavior to begin fading the intervention.
- If insufficient progress is being made, then modify or intensify the intervention and/or assess fidelity of the intervention's implementation.
- If sufficient progress has been made and the client has reached their goal(s), then fade and discontinue the intervention.

MONITORING TREATMENT INTEGRITY

Behavior analysts monitor treatment integrity to ensure interventions are consistently implemented precisely as designed. Implementing an intervention with treatment integrity carefully avoids administration of extraneous, confounding variables which, in turn, enables one to correctly infer the relationship between an intervention and a client's behavior, whether behavior is changed or unchanged.

Best practices for monitoring and ensuring treatment integrity include:

- To avoid experimenter bias, implement interventions in a manner that does not privilege one treatment condition over another (e.g., the baseline condition over the treatment condition).
- To avoid treatment drift, consistently deliver all elements of the treatment throughout the duration of the intervention.
- Develop a comprehensive, precise, clear, and explicit operational definition of the treatment procedures across the four dimensions of a treatment. That is, operationally define what should be said (verbal dimension) and/or physically done (physical dimension) when (temporal dimension) and where (spatial dimension).

- Simplify the intervention as much as possible to make it easy to implement.
- Standardize the intervention to the greatest degree possible. This could involve creating materials to guide those implementing the intervention (e.g., script of the procedures, a manual, a video, etc.) and/or automating the intervention using, for example, a video, app, or learning management system.
- Provide the individual who will be implementing the intervention with sufficient training, modeling, practice, feedback, and supervision in the skills and knowledge they need to competently implement the intervention with integrity.
- Collect, analyze, and review treatment integrity data regularly throughout intervention implementation.

TASK H.7

Make data-based decisions about the effectiveness of the intervention and the need for modification. Behavior analysts adhere to the evidence-based practice model of professional decision-making. This means they rely on the "best available evidence" coupled with clinical expertise to determine whether an intervention is effective and if a treatment needs to be revised.

Behavior analysts examine and interpret graphed data when determining the effectiveness of an intervention and need for treatment revision (Table 10.1). See Task C.11 (Chapter 5) for a review of graph interpretation.

Table 10.1 Interpretation of Graphed Data for Determining Intervention Effectiveness

If the trendline shows that the behavior is...	Then...
Being performed at a level that meets or exceeds the criterion for mastery	Monitor its maintenance and move to the next target.
Improving at the expected rate	Continue as-is.
Improving at a lower rate than expected	Modify prompts and/or add instructional time.
Not improving	Check implementation fidelity. If fidelity is adequate, consider breaking the targeted skill down further. If fidelity is inadequate, provide additional coaching/ feedback to implementers.
Variable	Check implementation fidelity. If fidelity is adequate, modify the reinforcer and/or schedule or reinforcement. If fidelity is inadequate, provide additional coaching/ feedback to implementers.

ADDITIONAL NOTE(S)

If the last 10 data points show little to no improvement, discontinuation of the intervention may be considered.

TASK H.8

Collaborate with others to support and enhance client services. Behavior analysts collaborate with others to serve clients, which helps to foster consistency in intervention implementation, improves the generalization of skills across settings, and enhances the overall quality of services. This approach not only supports the client's progress but also facilitates a more comprehensive understanding of the client's needs and promotes the sharing of valuable insights and strategies.

COLLABORATIVE TEAMING

Collaborative teaming strategies include: (a) developing and using a shared language, (b) employing the same data collection process, (c) displaying results in an understandable way, and (d) working together to develop and implement a behavior-change program.

Developing and Using a Shared Language

The guiding question for this strategy is, "How do we talk about behavior?" Steps for implementation are: (a) create a list of common terms related to observation, assessment, and intervention; (b) define them with the team; and (c) use those that are understood by all.

Employing the Same Data Collection Process

The guiding questions for this strategy are, "What type of data is needed?" "Who will collect it?" and "What resources (e.g., data collection skills, feasible data collection system) are needed?" Steps for implementation are: (a) determine method of data collection; (b) identify those responsible for collecting data; and (c) identify resources needed for data collection.

Displaying Results in an Understandable Way

The guiding question for this strategy is, "How will assessment results be shared with the team?" Steps for implementation are: (a) graph data (and/or use tables for descriptive data) and (b) use understandable language when discussing the results.

Working Together to Develop and Implement a Behavior-Change Program

The guiding questions for this strategy are, "What is an acceptable intervention?" "Have all team members been involved in the development of the behavior-change program?" and "Have all team members received the necessary training to implement the program?" Steps for implementation are: (a) identify skills to be taught to the client, and (b) identify supports and skills needed for team members to successfully implement the program.

In the event another nonbehavioral provider recommends a nonbehavioral treatment, the behavior analyst must determine whether it poses a risk to the safety of the client.

Safety Risk Is Present

If this is the case, directly address the issue with the nonbehavioral provider. Also, if the behavior analyst is unfamiliar with the nonbehavioral treatment, it is recommended that they learn about it and reassess the risk to safety.

Safety Risk Is Absent

If this is the case, then consider the underlying behavioral principles of the treatment and ask, "Is success possible?" If the answer is "yes" or "no, but it doesn't interfere with the client's goals," then do not address the treatment as an issue. If the answer is "no, but it does interfere with the client's goals," then consider the use of the Checklist for Analyzing Proposed Treatments (CAPT) to determine if the impact to the client is enough to warrant possible confrontation with the nonbehavioral provider.

ADDITIONAL NOTE(S)

Readers are encouraged to seek out further readings on other skills (e.g., business skills, assertiveness, leadership) that contribute to effective collaboration with others.

▶ PRACTICE QUESTION

Zaynab, a BCBA, is training Adam, a behavior technician, to implement a new behavior-change procedure for a 6-year-old client in the home setting. Zaynab breaks down the procedure into five discrete steps and, during an observation of Adam in session with the client, records data on the steps Adam did and did not complete successfully. After the observation session, Zaynab provides vocal and written feedback to Adam about his performance. Which of the following best describes the purpose of the data collection procedure Zaynab employed?

A. To assess client progress and performance on the targeted skill
B. To determine the environmental events affecting the behavior technician's performance
C. To evaluate treatment integrity
D. To calculate interobserver agreement

Before moving on to the following section for the solution, we recommend that you provide a brief explanation for the answer option you selected here:

____

____

When you're ready, move on to the next section for the solution!

Practice Question Breakdown

Step 1: Examine the question

The question calls for the identification of the purpose of the data collection procedure that Zaynab was described using (breaking down the steps of a procedure to be implemented by a behavior technician, and recording which steps were completed and which were missed).

Step 2: Analyze the answer options

A. Zaynab is recording data on the behavior technician's performance, not the client's performance. This answer option is a distractor.
B. In order for there to be any sort of evaluation of the effects of environmental events on personnel performance, data on these antecedent and consequent events must be gathered. Zaynab only recorded whether the steps of a procedure occurred. This answer option is a distractor.
C. Recording whether the steps of a procedure occurred is a method of collecting treatment integrity data. This information informs behavior analysts about the extent to which a given procedure is implemented as intended. This just might be the answer!
D. Interobserver agreement indicates the level of agreement between two or more independent observers recording the same event. This answer option is a distractor.

Step 3: Select the best answer

Among the four answer options presented, answer C (To evaluate treatment integrity) appears to be the best answer.

▶ CONCLUSION

In this chapter, we focused on TCO Tasks related to selecting and implementing interventions. This includes information on developing observable and measurable intervention goals; using assessment results and science to identify potential interventions; tailoring intervention goals and strategies to clients; selecting alternative behaviors; planning for unwanted effects;

progress monitoring; making data-based decisions; and collaborative teaming. This chapter's emphasis on selecting and implementing interventions nicely complements Chapter 9's focus on behavior-change procedures.

REFERENCE

Behavior Analyst Certification Board. (2024). *BCBA test content outline* (6th ed.). Author. https://www.bacb.com/wp-content/bcba-outline-6thEd

BIBLIOGRAPHY

Balsam, P. D., & Bondy, A. S. (1983). The negative side effects of reward. *Journal of Applied Behavior Analysis, 16*(3), 283–296. https://doi.org/10.1901/jaba.1983.16-283

Behavior Analyst Certification Board. (2012). *Guidelines, health plan coverage of applied behavior analysis treatment for autism spectrum disorder*. Author.

Brodhead, M. T. (2015). Maintaining professional relationships in an interdisciplinary setting: Strategies for navigating nonbehavioral treatment recommendations for individuals with autism. *Behavior Analysis in Practice, 8*(1), 70–78. https://doi.org/10.1007/s40617-015-0042-7

Brodhead, M. T., & Truckenmiller, A. (2021). Proof-of-concept evaluation of a decision-making algorithm. *Behavior Analysis: Research and Practice, 21*(1), 84–89. https://doi.org/10.1037/bar0000207

Christ, T. J., Riley-Tillman, T. C., & Chafouleas, S. M. (2009). Foundation for the development and use of direct behavior rating (DBR) to assess and evaluate student behavior. *Assessment for Effective Intervention, 34*(4), 201–213. https://doi.org/10.1177/1534508409340390

Cipani, E., & Schock, K. M. (2010). *Functional behavioral assessment, diagnosis, and treatment: A complete system for education and mental health settings*. Springer Publishing Company.

Cooper, J. O., Heron, T. E., & Heward, W. L. (2020). *Applied behavior analysis* (3rd ed.). Pearson Education.

Crone, D. A., Hawken, L. S., & Horner, R. H. (2010). *Responding to problem behavior in schools: The behavior education program*. Guilford Press.

Deno, S. L. (1997). Whether thou goest… Perspectives on progress monitoring. *Issues in educating students with disabilities* (1st ed., Vol. 16, pp. 213–235). Routledge.

Fuchs, L. S., & Fuchs, D. (2001). *What is scientifically-based research on progress monitoring?* National Center on Student Progress Monitoring.

Johnston, J. M. (2006). "Replacing" problem behavior: An analysis of tactical alternatives. *The Behavior Analyst, 29*(1), 1–11. https://doi.org/10.1007/BF03392114

Johnston, J. M., & Pennypacker, H. S. (1993). *Strategies and tactics of behavioral research* (2nd ed.). Erlbaum.

Kipfmiller, K. J., Brodhead, M. T., Wolfe, K., LaLonde, K., Sipila, E. S., Bak, M. S., & Fisher, M. H. (2019). Training front-line employees to conduct visual analysis using a clinical decision-making model. *Journal of Behavioral Education, 28*(3), 301–322. https://doi.org/10.1007/s10864-018-09318-1

Moulton, S., von der Embse, N., Kilgus, S., & Drymond, M. (2019). Building a better behavior progress monitoring tool using maximally efficient items. *School Psychology, 34*(6), 695–705. https://doi.org/10.1037/spq0000334

Sanetti, L. M. H., Kratochwill, T. R., Collier-Meek, M. A., & Long, A. C. J. (2014). *PRIME: Planning realistic implementation and maintenance by educators*. Neag School of Education, University of Connecticut.

Slocum, T. A., Detrich, R., Wilczynski, S. M., Spencer, T. D., Lewis, T., & Wolfe, K. (2014). The evidence-based practice of applied behavior analysis. *The Behavior Analyst, 37*(1), 41–56. https://doi.org/10.1007/s40614-014-0005-2

Wahman, C. L., Light-Shriner, C. L., & Pizzella, D. M. (2020). Effective teaming to bridge support for children with challenging behavior. *Young Exceptional Children, 25*(1), 15–29. https://doi.org/10.1177/1096250620950249

Wolf, M. M. (1978). Social validity: The case for subjective measurement or how applied behavior analysis is finding its heart. *Journal of Applied Behavior Analysis, 11*(2), 203–214. https://doi.org/10.1901/jaba.1978.11-203

Wolfe, K., McCammon, M. N., LeJeune, L. M., & Holt, A. K. (2021). Training preservice practitioners to make data-based instructional decisions. *Journal of Behavioral Education, 32*, 1–20. https://doi.org/10.1007/s10864-021-09439-0

KNOWLEDGE CHECK

1. A teacher writes a definition for a student's off-task behavior as "Any instance where the student is not working on their assignment." The definition is considered clear and complete, but the behavior analyst expresses concern that the definition might not be objective enough for consistent measurement. What is the issue with this definition?

   A. It is not clear, because "working" is difficult to define.

   B. It is not complete, because it doesn't specify the duration of "off-task" behavior.

   C. It is not objective, because "not working" can be interpreted differently by different observers.

   D. It is not concise, because it adds unnecessary details.

2. A teacher writes a behavior definition for a student's target behavior as "Any time the student throws objects when frustrated." A behavior analyst revises the definition to "Any instance in which the student throws objects to escape a difficult task." The revised definition is intended to be more function-based for the purpose of developing an effective intervention. Why is the revised definition considered function-based?

   A. It emphasizes the observable form of the behavior.

   B. It provides a reason behind the behavior.

   C. It focuses on the duration and intensity of the behavior.

   D. It tracks how often the behavior occurs.

3. A teacher is asked to define a student's target behavior for a behavior intervention plan. Instead of using vague terms like *disruptive behavior*, the teacher writes, "Any time a student stands up from their chair during class instruction without permission." What aspect of the definition will help ensure consistency among different observers?

   A. It is concise.

   B. It focuses on the function of the behavior.

   C. It describes a time-bound event.

   D. It includes objective and measurable criteria.

4. Which of the following is NOT a necessary component of a behavior goal statement?

   A. Criterion to be met

   B. Date by which it will be achieved

   C. Nonexample of the target behavior

   D. Target behavior to be increased or decreased

5. To set socially significant behavior-change goals:

   A. Evaluate the performance of those who are highly competent in the behavior and then use the normative data to set performance goals.

   B. Manipulate the behavior so that different performance levels are observed and then determine which specific level produces the best results.

   C. A or B

   D. None of the above

(*See answers on the next page.*)

1. **C) It is not objective, because "not working" can be interpreted differently by different observers.**
   In this scenario, the issue with the definition is that it is not objective enough because the phrase "not working" can be interpreted differently by different observers. Without specifying clear, observable criteria for what "not working" looks like (e.g., "The student is looking away from the assignment for more than 5 consecutive seconds"), the definition can lead to inconsistent measurement. The other options are incorrect because the definition is clear and complete but lacks the objectivity needed for reliable data collection.

2. **B) It provides a reason behind the behavior.**
   The revised definition is considered function-based because it provides a reason behind the behavior (escaping a difficult task), which helps to address the function or motivation driving the behavior. Function-based definitions focus on why the behavior occurs, guiding more effective interventions. The other options are incorrect because they emphasize the form, duration, or frequency of the behavior, which are not the focus of function-based definitions.

3. **D) It includes objective and measurable criteria.**
   In this scenario, the teacher's definition of the target behavior ensures consistency among different observers because it includes objective and measurable criteria. By clearly describing the observable action ("Any time a student stands up from their chair during class instruction without permission"), the teacher eliminates ambiguity, allowing all observers to consistently recognize and measure the behavior. The other answer options do not ensure consistency or provide the necessary clarity for accurate measurement.

4. **C) Nonexample of the target behavior**
   The criterion to be met, date by which it will be achieved, and target behavior to be increased or decreased are necessary components of a behavior goal statement. Nonexamples of the target behavior are sometimes included in definitions, but they are not a required component of goal statements.

5. **C) A or B**
   Behavior analysts may evaluate the performance of those who are highly competent in the behavior and then use the normative data to set performance goals, or they can manipulate the behavior so that different performance levels are observed and then determine which specific level produces the best results to set socially significant behavior-change goals.

6. When assessing the relevance of the scientific evidence, each of the following are considered in relation to the problem of interest, EXCEPT:

A. Client characteristics

B. The assessment procedures used

C. The context in which intervention is delivered

D. The forms of behavior and expected outcomes

7. When assessing the certainty of the scientific evidence, each of the following are considered, EXCEPT:

A. The consistency in replication of the outcomes

B. The functions of behavior and expected outcomes

C. The methodological rigor of the evidence

D. Both B and C

8. A behavior analyst implements a punishment procedure to reduce a client's hand-flapping behavior in one environment. While the behavior decreases in that environment, the client begins engaging in the same behavior more frequently in other environments where the punishment is not used, such as during free play time at home. What unwanted effect of punishment is the behavior analyst observing?

A. Evoking escape or avoidance

B. Overuse due to negative reinforcement

C. Behavioral contrast

D. Modeling of undesirable behavior

9. A teacher begins reinforcing a student's on-task behavior with tokens, but after a while, the student starts to exhibit an increase in off-task behaviors, such as talking to peers and fidgeting, while the frequency of on-task behavior decreases. What unwanted effect of reinforcement is the teacher observing?

A. Increase in the rate of problem behavior and decrease in other desirable behavior

B. Evoking aggression in others

C. Suppressing the desired response

D. Not being feasible for a client with little learning history

10. Which of the following is an unwanted effect of extinction?

A. It may be overused as it produces negative reinforcement for the individual using it.

B. It may initially increase the magnitude of the problem behavior.

C. It may produce behavioral contrast effects.

D. It may result in too much of the desired behavior.

(*See answers on the next page.*)

6. **D) The forms of behavior and expected outcomes**
The relevance of the scientific evidence refers to the extent to which it corresponds to the problem of interest in terms of client characteristics; the assessments and procedures used; functions of behavior and expected outcomes, rather than forms of behavior and expected outcomes; and the context in which intervention is delivered.

7. **B) The functions of behavior and expected outcomes**
The functions of behavior and expected outcomes are considered when assessing the relevance of scientific evidence. The consistency in replication of the outcomes and the methodological rigor of the evidence include considerations for assessing the certainty of the scientific evidence.

8. **C) Behavioral contrast**
In this scenario, the behavior analyst is witnessing behavioral contrast, which occurs when a behavior decreases in one setting where punishment is applied but increases in another setting where the punishment is not used. The hand-flapping behavior decreases in the environment where punishment is implemented but increases during free play at home, demonstrating this unwanted effect. The overuse of punishment, because it produces negative reinforcement for the individual using it, is a known and unwanted effect of punishment. The other answer options refer to unwanted effects of reinforcement but do not apply to this situation.

9. **A) Increase in the rate of problem behavior and decrease in other desirable behavior**
In this scenario, the teacher is observing an increase in the rate of problem behavior and a decrease in other desirable behavior. This occurs when reinforcement, intended to increase on-task behavior, inadvertently strengthens other problem behaviors, such as talking to peers or fidgeting, while reducing the targeted positive behavior (on-task behavior). The other answer options refer to unwanted effects of reinforcement but do not apply to this situation.

10. **B) It may initially increase the magnitude of the problem behavior.**
An initial increase in the magnitude of the problem behavior is an unwanted effect of extinction. The other answer options (it may be overused as it produces negative reinforcement for the individual using it, it may produce behavioral contrast effects, it may result in too much of the desired behavior) describe unwanted effects of reinforcement or punishment.

11. A behavior analyst is working with a 9-year-old client with autism spectrum disorder (ASD) who has successfully learned to use a communication device to express their needs and reduce frustration. The family is planning a vacation that involves a lot of travel and new environments. Which of the following strategies should the behavior analyst recommend?

A. Use a different communication method during the vacation

B. Rely on verbal communication alone during the vacation

C. Leave the communication device at home to evaluate how the client will cope without it

D. Bring the communication device and integrate its use into the vacation activities

12. A behavior analyst is working with a client for whom the most applicable interventions are based on limited scientific evidence. Given the uncertainty in the scientific evidence, what will the behavior analyst primarily rely on to guide future decisions about the intervention if it is implemented?

A. Caregiver interviews

B. Positive reinforcement-based procedures

C. Progress monitoring

D. Standardized testing

13. A behavior analyst is beginning to work with a client who frequently engages in out-of-seat behavior during class. Before developing an intervention plan or setting goals, the behavior analyst works with the teacher to define the behavior clearly as "Any instance in which the client leaves their seat during instruction without permission." Which of the following is the behavior analyst doing with the teacher?

A. Clearly operationalizing the behavior

B. Collecting baseline data and defining goals

C. Developing a progress monitoring plan

D. Selecting or creating data collection tools

14. A teacher and behavior analyst are preparing to address a student's off-task behavior. Before implementing any interventions, the behavior analyst spends a week observing the student and taking notes on how often the off-task behavior occurs during independent work. The teacher and behavior analyst plan to use this information to set appropriate targets for behavior improvement. What step in monitoring client progress are the teacher and behavior analyst engaging in?

A. Clearly operationalizing the behavior

B. Collecting baseline data and defining goals

C. Developing a progress monitoring plan

D. Selecting or creating data collection tools

(See answers on the next page.)

11. **D) Bring the communication device and integrate its use into the vacation activities**
Bringing the communication device and integrating its use into vacation activities allows the client to continue to use a familiar and effective tool to communicate, reducing the risk of frustration and relapse in challenging new environments. This approach maintains the consistency of the communication method that has already proven successful. The other answer options could disrupt the client's progress, increase frustration, and hinder their ability to express their needs effectively during the vacation.

12. **C) Progress monitoring**
The behavior analyst will primarily rely on progress monitoring because, when scientific evidence is limited, closely tracking the client's behavior and response to the intervention allows for data-driven decisions about whether to continue, modify, or discontinue the intervention. The other answer options can provide useful information, but they don't offer the same continuous feedback on the effectiveness of the intervention as progress monitoring does.

13. **A) Clearly operationalizing the behavior**
In this scenario, the behavior analyst is clearly operationalizing the behavior by working with the teacher to define the target behavior in specific, observable terms ("Any instance in which the client leaves their seat during instruction without permission"). This is the crucial first step in the process of monitoring client progress, as it ensures that the behavior is well-defined and measurable. The other options, such as collecting baseline data, developing a monitoring plan, or selecting data collection tools, are steps that occur later, after the behavior has been clearly defined.

14. **B) Collecting baseline data and defining goals**
In this scenario, the teacher and behavior analyst are collecting baseline data by observing and recording the student's off-task behavior over the course of a week before setting any goals or starting interventions. This step is essential for determining the current level of the behavior targeted for change and helps establish a benchmark for future progress. The other answer options refer to steps that occur before or after the baseline data collection and function as distractors.

15. A behavior analyst has been tracking a client's disruptive behavior during class for 2 weeks, noting that the behavior occurs an average of 10 times per class period. What can the behavior analyst do next based on the baseline data collected about the student's disruptive behavior?

    A. Set an initial intervention goal

    B. Select data collection tools

    C. Create a progress monitoring plan

    D. Define the target behavior

16. A behavior analyst is working with a client who frequently yells to get the teacher's attention. The behavior analyst suggests replacing the yelling behavior with raising their hand, a behavior the client already knows how to perform and is within their current skill level. What characteristic of an alternative behavior is the behavior analyst considering?

    A. The alternative behavior is within the teacher's control.

    B. The alternative behavior is more effortful than the problem behavior.

    C. The alternative behavior requires prompting from peers.

    D. The alternative behavior is already in the client's behavioral repertoire.

17. When evaluating progress monitoring data, it's observed that the gap between the trend line and the goal line is closing. This suggests:

    A. The client is making progress.

    B. The client is not making progress.

    C. The intervention should be modified.

    D. None of the above

18. When evaluating progress monitoring data, it's observed that the gap between the trend line and the goal line is closing. This suggests:

    A. The intervention should be discontinued.

    B. The intervention should be modified.

    C. The intervention should continue.

    D. None of the above

19. If progress monitoring data reveals sufficient progress has been made and the client has reached their goal, then:

    A. Assess the fidelity of the intervention's implementation

    B. Continue the intervention to support the maintenance of the behavior change

    C. Fade and discontinue the intervention

    D. Intensify the intervention for further gains

(*See answers on the next page.*)

15. **A) Set an initial intervention goal**
    The behavior analyst can use the baseline data to set an initial intervention goal based on the current frequency of the disruptive behavior (10 times per class period). Baseline data provides critical information about the starting point of the behavior, allowing the analyst to establish realistic and measurable goals. The other answer options are steps that occur earlier in the progress monitoring process and function as distractors.

16. **D) The alternative behavior is already in the client's behavioral repertoire.**
    In this scenario, the behavior analyst is selecting an alternative behavior (raising their hand) that is already in the client's behavioral repertoire, meaning the client knows how to perform the behavior and can do so without needing to learn a completely new skill. This increases the likelihood that the client will adopt the alternative behavior more easily. The other answer options do not apply to this situation and function as distractors.

17. **A) The client is making progress.**
    The closing of the gap between the trend line and the goal line is an indication of progress. The other answer options (the client is not making progress, the intervention should be modified) do not provide an accurate interpretation of the described data and serve as distractors.

18. **C) The intervention should continue.**
    The closing of the gap between the trend line and the goal line, which offers evidence of progress, indicates that the intervention should continue. The other answer options (the intervention should be discontinued and the intervention should be modified) do not describe recommended courses of action.

19. **C) Fade and discontinue the intervention**
    If progress monitoring data reveals sufficient progress has been made and the client has reached their goal, then the recommended next step is to fade and discontinue the intervention. The other answer options (assess the fidelity of the intervention's implementation, continue the intervention to support the maintenance of the behavior change, intensify the intervention for further gains) do not describe recommended courses of action.

20. Recommended practices for monitoring and ensuring treatment integrity include each of the following, EXCEPT:

A. Collect, analyze, and review treatment integrity data regularly

B. Deliver most of the elements of the treatment as consistently as possible throughout the duration of the intervention

C. Simplify the intervention as much as possible

D. Provide the implementers of the intervention with sufficient training and support

(*See answers on the next page.*)

20. **B) Deliver most of the elements of the treatment as consistently as possible throughout the duration of the intervention**
The aim is to consistently implement all elements of the treatment, rather than just some of them, throughout the time in which it is to be implemented to avoid treatment drift. The other answer options (collect, analyze, and review treatment integrity data regularly; simplify the intervention as much as possible; provide the implementers of the intervention with sufficient training and support) are recommended practices for monitoring and ensuring treatment integrity.

Personnel Supervision and Management

11

LEARNING OBJECTIVES

The following Test Content Outline (TCO) Tasks (Behavior Analyst Certification Board®, 2024, p. 3) related to supervision and management (I-1 through I-8) will serve as the learning objectives of this chapter:

- I.1 Identify the benefits of using behavior-analytic supervision (e.g., improved client outcomes, improved staff performance and retention).
- I.2 Identify and apply strategies for establishing effective supervisory relationships (e.g., executing supervisor-supervisee contracts, establishing clear expectations, giving and accepting feedback).
- I.3 Identify and implement methods that promote equity in supervision practices.
- I.4 Select supervision goals based on an assessment of the supervisee's skills, cultural variables, and the environment.
- I.5 Identify and apply empirically validated and culturally responsive performance management procedures (e.g., modeling, practice, feedback, reinforcement, task clarification, manipulation of response effort).
- I.6 Apply a function-based approach (e.g., performance diagnostics) to assess and improve supervisee behavior.
- I.7 Make data-based decisions about the efficacy of supervisory practices.

TASK I.1

Identify the benefits of using behavior-analytic supervision (e.g., improved client outcomes, improved staff performance and retention). Behavior-analytic supervision is a critical component of effective service delivery, providing numerous benefits that enhance both the performance of supervisees and, in turn, client outcomes.

BENEFITS OF USING BEHAVIOR-ANALYTIC SUPERVISION

These include (a) improved client outcomes, (b) improved staff performance, (c) increased staff retention, (d) enhanced professional development, (e) consistency and fidelity of interventions, and (f) maintenance of ethical practice.

Improved Client Outcomes

This is a primary benefit of behavior-analytic supervision. Through regular monitoring and feedback, supervisors can ensure that interventions are delivered correctly and are effective. This oversight allows for the early identification of any issues or deviations from the treatment plan, facilitating timely adjustments. As a result, clients are more likely to experience significant and sustained behavior changes, leading to better overall progress and goal achievement.

Improved Staff Performance

Supervisors provide ongoing training and support to staff, helping them develop and refine their behavior-analytic skills. This continuous professional development fosters a deeper understanding of behavioral principles and procedures, leading to more competent and confident practitioners. In addition, supervisors use performance data to provide objective feedback, reinforcing effective practices and addressing areas for improvement. This data-driven approach promotes accountability and encourages staff to strive for excellence in their work.

Increased Staff Retention

When staff feel supported and valued through consistent supervision, they are more likely to be satisfied with their job and remain with the organization. Supervisors who offer constructive feedback, recognize achievements, and provide opportunities for professional growth create a positive work environment that fosters loyalty and reduces turnover. This stability also benefits clients as they receive more consistent care from staff.

Enhanced Professional Development

Behavior-analytic supervision contributes to the fostering of a workplace environment that emphasizes continuous learning and professional development. Supervisors promote supervisees' engagement in ongoing education, facilitate skill-building activities, and provide regular and individualized feedback to help supervisees improve their knowledge and skills. This not only enhances the competencies of practitioners but also aids in establishing a culture of professional growth and excellence that ultimately benefits clients and the organization as a whole.

Consistency and Fidelity of Interventions

Behavior-analytic supervision can help to ensure that procedures are implemented consistently and with high fidelity. Supervisors set clear guidelines and protocols for intervention implementation, closely monitoring adherence to these standards. Regular observation and feedback sessions help identify and correct any deviations, ensuring that the interventions are delivered as designed. This is important for enhancing the reliability of outcomes.

Maintenance of Ethical Practice

Behavior-analytic supervision serves to provide oversight and guidance on ethical practice. Supervisors monitor the work of their supervisees, provide timely and corrective feedback, and offer guidance to ensure adherence to the standards of the Ethics Code. In addition, supervisors can serve as role models, exemplifying ethical behavior in their professional conduct.

ADDITIONAL NOTE(S)

Ineffective supervision poses several potential risks, including:

- degradation in the quality of behavior-analytic services
- supervisees developing faulty or inadequate professional skills, leading to poor performance
- negative impacts on client outcomes
- hindrance to the growth of the field of behavior analysis
- actionable violations of the Ethics Code

TASK I.2

Identify and apply strategies for establishing effective supervisory relationships (e.g., executing supervisor-supervisee contracts, establishing clear expectations, giving and accepting feedback). Key strategies for establishing effective supervisory relationships include (a) executing supervisor-supervisee contracts, (b) establishing clear expectations, (c) giving and accepting feedback, (d) building trust and rapport, (e) modeling professional behavior, (f) encouraging professional development, and (g) reviewing and adjusting the supervisory plan.

EXECUTING SUPERVISOR-SUPERVISEE CONTRACTS

This involves formalizing the supervisory relationship through a written agreement—a *supervision contract*. This contract should outline the roles and responsibilities of both parties, the frequency and duration of supervision meetings, and the goals and objectives of the supervision. The contract also serves as a reference point for resolving any disputes or misunderstandings that may arise.

ESTABLISHING CLEAR EXPECTATIONS

Clear expectations for the supervisor and supervisee should be communicated at the outset of a supervisory relationship. They serve to help prevent confusion and ensure that both parties are aligned in their goals and methods and should be documented in the supervision contract. For supervisors and supervisees, expectations may include and are not limited to:

- reviewing the Behavior Analyst Certification Board (BACB) experience standards
- adhering to the Ethics Code
- participating in supervision activities
- following the supervision schedule
- completing and maintaining required documentation

ADDITIONAL NOTE(S)

A strategy for enhancing a supervisee's professional behavior and providing the supervisor with an opportunity to better plan for an upcoming supervision meeting is to have the supervisee provide a draft agenda 24 hours in advance (Box 11.1).

Box 11.1 Example of a Draft Agenda

1. Check-in (5 min)
2. Discuss behavior-analytic activities in the past week (10 min)
3. Review progress on assignments and identify any problems along with possible solutions (15 min)
4. Discuss/practice previously reviewed or new competencies from the Task List (15 min)
5. Review feedback on performance (5 min)
6. Complete supervision documentation (5 min)
7. Final questions/comments (5 min)

The supervisor can also set expectations for notetaking, deadlines for assigned activities, and systems for managing supervision documentation.

GIVING AND ACCEPTING FEEDBACK

This is vital for continuous improvement and professional growth. Supervisors should provide constructive feedback that is specific, actionable, and supportive. Similarly, supervisees should be open to receiving feedback and willing to implement suggestions for improvement. Effective feedback should be timely, related to specific behaviors or skills, and balanced in terms of positive reinforcement and areas for growth.

BUILDING TRUST AND RAPPORT

This is essential for establishing an effective supervisory relationship. Supervisors should demonstrate empathy, active listening, and respect for the supervisee's perspectives and experiences. This can be achieved by taking the time to understand the supervisee's goals, challenges, and professional background, thereby fostering a supportive and collaborative environment. One practical strategy for this would be to schedule regular check-in meetings to discuss the supervisee's progress and any concerns they may have, ensuring they feel valued and heard.

MODELING PROFESSIONAL BEHAVIOR

Supervisors should exemplify the professional and ethical standards expected in the field. By modeling appropriate behavior, they set a standard for supervisees to emulate. This includes demonstrating professionalism and adhering to the BACB Ethics Code.

ENCOURAGING PROFESSIONAL DEVELOPMENT

This includes recommending relevant readings, attending workshops or conferences, and participating in professional organizations. By fostering a culture of continuous learning, supervisors help supervisees stay current with best practices and emerging research in behavior analysis.

REVIEWING AND ADJUSTING THE SUPERVISORY PLAN

Supervision should be a dynamic process that evolves based on the supervisee's progress and changing needs. Regularly reviewing and adjusting the supervisory plan ensures that it remains relevant and effective. This might involve setting new goals, introducing more advanced competencies, or adjusting the frequency of supervision meetings.

▶ PRACTICE QUESTION

You are a new trainee, working at an in-home applied behavioral analyst (ABA) agency. As part of this job, you will be acquiring fieldwork experience under the supervision of a BCBA® to meet BACB certification requirements. You meet with your new supervisor to establish a supervision contract that outlines the expectations of the professional relationship. What specific expectations are important to include in this written document?

A. Adhering to the Ethics Code
B. Following the supervision schedule
C. Completing and maintaining required documentation
D. All of the above

Before moving on to the following section for the solution, we recommend that you provide a brief explanation for the answer option you selected here:

____

____

When you're ready, move on to the next section for the solution!

Practice Question Breakdown

Step 1: Examine the question

The question calls for you to examine a supervision contract that outlines the expectations of the professional relationship between you and your BCBA supervisor. You are asked to identify the specific expectations that should be included in the written document.

Step 2: Analyze the answer options

A. This answer is an important expectation. Reviewing, discussing, and adhering to the Ethics Code for Behavior Analysts are essential to the professional requirements of the job and should be included in all supervision contracts.
B. This answer is an important expectation. Following a set supervision schedule from the initiation of the supervision relationship allocates time for this important activity to occur and should be included in all supervision contracts.
C. This answer is an important expectation. Completing and maintaining required documentation for supervision is not only important to ensure your supervisee is progressing and learning new skills, but also to meet BACB certification requirements.
D. This answer includes all of the previously listed answer options, which refer to important expectations that should be written into all supervision contracts. This is it!

Step 3: Select the best answer

Among the four answer options presented, answer D (All of the above) appears to be the best answer.

TASK I.3

Identify and implement methods that promote equity in supervision practices. Equity in supervision ensures that all supervisees receive the support and opportunities they need to succeed, regardless of their individual backgrounds or characteristics. Methods for promoting equity in supervision practices include (a) developing cultural competence, (b) providing individualized support, (c) communicating with transparency, (d) conducting regular evaluations, (e) addressing systemic barriers, and (f) promoting inclusivity.

DEVELOPING CULTURAL COMPETENCE

This involves supervisors developing and demonstrating an understanding and appreciation of diverse cultural backgrounds and experiences. Supervisors should make continuous efforts to enhance their cultural competence, engage in self-reflection to identify any biases they may hold, and use this understanding to inform their supervisory practices.

- **Example:** A supervisor takes time to learn about a supervisee's cultural background and consider how cultural factors may influence their work and interactions with clients. By doing so, the supervisor can tailor their guidance to be culturally relevant and sensitive.

PROVIDING INDIVIDUALIZED SUPPORT

This involves delivering support tailored to the unique needs and strengths of each supervisee. Supervisors should assess the individual learning styles, professional goals, and personal circumstances of their supervisees and adjust their supervisory approach accordingly.

- **Example:** A supervisee who is a working parent might benefit from flexible supervision meeting times, while another who is new to the field might need more frequent feedback and guidance on foundational skills.

COMMUNICATING WITH TRANSPARENCY

This involves maintaining open, honest, and respectful communication between supervisors and supervisees, which helps to build trust and ensures that supervisees feel heard and valued. Supervisors should encourage supervisees to share their experiences, challenges, and feedback openly.

- **Example:** Regular check-in meetings can be scheduled to discuss the supervisee's progress, address any concerns, and adjust the supervisory plan as needed.

Communicating with transparency also involves clearly articulating expectations, goals, and criteria for evaluation, ensuring that supervisees understand what is required for their professional development.

CONDUCTING REGULAR EVALUATIONS

This involves continuously assessing and adjusting supervisory practices to promote equity. Supervisors should use data and feedback to evaluate the effectiveness of their supervision and make any necessary changes. This could involve soliciting feedback from supervisees, reviewing supervision outcomes, and reflecting on their own practices.

ADDRESSING SYSTEMIC BARRIERS

This involves recognizing and addressing systemic barriers that may impact supervisees' opportunities and experiences. Supervisors should be aware of factors such as institutional biases, resource disparities, and socioeconomic challenges that may affect supervisees.

- **Example:** Seeing that a supervisee lacks access to necessary resources such as professional development materials or transportation to training sites, a supervisor advocates for institutional support and searches for alternative solutions.

PROMOTING INCLUSIVITY

This involves creating an inclusive supervisory environment where all supervisees feel welcome and valued. Supervisors should actively promote inclusivity by recognizing and celebrating diversity within their supervision team. This can be achieved by incorporating diverse perspectives into discussions, fostering a culture of respect and inclusion, and ensuring that all supervisees have a voice in decision-making processes.

TASK I.4

Select supervision goals based on an assessment of the supervisee's skills, cultural variables, and the environment. Assessment of the supervisee's skills, cultural variables, and the environment should precede the selection of supervision goals.

ASSESSMENT OF THE SUPERVISEE'S SKILLS

Methods for evaluating a supervisee's skills can include (a) self-assessment, (b) quizzes and interviews, and (c) review of permanent products and direct observation.

Self-Assessment

This involves having the supervisee rate their level of competence for each job and/or Task List item skill.

Quizzes and Interviews

Quizzes (i.e., brief tests of knowledge) and interviews (i.e., questions regarding the supervisee's level of competence across skills) can be presented orally or in written form to verify self-reported knowledge-based skills. Quizzes can include activities such as role-plays and in-vivo practice sessions.

Review of Permanent Products and Direct Observation

A review of permanent products (i.e., work samples) and direct observation can be used to verify self-reported performance-based skills. If a supervisee's skills can be sufficiently evaluated through a review of permanent products, direct observation may not be necessary. Direct observation can be used for skills that cannot be evaluated through other means (i.e., quizzes, interviews, or review of permanent products).

ADDITIONAL NOTE(S)

It is recommended that the previously described assessments are introduced in the sequence presented (i.e., self-assessment first, then quizzes/interviews, then observation and review of permanent products). Several other methods discussed in the literature include (a) reviewing the syllabi of relevant coursework completed by the supervisee, (b) meeting with the supervisee's previous supervisors to discuss the supervisee's skills, and (c) reviewing the Task List with the supervisee and using the document as a checklist of items mastered or not yet mastered.

ASSESSMENT OF CULTURAL VARIABLES

In addition to assessing skills, it is crucial to consider cultural variables that may influence the supervisee's learning and performance. Supervisors should gather information about the supervisee's cultural background, values, and beliefs. This can be done through open-ended conversations and culturally sensitive questionnaires. Understanding cultural factors helps supervisors tailor their approach to meet the unique needs of each supervisee, thereby fostering a more inclusive and supportive supervisory relationship.

ASSESSMENT OF THE ENVIRONMENT

The environment in which the supervisee works is another important consideration. Supervisors should assess the organizational culture, available resources, and any potential barriers to the supervisee's professional development. This includes evaluating the support systems in place, such as mentoring opportunities, access to continuing education, and the availability of necessary materials and tools. A supportive environment can significantly enhance the supervisee's ability to meet supervision goals and achieve professional growth.

SELECTION OF SUPERVISION GOALS

Based on the baseline performance data (i.e., results of the assessment of the supervisee's skills) and assessment of cultural variables and the environment, supervisors can collaboratively set realistic and attainable goals with the supervisee. See Chapter 2, "Preparing for the Exam," for a review of SMART goals, and Task H.1 (Chapter 10) for a review of stating goals in observable and measurable terms. Both long-term and short-term goals should be set.

Long-Term Goals

These are goals that are to be met after an extended period of time (e.g., 3 or 4 months). It is recommended that the following are considered when developing long-term goals: (a) the Task List items relevant to the supervisee's role, (b) their performance across those Task List items, and (c) the expected needs of the agency.

Short-Term Goals

These goals, which follow the determination of long-term goals, are to be met within a short period of time (e.g., 1 month). It is recommended that the following are considered when developing short-term goals: (a) the immediate needs of the agency and (b) the supervisee's ability to meet them.

TASK I.5

Identify and apply empirically validated and culturally responsive performance management procedures (e.g., modeling, practice, feedback, reinforcement, task clarification, manipulation of response effort). The identification and application of empirically validated and culturally responsive performance management procedures is essential for effective supervision and intervention. These procedures can include (a) modeling, (b) practice, (c) feedback, (d) reinforcement, (e) task clarification, (f) manipulation of response effort, and (g) behavior skills training (BST).

MODELING

This involves demonstrating the desired behavior for the supervisee or client to observe and imitate. Modeling is effective because it provides a clear example of what is expected. To ensure cultural responsiveness, supervisors should consider the cultural norms and values of the supervisee when selecting models. In a culturally diverse setting, using a variety of models that reflect the cultural backgrounds of the supervisee can enhance relatability and acceptance.

PRACTICE

This allows the supervisee or client to repeatedly perform the desired behavior, facilitating skill acquisition and fluency. This procedure should include opportunities for guided practice, where the supervisor provides immediate feedback, and independent practice. Culturally responsive practice sessions might incorporate culturally relevant scenarios or materials to make the practice more meaningful and engaging for the supervisee.

FEEDBACK

This involves giving specific, timely, and actionable information about performance. When delivering corrective feedback, consider the following guidelines:

- Find a way to incorporate praise (e.g., "That was a really good attempt").
- Provide instruction that the supervisee can use to improve their performance.
- Focus on one error at a time.
- Empathize and avoid labeling the error as "bad" or "wrong."

Feedback should be delivered in a manner that is respectful and considerate of the supervisee's cultural background.

REINFORCEMENT

This involves the delivery of reinforcement to increase the likelihood of the desired behavior being repeated. Reinforcers can be tangible (e.g., monetary reward) or intangible (e.g., praise). Culturally responsive reinforcement considers what is valued and motivating within the supervisee's cultural context.

TASK CLARIFICATION

This involves explicitly describing the expectations and steps required to complete a task successfully. Task clarification helps to prevent misunderstandings and ensure that the supervisee knows exactly what is expected. To be culturally responsive, task clarification should consider language proficiency and use culturally appropriate communication styles. Visual aids or bilingual instructions might be necessary for supervisees from different linguistic backgrounds.

MANIPULATION OF RESPONSE EFFORT

This involves altering the difficulty or effort required to perform a behavior. Making desirable behaviors easier to perform and undesirable behaviors more difficult can effectively manage performance. Cultural responsiveness in this context means considering the physical and cognitive demands placed on the supervisee and ensuring they are reasonable and achievable given the supervisee's cultural and personal circumstances.

BEHAVIOR SKILLS TRAINING

This is a procedure that uses a combination of instruction, modeling, practice, and feedback to teach new skills. The six steps of BST are (a) describing the target skill, (b) providing a written description, (c) demonstrating the target skill, (d) requiring the supervisee to practice the target skill, (e) providing feedback during practice, and (f) repeating the last two steps until mastery is achieved (Figure 11.1).

Describing the Target Skill

This involves explaining why a skill is to be targeted and then behaviorally defining it.

Providing a Written Description

This involves providing an explanation of why a skill is to be targeted and the behavioral definition of it in written form. It is recommended that the supervisee be given time to ask questions.

Demonstrating the Target Skill

This can involve role-playing activities, video models, and/or in-situ demonstrations with a client. During role-plays, the supervisor may stop at certain points to describe what is being done and why or wait until the end to provide feedback.

Requiring the Supervisee to Practice the Target Skill

This involves rehearsal of the targeted skill.

Providing Feedback During Practice

This involves providing supportive feedback (i.e., describing what was done correctly) and corrective feedback (i.e., specifying what was done incorrectly and providing instruction on how to do it correctly).

Repeating the Last Two Steps Until Mastery Is Achieved

Repeat the fourth step (requiring the supervisee to practice the target skill) and the fifth step (providing feedback during practice) until the skill meets the required performance criterion.

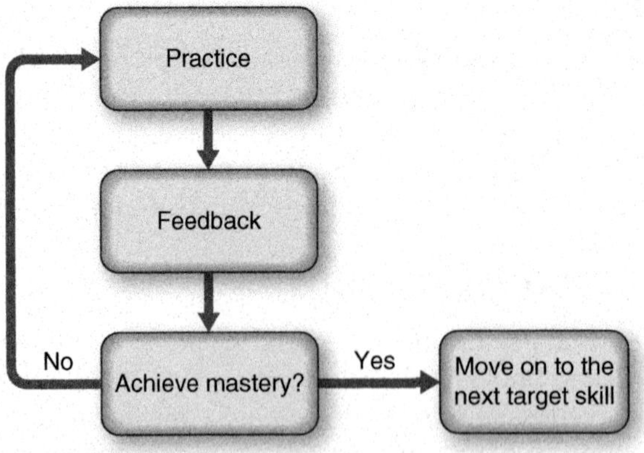

Figure 11.1 Behavior Skills Training Process

Culturally responsive BST considers the supervisee's cultural background during each step, ensuring that instructions are clear, models are relatable, and feedback is delivered in a culturally sensitive manner.

ADDITIONAL NOTE(S)

Performance monitoring is integral to performance management as it provides the data needed to inform decisions about which procedures to use and how to adjust them for maximum effectiveness. This involves ongoing collection of relevant performance data, including: (a) the number and rate of competencies that a supervisee acquires, (b) the number and rate of errors made in permanent products (e.g., data collection forms, assessment reports, and intervention plans), and (c) changes in the use of language (e.g., fluency and accuracy in the use of technical language, ability to explain concepts in nontechnical language).

TASK I.6

Apply a function-based approach (e.g., performance diagnostics) to assess and improve supervisee behavior. See Task F.6 (Chapter 8) for a review of functional analysis and common functions of behavior. Performance diagnostics (also known as *performance analysis*) uses a function-based approach to identify variables affecting personnel performance. The primary model used for performance diagnostics at the individual level is the antecedent-behavior-consequence (ABC) analysis. ABC analysis is recommended when (a) there is a desirable behavior that is not occurring often enough, and (b) there is some undesirable behavior that is occurring too often. There are seven steps to conducting performance diagnostics with an ABC analysis:

1. Describe the problem (undesirable behavior).
2. Describe what the person should be doing instead (desirable behavior).
3. Determine how severe the problem is.
4. Complete an ABC analysis for the problem behavior.
5. Complete an ABC analysis for the desirable behavior.
6. Determine the diagnosis (i.e., summarize the antecedent and consequences).
7. Determine the solution (i.e., add positive/immediate/certain consequences and antecedents for desirable behavior).

Performance diagnostics are conducted to allow behavior analysts to develop function-based strategies for improving personnel performance (Table 11.1).

Table 11.1 Possible Interventions for Problems Impacting Performance

PROBLEM	POSSIBLE INTERVENTION
Lack of training	Use behavioral skills training, improve personnel selection process
Lack of task clarification	Provide task clarification/checklists
Lack of visual aids & verbal/textual reminders	Provide prompts
Poor environment for task	Change task location
Lack of trained staff	Adjust staffing
Materials are disorganized or poorly designed	Organize/redesign materials
Materials are not available	Make materials more accessible
Lack of monitoring by supervisor	Increase presence of supervisor
Lack of feedback	Use performance feedback
Lack of association between accurate task completion and outcomes	Highlight task outcomes
Task is too difficult or requires too much effort	Decrease task difficulty/effort
Task competes with other priorities that take precedence	Decrease aversive task properties

ADDITIONAL NOTE(S)

The Performance Diagnostic Checklist—Human Services (PDC-HS) has been cited in the behavior-analytic literature as a tool that can be used to examine the variables that affect personnel performance in human-service settings.

TASK I.7

Make data-based decisions about the efficacy of supervisory practices. Behavior analysts are required to evaluate the effectiveness of their supervisory practices. This is crucial in ensuring that supervision supports the professional growth of supervisees and leads to positive client outcomes. By making data-based decisions, supervisors can enhance their practices, identify areas for improvement, and ensure that the goals of supervision are being met effectively. This approach relies on a systematic process that includes (a) establishing clear goals, (b) developing a data collection plan, (c) regularly monitoring and analyzing data, and (d) making informed adjustments based on the findings.

ESTABLISHING CLEAR GOALS

The first step in evaluating supervisory practices is to establish clear, measurable goals for the supervision process. These goals should align with the competencies required for effective practice and consider the specific needs and developmental levels of supervisees.

- **Example:** By the end of the next 3 months, the supervisee will correctly implement the steps of the assigned behavior intervention plan with 90% fidelity, as measured by biweekly direct observations using a fidelity checklist, achieving this level of performance on at least four consecutive observations.

See Chapter 2, "Preparing for the Exam," for a review of SMART goals, and Task H.1 (Chapter 10) for a review of stating goals in observable and measurable terms. Clear goals provide a framework for assessing progress and determining the effectiveness of supervision.

DEVELOPING A DATA COLLECTION PLAN

Once goals are established, a data collection plan must be developed. This involves determining what data will be collected, how it will be collected, and the frequency of collection. Data can be gathered from (a) direct observations of supervisee performance, (b) performance data, (c) self-reports, (d) client outcomes, and (e) feedback from supervisees.

Direct Observations of Supervisee Performance

This involves watching and recording the supervisee's performance in real time.

Performance Data

This includes data on (a) the number and rate of competencies that a supervisee acquires, (b) the number and rate of errors made in permanent products, and (c) changes in the use of language. Performance data can be gathered through direct observation or self-reports.

Self-Reports

This involves the supervisee reflecting on their own performance, typically using a structured form or checklist. Self-assessments encourage self-awareness and can help identify discrepancies between perceived and actual performance.

Client Outcomes

This measures the effectiveness of the behavior-analytic services provided by the supervisee, including changes in client behavior, skill acquisition, or other relevant metrics.

Feedback From Supervisees

Methods for gathering feedback from supervisees include (a) requesting feedback and (b) conducting a survey.

Requesting Feedback

This involves directly asking the supervisee the following questions:

"Are you getting what you need?" and "Am I teaching [knowledge/skill(s)] in the most effective way for you?" Asking these questions can occur regularly as a part of supervision meetings.

Conducting a Survey

This involves developing a brief structured survey that the supervisee can complete. Items should address specific areas such as the (a) supervisor's organization, knowledge, and use of feedback/reinforcement; and (b) relevance of knowledge/skills covered. Open-ended questions (e.g., "What would you change about supervision to enhance your learning?") can also be included. This approach may be particularly useful for supervisors who wish to collect feedback from a group of supervisees.

ADDITIONAL NOTE(S)

Supervisors should also collect some sort of data to learn about the effectiveness of the method(s) they choose to evaluate the effects of supervision.

REGULARLY MONITORING AND ANALYZING DATA

Supervisors should review data on an ongoing basis to assess progress toward goals and identify any emerging patterns or issues. Consistent monitoring ensures that any deviations from expected progress can be quickly identified and addressed.

MAKING INFORMED, DATA-BASED ADJUSTMENTS

Based on the analysis, supervisors can make informed adjustments to their practices. If data indicate that a supervisee is struggling with a particular skill, the supervisor might increase the frequency of direct observation and feedback, provide additional modeling, or offer targeted training sessions. Conversely, if data show that a supervisee has mastered certain competencies, the supervisor might reduce the level of direct supervision and focus on more advanced skills.

CONCLUSION

In this chapter, we reviewed key content for TCO Tasks related to personnel supervision and management. This included information related to setting performance expectations and goals; using performance monitoring, feedback, and reinforcement systems; using function-based strategies to improve personnel performance; and more. Given the role of behavior analysts as supervisors in the field, it is important that we acquire competencies and engage in practices that bring out the best in those we supervise. It is not an exaggeration to say that the generations of behavior analysts to come will, at least to some extent, be shaped by the supervision practices we adopt today.

REFERENCE

Behavior Analyst Certification Board. (2024). *BCBA test content outline* (6th ed.). Author. https://www.bacb.com/wp-content/bcba-outline-6thEd

BIBLIOGRAPHY

Austin, J. (2000). Performance analysis and performance diagnostics. In J. E. Carr & J. Austin (Eds.), *Handbook of applied behavior analysis* (pp. 321–349). Context Press.

Behavior Analyst Certification Board. (n.d.). *Sample supervision contract for BCBA/BCaBA trainees*. Author.

Carr, J. E., Wilder, D. A., Majdalany, L., Mathisen, D., & Strain, L. A. (2013). An assessment-based solution to a human-service employee performance problem. *Behavior Analysis in Practice, 6*(1), 16–32. https://doi.org/10.1007/BF03391789

Daniels, A. C. (2015). *The most powerful leadership tool: Positive reinforcement—5 Keys for effective delivery*. http://aubreydaniels.com/positive-reinforcement-most-powerful-leadership-tool

Garza, K. L., McGee, H. M., Schenk, Y. A., & Wiskirchen, R. R. (2018). Some tools for carrying out a proposed process for supervising experience hours for aspiring Board Certified Behavior Analysts®. *Behavior Analysis in Practice, 11*(1), 62–70. https://doi.org/10.1007/s40617-017-0186-8

Miltenberger, R. (2015). *Behavior modification: Principles and procedures*. Cengage Learning.

Parsons, M. B., Rollyson, J. H., & Reid, D. H. (2012). Evidence-based staff training: A guide for practitioners. *Behavior Analysis in Practice, 5*(2), 2–11. https://doi.org/10.1007/BF03391819

Sarokoff, R. A., & Sturmey, P. (2008). The effects of instructions, rehearsal, modeling, and feedback on acquisition and generalization of staff use of discrete trial teaching and student correct responses. *Research in Autism Spectrum Disorders, 2*(1), 125–136. https://doi.org/10.1016/j.rasd.2007.04.002

Sellers, T. P., Alai-Rosales, S., & MacDonald, R. P. (2016). Taking full responsibility: The ethics of supervision in behavior analytic practice. *Behavior Analysis in Practice, 9*(4), 299–308. https://doi.org/10.1007/s40617-016-0144-x

Sellers, T. P., Valentino, A. L., & LeBlanc, L. A. (2016). Recommended practices for individual supervision of aspiring behavior analysts. *Behavior Analysis in Practice, 9*(4), 274–286. https://doi.org/10.1007/s40617-016-0110-7

Turner, L. B., Fischer, A. J., & Luiselli, J. K. (2016). Towards a competency-based, ethical, and socially valid approach to the supervision of applied behavior analytic trainees. *Behavior Analysis in Practice, 9*(4), 287–298. https://doi.org/10.1007/s40617-016-0121-4

Valentino, A. L., LeBlanc, L. A., & Sellers, T. P. (2016). The benefits of group supervision and a recommended structure for implementation. *Behavior Analysis in Practice, 9*(4), 320–328. https://doi.org/10.1007/s40617-016-0138-8

KNOWLEDGE CHECK

1. A behavior analyst is supervising a group of behavior technicians. Through regular supervision sessions, the behavior analyst helps the behavior technicians improve their fidelity in implementing behavior intervention procedures, build professional skills, and apply ethical practices in their work with clients. As a result, the behavior technicians have improved their performance, developed stronger professional skills, applied ethical practices, and developed supportive workplace friendships within the team. Which of the following is NOT considered a direct benefit of behavior-analytic supervision?

   A. It contributes to the development of supportive workplace friendships.

   B. It contributes to the professional development of supervisees.

   C. It can enhance the fidelity of implementation of procedures.

   D. It can promote ethical practice.

2. Potential risks of ineffective supervision include all of the following, EXCEPT:

   A. It can degrade the quality of behavior-analytic services.

   B. It can negatively impact client outcomes.

   C. It can result in actionable violations of the Ethics Code.

   D. It can result in supervisor development of inadequate professional skills.

3. A behavior analyst is preparing to begin a new supervisory relationship with a supervisee. The supervisee is eager to start working but is unsure about what the performance expectations are. The behavior analyst needs to ensure that both parties understand the roles, responsibilities, and goals that will guide their work together. When should the behavior analyst communicate performance expectations to ensure clarity for both parties?

   A. At the outset of a supervisory relationship

   B. During the first performance evaluation

   C. Prior to the first supervision meeting

   D. Prior to the termination of the supervisory relationship

4. A trainee has completed their fieldwork experience and is preparing to submit their documentation to the Behavior Analyst Certification Board® (BACB®) for certification. While gathering the necessary paperwork, the trainee realizes they do not have a formal document outlining the specifics of their supervision arrangement, including the goals, responsibilities, and meeting schedule. What critical step was missed at the beginning of the supervisory relationship?

   A. Completing a declaration of supervision

   B. Signing a supervision contract

   C. Establishing a mentorship agreement

   D. Using the supervision verification system

(*See answers on the next page.*)

1. **A) It contributes to the development of supportive workplace friendships.**
The behavior analyst is focusing on important supervision goals such as improving procedural fidelity, building professional skills, and applying ethical practices. While friendships may form in the workplace, they are not a direct or intended outcome of supervision. The main objectives are to support professional development and ensure high-quality implementation of behavior intervention procedures. The other answer options all represent core benefits of behavior-analytic supervision.

2. **D) It can result in supervisor development of inadequate professional skills.**
Supervisor development of inadequate professional skills is not an identified potential risk of ineffective supervision. The other answer options (it can degrade the quality of behavior-analytic services, it can negatively impact client outcomes, it can result in actionable violations of the Ethics Code) are described in the professional literature as potential risks.

3. **A) At the outset of a supervisory relationship**
The supervising behavior analyst should clearly communicate performance expectations at the outset of the supervisory relationship to ensure that both parties have a shared understanding of their roles, responsibilities, and goals. This initial clarity helps prevent misunderstandings and sets a foundation for productive supervision. Waiting until the first evaluation or later in the relationship risks misalignment and confusion, while discussing expectations just prior to termination would be too late to benefit the supervisee's performance and development.

4. **B) Signing a supervision contract**
In this scenario, the trainee realizes that a supervision contract was never established, which is a critical step at the beginning of the supervisory relationship. The BACB® requires a formal contract to outline the goals, responsibilities, and expectations for both the supervisor and supervisee. Without this contract, there is no formal agreement documenting the supervisory relationship, expectations, roles, and responsibilities. The other answer options do not meet the BACB's requirement for a supervision contact that must be signed before fieldwork begins.

5. A behavior analyst is supervising a trainee and notices that the trainee is inconsistent in completing assigned tasks between supervision meetings. To help the trainee stay on track, the behavior analyst sets an expectation that the trainee must complete specific tasks by a designated time before the next supervision meeting. The supervisor will review the completed assignments during their next meeting to provide feedback. Is the behavior analyst appropriately setting an expectation in this situation?

A. Yes, setting deadlines for completing assigned tasks is appropriate for ensuring progress and accountability.

B. Yes, but the behavior analyst should not review the assignments during the supervision meeting.

C. No, it is unnecessary to set deadlines, as the supervisee should complete tasks at their own pace.

D. No, because the supervisee should focus only on learning during supervision meetings, not on completing tasks in between.

6. A behavior analyst is supervising a trainee and wants to evaluate the trainee's performance in working with clients. To do so, the supervisor decides to rely solely on the trainee's self-assessment, where the trainee rates their own skills and provides reflections on their work. The behavior analyst does not plan to observe the trainee in sessions or review any of the trainee's session data or other permanent products. Is the behavior analyst using appropriate methods to evaluate the trainee's skills?

A. Yes, self-assessment alone is sufficient for evaluating skills.

B. Yes, but the supervisor should include interviews with the trainee as well.

C. No, self-assessment should be supplemented with other methods like direct observation or review of permanent products.

D. No, the supervisor should only use quizzes and interviews to evaluate skills.

7. A supervisor is working with a trainee who is preparing for the Behavior Analyst Certification Board® (BACB®) Exam. Instead of reviewing the trainee's current performance levels, the supervisor sets goals based solely on the BCBA Task List without considering the trainee's strengths and weaknesses. As a result, some goals are either too easy or too difficult for the trainee, leading to slow progress. What step did the supervisor miss when setting the trainee's supervision goals?

A. Reviewing baseline performance data

B. Using the BCBA Test Content Outline to guide goal selection

C. Consulting the supervision contract for goal alignment

D. Focusing on the trainee's future career aspirations

8. A behavior analyst is working with a supervisee to develop supervision goals. The behavior analyst considers several factors, including the supervisee's current skill level, the environment in which they operate, cultural variables that may impact performance, and their own preferences for the types of skills they would like the supervisee to focus on. Which of the following factors should NOT have been considered when selecting supervision goals?

A. The environment in which the supervisee operates

B. The supervisee's current skill level

C. The cultural variables relevant to the supervisee

D. The supervisor's personal preferences

(See answers on the next page.)

5. **A) Yes, setting deadlines for completing assigned tasks is appropriate for ensuring progress and accountability.**
The behavior analyst is appropriately setting an expectation by requiring the trainee to complete tasks by a designated deadline. This helps ensure accountability and steady progress toward supervision goals. Reviewing the completed assignments in supervision meetings allows the behavior analyst to provide constructive feedback and address any issues. The other answer options suggest that deadlines or reviewing assignments are unnecessary, which is not correct, as these are essential components of effective behavior-analytic supervision.

6. **C) No, self-assessment should be supplemented with other methods like direct observation or review of permanent products.**
In this scenario, the behavior analyst is not using sufficient methods to evaluate the trainee's skills. While self-assessment can be a useful tool, it should be supplemented with more objective measures such as direct observation or review of permanent products to ensure an accurate assessment of the trainee's abilities. Relying solely on self-assessment provides a limited view and could miss critical areas that need improvement. The other answer options either incorrectly suggest that self-assessment alone is enough or recommend other methods without including key components of effective evaluation, such as direct observation.

7. **A) Reviewing baseline performance data**
In this scenario, the supervisor missed the critical step of reviewing baseline performance data before setting supervision goals. Baseline data allows the supervisor to understand the trainee's current skill level and tailor goals accordingly. By relying solely on the Behavior Analyst Certification Board® (BACB®) Task List, the supervisor overlooked the importance of setting goals that are achievable based on the trainee's actual performance, leading to goals that may be misaligned with the trainee's abilities. The other answer options may be useful but do not replace the need for baseline performance data when developing supervision goals.

8. **D) The supervisor's personal preferences**
The behavior analyst considered several valid factors, such as the supervisee's current skill level, the environment they work in, and cultural variables, which are all essential for setting effective supervision goals. However, the supervisor's personal preferences should not have influenced the goal-setting process. Supervision goals should be based on objective data and the supervisee's specific needs, not on what the supervisor personally favors. The other answer options are important for ensuring that the goals are realistic, achievable, and tailored to the supervisee's context, making them appropriate factors to consider.

9. A supervisor has been working with a supervisee for several months. During a feedback session, the supervisee expresses concern that while they are making progress on specific, immediate tasks, they are unsure how their current work aligns with their overall career development. The supervisor realizes that while they have focused on developing immediate skills, they may need to adjust the goal-setting process to provide the supervisee with a clearer path for long-term growth. What adjustment should the supervisor consider?

   A. Incorporating more specific short-term objectives

   B. Focusing exclusively on professional development without immediate skill-building

   C. Setting a balance of both short-term and long-term goals

   D. Reducing the number of short-term goals to make progress feel easier

10. A supervisor at a behavior analysis clinic sets a short-term goal for their supervisee to begin conducting client assessments independently within the next month. The clinic has an urgent need for new assessments, and the supervisor considered this when setting the goal. However, the supervisee has minimal experience in conducting assessments and requires more training before they can perform this task independently. What critical factor did the supervisor overlook when setting the short-term goal?

    A. The supervisee's ability to meet the goal based on their current skill level

    B. The clinic's immediate need for new assessments

    C. The long-term career goals of the supervisee

    D. The guidelines outlined in the supervision contract

11. A behavior analyst is working with a supervisee to help them learn how to implement a new behavior intervention plan. The behavior analyst begins by explaining each step of the intervention in detail and providing written instructions. Next, the behavior analyst demonstrates the intervention while the supervisee observes. Afterward, the supervisee practices the intervention while the analyst observes and provides feedback. The behavior analyst continues to provide feedback and gives opportunities for the supervisee to practice until they can implement the intervention independently. What training method is the behavior analyst using?

    A. Task analysis

    B. Behavior skills training (BST)

    C. Imitation training

    D. Cognitive behavioral therapy (CBT)

12. A behavior analyst is working with a supervisee on implementing a new behavior intervention procedure. To demonstrate the procedure, the behavior analyst role-plays with the supervisee, showing how to implement each step of the procedure, and then shows a video model of the procedure in action. Which step of the behavior skills training (BST) is the behavior analyst implementing with the supervisee?

    A. Describe the target skill

    B. Demonstrate the target skill

    C. Practice the target skill

    D. Provide written description of the target skill

(*See answers on the next page.*)

9. **C) Setting a balance of both short-term and long-term goals**
The supervisor needs to provide a balance between short-term and long-term goals to ensure the supervisee has a clear path for both immediate skill-building and overall career development. In this case, the supervisee feels unsure about how their current progress fits into their long-term growth. The other options either focus too narrowly on short-term goals, disregard the importance of immediate skill-building, or reduce the goals without addressing the supervisee's broader professional needs. Balancing both types of goals is essential for effective supervision.

10. **A) The supervisee's ability to meet the goal based on their current skill level**
The supervisor considered the clinic's immediate need for new assessments but overlooked the supervisee's current skill level and ability to meet the goal in the short term. Effective short-term goals should balance both the urgent needs of the agency and the supervisee's readiness to meet those needs. The other options, such as the clinic's immediate need or long-term career goals, are important but do not address the critical issue of whether the supervisee has the skills to achieve the goal within the given time frame.

11. **B) Behavior skills training (BST)**
The behavior analyst is using BST in this scenario, which involves explaining the skill, demonstrating it, allowing the supervisee to practice, and providing feedback until the skill is mastered. This structured training method is effective in teaching new skills by combining instruction, modeling, practice, and feedback. The other answer options refer to methods or approaches that do not include the process of instruction, modeling, practice, and feedback.

12. **B) Demonstrate the target skill**
The behavior analyst is demonstrating the target skill by role-playing and showing a video model of the procedure, allowing the supervisee to observe how each step of the procedure is implemented. This step in BST ensures the supervisee can see the correct behavior in action before practicing it themselves. The other answer options are part of BST but are not the focus of this scenario, which highlights the demonstration.

13. When delivering corrective feedback to a supervisee, a behavior analyst should do all of the following, EXCEPT:

A. Find a way to incorporate praise

B. Focus on one error at a time

C. Label the error as "wrong" to ensure the supervisee understands that it is to be avoided in the future

D. Provide instruction that the supervisee can use to improve their performance

14. A behavior analyst is working with a client whose staff performance has been declining. To identify the cause of the performance issues, the behavior analyst observes the staff member's behavior during sessions and reviews the antecedents and consequences surrounding the performance deficits. This analysis helps the behavior analyst pinpoint factors contributing to the staff member's poor performance. What model is the behavior analyst using to diagnose the staff member's performance issues?

A. ABC analysis

B. BST

C. Task analysis

D. FCT

15. The first step in conducting performance diagnostics with an antecedent-behavior-consequence (ABC) analysis is to:

A. Describe the desirable behavior

B. Describe the undesirable behavior

C. Determine the severity of the undesirable behavior is

D. Determine the diagnosis

16. A behavior analyst is evaluating the performance of staff members at a residential care facility. Some staff members have been inconsistently completing data collection tasks. To address this, the behavior analyst examines various factors, including the environment, tasks, and consequences that may be impacting staff performance. The aim is to identify which variables are contributing to the performance issues and implement targeted changes based on the findings. What type of approach is the behavior analyst using?

A. A skills acquisition approach

B. A function-based approach

C. A descriptive approach

D. A task analysis approach

17. What is a benefit of using a function-based approach to improve supervisee behavior?

A. It addresses the underlying reasons for performance issues.

B. It avoids specific behavior targets.

C. It provides a one-size-fits-all solution to performance issues.

D. It relies on anecdotal evidence for decision-making.

(See answers on the next page.)

13. **C) Label the error as "wrong" to ensure the supervisee understands that it is to be avoided in the future**
When delivering corrective feedback, a behavior analyst should find a way to incorporate praise, focus on one error at a time, and provide instruction that can be used by the supervisee to improve their performance. They should also empathize and avoid labeling errors as "wrong."

14. **A) ABC analysis**
In this scenario, the behavior analyst is using ABC analysis to diagnose the staff member's performance issues by examining the antecedents, behavior, and consequences surrounding the performance deficits. This model is effective for identifying factors that influence performance at the individual level. The other answer options (BST [behavior skills training], task analysis, FCT [functional communication training]) are not performance diagnostic models.

15. **B) Describe the undesirable behavior**
The first step in conducting performance diagnostics with an ABC analysis is to describe the undesirable behavior. The other answer options (describe the desirable behavior; determine the severity of the undesirable behavior; and determine the diagnosis) describe later steps in the process.

16. **B) A function-based approach**
The behavior analyst is using a function-based approach to analyze the variables that impact staff performance. This approach identifies environmental and task-related factors and the consequences affecting performance. The other answer options refer to approaches that are not used to comprehensively analyze the variables influencing performance.

17. **A) It addresses the underlying reasons for performance issues.**
A function-based approach to improving supervisee behavior focuses on identifying and addressing the underlying reasons for performance issues by analyzing environmental factors, task demands, and consequences that impact performance. The other options are incorrect because this approach does not avoid specific behavior targets, does not rely on a one-size-fits-all solution, and is based on objective data rather than anecdotal evidence.

18. A supervisor notices that despite following a structured supervision plan, several supervisees are not making the expected progress in mastering key skills. The supervisor decides to review supervision data, observe the supervisees during practice, and evaluate their own supervision strategies to identify areas where their supervisory methods may need improvement. What step is the supervisor taking in this situation?

A. Adjusting intervention goals based on client progress
B. Providing feedback to supervisees on their performance
C. Evaluating the effectiveness of their supervisory practices
D. Revising the supervision contract to include additional requirements

19. Methods for assessing the effects of supervision include all of the following, EXCEPT:

A. Conducting a survey
B. Interviewing peers
C. Requesting feedback
D. Tracking relevant performance data

20. Data that may be tracked by a behavior analyst to assess the effects of their supervision can include:

A. Changes in the use of language
B. The number and rate of competencies that a supervisee acquires
C. The number and rate of errors made in permanent products
D. All of the above

(*See answers on the next page.*)

18. **C) Evaluating the effectiveness of their supervisory practices**
    In this scenario, the supervisor is addressing the lack of progress among supervisees by reviewing data and observing performance, which indicates they are evaluating the effectiveness of their supervisory practices. This step is essential for identifying areas where supervision strategies may need adjustment. The other answer options refer to solutions that are not the main focus here, as the scenario specifically describes actions aimed at assessing the supervisor's methods, not altering supervisee goals or feedback.

19. **B) Interviewing peers**
    Conducting surveys, requesting feedback, and tracking relevant performance data are methods for assessing supervision. Interviewing peers, however, is not.

20. **D) All of the above**
    Data that may be tracked by a behavior analyst to assess the effects of their supervision can include changes in the use of language, the number and rate of competencies that a supervisee acquires, and the number and rate of errors made in permanent products.

12

Practice Exam

Preparing for the BCBA® exam requires a strong understanding of behavior-analytic concepts, principles, and applications. This practice exam is designed to help you assess your knowledge and reinforce key topics outlined in the BACB® Test Content Outline (TCO). By working through these multiple-choice questions, you can test your recall, comprehension, and application of essential behavior-analytic principles.

Taking this practice exam is a great way to measure your readiness, refine your test-taking strategies, and build confidence before the actual exam. Use this as a tool to identify areas of strength and focus your studies on concepts that may require additional review.

You have up to 4 hours to complete this 185-item examination. Read each question carefully and consider all response options before selecting your answer. Answers and explanations are provided in the next section to support your learning and reinforce key concepts.

Start the timer, stay focused, and do your best. Good luck!

1. ________________ is a measure of the number of response opportunities required to achieve a predetermined level of performance.

   A. Count

   B. Event recording

   C. Percentage

   D. Trials to criterion

2. This scientific attitude emphasizes that all knowledge should be viewed as tentative and subject to change, requiring scientists to maintain a skeptical stance toward existing knowledge and to be willing to revise their beliefs in light of new evidence and discoveries. Which attitude of science does this statement BEST describe?

   A. Philosophic doubt

   B. Replication

   C. Parsimony

   D. Empiricism

3. A behavior analyst is considering whether a client needs ongoing services. Best practice is for the behavior analyst to carefully consider all of the following EXCEPT:

   A. The ethical guidelines addressing termination of services

   B. Assessment results and ongoing progress monitoring data

   C. Their clinical expertise

   D. Insurance reimbursement

4. As part of performance monitoring, supervisors assess the quality of supervisee work by examining permanent products. Which of the following is the clearest example of a permanent product?
   - **A.** Skeptical attitude
   - **B.** Awareness of the Ethics Code for Behavior Analysts
   - **C.** A behavior intervention plan
   - **D.** Conceptual understanding client rapport

5. Behavior analysts are required to maintain appropriate professional relationships with clients. Which of the following scenarios presents an ethical problem?
   - **A.** Esther is a behavior analyst who is very well-liked by her clients. However, one of the families she works with was offended when they asked her to stay for lunch and she politely declined the invitation.
   - **B.** Harold is a behavior analyst who lives next door to a family with a child who struggles with behavior issues. He wants to help but is uncomfortable charging his neighbors for his services, so he instead provides them with free behavioral advice.
   - **C.** Kamala is a behavior analyst who has been experiencing some personal problems. When she noticed that they began to impact her performance at work, she contacted her supervisor, requested a leave of absence, and arranged for another behavior analyst to cover her cases.
   - **D.** Leonard is a behavior analyst who is very familiar with the research literature on behavior change procedures. However, he only uses very simple language when speaking with clients.

6. Behavior analysts couple their clinical expertise with which of the following to determine whether an intervention is effective and if a treatment needs to be revised?
   - **A.** The best available evidence
   - **B.** Philosophic doubt
   - **C.** Grounded theory
   - **D.** Experimental analysis of behavior

7. Ms. Keyes is a third-grade teacher who describes one of her students as "highly defiant." When questioned about what this meant, Ms. Keyes reported that the student would throw tantrums, pinch their peers, be disrespectful to adults, and occasionally leave the classroom without permission. Which of the following is NOT an appropriate target for intervention?
   - **A.** Being disrespectful to adults
   - **B.** Leaving the classroom without permission
   - **C.** Pinching peers
   - **D.** Throwing tantrums

8. In which branch of behavior analysis do researchers focus on controlled experiments in a laboratory setting to study the fundamental principles of behavior?
   - **A.** Applied behavior analysis (ABA)
   - **B.** Experimental Analysis of Behavior (EAB)
   - **C.** Behaviorism
   - **D.** Professional practice guided by the science of behavior analysis

9. BCBAs® are encouraged to develop definitions of behavior that describe responses in terms of their effect on the environment (e.g., "Any behavior that results in X"). This statement BEST describes which of the following definitions of behavior?

   A. Topography-based definitions

   B. Gestalt-based definitions

   C. Outcome-based definitions

   D. Function-based definitions

10. Mrs. Johnson, a second-grade teacher, has implemented a token economy system in her classroom to improve student behavior. Each student starts the day with a "token card" that has five spaces for tokens. Throughout the day, students earn tokens for displaying positive behaviors such as raising their hand before speaking, completing assignments on time, and helping their classmates. At the end of the week, students can exchange their tokens for small prizes such as extra recess time, stickers, or a pencil. In this example, the tokens served as:

    A. Primary reinforcers

    B. Secondary reinforcers

    C. Noncontingent reinforcers

    D. Unconditioned reinforcers

11. Ashley is a graduate student studying behavior analysis. She just started a new fieldwork experience at a local healthcare center serving children with behavior problems. Her supervisor, Sam, is a BCBA® who sometimes seems a bit scattered. Sam was scheduled to conduct his first observation of Ashley at her site last week, but he never showed up. The observation was then rescheduled for earlier this week; however, just minutes before the start of the session, Ashley received an email from Sam about canceling the session. "I'm stuck in a meeting and probably won't be able to come see you today," he said. "It seems like you're doing fine. If any problems come up, just ask one of the other behavior support staff at the center. I'll get in touch with you later after things quiet down." Ashley is concerned about the supervision she is receiving. What should she do first?

    A. Proceed in conducting fieldwork with or without Sam's supervision; if problems arise, there are other staff that can help.

    B. Document the missed sessions and report Sam to the Behavior Analyst Certification Board®; Sam is not following the Board's requirements for providing supervision.

    C. Find another supervisor; Sam is clearly lacking availability and does not seem able to meet Ashley's supervision needs.

    D. Contact Sam and be persistent in finding a time to meet; Ashley should express her concern to Sam and ask if it can be immediately resolved.

12. Valid measurement requires all of the following, EXCEPT:

    A. Data representing the behavior's occurrence under relevant conditions

    B. Direct measurement of a socially significant behavior

    C. Measurement of a relevant dimension of the behavior

    D. Repeated measurement that yields the same results

13. According to radical behaviorism, which statement BEST reflects its perspective on the nature of private events, such as thoughts and feelings?

A. Private events are not real and should not be studied.

B. Public events are private events and vice versa.

C. Private events are behaviors that can be influenced by environmental factors.

D. Private events are beyond the scope of behavior analysis.

14. When Shelly wanted attention, she generally screamed at her father until he paid attention to her. Now, her father is ignoring her screams. Which of the following MOST accurately describes the procedure used in this situation?

A. Extinction of behavior maintained by positive reinforcement

B. Extinction of behavior maintained by negative reinforcement

C. Extinction of behavior maintained by positive punishment

D. Extinction of behavior maintained by automatic reinforcement

15. Darius is only 2 years old and cannot reach the kitchen counter where a dish of walnuts was placed. After some experimentation, he learned to use the shelves of the cupboard as a ladder to get on top of the kitchen counter and retrieve a handful of walnuts from the dish. Darius never received any training to perform these steps, nor were walnuts ever paired with another reinforcer. What type of reinforcer did the walnuts MOST likely serve as?

A. Conditioned

B. Generalized

C. Secondary

D. Unconditioned

16. Which of the following BEST describes the philosophical assumption of determinism?

A. All behavior is random and unpredictable.

B. Behavior is influenced by free will and choice.

C. Behavior is determined by past events and environmental factors.

D. Behavior is influenced by innate biological factors alone.

17. Liam conducted an observation of a client, Gus. Before the start of the observation, Liam spent time arranging the environment to include different objects and activities that Gus might like, such as puzzles, blocks, and musical games. During the observation, Liam recorded the length of time Gus would approach, contact, or engage with the different objects and activities available. What type of preference assessment did Liam conduct?

A. Single stimulus

B. Contrived free-operant observation

C. Naturalistic free-operant observation

D. Multiple stimulus without replacement

18. Which of the following is NOT an element of baseline logic?

A. Prediction

B. Replication

C. Generalization

D. Verification

19. What type of validity refers to the degree the changes in the dependent variable (DV; i.e., target behavior) can be attributed to the manipulation of the independent variable (IV; i.e., intervention) and not the result of uncontrolled/extraneous factors?

A. Criterion validity

B. Internal validity

C. Construct validity

D. External validity

20. Emma's parents want to work on decreasing the amount of time it takes for her to eat her lunch. The behavior technician collects baseline data to determine the amount of time it takes Emma to eat her lunch. The timer starts after Emma's mother places the lunch on the table in front of Emma and she begins to eat it. The timer is stopped when she has consumed all edible parts of the lunch. The time elapsed is recorded for each occurrence. The measurement procedure described in this scenario involves the recording of what dimensional quantity of behavior?

A. Response latency

B. Interresponse time

C. Duration

D. Frequency

21. As supervisors, behavior analysts must monitor the performance of supervisees and provide timely feedback and reinforcement. These practices enhance supervisees' performance and help to:

A. Support procedural integrity

B. Support affective commitment

C. Support resiliency efforts

D. Support organizational constraints

22. When using reinforcement, extinction, and punishment procedures, behavior analysts must consider and plan for the possibility of unwanted effects. Of these, ________________ is associated with the following unwanted effects: emotional/aggressive reactions, an initial increase in the rate of the problem behavior, an initial increase in the magnitude of the problem behavior, the reappearance of the problem behavior after it has been reduced/eliminated, and the reappearance of a previously extinguished problem behavior that was replaced by the targeted problem behavior.

A. Reinforcement

B. Punishment

C. Extinction

D. None of the above

23. Which of the following BEST describes what the Ethics Code says about bartering as a substitute for the collection of fees for behavior-analytic services?

A. Bartering with goods (but not services) is prohibited.

B. Bartering of services (but not goods) is prohibited.

C. Bartering may be acceptable when certain conditions are met.

D. Bartering of any kind is prohibited.

24. During a meeting, a BCBA® discusses a new intervention plan with a teacher. The BCBA emphasizes that the plan's success will be measured by observing specific changes in the student's behavior over time. Which philosophical assumption does the behavior analyst's approach illustrate?

A. Determinism

B. Pragmatism

C. Empiricism

D. Parsimony

25. Behavior analysts identify potential interventions based on assessment results and the best available scientific evidence. When evaluating the scientific evidence to guide intervention selection decisions, a BCBA® prioritizes its:

A. Relevance and certainty

B. Scope and parsimony

C. Testability and rigor

D. Classification and certainty

26. A group of inmates in a correctional facility frequently exhibit aggressive behavior. A behavior analyst consulting with the facility conducts systematic observations and suggests implementing a contingency management system. A token economy is devised where inmates earn vouchers for displaying nonaggressive, socially appropriate behavior. Vouchers are withheld for any incidents of aggressive behavior. Data collected during the intervention shows a decrease in aggressive behavior and an increase in prosocial behavior. What is the dependent variable (DV) in this intervention?

A. Contingency management system

B. Prosocial behavior

C. Systematic observations

D. Vouchers

27. Which of the following is not an advantage of utilizing continuous measurement methods?

A. They can detect all occurrences of the target behavior during an observation period.

B. They can be highly accurate.

C. They are more sensitive to small improvements in performance not captured by other methods of measurement.

D. They require less attention from the observer, are time-consuming, and require less training for users.

28. Ms. Charlotte, a fourth-grade teacher, tells her students that they are to line up by the classroom door to walk to the cafeteria after the lunch bell rings, but only after she calls their name. When the lunch bell rings, students eagerly wait at their desks until they hear Ms. Charlotte call their name before standing up and lining up by the door. In the example, the students are demonstrating:

A. Conditional discrimination

B. Compound discrimination

C. Simple discrimination

D. Conditional verbal discrimination

29. Which type of validity assesses the degree to which the results of an intervention (i.e., functional relationship demonstrated in an experiment) can be generalized to other behaviors, environments, and individuals/populations?

A. Internal validity

B. External validity

C. Construct validity

D. Concurrent validity

30. One component of a sound definition of a target behavior is that it refers to observable aspects of the behavior (and environment, when applicable). This means the definition is:

A. Complete

B. Functional

C. Objective

D. Clear

31. A behavior analyst is consulting with a client, Lily, who frequently refuses to participate in group activities by sitting in a corner and crying. When Lily cries, staff members often allow her to leave the group activity and go to a quiet area with her favorite toys. Lily's crying rarely happens during one-on-one sessions or free play time. Which of the following is MOST likely the function of Lily's crying behavior?

A. Sensory stimulation

B. Attention from caregivers

C. Escape from group activities

D. Access to preferred toys

32. A client is taught that the spoken word "bicicleta" is the same as the spoken word "bicycle." The client is also taught that the spoken word "bicycle" is the same as a physical, two-wheeled vehicle. Without any training to do so, the client then calls a physical, two-wheeled vehicle a "bicicleta." What type of derived stimulus relation does this example illustrate?

A. Reflexivity

B. Substitution

C. Symmetry

D. Transitivity

33. Carey, a behavior analyst, is working with a student who engages in elopement behavior from the classroom. Carey defines elopement as any unauthorized departure from the classroom, excluding instances such as restroom breaks with permission or leaving for scheduled activities like lunch. Carey uses 1-minute intervals to observe and record whether elopement is occurring at the exact moment the interval ends. What measurement procedure is Carey employing to monitor the frequency of this behavior?

A. Event recording

B. Momentary time sampling

C. Partial interval recording

D. Whole interval recording

34. Sunni, a trainee acquiring fieldwork experience to meet Behavior Analyst Certification Board® (BACB®) certification requirements, meets with Erin, a BCBA®, for behavior-analytic supervision. It is their first meeting, so Erin takes the opportunity to review her expectations of Sunni. These include providing a draft agenda 24 hours in advance of supervision meetings, following firm deadlines for assigned activities, taking notes during feedback meetings, and sharing personal reflections on work with clients. All of these are reasonable EXCEPT for the requirement for Sunni to:

A. Provide a draft agenda 24 hours in advance of supervision meetings

B. Follow firm deadlines for assigned activities

C. Take notes during feedback meetings

D. Provide ongoing evaluation of the effects of supervision

35. Chelsea does not particularly enjoy doing household chores (e.g., doing the dishes, folding laundry), but she would frequently volunteer to do them because her father would give her a small amount of money for each one that she completed. One day, Chelsea's father decides that "doing things to help out around the house should be inherently rewarding" and stops paying Chelsea for completing chores. Subsequently, Chelsea completes fewer chores. This change in behavior is MOST likely the result of:

A. Extinction

B. Negative punishment

C. Negative reinforcement

D. Positive punishment

36. A 2-year-old named Sully is working with his father to learn new words. Sully's father is using simple discrimination. Select the option that BEST exemplifies simple discrimination.

A. Sully's father presents him with a blueberry. When Sully says "Blueberry," his father delivers reinforcement. Sully's father then presents him with an apple. When Sully says "Apple," his father delivers reinforcement; if Sully says "Blueberry" when presented with an apple, reinforcement is not delivered.

B. Sully's father presents him with a blueberry. When Sully says "Blueberry," his father models how to place the blueberry in his mouth, chew the blueberry, and swallow it.

C. Sully's father presents him with a blueberry. When Sully says "Blueberry," his father delivers reinforcement. When Sully says any word other than blueberry, his father does not deliver reinforcement.

D. Sully's father presents him with a bowl of fruit that includes blueberries, strawberries, blackberries, and raspberries. When Sully picks up a berry, his father verbally identifies it by its name.

37. Roberto, a behavior analyst, has a new client, Araceli, who exhibits frequent aggressive behaviors at school. Roberto is crafting an operational definition for these aggressive behaviors that Araceli's teachers will use to track their occurrence during school hours. Which of the following would be considered a strong operational definition for Roberto to share with Araceli's teachers?

A. Any physical contact between Araceli's body and another person's body

B. Any physical contact between Araceli's hands or feet and another person's body

C. Any physical contact between Araceli's body and another person's body with enough force to be audible or leave a mark

D. Any physical contact between Araceli's body and another person's body with enough force to be audible or leave a mark, outside of activities in which such contact would be appropriate

38. Darnell, a behavior analyst, is developing a treatment plan that targets a client's problem behavior for reduction. The targeted behavior is problematic, but it is not severe, does not occur frequently, and does not have a significant impact on the environment. In the treatment plan, Darnell plans to supplement reduction contingencies with reinforcement contingencies. When selecting an acceptable alternative behavior, Darnell should do all of the following EXCEPT:

A. Select an alternative behavior that is already in the client's behavioral repertoire

B. Select an alternative behavior that is incompatible with the problem behavior

C. Select an alternative behavior that is within the client's current abilities

D. Select an alternative behavior that is less effortful than the problem behavior

39. Farah, a behavior analyst, is exploring the impact of different frequencies of reinforcement on student engagement in a classroom. Farah tests reinforcement given every 5 minutes, 10 minutes, and 15 minutes. What type of analysis does this represent?

A. Comparative analysis

B. Add-in component analysis

C. Parametric analysis

D. Drop-out component analysis

40. Behavior analysts assess client progress to evaluate responsiveness to interventions by observing changes in behavior over time. All of the following are integral to this process EXCEPT:

A. Evaluating and utilizing data for decision-making

B. Collecting baseline data and defining goals

C. Experimenting to identify the function of the target behavior

D. Clearly operationalizing the target behavior

41. Sam is a behavior technician who works with a client, Frank, in a school setting. In the classroom, Sam observes Frank's teacher vocally instruct him to walk to and stand behind the last student in line by the door to go to the library. Instead of walking toward the line, Frank walks in the opposite direction toward the back of the classroom where the computer station is situated. The teacher quickly positions themselves between Frank and the computer station and instructs him again to line up by the door. Frank proceeds to cry and kick his teacher, who then physically prompts him to walk over to a designated "cool down" area of the classroom. Examine the antecedent-behavior-consequence (ABC) data recorded by Sam in the following table. What is the MOST significant limitation of this recorded narrative?

ANTECEDENT	BEHAVIOR	CONSEQUENCE
Teacher instructs Frank to walk to and line up behind his classmates by the door.	Frank cries and kicks his teacher.	Teacher physically prompts Frank to walk over to the "cool down" area.

A. Relevant antecedent details were left out.

B. The target behavior is not accurately described.

C. The function of the behavior is not included.

D. It is not positively and objectively worded.

42. Darcy is using an instructional arrangement that allows for her client, Freya, to freely emit one or more responses. Darcy allows Freya to interact with the environment with naturally occurring motivating operations (MOs). What instructional arrangement is Darcy using with Freya?

A. Naturalistic teaching approaches (NTAs)

B. Free-operant arrangement (FO arrangement)

C. Discrete-trial teaching (DTT)

D. Incidental teaching (IT)

43. Emily, a behavior analyst, has been working with her client, Marlowe, on developing social skills throughout the school year. With the end of the school year approaching, Emily is preparing to ensure Marlowe maintains these skills over the summer break. Which of the following strategies is LEAST likely to support the maintenance of these skills?

A. Conducting weekly family meetings to practice social communication

B. Giving Marlowe a checklist of social skills to practice independently

C. Coordinating playdates with peers

D. Engaging Marlowe in community service activities where she can interact with others

44. Simon, a BCBA®, is taking on a new 7-year-old client who engages in tantrum behavior in school. After collecting preliminary background information and establishing a contract for services, Simon conducts a functional analysis (FA) of the tantrum behavior. Results of the FA showed undifferentiated responding, so Simon developed an intervention plan to address multiple functions. After implementing the plan for over a month, the tantrum behavior remained unchanged. Upon further consultation with the client's teacher, Simon learned that there was an untreated medical condition that may be contributing to the occurrence of the tantrum behavior. What activity did Simon MOST likely neglect to conduct in the assessment process?

A. Antecedent-behavior-consequence (ABC) recording and analysis

B. Interview with relevant stakeholders

C. Review of records

D. Standardized testing

45. Behavior analysts incorporate transition and discharge planning into the overall treatment planning process. As such, termination of services should never come as a surprise to the client or their network of support; rather, services should be gradually stepped down. How long does the process of gradually decreasing services over time typically take?

A. At least 6 months

B. At least 1 week

C. At least 12 weeks

D. At least 1 month

46. When considering observable behavior, topography can BEST be defined as:

A. A method for identifying the impact of the behavior on the environment

B. A set of behaviors that the individual can perform

C. The physical form of the behavior

D. The sense organ that is used to identify external stimuli through hearing, vision, taste, smell, and cutaneous touch

47. Nico, a 9-year-old client, displays tantrum behavior during morning circle time in his classroom. His teacher notices that Nico becomes agitated and starts crying loudly when asked to participate in group activities that involve sharing personal stories with peers. This behavior does not occur during other classroom activities. To avoid disruption, the teacher allows Nico to sit quietly and draw in a corner of the classroom when he engages in tantrum behavior. Based on this information alone, what would you hypothesize to be the function of Nico's tantrum behavior?

A. Attention

B. Escape

C. Sensory

D. Tangible

48. Of the following, which is NOT an advantage afforded by single-subject experimental designs for behavior analysts' measurement of individual behavior?

A. It reveals the performance of individual subjects.

B. It allows for replication of effects within and across individual subjects.

C. Data for subjects are not combined/averaged, which helps to prevent distortion/masking of variability in the data.

D. It provides strong evidence of external validity and the generalization of results to a broader population.

49. Terri, a BCBA®, teaches Heather, a client, how to implement an intervention procedure to decrease her dog's behavior of chewing on her shoes. Terri instructs Heather to physically block her dog every time it tries to get a shoe in its mouth, redirect the dog to a chew toy, and deliver vocal praise and pet her dog when it engages with a chew toy. Heather's dog responds favorably to this intervention when it is in effect. However, when the intervention is removed, the dog returns to chewing on her shoes. When Heather reimplements the intervention, the dog again stops chewing on her shoes. This fact pattern BEST exemplifies which type of validity?

A. Internal validity

B. Face validity

C. External validity

D. Content validity

50. A behavior analyst conducts a latency-based functional analysis of a client's aggressive behavior. Examine the latency data (in seconds) in the following table. Based on this alone, what would you hypothesize to be the function of the aggressive behavior?

CONDITION	TRIAL 1	TRIAL 2	TRIAL 3
Tangibles	180	165	210
Attention	160	170	185
Escape	20	25	15
Alone	200	190	205

A. Access to tangibles

B. Attention

C. Escape from demands

D. Automatic reinforcement

51. Identify the type of experimental design displayed in the following graph.

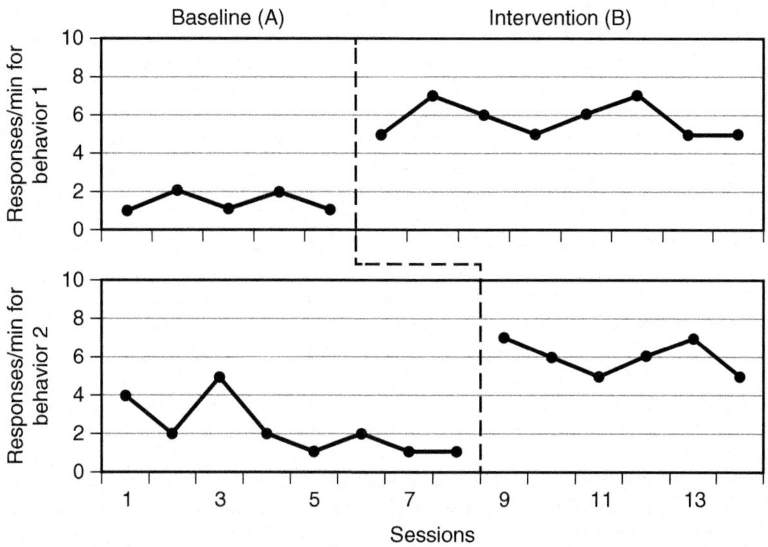

A. AB design

B. Changing criterion design

C. Multielement design

D. Multiple baseline design

52. Warner is a behavior analyst working in a special education classroom with Derrick, a 12-year-old student with autism spectrum disorder (ASD). Warner determines that attention is the function of Derrick's table-hitting behavior, so he plans to ignore it when it occurs. Warner implements the intervention with Derrick for 5 days, during which time Derrick's table-hitting behavior drops from an average of 12 times to an average of three times. The following 5 days, Warner stops implementing the intervention; in this phase, Derrick engaged in table-hitting behavior an average of 13 times. Warner then resumes the intervention, and Derrick's table-hitting behavior again drops to an average of two times. Identify the element of experimental reasoning this scenario exemplifies.

   A. Prediction

   B. Replication

   C. Generalization

   D. Verification

53. When considering the solicitation of testimonials from clients, which of the following is true?

   A. Behavior analysts may not solicit testimonials from current or former clients.

   B. Behavior analysts may solicit testimonials from current clients but not former clients.

   C. Behavior analysts may solicit testimonials from current and former clients.

   D. Behavior analysts may solicit testimonials from former clients but not current clients.

54. A teacher is interested in tracking her students' engagement with class activities. After developing an operational definition of "on-task" behavior, she decides to record the number of students that are on-task at the end of every hour throughout the school day. What type of measurement system is the teacher using?

   A. Event recording

   B. Partial interval recording

   C. Planned activity check (PLACHECK)

   D. Whole interval recording

55. Sometimes clients show a preference for reinforcers that are known to be harmful (e.g., cigarettes). What should behavior analysts do in these situations?

   A. Minimize the use of items as reinforcers when they may be harmful to clients

   B. Plan to use the reinforcers in treatment, even if known to be harmful, when the client has already been accessing it

   C. Use harmful reinforcers only when the behavior-change program is short in duration

   D. Use harmful reinforcers when needed for individual behavior plans

56. A BCBA® is planning to implement a 6-week social skills training program for five elementary school students. To evaluate the effectiveness of their efforts, the BCBA develops a plan to monitor each student's social skills performance by asking the students' teachers to provide a daily report on their demonstration of target skills in their classrooms. Data collection is to begin a week before the social skills training program commences and end 2 weeks after the program concludes. Select the visual display format MOST appropriate for the data to be collected in this scenario.

A. Cumulative record

B. Histogram

C. Line graph

D. Standard celeration chart

57. A behavior analyst is assisting a client in learning how to operate a cash register at a retail store. The client needs to perform tasks such as entering items correctly, processing payments, providing change, and issuing receipts. The behavior analyst monitors the number of attempts it takes for the client to complete each transaction accurately. What method of measurement is MOST suitable for tracking progress in mastering this skill?

A. Event recording

B. Time sampling

C. Trials to criterion

D. Interval recording

58. Pedro, a BCBA®, is preparing to provide behavior-analytic supervision to João, a trainee acquiring fieldwork experience to meet BCBA certification requirements. To select supervision goals based on an assessment of João's skills, Pedro performs which of the following tasks in sequence?

A. Select long- and short-term supervision goals, review João's permanent products (and conduct direct observations if needed), administer quizzes and interviews to assess his knowledge-based skills, and have João perform a self-assessment

B. Administer quizzes and interviews to assess his knowledge-based skills, have João perform a self-assessment, review João's permanent products (and conduct direct observations if needed), and select long- and short-term supervision goals

C. Have João perform a self-assessment, administer quizzes and interviews to assess his knowledge-based skills, review João's permanent products (and conduct direct observations if needed), and select long- and short-term supervision goals

D. Have João perform a self-assessment, select long- and short-term supervision goals, review João's permanent products (and conduct direct observations if needed), and administer quizzes and interviews to assess his knowledge-based skills

59. Erica, a behavior technician, is working with a client, Joseph, on a matching task. She places several objects on a table in front of Joseph, one of which is a crayon. Erica then hands Joseph a crayon that matches the one on the table and says, "Find the match." Joseph initially requires prompting but, after multiple trials, learns to independently and correctly match the crayon in his hand to the crayon on the table. Erica then hands Joseph a different object, which he independently and correctly matches to an identical object on the table. What type of stimulus-stimulus relation is demonstrated in this example?

A. Congruency

B. Reflexivity

C. Symmetry

D. Transitivity

60. Whitney, a client, used to run down the steps in front of her home quickly, which often led to tripping and falling. After experiencing several falls, she now walks down the steps slowly and carefully to avoid accidents. Which of the following BEST describes her cautious behavior on the steps?

A. Contingency-shaped

B. Pivotal

C. Rule-governed

D. Reflexive

61. Jessica is a 22-year-old client with cognitive deficits who engages in severe self-injurious behavior (SIB). Recently, the intensity and rate of the behavior has markedly increased. An assessment has not been conducted to identify its function, so the behavior analyst overseeing the case has recommended a functional analysis (FA). However, there is concern among members of Jessica's treatment team that evoking the behavior will endanger Jessica's safety and may result in undesirable long-term effects. What type of FA should the supervising behavior analyst proceed to conduct on Jessica's SIB?

A. Brief FA

B. FA of precursor behavior

C. Indirect assessment of the behavior

D. Latency-based FA

62. Orion is a 48-year-old who still frequently asks his parents for financial assistance. Though his parents wish he would stop asking for money and achieve financial independence, they nevertheless give him money whenever he asks for it. Which behavior-change procedure are Orion's parents unwittingly implementing with Orion?

A. Positive punishment

B. Negative reinforcement

C. Positive reinforcement

D. Negative punishment

63. A behavior analyst is working with a client, Alex, who frequently engages in head-banging behavior. This behavior occurs most often when Alex is left alone in his room, but it occasionally happens in other settings as well. When Alex engages in head-banging, staff members rush to him and provide comfort and attention. Alex's head-banging behavior decreases significantly when he is engaged in group activities or when someone is interacting with him directly. Which of the following is MOST likely the function of Alex's head-banging behavior?

A. Access to tangible items

B. Sensory stimulation

C. Attention from caregivers

D. Escape from tasks

64. When conducting a behavior assessment, a behavior analyst plans to use both direct and indirect measures. Which of the following would NOT be considered an indirect measure?

A. Structured interviews with caregivers

B. Direct observations

C. Standardized questionnaires

D. Review of historical records

65. Ms. Jackson asks Amalie to pick up the toys at the end of a free play period and put them away in the correct bins. After giving this prompt, she walks away and leaves Amalie alone with the toys. Ms. Jackson returns after 5 minutes, and all the toys are put away. She provides verbal praise to Amalie for cleaning up the toys and marks the task as complete on Amalie's data sheet. Which of the following MOST likely represents the type of data collection Ms. Jackson is using?

A. Duration recording

B. Latency recording

C. Momentary time sampling

D. Permanent product recording

66. Michael is a BCBA® who runs a private practice that offers behavioral consultation services to various types of organizations. To promote his practice, he created an attractive website with testimonials from former clients who had wonderful things to say about him and his business. The testimonials were identified as solicited, state the relationship with clients, and do not violate any laws. Is this ethical?

A. Yes, because the Ethics Code does not address the use of testimonials for advertising.

B. Yes, because the testimonials were identified as solicited, state the relationship with clients, and comply with the law.

C. No, because behavior analysts do not solicit or use testimonials about their services.

D. No, because the Ethics Code strictly forbids the use of technology to promote one's business.

67. Lupe often talks to her peers during a 50-minute group activity. A behavior technician records the number of times Lupe initiates conversation during three group activities: five, seven, and nine times. What is the average rate of Lupe's conversation-initiating behavior?

A. Five times per group activity

B. Six times per group activity

C. Seven times per group activity

D. Eight times per group activity

68. ________________ is the provision of differential reinforcement for a progression of responses that are more similar to the target response. In other words, it is a process through which reinforcement is delivered for successive approximations of a terminal behavior.

A. Training

B. Shaping

C. Modeling

D. Chaining

69. A behavior technician, Carl, is working with a 5-year-old client, Renee, to enhance her communication skills. During a lesson, Carl asked Renee a series of simple questions to which she would provide an answer. For example, Carl asked, "What is your name?" to which Renee answered, "Renee." Appropriate responses were reinforced with verbal praise. What verbal operant does the lesson appear to be targeting for instruction?

A. Codic

B. Intraverbal

C. Mand

D. Tact

70. Maria, a BCBA®, observes that her supervisee, Daniel, consistently misses deadlines for submitting data. To effectively address this issue, Maria decides to conduct a performance diagnostic to uncover the root causes of Daniel's behavior. What specific approach is Maria utilizing in this scenario?

A. Cultural adaptation

B. Function-based approach

C. Standard performance

D. Transformational

71. Examine the following graph of the frequency of three different behaviors across seven sessions. Which of the following descriptions is MOST accurate for Behavior 3?

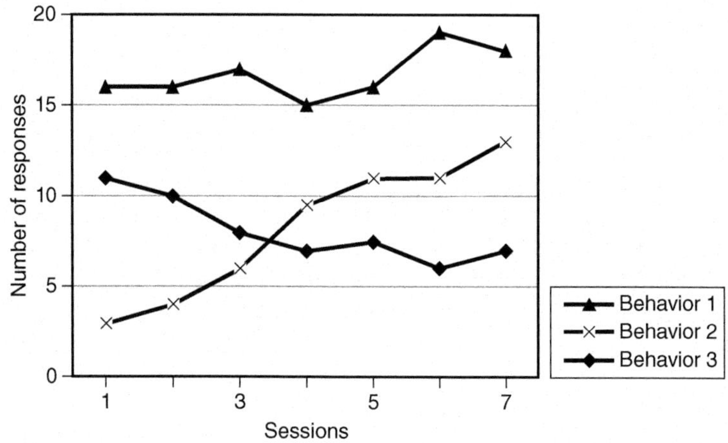

A. High-level responding, low variability, increasing trend

B. Low-level responding, low variability, decreasing trend

C. Mid-level responding, high variability, increasing trend

D. Mid-level responding, low variability, decreasing trend

72. Hillary, a BCBA®, is about to start her first day on the job at a new behavior analysis service agency. On the morning of her first day, she leaves the house at 8:30 a.m. and runs into traffic on the road. The next day, she leaves half an hour earlier—at 8:00 a.m.—resulting in avoiding traffic. Subsequently, Hillary leaves for work every weekday morning at 8:00 a.m. In this example, traffic functioned as:

A. A negative punisher for leaving the house at 8:00 a.m.

B. A negative reinforcer for leaving the house at 8:00 a.m.

C. A positive punisher for leaving the house at 8:00 a.m.

D. A positive reinforcer for leaving the house at 8:00 a.m.

73. Mateo is a second-grade student who has trouble making friends at school. One day, Mateo's teacher encourages him to play a game with another student in his class. While initially hesitant, Mateo approaches the other student. During that recess period, they play a ball game together which Mateo seems to really enjoy. At the start of the next recess period, Mateo approaches the same peer and asks to play a ball game together. Which of the following BEST explains Mateo's behavior?

A. Automatic reinforcement

B. Graduated guidance

C. Socially mediated reinforcement

D. Tact-to-mand transfer

74. Which of the following is NOT a condition for discontinuing services established in a service agreement?

A. Funding is discontinued for services.

B. Behavioral staff are exposed to harmful conditions that cannot be changed.

C. The client met all their goals.

D. The client only receives some benefit from services.

75. Ms. Carson is a seventh-grade science teacher. In her classroom, when she performs a cadence clap, students will stop what they are doing, repeat the cadence clap, and then direct their eyes toward her for instructions. In the absence of her cadence clap, students will simply continue with whatever activity they are engaged with. Which of the following BEST explains the students' response to Ms. Carson's cadence clap?

A. Automatic contingency

B. Reflexivity

C. Stimulus control

D. Stimulus equivalence

76. A behavior analyst is working with a 5-year-old client, Everett, who emits various responses to gain his parents' attention. These include pulling them toward his toys, saying "Come play," climbing on furniture, pushing items off counters, and crying with tears. These behaviors are BEST described as:

A. A stimulus class

B. A functional response class

C. An equivalence class

D. A topographical response class

77. Mia, a BCBA®, is working with Marley, a young student with an intellectual disability. Before conducting imitation training, Mia evaluates whether Marley is sufficiently able to attend to the model stimulus and discovers that she needs to begin by teaching Marley basic attending skills. Identify the skill that is NOT essential for Marley to possess in order for Mia to conduct imitation training.

A. Ability to imitate verbal models

B. Looking at the teacher

C. Looking at the objects

D. Complying with instructions

78. Examine the following graph of the cumulative frequency data collected for a target response over the course of 10 treatment sessions. During which session was the frequency of the target response equal to 2?

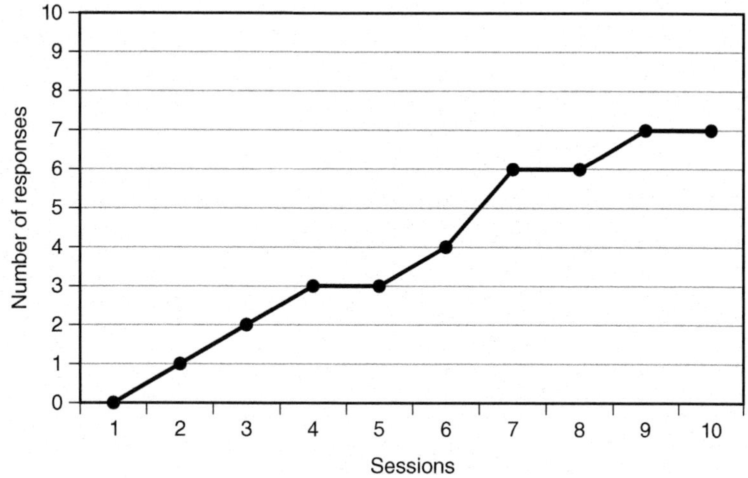

A. Session 3

B. Session 6

C. Session 7

D. Session 9

79. During the first week of school, Ms. Hart, a fourth-grade teacher, conducts morning meetings with her students. In these meetings, the students first share their goals and aspirations for the year. Next, they discuss how these goals relate to classroom behavior norms, the importance of these behaviors, and the rewards for following them, as well as the consequences for not doing so. Together, they create a poster listing all the agreed-upon classroom norms. They display the poster prominently on the classroom wall and hold a celebratory ceremony where all the students and Ms. Hart sign it. Ms. Hart and her students refer to this as their "Commitment to Caring," but a behavior analyst would refer to it as a:

A. Positive practice

B. Contingency contract

C. Response cost system

D. Premack principle

80. A behavior analyst is a member of a multidisciplinary treatment team at a community behavioral health clinic. A client at the clinic is receiving services from the behavior analyst to address self-injurious behavior. The client also receives services from the clinic's psychiatrist and an intern earning his licensed professional counselor (LPC). During a treatment team meeting, the LPC recommends a nonbehavioral treatment that the behavior analyst is unfamiliar with. What is the MOST pressing question the behavior analyst must answer?

A. Does the treatment interfere with the client's goals?

B. Is the treatment supported by peer-reviewed research?

C. Does the treatment allow for quantitative data collection?

D. Does the treatment pose a risk to the safety of the client?

81. Examine the following graph. What type of experimental design was used?

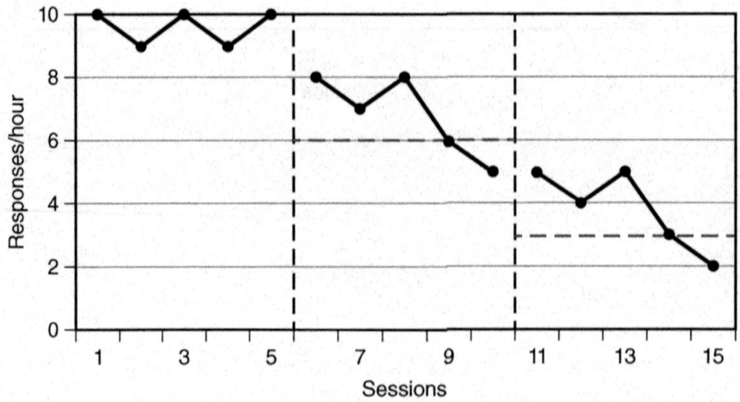

A. Changing criterion design

B. Multielement design

C. Multiple baseline design

D. AB design

82. A behavior analyst is concerned about the services provided by a nonbehavioral professional. They should:

A. Discontinue services

B. Refer the client to another professional for relevant services

C. Report the other professional to the Behavior Analyst Certification Board® (BACB®)

D. Take steps to resolve the issue with the other professional

83. Bart is a fourth-grade student who has been leaving his assigned seat in the classroom without permission. His teacher, Ms. Andrews, decides to implement a strategy to address his out-of-seat behavior. There is a token system in the classroom that rewards students for desirable behaviors throughout the school day. Each time Bart leaves his seat without permission, Ms. Andrews takes away one of the tokens that Bart has earned. It's not long before Bart's out-of-seat behavior sharply declines. Which of the following BEST explains the change in target problem behavior?

A. Negative punishment

B. Negative reinforcement

C. Positive punishment

D. Positive reinforcement

84. Ms. Said is a special education teacher implementing a behavior change system with her students. If the students stop talking when she rings a bell, she gives them points. If the students earn a certain amount of points, they get an extra recess at the end of the day on Friday. If they do not stop talking when she rings a bell, she removes points. Which of the following BEST describes the behavior change system Ms. Said is implementing?

A. Token economy with backup reinforcers

B. Token economy with level system

C. Token economy with response cost

D. Token economy with generalized conditioned reinforcer

85. Respondent conditioning involves pairing an unconditioned stimulus (US) with a neutral stimulus (NS) until the NS becomes a ________________ that elicits a ________________.

A. Conditioned stimulus (CS); conditioned response (CR)

B. Conditioned stimulus (CR); unconditioned response (UR)

C. Unconditioned stimulus (US); conditioned response (CR)

D. Unconditioned stimulus (US); unconditioned response (UR)

86. Shaan, a behavior technician, is working with a client to help them recognize their written name, "Rory." In the initial trial, he places the written name "Rory" among shapes. Gradually, he replaces these shapes with letters and words until the client recognizes all the letters in the written name "Rory." What type of stimulus prompting is being used?

A. Response prompting

B. Least-to-most prompting

C. Stimulus shaping

D. Stimulus fading

87. Georgia, a BCBA®, wants to measure how often Mark, a client, displays inappropriate vocalizations during treatment sessions. Which of the following BEST describes how Georgia can accurately measure the rate of the target behavior?

   A. Record each occurrence of the target behavior, then count the total number of occurrences at the end of the treatment session

   B. Record whether the target behavior occurred or did not occur at the end of each 5-minute interval for the duration of the treatment session

   C. Record each occurrence of the target behavior, then count the total number of occurrences and divide it by the length of the observation period at the end of the treatment session

   D. Record the length of time between the onset and offset of the target behavior, then add up the amount of time across all occurrences at the end of the treatment session

88. Jason is a BCBA® who works at an elementary school. One day, a teacher enters his office at the school and says, "Hi, I'm wondering if you might be able to help me. I know you're the behavior specialist here, and I've been struggling with a student in my class. Can you just stop by briefly, have a look at him, and maybe give me some tips for dealing with his behavior? I would really appreciate your support!" What should Jason do?

   A. Agree to conduct the observation

   B. Agree to conduct the observation, but only after obtaining permission from his supervisor

   C. Decline to observe the student

   D. Decline to observe the student, but instead offer to schedule a visit to begin a functional assessment of the problem behavior

89. A behavior analyst is considering terminating services with a client. It is unclear whether services are appropriate or effective for the client. What is the BEST course of action?

   A. Consult with the client's network of support (e.g., caregiver, teacher, or employer)

   B. Convene an expert panel of behavior analysts and other relevant professionals to review the treatment program

   C. Conduct a systematic interview with the client

   D. Consult the client's insurance company

90. Morgan, a behavior technician, is teaching a 5-year-old client to identify colors. She sits at a table with the client and presents a red card, asking, "What color is this?" The client responds, "Red," and Morgan immediately says, "Great job!" and gives the client a token. She then repeats the process with a blue card. What instructional procedure is Morgan using?

   A. Discrete-trial teaching (DTT)

   B. Free-operant arrangement (FO arrangement)

   C. Incidental teaching (IT)

   D. Naturalistic teaching approaches (NTAs)

91. Amy, a behavior analyst, is providing behavior-analytic supervision to Tyler, who is providing applied behavior analysis services to children with autism spectrum disorder (ASD) in a university-based clinic. To monitor Tyler's performance and acquisition of skills, Amy is collecting relevant performance data. Amy should collect all of the following forms of performance data EXCEPT:

A. The number and rate of competencies Tyler acquires

B. The number and rate of errors Tyler makes in permanent products

C. The impact of the Hawthorne effect on Tyler's performance

D. Progress in Tyler's fluent and accurate use of technical language

92. Examine the following graph of the results from a functional analysis (FA) of Arya's tantrum behavior. Based on this alone, what would you hypothesize to be the function of the tantrum behavior?

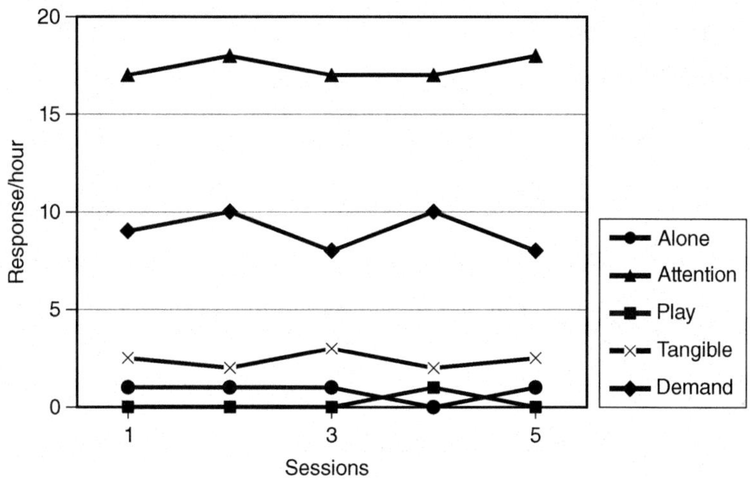

A. Social positive reinforcement

B. Social positive reinforcement and social negative reinforcement

C. Social negative reinforcement and access to tangibles

D. Inconclusive; the pattern is undifferentiated

93. In the course of developing intervention goals and strategies, a behavior analyst working in a psychiatric treatment facility for adolescent males pays particular attention to the level of support available in the facility (e.g., physical space, staffing), as well as elements that may inhibit successful implementation of the treatment program. In other words, the behavior analyst is considering which two factors prior to making recommendations?

A. Risks and social validity

B. Supporting environments and constraints

C. Supporting environments and social validity

D. Social validity and supporting environments

94. During a paired stimulus preference assessment, a behavior analyst presents two items at a time to a client and records the client's choice. What is the PRIMARY data the analyst should collect?

A. Duration of engagement with nonpreferred items

B. Number of times each item is chosen over others

C. Frequency of requests for additional items

D. Duration of engagement with each chosen item

95. One day at school, Tim drew an obnoxious picture on the whiteboard in his classroom and the entire class laughed. As a result of the attention that he received from the other students, Tim continued to draw obnoxious pictures on the whiteboard at every opportunity throughout the school day for the rest of the week. Tim's behavior is the result of:

A. Negative punishment

B. Negative reinforcement

C. Positive punishment

D. Positive reinforcement

96. Negative reinforcement involves the ________________ of a stimulus immediately following a behavior that serves to ________________ the future frequency of the behavior.

A. Addition; decrease

B. Addition; increase

C. Removal; decrease

D. Removal; increase

97. Taylor, a behavior analyst, receives a new client referral. After verifying that the case is within her area of expertise, she meets with the client to collect initial information, explain behavior-analytic services, and go over the service agreement. Once written consent is obtained, what should Taylor do next?

A. Conduct a functional analysis

B. Conduct a preference assessment

C. Develop an intervention plan based on initial observations

D. Request and review relevant client records

98. A behavior analyst administers a series of structured interviews to parents and teachers to gather information about a child's daily routines, preferences, and responses to specific antecedents and consequences. What type of assessment method is the behavior analyst using?

A. Direct

B. Functional

C. Indirect

D. Descriptive

99. Gus is a client who engages in physical aggression toward others. During treatment sessions, vocal attempts from staff to redirect Gus when he engages in the problem behavior have been unsuccessful. When staff resorts to using physical restraints to prevent Gus from engaging in physical aggression, he almost immediately relaxes and becomes noticeably calmer; but when he is released from the restraint, Gus will rapidly escalate and engage in the problem behavior again. Given this information, what would you hypothesize to be the function of Gus's aggressive behavior?

A. Attention

B. Escape

C. Sensory

D. Tangible

100. A behavior analyst is consulting with the parents of a 10-year-old boy, Gary, about his extreme resistance to completing homework. When Gary's parents ask him to do his homework, he refuses and, quite often, has a temper tantrum. The behavior analyst meets with Gary and, in the course of their conversation, asks where he likes to do homework; what pen or pencil he likes to use; if he likes to listen to music while doing homework; if he likes to work in bright or soft light; which subjects he likes to work on first; how often he feels he needs a break; and what he likes to do when he takes a break from doing homework. This best exemplifies the consideration of which factor when recommending intervention goals and procedures?

A. Constraints

B. Supporting environments

C. Risks

D. Client preferences

101. After the start of services, a behavior analyst decides there is a need for a change to the intervention plan. What should the behavior analyst do to enact the change?

A. Document the change and explain it to clients/stakeholders

B. Document the change and proceed to implement it

C. Explain the change to clients/stakeholders

D. Explain the change to clients/stakeholders and obtain informed consent as appropriate

102. A behavior analyst, Mieka, is working with a fifth-grade student, Randolph, to improve his initiation of in-class writing activities. Mieka observes Randolph during his English Language Arts (ELA) class and found that, on average, it takes Randolph 104 seconds to begin writing tasks, whereas randomly selected peers take 47 seconds to begin. The measurement starts when the teacher finishes providing instructions for the activity and ends when Randolph uses his writing utensil to write assignment-appropriate information on his paper (e.g., name, date, letters). Which temporal dimension of behavior is measured in this scenario?

A. Duration

B. Interresponse time

C. Latency

D. Whole interval

103. Which of the following is a contingency-dependent antecedent intervention that involves presenting a series of simple requests followed by a target request?

A. Functional communication training

B. Noncontingent reinforcement with positive reinforcement

C. Noncontingent reinforcement with negative reinforcement

D. High-probability request sequence

104. Paul, the CEO of a major corporation, was arrested after he flew into a rage while driving and deliberately forced another driver's car off the road. As a result, Paul was sentenced to attend weekly group therapy meetings for anger management, which he despises and thinks are a waste of time. During each meeting, Paul makes offensive remarks to the other participants and the group leader until he is asked to take a 10-minute break outside to calm down and reconsider his behavior. Once outside, Paul smokes cigarettes and responds to emails on his phone. The group leader notices that, rather than stopping, Paul's aggressive and offensive remarks are beginning earlier in the session and occurring with greater frequency. What is the MOST likely reason that Paul's aggressive behavior is increasing?

A. Paul's behavior is reinforced by access to escape from the group.

B. The group leader lacks group management skills.

C. Paul's behavior is reinforced by attention from the other members of the group.

D. The group leader fails to reinforce Paul's participation in the anger management group.

105. Examine the following graph of the results from a functional analysis (FA) of Walter's scratching behavior. Based on this alone, what would you hypothesize to be the function of the scratching behavior?

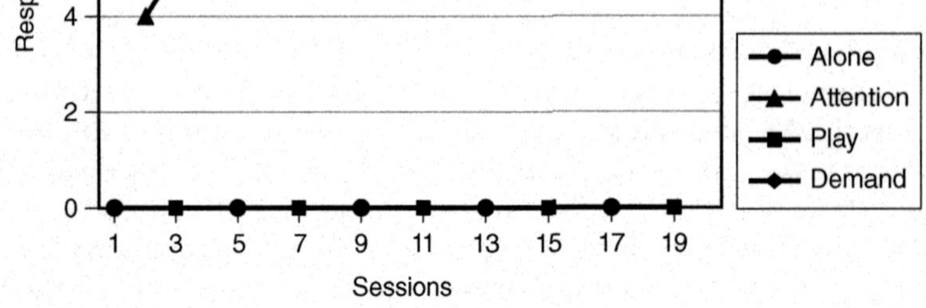

A. Automatic reinforcement

B. Automatic reinforcement and social negative reinforcement

C. Social positive reinforcement and social negative reinforcement

D. Inconclusive; the pattern is undifferentiated

106. Ashton, a behavior analyst, is initiating a supervisory relationship with a new supervisee. Ashton is aware that supervisors must assess the outcomes of their behavior-analytic supervision activities and decides to create an assessment plan that uses recommended methods. Consequently, she considers all of the following methods EXCEPT:

A. Conducting a survey

B. Engaging in covert third-party observation

C. Tracking relevant data

D. Requesting feedback

107. A behavior analyst is working with a fifth-grade teacher in a general education classroom to gather data on a particular student's frequent question-asking behavior. According to the teacher, the student asks questions constantly throughout the day and sometimes strings questions together so much that it is difficult to identify when an instance of questioning ends and another begins. Based on this information, which of the following measurement procedures should the behavior analyst recommend for collecting data on this student's question-asking behavior?

A. Frequency recording

B. Interresponse time recording

C. Partial interval recording

D. Whole interval recording

108. Olivia, a BCBA®, is taking on a new 3-year-old client who engages in food refusal behavior. She has already met with the parents to collect preliminary background information about the client and review the contract for professional services. After obtaining written consent from parents to proceed with services, what should Olivia do next?

A. Conduct a functional analysis

B. Obtain consent from the 3-year-old client

C. Refer the client to a healthcare professional

D. Review records and available data

109. Which of the following is not a defining feature of single-subject experimental designs?

A. The subject is the unit of intervention and data analysis.

B. Subjects are randomly selected from a population of interest.

C. The subject provides its own control for comparison.

D. The target behavior is measured repeatedly across different levels or conditions of the intervention.

110. Corey is a BCBA® who is supervising Steven, a graduate student in a behavior analysis training program. Corey discovered that Steven had submitted falsified fieldwork experience verification forms, counting many more hours than he would have been able to complete given his schedule. When Corey confronted Steven about this issue, Steven refused to admit any wrongdoing and claimed that he had indeed completed the hours reported on his experience verification forms. How should Corey proceed?

A. Ask Steven to make up the extra hours reported; if he agrees, then consider this a lesson learned and the matter closed

B. Ask Steven to seek out another supervisor; if he agrees, then consider this a lesson learned and the matter closed

C. Report Steven to his university; he is a graduate student, so this is a university problem

D. Report Steven to the Behavior Analyst Certification Board® (BACB®); this is a serious breach of the Ethics Code

111. Maggie is a BCBA® who has obtained training in supervision. She supervised several graduate students for her agency who complained about her supervision practices. Some of the students reported that Maggie failed to even provide an adequate number of supervisory contacts. As a result, Maggie was eventually reported to the Behavior Analyst Certification Board® for multiple ethical violations. When questioned about the reported issues, she argued that the training she received did not cover all aspects of her responsibilities as a supervisor. "If my training didn't cover it, how am I supposed to know?" she asked. What would the Ethics Code's position on this matter be?

A. BCBAs are obligated to be familiar with the Ethics Code.

B. BCBAs are obligated to be familiar with only those parts of the Ethics Code that are relevant to the work they're doing.

C. BCBAs cannot be held liable for their professional conduct if they have not been properly trained.

D. BCBAs should immediately take steps to resolve problems when notified that they are out of compliance with the Ethics Code.

112. A behavior analyst designs an intervention plan to reduce off-task behavior in a fifth-grade classroom. The intervention involves providing specific instructions and modeling to the teacher. The behavior analyst periodically observes the classroom during instructional time, noting any deviations from the intervention plan. During recess, the behavior analyst meets with the teacher to provide feedback based on these observations. Why does the behavior analyst conduct these observations?

A. To evaluate the social validity of the intervention

B. To monitor and support fidelity of implementation

C. To assess the social significance of the behaviors targeted

D. To establish criteria for behavior change

113. Stewart is a BCBA® who is working with a 15-year-old client who engages in several problem behaviors at school. These include shouting at his peers, scribbling in his textbooks, stealing items from his teacher's desk, and leaving the school building without permission. Which of these behaviors should be targeted first?

A. Shouting at peers

B. Scribbling in books

C. Stealing items from teacher's desk

D. Leaving school building without permission

114. A BCBA® is the main author of a published study. A researcher contacts the BCBA and asks to see the original data gathered from the study. How should the BCBA respond?

A. Share the data, excluding confidential client information

B. Share the data, including all information on clients

C. Refuse to share the data as it is not required

D. Refer the researcher to the data published in the journal article; the original data does not have to be shared

115. Alex is a behavior analyst who is evaluating the effectiveness of two different instructional procedures for increasing intraverbal behavior. To do this, he measures the number of response opportunities needed to acquire a target behavior for each of the two procedures. The first procedure resulted in acquisition of the target skill after an average of six trials, but the second procedure resulted in acquisition of the target skill after an average of only two trials. What measurement method is Alex using to compare the two instructional procedures?

A. Baseline probe trials

B. Component analysis

C. Task analysis

D. Trials to criterion

116. Ezra is a BCBA® who supervises several students enrolled in an applied behavior analysis training program at a local university. She has been careful about taking on only the number of supervisees that allows her to be effective as a supervisor and ensures that the training she provides is well within her defined scope of competence. To evaluate the effects of her supervision, what does Ezra need to do?

A. Nothing else; Ezra has already taken the necessary steps for ensuring that she provides high-quality supervision

B. Conduct regular meetings with supervisees to discuss supervision and allow opportunities for them to report any concerns

C. Conduct regular evaluations of supervisory performance using feedback from others, clients' outcomes data, and supervisees' outcomes data

D. Examine quarterly and annual evaluation reports from her supervisor to identify areas of concern and set goals for addressing them

117. Mr. Gupta, a middle school teacher, notices that his students are often off-task during class. He seeks help from Ms. Lim, the school's BCBA®, who observes and records the rate of students' off-task behavior and Mr. Gupta's use of corrective feedback. Ms. Lim's analysis shows that off-task behavior decreases when Mr. Gupta increases his use of corrective feedback. After following Ms. Lim's advice to provide more corrective feedback, Mr. Gupta notices a significant improvement in his students' behavior. At what level, according to the science of behavior analysis, is Ms. Lim and Mr. Gupta's understanding of these students' behavior in class?

A. Prediction and control

B. Description and prediction

C. Control

D. Description

118. A teacher is implementing a new reward system in her classroom. This system involves having students earn tickets for completing assigned tasks. The students then write their names on the tickets they have earned and place them in a box located on the teacher's desk throughout the week. At the end of the week, the teacher draws a ticket from the box, declares the student whose name is on the ticket as the winner, and gives the winning student a prize. The more tickets the students earn, the greater the chance that one of their tickets will be drawn. What schedule of reinforcement does this system use?

A. Fixed interval (FI)

B. Fixed ratio (FR)

C. Variable interval (VI)

D. Variable ratio (VR)

119. Peyton, a behavior technician, is working with a client named Gabriel to increase his compliance with brushing his teeth. To achieve this, Peyton first asks Gabriel to perform a series of simple tasks he is likely to comply with, such as giving a high five, touching his nose, and making a silly face. After Gabriel successfully completes these tasks, Peyton then requests that he brush his teeth. When Gabriel complies, Peyton delivers a high-quality reinforcer. What type of procedure is Peyton implementing?

A. Errorless learning

B. Graduated guidance

C. High-probability instructional sequence

D. Task analysis

120. A behavior analyst assesses a client's communication abilities using a structured test that requires following specific guidelines. What type of assessment is this?

A. Functional

B. Criterion-referenced

C. Indirect

D. Standardized

121. Mackenzie is a client who has been engaging in problem behavior at school. The BCBA® assigned to her case, Eli, conducts an observation of Mackenzie in the school setting and records each occurrence of the target behavior and the environmental events surrounding it. What type of assessment is Eli conducting?

A. Descriptive

B. Criterion-referenced

C. Free operant

D. Indirect

122. Each of the following behaviors can be measured using permanent product recording EXCEPT:

A. Completing homework assignment sheets

B. Making eye contact with peers

C. Placing toys in toy bins after free play periods

D. Urinating in diapers

123. A 52-year-old person receiving care in a psychiatric residential treatment facility stands still in silence, holding a broom for several hours daily. In a treatment team discussion, a BCBA® learns that this person used to sweep the common room while singing every day. One member of the treatment team expresses the view that the person's change in behavior may just be a mystery with no rational explanation or cause. Another team member speculates that the person's change in behavior may be caused by their experience as a young child and repressed emotions that have resurfaced into their consciousness. The BCBA is committed to a scientific approach to understanding and intervening in human behavior. As such, she respectfully shares with the team that all behavior possesses an identifiable cause and, as a result, is to some degree determinable. She then encourages the team to (a) focus on explanations of the person's behavior based on the person's known experiences and the consequences of their behavior; and (b) rule out simple, logical explanations for the person's behavior before entertaining more complex or abstract explanations. In her comments, the BCBA is promoting which three attitudes of science?

A. Empiricism, parsimony, and philosophic doubt

B. Determinism, selectionism, and parsimony

C. Selectionism, determinism, and empiricism

D. Parsimony, philosophic doubt, and determinism

124. Amy is a BCBA® who works at a local clinic for young children with developmental disabilities. Each morning when she arrives at the clinic, she checks her calendar to review the day's planned work activities. On days when she sees an event with the label "supervision meeting" on her calendar, she immediately spends the first 15 minutes of her workday reviewing the discussion points and activities that she will go over with her supervisee at their next meeting. However, when no such event is seen on her calendar, Amy does not spend any time reviewing the discussion points and activities that she will go over with her supervisee at their next meeting. Amy's behavior is likely the result of:

A. Response generalization

B. Socially mediated reinforcement

C. Stimulus control

D. Stimulus generalization

125. What position does the Ethics Code for Behavior Analysts take on the use of punishment procedures in behavioral interventions?

A. Recommend reinforcement rather than punishment whenever possible

B. Use either reinforcement or punishment, not both

C. When attempting to decrease behavior, use punishment first to achieve quick results

D. Use reinforcement only; punishment is bad practice and should never be used

126. Which of the following is an example of an automatically reinforced response?

A. Eating quinoa because you read that it's a healthy thing to do

B. Knocking on a door because you want someone to open it

C. Scratching a spot on your leg because it itches

D. Washing your hands because you were told to

127. Ian is a 3-year-old boy who does not communicate using language very often. He knows many basic words, but he often screams or makes physical gestures to communicate with his parents instead of using words—especially when he wants something. Kelly is a BCBA® working with Ian and his parents in their home to increase Ian's use of vocal mands. Which procedure is the MOST appropriate for Kelly to employ?

A. Shaping latency within a response topography

B. Shaping across response topographies

C. Shaping frequency within a response topography

D. Shaping magnitude within a response topography

128. Wanda, a BCBA®, works in a school with other nonbehavioral professionals. One day, the school counselor tells Wanda that one of her clients was banging her head against a desk during a counseling session. When Wanda asked the counselor what he did about it, the counselor said, "She seemed like she was having a rough day, so I just let her. She needed to release her frustrations out somehow." In a situation such as this, what should a BCBA do?

A. Attempt to resolve the issue directly with the counselor; if it cannot be resolved, report it to the appropriate authority (e.g., administrator, supervisor)

B. File a report with details of the issue to the Behavior Analyst Certification Board®

C. Avoid conflict with nonbehavioral colleagues; do not report the incident or attempt to resolve it directly with the counselor

D. Notify the client's parent or legal guardian of the incident

129. Daria, a behavior technician, is teaching a 4-year-old client, Milo, to say the word "apple." Daria emits the vocal response of "apple" as a model, then prompts Milo to replicate the response. Milo's vocal response of "apple" is under the control of Daria's vocal response of "apple." Milo's vocal response is an example of which of the verbal operants?

A. Codic

B. Echoic

C. Mand

D. Tact

130. Examine the following graph of the results from a functional analysis (FA) of Cary's yelling behavior. Based on this alone, what would you hypothesize to be the function of the yelling behavior?

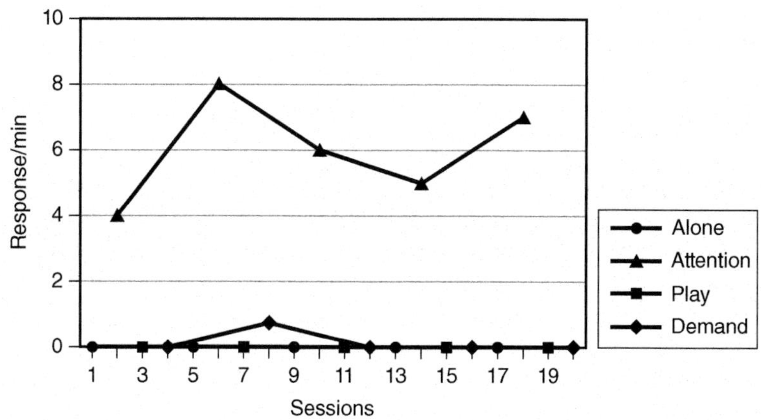

A. Automatic reinforcement

B. Social positive reinforcement

C. Automatic reinforcement and social positive reinforcement

D. Social negative reinforcement

131. Mr. Caretto, a fourth-grade teacher, explains to his students that they will have a pizza party once every student has memorized all of the multiplication facts. What type of group contingency is this?

A. Dependent group contingency

B. Intradependent group contingency

C. Independent group contingency

D. Interdependent group contingency

132. As supervisors, behavior analysts must provide supervisees with timely feedback and reinforcement to enhance their performance. Dr. Digable, a BCBA®, conducts observations of her supervisee, Toni, to offer performance feedback. After each observation, Dr. Digable will carefully write up her notes describing what Toni performed correctly, which can take several days, and then praise Toni for it the next time they meet. Despite Dr. Digable's efforts to praise Toni for his good work, she notices that his performance is not improving over time. What might account for this?

A. Dr. Digable is not delivering feedback in a timely enough manner.

B. Dr. Digable's feedback is unclear.

C. Dr. Digable uses too many technical terms.

D. Dr. Digable focuses on too many errors at a time.

133. Sarah, a behavior analyst, conducts a training session for her staff on a new intervention strategy. After the training, she periodically observes the staff implementing the strategy and records data on their adherence to the protocol. Sarah uses these data to provide ongoing feedback and additional training as needed. What is Sarah's PRIMARY goal with these observations and data recordings?

A. Assess the social validity of the intervention

B. Evaluate the impact of the intervention on client behavior

C. Determine the level of interobserver agreement

D. Ensure the intervention is being implemented with high fidelity

134. A floor sign with the words "Out of service for maintenance" is positioned directly in front of a restroom entrance. Cooper needs to use the restroom and approaches the entrance but, because he sees the sign, does not go inside. Cooper's behavior is an example of:

A. Contingency-shaped behavior

B. Negative reinforcement

C. Rule-governed behavior

D. Premack principle

135. Danielle has been taught to use a hand signal to communicate to her teacher that she needs to go to the restroom. This usually results in the teacher looking at Danielle and nodding, thereby giving her permission to go to the restroom. Recently, Danielle has started to wave her arms in the air and silently mouth the word "bathroom" when the teacher looks in her direction to ask for permission to go to the restroom. Which of the following BEST explains this new untrained behavior?

A. Functional response class

B. Response generalization

C. Setting/situation generalization

D. Stimulus generalization

136. Conducting a descriptive assessment of problem behavior can involve any of the following activities EXCEPT:

A. Administering checklists or rating scales at regular intervals to stakeholders who most frequently observe the problem behavior

B. Continuously recording the occurrence of the problem behavior in relation to environmental events

C. Writing a narrative description of the problem behavior under the conditions in which it occurs

D. Recording when the problem behavior occurs in a scatter plot

137. The format of a goal statement can include several components. Identify the criterion in the following example: After recess, when asked to complete independent writing tasks, Sam will remain seated at his desk at least 80% of the time as measured by interval recording data by 1/1/2023.

A. The phrase, "when asked to complete independent writing tasks."

B. The phrase, "Sam will remain seated at his desk."

C. The phrase, "at least 80% of the time."

D. The phrase, "as measured by interval recording data."

138. A client yells during therapy sessions to avoid difficult tasks. The behavior therapist implements an extinction procedure where the client must continue with the tasks despite the yelling. What type of extinction procedure is this?

A. Extinction of behavior maintained by positive reinforcement

B. Extinction of behavior maintained by negative reinforcement

C. Extinction of behavior maintained by automatic reinforcement

D. Extinction of behavior maintained by secondary reinforcement

139. Hector is a graduate student in an applied behavior analysis (ABA) program and works at a preschool for children with disabilities. Several children in the classroom have feeding problems and Hector thinks he may have an intervention idea to help them eat during snack times. Knowing that he will need to complete a research project for graduate school, Hector plans to ask the classroom teacher for permission to conduct a small research project. Once the teacher agrees, he can then begin to take baseline data and implement the snack time intervention. Hector's goal is to have a completed research project ready to submit to his university when it is due. What should Hector do to act in accordance with the Ethics Code?

A. Proceed as planned as he is not required to obtain approval from the university or school to conduct the study

B. Obtain the teacher's permission to proceed with data collection and implementation of the intervention

C. Conduct the project as an employee in the context of his job and have the teacher notify parents of the intervention

D. Notify his university and obtain approval from the institutional review committee before collecting any data

140. A BCBA® for a school is assessing a student's preferences using an interest inventory. After asking the student to identify activities that may serve as reinforcers, the BCBA groups the activities into different categories: board games, books, and puzzles. The BCBA wants to calculate the total number of activities for each category and graph the results to discuss with the student's teachers. Which of the following data display options is MOST appropriate for the BCBA to use in this instance?

A. Bar graph

B. Cumulative record

C. Line graph

D. Semilogarithmic chart

141. A behavior analyst is reviewing classroom observation notes taken by an applied behavior analysis (ABA) student who they are supervising. The student notes that the teacher heavily relies on negative punishment procedures for classroom management. If the behavior analyst conducts a follow-up observation, which two negative punishment procedures might they expect to see the teacher implementing?

A. Response cost and time-out

B. Reprimands and response cost

C. Time-out and response blocking

D. Contingent exercise and overcorrection

142. Martin, a BCBA®, is teaching a paraprofessional, Sam, in a special education classroom how to competently implement an intervention with integrity. Martin employs behavioral skills training (BST); he describes the target skill, demonstrates it, requires Sam to practice it, provides feedback during practice, and repeats the final two steps (requiring Sam to practice it and providing feedback during practice) until mastery is achieved. Which step of the BST process did Martin miss?

A. Role-play the skill with the client

B. Behaviorally define the target skill

C. Provide a written description of the target skill

D. None of the above; all steps of BST were followed

143. Dinah is a behavior analyst who works with a 12-year-old client with Down syndrome in the home setting to reduce incidents of physical aggression and improve social skills. Prior to the start of services, the client's parents agreed to actively participate in parent training sessions and follow agreed upon intervention procedures. After several months, the parents filed for a divorce and began living in different homes. The client's mother has stopped using the planned reinforcement schedule, arguing, "My child should behave without needing constant rewards." At the same time, the father frequently interrupts sessions, saying, "My child is under a lot of stress; let's just give him a break." The client is no longer making progress, and the parents have missed multiple training sessions. What should Dinah do next?

A. Continue to work with the client because behavior analysts cannot abandon clients. Dinah should make additional attempts to work with the parents.

B. Continue to work with the client and leave the parents out of the process. It is likely that the parents' behaviors are a result of the divorce, and the situation may improve over time.

C. Call a meeting with her supervisor and the client's parents to discuss how they can solve the issue. If parents fail to attend, it may be appropriate to begin terminating services.

D. Suggest to the parents that she work with the client at school since therapy in the home is not going well and clients have a right to effective treatment.

144. A client is taught to select a physical ball when the picture of a ball is presented. The client is then taught to select the picture of a ball when the spoken word "ball" is presented. A relation of symmetry would be demonstrated if a ball is presented and the client:

A. Says "Ball"

B. Selects a physical ball

C. Selects a picture of a ball

D. Selects the sample stimulus

145. Miya is a behavior analyst who is working with a third-grade teacher, Ms. April, to enhance her classroom management practices. Miya conducts an observation of Ms. April during the school day. At the start of the day, Ms. April reviewed a visual schedule displayed at the front of the room. Throughout the day, Ms. April intermittently praised students with statements like, "I like how you're following my directions," and awarded tokens to students who followed her directions. In addition, she consistently used an egg timer to give an audible warning before each transition. Which of Ms. April's observed behaviors belong to the same stimulus class?

A. Giving tokens and providing a transition warning

B. Saying "I like how you're following my directions" and giving tokens

C. Giving tokens and reviewing a visual schedule

D. Transition warning and reviewing a visual schedule

146. Eddie's dad discovered that he plays video games before completing his homework, so he sat him down for a talk to communicate the expectation that Eddie is to prioritize schoolwork and only play video games after finishing his homework assignments. When Eddie argued, his dad took away his video game controllers for the remainder of the day without hesitation. The next time Eddie's dad has a talk with him about what he is expected to do, Eddie does not argue. What basic principle is likely to be responsible for the change in Eddie's behavior?

A. Extinction

B. Negative punishment

C. Negative reinforcement

D. Positive punishment

147. As a first-year college student with autism spectrum disorder (ASD), Andy rarely spoke to others and stayed in his dorm room playing video games alone when not in class. He was disengaged from school and lacked friends; as a result, he seriously considered dropping out. In the spring term of that academic year, he worked with a BCBA® who implemented an intervention for Andy that involved attendance and engagement in a swing dancing class. Over the course of the intervention, Andy increased the amount of time he spent with others and greatly enhanced his willingness to communicate with others and his conversation skills. Two years later, Andy was involved in several clubs on campus, had numerous friends, was successful in school and work, and was on track to graduate. This is an example of which core dimension of applied behavior analysis (ABA)?

A. Technologic

B. Analytic

C. Replicable

D. Generality

148. John is a behavior analyst working with a client who exhibits frequent elopement behavior, typically occurring during transitions between activities. John determines that the function of the behavior is to escape from nonpreferred tasks. He implements a plan involving redirection and positive reinforcement for remaining in the activity area. Despite consistent implementation, there is minimal reduction in elopement incidents. What treatment component might be missing from John's plan?

A. Antecedent manipulation to decrease task demands

B. Increased use of redirection prompts

C. Implementation of differential reinforcement of alternative behavior

D. Establishment of a token economy system

149. Leslie is an 11-year-old client who engages in physical aggression at school. Her teacher reported that she "Scratches, bites, and kicks the other students during recess." When asked what occurs after the problem behavior, the teacher shared that those other students will typically abandon their toys, which Leslie then picks up and engages in play with. What is likely to be the function of Leslie's physically aggressive behavior at school during recess?

A. Access to social reinforcement

B. Access to tangible reinforcement

C. Escape from task demands

D. Sensory reinforcement

150. Nic is a 9-year-old student in the fourth grade who often refuses to complete his academic work, especially in-class math assignments, which he finds very challenging. Frank, a behavior analyst in training, is tasked with developing an intervention to address Nic's work refusal. Which of the following is the MOST appropriate independent variable (IV) for Frank to include in the behavioral intervention for addressing the problem?

A. Access to a preferred activity after completing a reduced math assignment

B. Increasing on-task behavior during math instruction

C. Reducing inattentive behavior

D. Implementation of the Good Behavior Game

151. John and Kim's 5-year-old son, Sam, refuses to use the toilet for urination. Instead, he insists on using a training potty in his bedroom. When he's finished, he calls for one of his parents to clean up. After John and Kim promise a new storybook each time Sam uses the bathroom in the toilet, Sam starts doing so. However, this reward system becomes unsustainable as it's costly and Sam now has a large collection of storybooks. When they stop rewarding him with books, he returns to using the training potty. John and Kim are at a loss and seek advice from a behavior analyst. Which is the BEST strategy for John and Kim to try to solve their problem?

A. Conduct a functional analysis (FA) of Sam's behavior.

B. Teach Sam to let his parents know when he needs to go to the bathroom.

C. Talk with Sam about why he won't use the toilet.

D. Implement an intermittent schedule of reinforcement.

152. Anders, a trainee, asks Tiana, a BCBA®, if she will provide him with behavior-analytic supervision. Tiana is quite busy, but she considers Anders' request. All of the following are sound reasons for Tiana to provide Anders with behavior-analytic supervision EXCEPT:

A. It will contribute to Anders' professional development.

B. It will enable them to further enhance their relationship.

C. It is required per the Professional and Ethical Compliance Code for behavior analysts.

D. It is supported as best practice by the field's professional literature.

153. Examine the following graph of the frequency of three different behaviors across seven sessions. Which of the following descriptions is MOST accurate for Behavior 2?

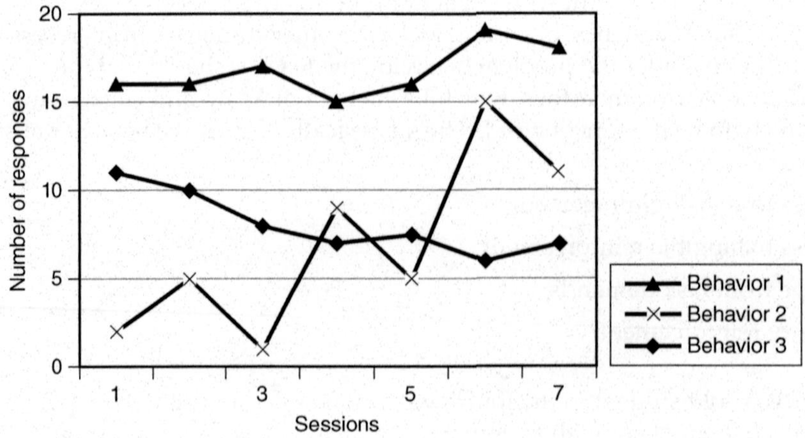

A. High-level responding, low variability, increasing trend

B. Mid-level responding, high variability, increasing trend

C. Mid-level responding, low variability, decreasing trend

D. Low-level responding, high variability, increasing trend

154. Nicole, a behavior analyst, is working with a 42-year-old client, Grayson, who has been struggling to fall asleep at night. To address this issue, Nicole recommends manipulating motivating operations (MOs). Which of the following strategies is an example of this approach?

A. Only sleeping in the bedroom

B. Setting a reminder to go to bed at 11:00 p.m.

C. Removing the television from the bedroom

D. Refraining from taking a nap during the day

155. Examine the following graph. What type of experimental design was used?

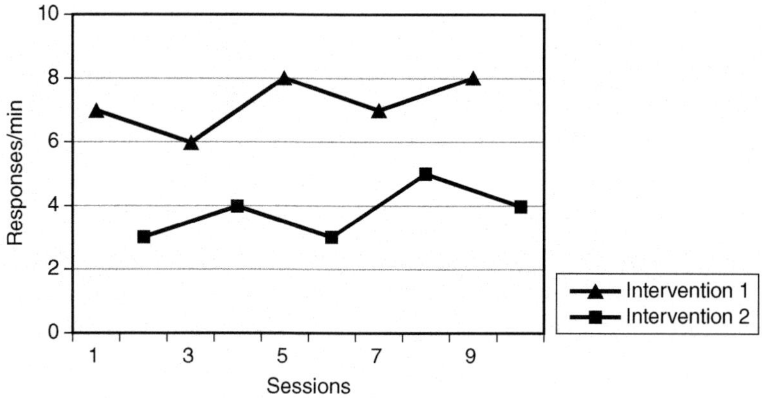

A. AB design

B. Changing criterion design

C. Multielement design

D. Multiple baseline design

156. Bennett is a behavior analyst and clinic director who focuses on early intervention programs for children with developmental delays. His clinic requests that he develop a new program for adolescents with emotional and behavioral disorders. How should Bennett respond to this request?

A. Agree to develop the program and begin studying the relevant literature on emotional and behavioral disorders.

B. Agree to develop the program and start outlining the curriculum.

C. Agree to develop the program and gather a team to help with the design.

D. Decline to develop the program and recommend finding a professional with relevant experience.

157. Martika is a trainee who has recently been hired by a private school to provide a fourth-grade student with daily applied behavior analysis (ABA) services. Martika would like to count these hours toward meeting her fieldwork requirements for the BCBA® certification, so she asks Traci, a BCBA, to provide her with behavior-analytic supervision. Traci agrees, and they establish a supervisor–supervisee relationship. Which of these must be clearly communicated at the outset of this new supervisory relationship?

A. Performance expectations for the supervisor and the supervisee in the form of a supervision contract

B. Martika's approach to delivering school-based behavior-analytic services

C. When and where supervision meetings will take place

D. Traci's approach to providing Martika with skill-based feedback

158. Rosalie is a BCBA® who works at a residential facility for physically disabled clients with severe developmental disabilities. One of her clients, Albert, is 24 years old, nonverbal, and uses a wheelchair. Albert has no prior history of engaging in self-injurious behaviors, but he suddenly begins to engage in multiple episodes of a new behavior: hitting himself in the head with his fists and screaming. Rosalie consults with her supervisor and they both agree there may be a medical cause given the sudden onset of this new behavior. How should Rosalie proceed?

A. Implement an emergency procedure to maintain his safety and refer him to an appropriate professional for assessment; programming can be placed on hold

B. Refer him to an appropriate professional for assessment but continue providing his regular program

C. Conduct a functional assessment to identify the controlling variables

D. Try some activities that may help Albert calm down, such as seating him in a comfortable lounge chair or playing relaxing music

159. It is recommended that behavior analysts use which strategic approach to improving personnel performance?

A. Human engineering

B. Behavioral consultation

C. Organizational manding

D. Function-based strategies

160. Suri, a behavior technician, is working with a client, Anita. Suri gets Anita's attention and then says, "If you wash your hands, then you can have a snack." What is this an example of?

A. Norm

B. Rule

C. Command

D. Instruction

161. Frank is a behavior analyst at a company that provides applied behavior analysis (ABA) services for youth with autism spectrum disorder (ASD). He has supervised numerous supervisees over the years. The company recently conducted an internal review, which surfaced anonymous feedback from Frank's previous supervisees indicating that he possesses strong ABA skills and knowledge, but that his supervision was not tailored to their specific needs. Of the following practices, which is MOST likely to enhance Frank's ability to meet his supervisees' unique needs?

A. Conducting an anonymous and brief structured survey of supervisees

B. Gathering and reviewing relevant performance data

C. Directly requesting feedback

D. Collecting data on the effectiveness of the methods they use to evaluate the effects of supervision

162. A behavior analyst develops an intervention plan to reduce a student's frequent outbursts during class. The plan is introduced to the school staff in a training session, and a detailed written copy is distributed to all relevant teachers. Despite these efforts, data collected over 8 weeks show no significant reduction in the student's outbursts. What should the behavior analyst suggest as the next step?

A. Increase the intensity of the intervention

B. Continue implementing the current intervention

C. Assess the implementation fidelity of the intervention

D. Modify the intervention based on initial feedback

163. During the presentation of a functional analysis (FA) condition, the experimenter ignores the client but delivers social positive reinforcement when the client engages in problem behavior. What experimental condition does this describe?

A. Alone

B. Contingent attention

C. Contingent escape

D. Play

164. Rebecca, a BCBA®, is reviewing the results of the skill assessments her supervisee, Ian, recently completed in order to set achievable supervision goals. When developing long-term goals for Ian, Rebecca should consider all of the following EXCEPT:

A. Task List items relevant to Ian's role

B. Expected needs of the agency

C. Immediate needs of the agency

D. Ian's performance across the Task List items

165. A behavior analyst cannot accept as a supervisee an individual with whom they have had a romantic/sexual relationship within the last ________________.

A. 3 months

B. 6 months

C. 12 months

D. 24 months

166. A behavior analyst supervising a trainee observes that the trainee struggles with implementing behavior intervention plans consistently across different settings. What should the behavior analyst do?

A. Assign the trainee to work exclusively in a single setting to minimize variability

B. Provide training on generalization strategies and monitor implementation fidelity

C. Ignore the inconsistencies to avoid demoralizing the trainee

D. Revoke the trainee's supervision until they demonstrate competency

167. Clive, a client, is learning how to strap the velcro on his shoes. He already knows how to sit down, put his foot in the shoe, and take hold of the velcro with his hand, so these steps do not require teaching. Which of the following is the MOST appropriate procedure to use?

A. Backward chaining

B. Total-task chaining

C. Backward chaining with leap aheads

D. Forward chaining

168. This branch of behavior analysis focuses on the systematic application of behavioral principles and experimental techniques to enhance socially significant behaviors. It relies on experimentation to identify the environmental variables affecting behavior. What is this branch?

A. Applied behavior analysis (ABA)

B. Behaviorism

C. Experimental Analysis of Behavior (EAB)

D. Empiricism

169. Select the example that BEST exemplifies response generalization.

A. A 10-year-old, Shefali, regularly brushes her teeth before bed in the bathroom at home. When she goes to 2-week summer camp she continues to brush her teeth before bed in the shared camp bathroom.

B. Harold's basketball coach teaches him techniques to jump higher during the winter season. In the spring season, Harold employs those techniques to jump higher when blocking in volleyball.

C. Betty, a first-year college student with autism spectrum disorder, takes a ballroom dancing class with a BCBA® during which she learns and practices how to ask people to dance and make small talk. In her second year of college, Betty regularly asks questions in class and responds to professors' questions.

D. Friedrich, a 1-year-old Austrian, learns how to make a guttural R sound when learning how to say his name, one of the first words he learns. He later applies this skill when pronouncing other German words with a guttural R sound.

170. A behavior analyst has been working with a client, Lincoln, on how to respond appropriately in class—raising his hand, waiting for his turn, and providing answers. Observational data suggests he consistently demonstrates this behavior sequence. However, when called upon, Lincoln tends to shout out his answers, which draws negative attention from his peers. What dimension of the behavior should the behavior analyst target for improvement?

A. Topography

B. Magnitude

C. Latency

D. Function

171. Pat is a dog trainer developing an online course. She wants to teach dog owners how to create a conditioned response (CR) using a clicker. Which method should Pat employ to teach her students?

A. Give the dog a treat, then click the clicker; repeat several times

B. Click the clicker as the dog is given a treat; repeat several times

C. Click the clicker, then give the dog a treat; repeat several times

D. Hide a treat and click the clicker when the dog finds it; repeat several times

172. What type of assessment do behavior analysts use to identify the variables that affect personnel performance?

A. Analogue

B. Function-based

C. Idiographic

D. Skills-based

173. Examine the antecedent-behavior-consequence (ABC) data describing Arya's crying behavior in the following table. Based on this alone, what would you hypothesize to be the function of the crying behavior?

ANTECEDENT	BEHAVIOR	CONSEQUENCE
Teacher reads to class.	Arya cries.	Teacher tells Arya to be quiet.
Teacher assists another student on worksheet activity.	Arya cries.	Teacher walks over to Arya and asks, "What's wrong?"
Teacher speaks on the phone.	Arya cries.	Teacher looks at Arya and whispers, "Hush, Arya! Hush!"
Teacher walks toward another student.	Arya cries.	Teacher turns toward Arya and asks, "What's wrong, Arya?"
Teacher reviews instructions for class assignment.	Arya cries.	Teacher tells Arya to stop crying.

A. Access to social reinforcement

B. Access to tangible reinforcement

C. Escape from task demands

D. Sensory reinforcement

174. A behavior analyst wants to assess the effectiveness of their supervisory practices. Which of the following measures should be prioritized when evaluating the impact of supervision on supervisee performance?

A. Number of supervision sessions held per week

B. Feedback from supervisors on supervisee performance

C. Objective measures of supervisee skill acquisition

D. Length of time each supervisee has been employed

175. Velvet, a behavior analyst in training, is preparing to teach a client how to tie their shoes, which involves linking behaviors in a chain. However, to do so, Velvet must first develop which of the following?

A. Action plan

B. Treatment plan

C. Skinner's analysis

D. Task analysis

176. Abigail, a behavior analyst, is working with an 8-year-old client, Bexley, who refuses to do her homework and instead whines and complains. In response to Bexley's whining, her parents usually allow her to watch TV instead. Abigail advises Bexley's parents to ignore her whining and complaints during homework time. After a few challenging evenings during which Bexley 's whining was ignored, she stopped complaining and started doing her homework. What procedure did Abigail advise Bexley's parents to use?

A. Positive reinforcement

B. Negative reinforcement

C. Extinction

D. Response cost

177. Liam arranged six objects on a table in front of a client, Gus. Liam allowed Gus to select a single object from the array and interact with it for 10 seconds, at which point Liam would then remove the object and allow Gus to select another object from those remaining. This process was repeated until no objects were left on the table. What type of preference assessment did Liam conduct?

A. Single stimulus

B. Paired stimulus

C. Multiple stimulus with replacement

D. Multiple stimulus without replacement

178. Which of the following statements is not true about behavior analysts and their responsibility in selecting and designing assessments?

A. They conduct assessments that prioritize reinforcement procedures.

B. They conduct assessments that consider the needs, context, and resources of clients and stakeholders.

C. They conduct assessments that are conceptually consistent with behavior principles.

D. They conduct assessments with a focus on maximizing benefits and minimizing risk of harm to clients and stakeholders.

179. Antecedent interventions based on motivating operations (MOs) and discriminative stimuli (S^Ds) are considered ________________. Those based on MOs are ________________, whereas those based on stimulus control are ________________. Fill in the blanks in the correct order.

A. Contingency-independent; function-based; contingency-dependent

B. Function-based; contingency-independent; contingency-dependent

C. Contingency-dependent; function-based; contingency-independent

D. Function-based; contingency-dependent; contingency-independent

180. Michaela, a supervisor in a behavioral health clinic, has a team of supervisees who come from diverse cultural backgrounds and have varying levels of experience. She aims to create an equitable supervision environment that supports the growth and development of all her supervisees. Which practice should Michaela implement to promote equity in her supervision?

A. Applying the same supervision strategies to all supervisees to ensure fairness

B. Utilizing culturally responsive performance management techniques tailored to each supervisee

C. Focusing her attention primarily on supervisees who have been with the clinic the longest

D. Implementing a standardized supervision plan for all supervisees regardless of their backgrounds

181. Toby, a BCBA®, is working with a 4-year-old client in the home setting. The child's mother, Kirsten, is single. One day, Toby runs into Kirsten in a small café. Kirsten invites Toby to sit with her and he does. During the chance encounter at the café, Kirsten asks Toby if he would like to join her for a drink after his next session with her child, and he promptly says that he would. Before the next session, Toby notices that he's spending extra time styling his hair and feeling excited about seeing Kirsten. How should Toby proceed?

A. Continue to meet with Kirsten; if they develop a romantic relationship, Toby will just need to be discreet so that there is no impact on services

B. Continue to meet with Kirsten; if they develop a romantic relationship, there is no issue with exploitation as the Ethics Code is only concerned with exploitative relationships between supervisors and supervisees

C. Avoid these social events and end the potential relationship before it starts; if Toby wants to pursue a relationship, he should wait at least 2 years after services have been discontinued

D. Tell his supervisor as soon as possible if he is interested in pursuing a romantic relationship and request to be removed from the case so there would not be any conflict of interest

182. Alvin is a behavior analyst overseeing the work of several behavior technicians in a residential treatment facility. One of his supervisees, Corinna, has been struggling with managing challenging behaviors during therapy sessions. Alvin decides to conduct a function-based assessment to determine the reasons behind Corinna's difficulties and discovers that she lacks clear guidance and reinforcement for handling challenging behaviors. What should Alvin do to enhance Corinna's performance?

A. Increase Corinna's supervision hours

B. Provide Corinna with articles on effective behavioral management techniques

C. Implement a performance management plan that includes modeling, practice opportunities, feedback, and reinforcement

D. Rotate Corinna to different clients

183. Aziz is a behavior analyst working with a client, Malcolm, who engages in exhibitionistic behavior at the retirement facility where he lives. Aziz conducts a functional analysis of Malcolm's behavior and determines that attention is the function. To address the issue, Aziz develops and implements an intervention with Malcolm that includes a schedule of noncontingent access to attention to decrease his motivation to engage in exhibitionistic behavior. After implementing the intervention for 4 weeks, progress monitoring data reveals only a very small reduction in Malcolm's exhibitionistic behavior. As a result, the retirement facility has begun the process of evicting Malcolm. Unfortunately, Aziz's intervention was ineffective because he neglected a critical component of an effective treatment plan. Identify the component Aziz neglected to incorporate.

A. Aziz neglected to incorporate a skill training component to help Malcolm acquire a functionally equivalent replacement behavior.

B. Aziz neglected to incorporate an extinction procedure that would impede reinforcement for Malcolm's exhibitionistic behavior.

C. Aziz neglected to provide differential reinforcement of other behaviors.

D. Aziz neglected to consult and describe the research on the efficacy of behavioral interventions for exhibitionistic behavior.

184. A healthcare facility hires Jeremy, a behavior analyst, to develop a behavior intervention plan for Karson, a 17-year-old client with aggressive behaviors. To ensure the plan's success, it is crucial that all staff members implementing the plan are adequately trained and follow the procedures precisely. What training method should Jeremy use to best prepare the staff for implementing the behavior intervention plan?

A. Behavioral skills training (BST)

B. Didactic instruction

C. Group-based training

D. Simulation training

185. A BCBA® is working with a 7-year-old child with autism spectrum disorder (ASD) who presents with some motor skills problems and tantrum behavior where they scream and hit their head against hard surfaces. During a treatment team meeting to discuss programming for this client, another professional recommends the use of sensory integration therapy as the primary approach to address the problem behaviors. The BCBA should say:

A. "I agree, we should implement sensory integration therapy to address the motor skills problems and tantrum behavior."

B. "It may be helpful to try sensory integration therapy for addressing the motor skills problems. For the tantrums, however, I would suggest that we begin with a functional assessment."

C. "I completely disagree, this recommendation is not evidence-based."

D. "Please explain to the team how performing exercises like bouncing on a trampoline can decrease the tantrums."

13

Practice Exam: Answer Key and Rationales

This section provides the correct answers along with detailed rationales to help reinforce your understanding of key behavior-analytic concepts. Reviewing the explanations will allow you to identify patterns in your reasoning, clarify misunderstandings, and strengthen your grasp of the BACB® Test Content Outline (TCO) material.

As you go through the answer key, take time to reflect on any incorrect responses and consider why the correct option is the best choice. Use this as a learning tool to refine your test-taking strategies and improve your overall comprehension.

Keep learning, stay focused, and continue building your confidence. You're one step closer to success!

1. **D) Trials to criterion**
   Trials to criterion is a measure of the number of response opportunities required to achieve a predetermined level of performance. Count simply refers to the total number of occurrences of a behavior, not the number of opportunities required to reach a criterion. Event recording measures the frequency of behavior but does not focus on the number of response opportunities needed to reach a predetermined performance level. Percentage measures the proportion of correct responses but does not reflect the number of opportunities required to achieve a set level of performance.

2. **A) Philosophic doubt**
   Philosophic doubt refers to the attitude of viewing scientific knowledge as tentative and continually developing. Consequently, scientists remain skeptical about the validity and truthfulness of all scientific knowledge and are open to revising their beliefs when new evidence emerges. Replication refers to repeating experiments to confirm findings, not the skeptical stance or willingness to revise beliefs based on new evidence. Parsimony emphasizes selecting the simplest explanation consistent with the evidence, not the tentativeness or revision of knowledge. Empiricism focuses on knowledge derived from observation and experience, not the questioning of existing knowledge or openness to change.

3. **D) Insurance reimbursement**
   Determining a client's need for ongoing services is a broader question than whether a particular intervention should be ended and, consequently, involves a multidimensional assessment of needs and progress. Behavior analysts rely on clinical expertise and adhere to relevant ethical guidelines when determining whether services remain clinically or medically necessary. Factors to consider include the client's progress toward treatment goals as evidenced by assessment results and other forms of data collection, and the degree to which the client has made socially significant progress. Insurance reimbursement is not relevant to this decision.

4. **C) A behavior intervention plan**
Permanent products are tangible outputs that result from behavior-analytic practices and can be objectively reviewed. Among the answer options presented, a behavior intervention plan best exemplifies a permanent product as it represents a concrete documentation of strategies devised for client intervention. This document allows supervisors to evaluate the quality and effectiveness of the intervention strategies implemented by the supervisee. An attitude is an internal state, not a tangible, measurable product that can be reviewed later. Awareness is a cognitive process and not a physical product that can be assessed directly. Conceptual understanding of rapport is an abstract quality, not a physical product or document.

5. **B) Harold is a behavior analyst who lives next door to a family with a child who struggles with behavior issues. He wants to help but is uncomfortable charging his neighbors for his services, so he instead provides them with free behavioral advice.**
While it is understandable that Harold wants to help his neighbors, the Ethics Code requires that behavior analysts only provide services after having defined and documented their professional role with relevant parties. The behavior analysts in the other scenarios presented are behaving according to ethical principles. Esther declining a lunch invitation is not an ethical problem because politely declining personal social interactions maintains appropriate professional boundaries. Kamala addressing personal problems is not an ethical issue either, as Kamala appropriately managed her situation by notifying her supervisor, requesting a leave, and ensuring continuity of care for her clients. Leonard using simple language also does not present an ethical issue, as using clear, simple language can improve client understanding and collaboration.

6. **A) The best available evidence**
Behavior analysts adhere to the evidence-based practice model of professional decision-making. This means they rely on the "best available evidence" coupled with clinical expertise to determine whether an intervention is effective and if a treatment needs to be revised. Behavior analysts examine and interpret graphed data when determining the effectiveness of an intervention and need for treatment revision. Philosophic doubt refers to maintaining skepticism and openness to revising knowledge but does not directly relate to assessing intervention effectiveness. Grounded theory, a qualitative research method focused on developing theories based on data, is unrelated to clinical decision-making for behavior analysts. Experimental analysis of behavior, while foundational to behavior analysis, primarily concerns basic research rather than the applied process of evaluating and revising interventions.

7. **A) Being disrespectful to adults**
When selecting behaviors to target with intervention, it is necessary to focus on those that are observable and measurable. In other words, behaviors targeted for intervention must be observable and measurable in terms of one of the measurable dimensions of behavior (e.g., topography, duration, rate/frequency). Leaving the classroom without permission, pinching peers, and throwing tantrums are all observable behaviors. "Being disrespectful to adults" is a subjective description of behavior that does not lend itself to observation and valid/reliable measurement.

8. **B) Experimental Analysis of Behavior (EAB)**
Founded by B. F. Skinner with the publication of *The Behavior of Organisms* in 1938, EAB is the basic research branch of behavior analysis. EAB takes a natural science approach to research that defines and clarifies the basic processes and principles of behavior. This stands in contrast with ABA, which applies these principles in practical settings, and behaviorism, which is the broader philosophy of the science.

9. D) Function-based definition
An intervention goal may target a behavior that is functionally or topographically defined. Function-based definitions describe responses in terms of their effect on the environment (e.g., "Any behavior that results in X") whereas topography-based definitions describe responses in terms of their form. Whether functionally or topographically defined, definitions should be objective, clear, and complete.

10. B) Secondary reinforcers
The tokens are secondary reinforcers because they acquire their reinforcing properties through their association with primary or other strong reinforcers (extra recess time, stickers, pencils). The tokens themselves do not satisfy any physiological or primary needs but become reinforcing through their link to desirable outcomes. Primary reinforcers are inherently reinforcing and do not rely on learning or association, unlike tokens. Noncontingent reinforcers is an incorrect choice because tokens in this example are earned contingent on specific behaviors, not given independently of behavior. Unconditioned reinforcers is an incorrect choice because these are natural reinforcers that do not require learning, whereas tokens are learned reinforcers.

11. D. Contact Sam and be persistent in finding a time to meet; Ashley should express her concern to Sam and ask if it can be immediately resolved.
Behavior analysts should address concerns about the professional misconduct of others directly with them whenever possible. Reporting Sam to the BACB® for his actions or finding another supervisor thus far does not seem warranted until Ashley attempts to reach out to Sam to problem-solve the issue first. Proceeding without supervision does not address the misconduct and may lead to undue risk.

12. D) Repeated measurement that yields the same results
Validity refers to the degree to which we are measuring what we intend to measure. Requirements for valid measurement include direct measurement of a socially significant behavior, measurement of its relevant dimension for answering the question, and data representing its occurrence under relevant conditions (e.g., time, place) for answering the question. Repeated measurement that yields the same results is an indicator of reliability, not validity.

13. C) Private events are behaviors that can be influenced by environmental factors.
Radical behaviorism views private events, such as thoughts and feelings, as behaviors that occur within an individual and are influenced by environmental variables. This perspective stands in contrast with the view that private events do not exist or that they are equivalent to observable public events. Because private events are behaviors, according to radical behaviorism, they are within the scope of behavior analysis.

14. A) Extinction of behavior maintained by positive reinforcement
In the scenario presented, Shelly engages in a problem behavior (screaming) that is maintained by positive reinforcement (attention from her father). By ignoring the screams, Shelly's father is withholding reinforcement (attention) for the previously reinforced behavior (screaming). This is an example of an extinction procedure for a behavior maintained by positive reinforcement. Extinction behavior maintained by negative reinforcement applies to behaviors reinforced by escaping an aversive stimulus, not attention-seeking. Extinction involves withholding reinforcement, not introducing punishment. Extinction of behavoir maintained by automatic reinforcement refers to behaviors reinforced by sensory stimulation, not social attention.

15. **D) Unconditioned**
Also known as a primary or natural reinforcer, unconditioned reinforcers are stimuli that increase the future frequency of the behavior that it immediately follows independent of the individual's learning history. These reinforcers satisfy basic life needs (e.g., food) and do not need to be learned. In the scenario presented, the walnuts served as unconditioned reinforcers. Darius did not need to learn that walnuts were reinforcing. Conditioned, generalized, and secondary are incorrect because the walnuts were not paired with other reinforcers or learned through association.

16. **C) Behavior is determined by past events and environmental factors.**
The philosophical assumption of determinism holds that behavior is lawful and orderly, influenced by past events and environmental factors. This concept contrasts with the idea of free will and emphasizes that behavior is predictable based on prior experiences and contextual variables. The idea that all behavior is random and unpredictable contradicts determinism, as it assumes behavior is causally influenced by prior events. The option indicating behavior is influenced by free will and choice is incorrect because determinism rejects the idea of free will, instead emphasizing causality. The option indicating behavior is influenced by innate biological factors alone is incorrect because determinism recognizes the influence of past events and environmental factors, not just biology.

17. **B) Contrived free-operant observation**
Free-operant observation preference assessments involve observing and recording the duration of engagement with each object/activity available. Free-operant observations can be contrived, involving prearrangement of the environment, or naturalistic, involving no prearrangement of the environment. Liam prearranged the environment to include different objects and activities that Gus may like and can engage, so this is an example of a contrived free-operant observation rather than a naturalistic one. Single stimulus involves presenting one item at a time to measure engagement, but Liam observed engagement with multiple items in the environment simultaneously. Multiple stimulus without replacement does not apply because this method involves presenting multiple items and removing selected ones in a structured format, not free interaction with items in the environment

18. **C) Generalization**
Baseline logic is a powerful form of experimental reasoning that calls for three elements: prediction (anticipated outcome of an unknown/future measurement), verification (demonstration of a functional relationship between the intervention and target behavior), and replication (repeating of IV manipulations and obtaining outcomes similar to that of a previous study).

19. **B) Internal validity**
Internal validity refers to the degree the changes in the dependent variable (i.e., target behavior) can be attributed to the manipulation of the independent variable (i.e., intervention) and not the result of uncontrolled/extraneous factors. Experiments that reliably demonstrate a cause-and-effect relationship between the IV and DV are said to have a high degree of internal validity. Internal validity is threatened when there is the possibility that results are affected by uncontrolled/extraneous factors. Criterion validity refers to how well a measure correlates with a specific outcome or criterion, not the causal relationship between variables. Construct validity assesses whether a measure accurately represents the concept it claims to measure, rather than addressing causal attribution. External validity refers to the generalizability of findings across settings or populations, not the control of extraneous variables within a study.

20. C) Duration

Duration refers to the amount of time a behavior lasts from start to finish. By starting the timer at the beginning of the behavior, stopping at its end, and then recording the elapsed time for its occurrence, the behavior technician is documenting the duration of the behavior. Response latency measures the time between a stimulus and the start of a behavior, inter-response time measures the time between behaviors, and frequency counts how often a behavior occurs.

21. A) Support procedural integrity

When behavior analysts monitor the performance of supervisees and provide timely feedback and reinforcement, it enhances supervisees' performance and supports procedural integrity. The option to support affective commitment relates to emotional attachment, the option to support resiliency efforts relates to coping with challenges, and the option to support organizational constraints relates to workplace limitations, none of which address the accuracy of implementation.

22. C) Extinction

Of the procedures listed, the set of unwanted effects presented (i.e., emotional/aggressive reactions, an initial increase in the rate of the problem behavior, an initial increase in the magnitude of the problem behavior, the reappearance of the problem behavior after it has been reduced/eliminated, and the reappearance of a previously extinguished problem behavior that was replaced by the targeted problem behavior) are uniquely associated with the use of extinction. Reinforcement and punishment do not align with the specific unwanted effects described

23. C) Bartering may be acceptable when certain conditions are met.

The Ethics Code states that bartered services can be provided but only under a specific service agreement. The barter should be requested by the client, considered customary in the area where services are provided, and fair (i.e., commensurate with the value of the BCBA®'s services).

24. C) Empiricism

The behavior analyst's focus on measuring specific changes in the student's behavior over time aligns with empiricism, which involves relying on objective, systematic observation and measurement to understand and evaluate behavior. Determinism relates to the belief that behavior is caused by prior events, not about measuring changes in behavior. Pragmatism focuses on the practical application of ideas, not on observing and measuring behavior changes over time. Parsimony involves selecting the simplest explanation, which is not directly related to the approach of measuring behavioral changes.

25. A) Relevance and certainty

Behavior analysts consider the scientific literature's relevance and certainty. Relevance refers to the extent to which the evidence corresponds to the problem in terms of client characteristics, the assessments and procedures used, functions of behavior and expected outcomes, and the context in which intervention is delivered. Certainty refers to the extent to which the evidence supports the use of a procedure and rules out alternative explanations. It is based on two factors: (a) the methodological rigor of the evidence, and (b) consistency in replication of outcomes. Scope and parsimony are not directly related to evaluating the quality of scientific evidence for intervention decisions. Testability and rigor, while important in research, do not directly address the key factors of applying evidence to guide intervention. Classification and certainty are not a priority when evaluating scientific evidence for intervention, although certainty is important.

26. **B) Prosocial behavior**
The DV is the behavior that is measured to determine the effects of the intervention. In this case, the behavior analyst implemented a token economy where prosocial behavior (earning vouchers) was contingent upon displaying nonaggressive behavior. The intervention's success is evaluated by changes in the frequency of prosocial behavior, making it the DV. The contingency management system is part of the intervention (independent variable), not the outcome being measured. Systematic observations refer to the method used to collect data, not the variable being studied. Vouchers are a component of the token economy and act as reinforcers, not the behavior being measured.

27. **D) They require less attention from the observer, are time-consuming, and require less training for users.**
There are noted advantages to using continuous measurement methods, such as increased accuracy of measurement and sensitivity to small improvements in performance that may be missed by discontinuous methods. However, they are not without limitations. Continuous methods are criticized for being time-consuming, requiring the undivided attention of the observer, and potentially requiring multiple trained personnel for adequate implementation.

28. **A) Conditional discrimination**
Conditional discriminations are established by reinforcing certain responses in the presence of certain antecedents only if they are preceded by certain other stimuli. In this example, students display conditional discrimination when they notice that the lunch bell has rung (preceding stimulus) and then they wait for Ms. Charlotte to call their name (antecedent) to line up to walk to the cafeteria. Allowing students to line up to walk to the cafeteria for demonstrating conditional discrimination and responding correctly reinforces their behavior. Compound discrimination involves responding to a combination of two or more stimuli, which is not the case here. Simple discrimination involves responding to one specific stimulus in isolation, whereas the scenario requires responding based on a combination of stimuli (the bell and hearing their name). Conditional verbal discrimination is not being demonstrated here because the students' behavior is not solely based on verbal stimuli; it is conditional upon the bell ringing and their name being called.

29. **B) External validity**
External validity addresses the extent to which the results of a study can be extrapolated to other contexts, behaviors, or populations beyond those directly studied. This type of validity helps behavior analysts determine the robustness and applicability of their interventions in real-world scenarios, providing insights into whether similar outcomes can be expected under different conditions or with different individuals. Internal validity assesses whether changes in the dependent variable are caused by the independent variable, not generalization. Construct validity measures how well a test or intervention reflects the theoretical construct it is intended to represent. Concurrent validity evaluates the degree to which results align with another established measure taken at the same time, not generalization.

30. **C) Objective**
Intervention goals must be stated in observable and measurable terms to allow for the accurate measurement of behavior change. To accomplish this, behavior analysts define target behaviors and set criteria for behavior change. Definitions of target behaviors should be objective, clear, and complete. To be objective, the definition must refer to observable aspects of the behavior (and environment, when applicable). To be clear, the definition must present sufficient detail, leaving no room for confusion or doubt. And to be complete, the definition must accurately and concisely describe the target behavior, allowing for discrimination between occurrences and nonoccurrences.

31. C) Escape from group activities

Lily's crying behavior is most likely maintained by escape from group activities. This is evidenced by the behavior occurring primarily during group activities and leading to Lily being allowed to go to a quiet area, thus avoiding the aversive group setting. Sensory stimulation is unlikely because Lily's crying occurs in response to group activities, not for self-reinforcing sensory input. Attention from caregivers is incorrect because the scenario does not indicate that staff attention is reinforcing her crying. Access to preferred toys is incorrect because while she gains access to toys, the primary trigger for her crying appears to be group activities, suggesting another function.

32. D) Transitivity

This is an example of the emergence of a transitive stimulus relation, which is demonstrated when there is a derived stimulus-stimulus relation following the training of two other stimulus-stimulus relations (e.g., if A = B and B = C, then A = C and C = A). In the example presented, the client is taught that the spoken word "bicicleta" (stimulus A) corresponds with the spoken word "bicycle" (stimulus B), and that the spoken word "bicycle" corresponds with the physical bicycle (stimulus C). Then, without training, the client associates the physical bicycle (stimulus C) with the spoken word "bicicleta" (stimulus A).

33. B) Momentary time sampling

In the scenario presented, the session is broken into smaller time intervals and the behavior is not continuously measured. Carey is recording whether the eloping behavior occurred only at the end of each interval. Thus, Carey is using momentary time sampling to record how much the target behavior is occurring. Unlike whole or partial interval recording, this method does not require the observer's undivided attention to measurement, but a significant amount of behavior will be missed as a result.

34. D) Provide ongoing evaluation of the effects of supervision

Supervisors can set expectations for the supervisee to develop a draft agenda in advance of the scheduled supervision meeting, follow scheduled deadlines for assigned activities, and take notes during feedback meetings. Additionally, they can set expectations for the supervisee to review BACB® experience standards, adhering to the Ethics Code, completing and maintaining required supervision documentation, and so on. However, providing ongoing evaluation of the effects of supervision is an expectation for the supervisor rather than the supervisee.

35. A) Extinction

Extinction procedures involve withholding reinforcers that maintain behavior, resulting in the reduction of the behavior. In the scenario presented, Chelsea's behavior (completing chores) resulted in positive reinforcement (money). After her father decides to withhold money for completing chores, a reduction in completion of chores was observed. Thus, the change in Chelsea's behavior is likely the result of extinction. Negative punishment involves removing a desirable stimulus as a consequence, negative reinforcement involves removing an aversive stimulus to increase behavior, and positive punishment involves adding an aversive stimulus to decrease behavior.

36. **C) Sully's father presents him with a blueberry. When Sully says "Blueberry," his father delivers reinforcement. When Sully says any word other than blueberry, his father does not deliver reinforcement.**
This example best exemplifies simple discriminations, which are established by reinforcing certain responses only in the presence of certain antecedents. Thus, teaching a discriminative response involves the presentation of a defined antecedent stimulus (e.g., blueberry), as well as the delivery of reinforcement if the response is emitted. Response A is an example of conditional discriminations, which are established by reinforcing certain responses in the presence of certain antecedents only if they are preceded by certain other stimuli.

37. **D) Any physical contact between Araceli's body and another person's body with enough force to be audible or leave a mark, outside of activities in which such contact would be appropriate**
Recall that a well-written operational definition allows for a behavior analyst to gather complete information about its occurrence and nonoccurrence, precisely apply procedures in a timely manner, and produce an accurate evaluation of intervention effectiveness. Consequently, it is necessary that the operational definition is an objective, clear, and complete description of an observable and measurable target behavior. Among the options presented, "Any physical contact between Araceli's body and another person's body with enough force to be audible or leave a mark, outside of activities in which such contact would be appropriate" is the definition that best meets the requirements of a strong operational definition as it describes the topography and magnitude of Araceli's behavior and clarifies which instances of contact should be excluded from measurement.

38. **B) Select an alternative behavior that is incompatible with the problem behavior**
Behavior analysts select acceptable alternative behaviors that are already in the client's behavioral repertoire, within the client's current abilities, and less effortful than the problem behavior. Darnell should only consider selecting an alternative behavior that is incompatible with the problem behavior when the problem behavior is severe, occurs frequently, and has a significant impact on the environment.

39. **C) Parametric analysis**
Rationales for the use of parametric analysis include: (a) to evaluate the differential effects of a range of values of an intervention on behavior, and (b) to answer the questions, "How much intervention is required to be effective?" and "How much intervention is most effective?" This scenario represents parametric analysis, where the behavior analyst is systematically varying the frequency of reinforcement to assess its effect on student engagement. By testing different reinforcement intervals (5 minutes, 10 minutes, and 15 minutes), Farah can identify the most effective frequency for maintaining high levels of engagement, thereby optimizing the reinforcement schedule for the classroom setting. Comparative analysis compares different interventions, add-in component analysis tests additional treatment components, and drop-out component analysis looks at removing components.

40. **C) Experimenting to identify the function of the target behavior**
Progress monitoring involves a series of steps that include clearly operationalizing the behavior, collecting baseline data and defining goals, and evaluating and utilizing data for decision-making. While experimenting to identify the function of the target behavior (i.e., functional analysis) is important for determining the cause of behavior, it is not a component of ongoing progress monitoring.

41. **A) Relevant antecedent details were left out.**
The narrative recording fails to capture pertinent antecedent details. As described in the scenario, the teacher redirected Frank when he walked toward the back of the classroom, physically standing between Frank and the computer station. This is important information that Sam should have included in the narrative.

42. **B) Free-operant arrangement (FO arrangement)**
Darcy is employing an FO arrangement with Freya. In an FO arrangement such as this, Darcy would not have specifically programmed reinforcement, but rather would allow Freya to engage in responses that naturally produce reinforcement continuously or intermittently. In an FO arrangement, Darcy might make Freya's access to objects contingent upon performance of a specific behavior (e.g., saying the name of the object), and Darcy would strive to turn interactions with Freya into teaching moments. NTAs, DTT, and IT involve structured or teacher-directed methods, not the free response emission with natural MOs.

43. **B) Giving Marlowe a checklist of social skills to practice independently**
An independent checklist does not provide the same level of interactive, real-world practice and feedback that the family meetings, playdates, and community service activities offer. Thus, it is the least likely to effectively support the maintenance of Marlowe's social skills over the summer break.

44. **C) Review of records**
Behavior analysts should, at the outset of a case, examine the client's records for relevant data. This includes medical information related to the client's health (e.g., clinical findings, diagnostic test results, care plans, and medication) to rule out medical reasons for behavior. If a medical reason is found, treatment of the condition may be necessary before implementing behavioral interventions. In this scenario, the behavior analyst did not learn about the medical issue until after the intervention plan was already implemented.

45. **A) At least 6 months**
The process of terminating services typically requires at least 6 months and involves the titration of services; during this time services are gradually decreased.

46. **C) The physical form of the behavior**
Topography refers to the physical characteristics of the behavior. Thus, topography-based definitions of behavior describe instances of the response by the way it looks or sounds. The impact of the behavior, the individual's overall repertoire, or sensory functions do not describe the behavior's physical characteristics.

47. **B) Escape**
The function of Nico's tantrum behavior in this scenario appears to be escape-maintained. When Nico is asked to participate in activities that involve sharing personal stories during circle time, he displays tantrum behavior characterized by crying and agitation. The teacher's response to allow Nico to sit quietly and draw in a corner when he engages in tantrums effectively removes him from the aversive demand of participating in group activities, thereby reinforcing the escape behavior. This escape-maintained function is supported by the behavior occurring specifically during circle time activities that involve sharing personal stories, without occurrences during other classroom activities. The tantrum behavior seems to occur in response to a demand (group activity), not to gain attention, so it does not appear to be maintained by attention-seeking behavior. There is no indication that Nico is engaging in tantrums due to sensory stimulation or a sensory need in this context. The behavior is not related to accessing a specific object or item, so it is not likely maintained by the desire for a tangible item.

48. **D) It provides strong evidence of external validity and the generalization of results to a broader population.**
Providing strong evidence of external validity and the generalization of results to a broader population is an advantage afforded by group experimental designs. The advantages of single-subject experimental design include: subjects serve as their own control; it reveals the performance of individual subjects; data for subjects are not combined/averaged, which helps to prevent distortion/masking of variability in the data; it enables the demonstration of behavior-environment relations at the level of the individual; and it allows for replication of effects within and across individual subjects.

49. **A) Internal validity**
In the case example presented, the dog's behavior of chewing on its owner's shoes reliably occurs at a higher rate when the intervention is not in effect but ceases when the intervention is in effect. Experiments that reliably demonstrate a cause-and-effect relationship between changes in a behavior (dependent variable) and the implementation of an intervention (independent variable) and not the result of uncontrolled/extraneous factors are said to have a high degree of internal validity. Face validity concerns subjective appearance; external validity pertains to generalizability; and content validity evaluates whether a measure fully represents a construct—these are all unrelated to the described scenario.

50. **B) Attention**
In a latency-based functional analysis, shorter latencies to the problem behavior suggest that the behavior is more likely to occur under that condition. The data show that the aggressive behavior occurs much more quickly in the attention condition compared to the other conditions. This indicates that the behavior is most likely maintained by social attention.

51. **D) Multiple baseline design**
The graph presented shows the use of a multiple baseline design. This type of experimental design is commonly used when a reversal is determined to be impractical or unethical. This involves establishing two or more independent baselines and introducing the intervention in a staggered fashion for each baseline. When the behavior for the first baseline is stable, the intervention is then introduced to the second baseline, and so forth. This design can be used to compare responding across different behaviors for a client, a behavior across different clients, or a behavior across different settings.

52. **D) Verification**
Verification is the demonstration of a functional relationship between the intervention and target behavior. This would require observing changes in the target behavior associated with the introduction and withdrawal of the intervention. It is accomplished when data convincingly shows that baseline responding would remain as-is without introduction of the intervention.

53. **D) Behavior analysts may solicit testimonials from former clients but not current clients.**
Behavior analysts are prohibited from soliciting testimonials from current clients due to the potential for exploitation and the impact on the professional relationship. However, it is permissible to solicit testimonials from former clients as they are no longer in a professional relationship with the behavior analyst and the potential for exploitation and undue influence is minimized.

54. C) Planned activity check (PLACHECK)

In the scenario presented, the teacher is using the PLACHECK method. PLACHECK is a variation of momentary time sampling that involves recording the count of individuals in a group that are engaged in the target behavior only at the end of the interval. Event recording tracks frequency, partial interval recording records if behavior occurs at any point during an interval, and whole interval recording requires behavior to occur continuously throughout an interval.

55. A) Minimize the use of items as reinforcers when they may be harmful to clients

The general rule is to select and implement behavior-change interventions with a focus on minimizing risk of harm to the client. However, this may not always be possible, and a reinforcer known to be harmful may be selected if it is determined by the treatment team that the benefits of doing so outweigh its risks. The other answers either justify the use of harmful reinforcers based on prior access, program duration, or individual plans, which contradicts ethical guidelines that emphasize client well-being and avoiding harmful reinforcers whenever possible.

56. C) Line graphs

The line graph, which is the most appropriate visual display format for the data collected in the scenario presented, is used to display behavior change over time. The BCBA® can plot the students' performance on target skills in response to the social skills training program on a line graph to analyze each student's performance of target skills across time (i.e., level, variability, and trend of their data paths). A cumulative record shows the total accumulation of a behavior over time and is most appropriate for monitoring behaviors that increase cumulatively, such as the number of items completed. It's not ideal here because the focus is on social skills performance over specific time periods, not cumulative changes. A histogram is useful for summarizing data in discrete categories or showing frequency distributions, not for tracking performance trends over time, which is the objective of the scenario. Standard celeration charts are designed to display changes in the rate of behavior over time on a logarithmic scale, typically in precision teaching contexts. It is not necessary here as the data does not require such precise scaling or analysis.

57. C) Trials to criterion

Trials to criterion, which can be used to assess progress toward the acquisition of new skills, is a measure of the number of response opportunities (i.e., trials) required to achieve a predetermined level of performance (i.e., mastery criterion). In this scenario, the behavior analyst is interested in measuring the client's ability to complete all steps of a transaction correctly within a certain number of trials. This approach allows for a precise measurement of skill acquisition over repeated trials, ensuring the client reaches a set criterion before considering the skill mastered. Event recording tracks frequency, not attempts to achieve accuracy; time sampling estimates behavior presence, not skill progression; and interval recording captures occurrences within intervals but does not evaluate attempts to meet performance criteria.

58. C) Have João perform a self-assessment, administer quizzes and interviews to assess his knowledge-based skills, review João's permanent products (and conduct direct observations if needed), and select long- and short-term supervision goals

Assessment of the supervisee's skills should precede the selection of supervision goals. To assess a supervisee's skills, the recommended process is to start with a supervisee's self-assessment, then administer quizzes/interviews to assess skills, then review permanent products (and conduct direct observations if necessary).

59. **B) Reflexivity**
Reflexivity is indicated when, in this type of stimulus-stimulus relation, the selection of a comparison stimulus matches the sample stimulus (e.g., A = A) without training to do so. In the scenario presented, Erica teaches Joseph to match a crayon (A) to a crayon (A). Joseph is then handed a different object and, without training to do so, matches it to its identical twin on the table. This is an example of reflexivity. Congruency is not a behavior analysis term. Symmetry requires reversing the relation, which isn't demonstrated here. Transitivity requires deriving new relations among three stimuli.

60. **A) Contingency-shaped**
Whitney's shift to walking down the steps slowly and carefully is best described as contingency-shaped behavior. This term reflects how her behavior changed as a direct result of experiencing the unpleasant and painful consequences (the falls) of her previous actions, rather than being influenced by explicit rules, verbal instructions, or automatic responses as it would be for pivotal, rule-governed, or reflexive behaviors.

61. **B) FA of precursor behavior**
Behavior analysts are ethically obligated to consider the safety and welfare of the client when planning for assessment. As noted in the scenario presented, members of the treatment team are concerned about the use of an FA that evokes the problem behavior. To effectively address this concern, the behavior analyst can instead plan for an FA of precursor behavior, which involves presenting the establishing operation and then immediately terminating the session when a precursor behavior (i.e., a behavior that reliably precedes the problem behavior) occurs.

62. **C) Positive reinforcement**
Reinforcement is a stimulus change that maintains a behavior or increases the likelihood that the behavior will occur again in the future. Positive reinforcement involves the addition of a stimulus that increases the likelihood that a behavior will occur again in the future. In this scenario, receiving money from his parents serves as a positive reinforcer for Orion's behavior. This scenario is not an example of positive punishment because nothing aversive is introduced to reduce the behavior. It is not an example of negative reinforcement because nothing aversive is removed to increase behavior, and it is not negative punishment because nothing desirable is removed to decrease behavior.

63. **C) Attention from caregivers**
The most likely function of Alex's head-banging behavior is attention from caregivers. This conclusion is based on the observation that the behavior occurs primarily when Alex is left alone and significantly decreases when he is engaged with others. The staff's response of rushing to provide comfort and attention reinforces the behavior.

64. **B) Direct observations**
Direct observations involve the behavior analyst directly watching and recording the client's behavior in real time, making it a direct measure. The other answer options (structured interviews, standardized questionnaires, review of historical records) are all indirect measures that gather information through reports, surveys, or existing records.

65. **D) Permanent product recording**
Product measures refer to the measurement of behavior through examination of its effects produced on the environment (i.e., permanent product). This form of measurement takes place after the behavior has occurred. Although Ms. Jackson did not directly observe Amalie's cleaning up behavior, she looked to tangible artifacts that resulted from Amalie's behavior for determining the occurrence of the cleaning up behavior. This scenario accurately describes the use of permanent product recording. Event recording tracks the frequency of behaviors rather than completed tasks; interval recording focuses on whether behaviors occur during specific time intervals; and duration recording measures how long a behavior lasts, none of which apply to evaluating the outcome of cleaned toys.

66. **B) Yes, because the testimonials were identified as solicited, state the relationship with clients, and comply with the law.**
There is no indication of an ethics violation in this situation. While behavior analysts cannot solicit testimonials from current clients for advertising, they can solicit testimonials from former clients for advertising when certain conditions are met. Testimonials from former clients used to promote a business must be identified as solicited or unsolicited, include a statement of the relationship between the BCBA® and the person giving it, and meet legal requirements.

67. **A) Five times per group activity**
Rate is the number of responses over the length of time of the observations. To calculate the average rate of Lupe's conversation-initiating behavior, count the number of times the behavior occurred across the three observation periods ($5 + 7 + 9 = 21$) and divide by the number of group activities (3). Therefore, the average rate is $21 \div 3 = 7$ times per group activity.

68. **B) Shaping**
Shaping is the provision of differential reinforcement for a progression of responses that are more similar to the target response. In other words, shaping is the reinforcement of successive approximations of a terminal behavior. While training refers to teaching a skill or behavior, it is a broad term and does not specifically involve reinforcing successive approximations to reach a target behavior. Modeling involves demonstrating a behavior for the learner to imitate, rather than reinforcing incremental steps toward a terminal behavior. Chaining involves teaching a sequence of behaviors, not reinforcing gradual approximations of a single behavior.

69. **B) Intraverbal**
The intraverbal is a verbal operant that is under the control of a verbal stimulus without point-to-point correspondence and is maintained by generalized reinforcement. In the example presented, Carl's question ("What is your name?") served as the discriminative stimulus that evoked Renee's verbal response ("Renee"). Renee's appropriate verbal response to Carl's question resulted in the delivery of a generalized reinforcer (praise), and there is no point-to-point correspondence between Carl's question and Renee's response. Codic involves textual behavior, mand involves requesting, and tact involves labeling stimuli, none of which align with Renee's conversational responses to verbal prompts.

70. **B) Function-based approach**
By conducting a performance diagnostic to identify the underlying reasons for Daniel's behavior, Maria is using a function-based approach. This method focuses on understanding the specific factors that contribute to the behavior in order to develop targeted strategies for improvement. Cultural adaptation involves aligning interventions with cultural norms, standard performance compares behavior to set standards without root cause analysis, and transformational relates to motivational leadership, not diagnostic assessment.

71. D) Mid-level responding, low variability, decreasing trend
The graph presented displays the data paths for three different behaviors, all of which can be visually analyzed across the characteristics of level, trend, and variability. Level relates to the position along the vertical *y* axis where a series of data points converge, variability relates to the amount of discrepancy between the values of a series of data points, and trend relates to the direction of a series of data points. When examining Behavior 3, the path of the data shows mid-level responding with a decreasing trend. Furthermore, the data appears to decrease in a relatively stable, low variability pattern.

72. B) A negative reinforcer for leaving the house at 8:00 a.m.
Negative reinforcement refers to the removal or reduction in intensity of a stimulus immediately following a behavior that serves to increase the future frequency of the behavior. Again, it may be helpful to think of "positive" and "negative" in the mathematical sense where "negative" involves the subtraction of a stimulus. In the scenario presented, the removal of aversive stimuli (traffic) followed her leaving-the-house-at-8:00 a.m. behavior. Thus, traffic functioned as a negative reinforcer for leaving the house at 8:00 a.m.

73. C) Socially mediated reinforcement
Recall that socially mediated contingencies are environmental contingencies that can affect behavior with the mediation or deliberate actions of another person. Socially mediated reinforcement occurs when reinforcement is a product of the actions of another person resulting from a behavior. In the scenario presented, asking to play a ball game with the same peer indicates that the activity was reinforcing for Mateo. Because this reinforcement was mediated by a peer, this is considered an example of socially mediated reinforcement. Automatic reinforcement is incorrect because Mateo's behavior (approaching the peer to play) is socially driven, not self-reinforced by the activity itself. Graduated guidance is incorrect because it refers to a fading process used to teach skills, not Mateo's spontaneous social interaction. Tact-to-mand transfer is incorrect because this concept involves a verbal behavior transition from labeling (tact) to requesting (mand), which doesn't apply to this scenario.

74. C) The client met all their goals.
Discontinuation is considered if the client is not benefiting from services, but this answer option clearly indicates that there is at least "some" benefit received from services. The other answer options describe conditions indicated in the Code as those in which discontinuation is considered.

75. C) Stimulus control
Stimulus control refers to the alteration of the frequency, duration, latency, or magnitude of behavior by the presence or absence of an antecedent stimulus. In short, behavior changes based on whether or not a particular stimulus is present. In the scenario presented, the students' response (stopping what they were doing, performing the cadence clap, and then looking at Ms. Carson) only occurred after a specific stimulus (Ms. Carson's cadence clap) was presented. Automatic contingency involves natural outcomes, reflexivity involves a stimulus matching itself, and stimulus equivalence relates to the formation of relations between multiple stimuli, none of which apply to the students responding to a specific cue.

76. B) A functional response class
The various behaviors Everett exhibits (pulling toward toys, saying "Come play," climbing on furniture, pushing objects off counters, and crying) all serve the same function of gaining attention from his parents. These behaviors, although topographically different, form a functional response class because they achieve the same outcome.

77. **A) Ability to imitate verbal models**
Imitation requires that the client attends to the model stimulus. Thus, it is important for Mia to evaluate and, if necessary, teach Marley basic attending skills (i.e., staying seated, looking at the teacher/objects, complying with instructions) before conducting imitation training. The client's ability to imitate verbal models is not an essential prerequisite skill for imitation training; modeling and imitation training are often utilized to teach nonverbal behaviors.

78. **C) Session 7**
A cumulative graph is used to display the running total of responses over time. The slope of the line represents the response rate; the steeper it is, the higher the response rate. Unlike those between any other two consecutive sessions, the slope of the line between Sessions 6 and 7 is steep and indicates a difference of 2 in the number of responses between them as measured by the markers along the vertical axis. This means that two additional responses occurred during Session 7.

79. **B) Contingency contract**
A contingency contract (or behavioral contract) is a document that specifies a contingent relationship between the completion of a specific task and access to a specified reinforcer. Ms. Hart is creatively implementing a contingency contract with her students that outlines specific classroom behaviors and the corresponding rewards and consequences. By collaboratively creating and signing the poster, the students and teacher establish clear, mutual expectations, which is a defining feature of a contingency contract.

80. **D) Does the treatment pose a risk to the safety of the client?**
In the event another nonbehavioral provider recommends a nonbehavioral treatment, the behavior analyst must determine whether it poses a risk to the safety of the client. If a safety risk is present, the behavior analyst should directly address the issue with the nonbehavioral provider. If a safety risk is not present, the behavior analyst should consider the underlying behavioral principles of the treatment and ask, "Is success possible?" If the answer is "yes" or "no, but it doesn't interfere with the client's goals," then do not address the treatment as an issue. If the answer is "no, but it does interfere with the client's goals," then consider the use of the Checklist for Analyzing Proposed Treatments (CAPT) to determine if the impact to the client is enough to warrant possible confrontation with the nonbehavioral provider.

81. **A) Changing criterion design**
The graph presented shows the use of a changing criterion design, which is an experimental design that uses stepwise benchmarks for altering a measurable dimensional quantity (i.e., frequency, duration, latency, magnitude) of a behavior. The initial baseline phase is followed by a series of intervention phases with successive/gradual criteria for change.

82. **D) Take steps to resolve the issue with the other professional**
The behavior analyst should attempt to resolve concerns directly with the nonbehavioral professional to maintain collaboration and address the issue constructively. This is important for preserving the integrity of client services.

83. **A) Negative punishment**
Negative punishment involves the removal of a stimulus immediately following a behavior, which decreases the future frequency of the behavior. In the scenario presented, Ms. Andrews removes a token contingent on the occurrence of Bart's target problem behavior (getting out of his seat without permission) which decreases the future frequency of the target problem behavior.

84. **C) Token economy with response cost**
Ms. Said is implementing a token economy with response cost, which involves the implementation of a negative punishment procedure in which undesirable behavior results in the loss of tokens—in this case, points.

85. **A) Conditioned stimulus; conditioned response**
Respondent conditioning is a type of learning whereby new stimuli develop the capacity to elicit responses through the pairing process. It focuses on involuntary responses and involves stimulus-stimulus pairing of an US with an NS until the NS becomes a CS that elicits a CR.

86. **D) Stimulus fading**
Stimulus fading involves gradually changing the physical properties of the surrounding stimuli to help the learner focus on the target stimulus. In this scenario, Shaan initially presents the name "Rory" among shapes and then systematically replaces these shapes with letters and words. This gradual alteration of the context until only the target stimulus remains helps the client recognize and focus on the relevant features of "Rory."

87. **C) Record each occurrence of the target behavior, then count the total number of occurrences and divide it by the length of the observation period at the end of the treatment session**
To measure rate, Georgia needs to collect the count of the target behavior over some unit of time (e.g., per minute, per hour, or per day). This is calculated by dividing the number of occurrences of Mark's inappropriate vocalizations by the unit of time in which the observations are conducted.

88. **C) Decline to observe the student**
Behavior analysts are responsible for obtaining informed consent before conducting assessments. In this situation, the student's parents or legal guardian would need to give permission for an observation. Jason should not agree to conduct an observation, informal or not, until informed consent has been obtained.

89. **B) Convene an expert panel of behavior analysts and other relevant professionals to review the treatment program**
If it is unclear whether services are appropriate or effective for a client, an expert panel of behavior analysts and other relevant professionals should review the treatment program.

90. **A) Discrete-trial teaching (DTT)**
DTT involves a structured teaching method with clear, distinct trials that include an instruction, a response from the learner, and immediate feedback. In this scenario, Morgan is using a structured approach with a clear instruction ("What color is this?"), a response ("Red"), and immediate feedback (praise and candy), which characterizes DTT. The other options (FO arrangement, IT, and MTA) are distractors.

91. **C) The impact of the Hawthorne effect on Tyler's performance**
Performance monitoring involves ongoing collection of relevant performance data, including the number and rate of competencies that a supervisee acquires, the number and rate of errors made in permanent products (e.g., data collection forms, assessment reports, and intervention plans), and changes in the use of language (e.g., fluency and accuracy in the use of technical language, ability to explain concepts in nontechnical language).

92. B) Social positive reinforcement and social negative reinforcement
The graph displays the results of an FA that included five conditions: alone, attention, play, tangible, and demand. The rate of the tantrum behavior is relatively low in the alone, play, and tangible conditions. While the data paths for the attention and demand conditions vary in terms of level, they are both elevated and show high levels of responding. Thus, the function of the behavior is likely to be maintained both by social positive reinforcement (i.e., access to attention) and social negative reinforcement (i.e., escape from demand).

93. B) Supporting environments and constraints
Behavior analysts consider client preferences, supporting environments, risks, constraints, and social validity when recommending intervention goals and procedures. When considering "supporting environments" (i.e., level of support available in the location where treatment is to occur), there are a wide variety of environmental variables to consider (e.g., physical space, materials, staffing, and abilities of individuals implementing the procedures). Constraints refer to factors that may inhibit successful implementation of a treatment program.

94. B) Number of times each item is chosen over others
In a paired stimulus preference assessment, the primary data collected is the number of times each item is chosen over others. This information helps establish a preference hierarchy, indicating which items are likely to be the most reinforcing for the client.

95. D) Positive reinforcement
Positive reinforcement refers to the presentation of a stimulus following a behavior that serves to increase the future frequency of the behavior. In the scenario presented, Tim's behavior (drawing an obnoxious picture on the whiteboard) was followed by his peers' attention (laughter). As a result of the presentation of his peers' attention, the future frequency of the behavior increased.

96. D) Removal; increase
Negative reinforcement involves removal, or reduction in intensity, of a stimulus immediately following a behavior that serves to increase the future frequency of the behavior. This stimulus is often referred to as an aversive stimulus whose removal results in relief. In contrast, positive reinforcement involves the presentation of a stimulus immediately following a behavior that serves to increase the future frequency of the behavior.

97. D) Request and review relevant client records
Before conducting any direct assessments and developing a treatment plan, it's important to gather all relevant information, including educational, medical, and historical records. This helps to form a comprehensive understanding of the client's background and any factors that may influence the assessment and treatment process.

98. C) Indirect
The behavior analyst is using an indirect assessment method. Indirect assessments involve gathering information through interviews, surveys, or checklists to understand behavior patterns, environmental influences, and potential functions of behaviors. This approach relies on reports and observations provided by others who have knowledge of the individual's behavior and environment.

99. C) Sensory

As described in the scenario, Gus calms down when he is physically restrained but reengages in the problem behavior when he is released. Vocal attempts from staff to redirect Gus (i.e., attention from others) were unsuccessful. This suggests that the problem behavior is used to obtain access to reinforcing sensory stimulation produced by the physical restraints.

100. D) Client preferences

Behavior analysts consider client preferences, supporting environments, risks, constraints, and social validity when recommending intervention goals and procedures. Considering client preferences means collaborating with the client and/or caregivers on the selection of intervention goals and procedures. In this instance, the behavior analyst is interviewing Gary to determine his preferences around doing homework in order to build his preferences into the intervention procedures.

101. D) Explain the change to clients/stakeholders and obtain informed consent as appropriate

Ethical practice requires that any changes to the intervention plan be clearly communicated to clients and stakeholders. This involves explaining the reasons for the change, identifying its potential impact, and obtaining informed consent. This ensures that clients are fully aware and agree to the modifications before implementation, which is a cornerstone of ethical and client-centered practice.

102. C) Latency

Latency measures the time between the presentation of a stimulus and the onset of a targeted response. This scenario describes a measurement of time between the given opportunity to emit writing behavior (i.e., end of teacher's delivery of instructions) and when the targeted response is initiated (i.e., Randolph begins to comply by writing appropriate information on the assignment paper).

103. D) High-probability request sequence

The high-probability request sequence (high-*p*) is a contingency-independent antecedent intervention that involves presenting a series of easy-to-follow requests for which the client has a history of compliance (i.e., high-*p* requests), and presenting the target request (i.e., low-*p* request) after the client has complied with the high-*p* requests. Typically, two to five high-*p* requests precede the presentation of a low-*p* request. To effectively implement this procedure, the following guidelines should be followed: present high-*p* requests that the client is currently able to comply with, present requests in rapid succession, acknowledge compliance with each request, and use high-quality reinforcers. The procedure may function as an abolishing operation and decrease the motivation to escape from requests.

104. A) Paul's behavior is reinforced by access to escape from the group.

Per the scenario, Paul despises the group meetings and thinks they are a waste of time. When he is asked to take a break outside, he escapes from the meeting and is then able to smoke cigarettes and respond to emails on his phone. Given that Paul's aggressive behavior is increasing, it is reasonable to hypothesize that the group leader's current strategy is reinforcing Paul's behavior.

105. C) Social positive reinforcement and social negative reinforcement
The graph displays the results of an FA that included four conditions: alone, attention, play, and demand. The rate of the scratching behavior is at zero in the alone and play conditions, but the data paths in both the attention and demand conditions are elevated and show high levels of responding. Thus, the function of the behavior is likely to be maintained both by social positive reinforcement (i.e., access to attention) and social negative reinforcement (i.e., escape from demand).

106. B) Engaging in covert third-party observation
Covert third-party observation is not a method used for assessing the effects of supervision. To evaluate the effects of supervision activities, supervisors can track relevant performance data of supervisees (i.e., rate of skill acquisition, rate of errors made in permanent products, and use of language), request feedback from supervisees, and administer brief structured surveys including items related to supervisor performance (e.g., organization, knowledge, and use of feedback/reinforcement).

107. C) Partial interval recording
Based on the information presented in the scenario, partial interval recording is the most appropriate measurement system for collecting data on the student's question-asking behavior. Partial interval recording can be used when the behavior cannot be easily counted (i.e., it is difficult to tell when it begins and ends, or it occurs at too high of a rate) and is oftentimes employed to target behaviors that are to be decreased. Also, in a class full of fifth-grade students and only one teacher, partial interval recording may be more feasible to implement than some of the other methods available that require more time and attention (e.g., whole interval recording). Using this method, the teacher would record whether the question-asking behavior occurred at any time during the interval at the end of the interval.

108. D) Review records and available data
Before conducting a formal assessment, Olivia needs to request and review the available records and data on the new client. Records of interest include those that contain educational, medical, and historical information. This is an important task completed at the outset of a case that can serve to provide behavior analysts with relevant background information that may be used to inform decisions related to assessment and treatment.

109. B) Subjects are randomly selected from a population of interest.
The defining features of experimental designs include: (a) the subject is the unit of intervention and data analysis, (b) the subject provides its own control for comparison, and (c) the target behavior is measured repeatedly across different levels or conditions of the intervention. Randomly selecting subjects from a population of interest is a feature of group experimental designs.

110. D) Report Steven to the Behavior Analyst Certification Board® (BACB®); this is a serious breach of the Ethics Code
This is a serious violation of the Ethics Code that warrants a report to the BACB®. Behavior analysts are to be honest and report only accurate information. Even as a student, Corey is obligated to abide by the Ethics Code for behavior analysts. With a report from Corey, it is quite likely that Steven will not be able to count his reported fieldwork experience hours.

111. A) BCBAs are obligated to be familiar with the Ethics Code.
Saying "I didn't know" does not excuse an ethical violation. As stated in the Ethics Code, behavior analysts are expected to know and comply with all parts of the Code. Having a lack of awareness, training, or misunderstanding of the Code is never a justifiable excuse for violating it.

112. B) To monitor and support fidelity of implementation
The behavior analyst conducts these observations to monitor and support fidelity of implementation. By observing the classroom and noting any deviations from the intervention plan, the behavior analyst can provide feedback and support to the teacher to ensure that the plan is being implemented as intended. This process helps maintain consistency and effectiveness in the use of behavioral procedures to address the off-task behavior in the classroom.

113. D) Leaving school building without permission
This scenario describes Stewart as a student who engages in four problem behaviors: shouting at his peers, scribbling in his textbooks, stealing items from his teacher's desk, and leaving the school building without permission. When selecting a target behavior to prioritize, it is important to consider whether the behavior poses a danger to the client or to others. The greater the threat, the higher the priority. Among the behaviors listed, leaving the school building without permission is the behavior that poses the greatest threat to the safety of the client and/or others.

114. A) Share the data, excluding confidential client information
Behavior analysts are expected to share their data directly with other professionals when possible. This practice may allow other researchers to verify our analyses and conclusions. However, the confidentiality of research participants must be protected.

115. D) Trials to criterion
In the scenario presented, Alex is evaluating the effectiveness of two instructional procedures for teaching a target intraverbal behavior. Trials to criterion, a measurement system that can be used to compare two or more treatments, is used to measure the number of response opportunities (i.e., trials) required to achieve a predetermined level of performance (i.e., mastery criterion).

116. C) Conduct regular evaluations of supervisory performance using feedback from others, clients' outcomes data, and supervisees' outcomes data
Ensuring supervisory competence and appropriate supervisory volume is good, but Ezra should not make any assumptions about the effectiveness of her supervisory practices. Behavior analysts are responsible for designing and implementing a system for obtaining and using regular performance feedback data from others (e.g., supervisees, supervisors), clients' outcomes data, and supervisees' outcomes data to inform their supervisory practices.

117. B) Description and prediction

The knowledge learned from science allows for one or more of three levels of understanding: description, prediction, and control. Ms. Lim's systematic observations of the classroom enabled her to describe classroom events in quantifiable terms and develop a hypothesis about the potential relationship between students' off-task behavior and Mr. Gupta's use of corrective feedback (description). Her repeated observations enabled her to demonstrate that the two events covaried; this correlation between events did not provide evidence of causation between the variables, but did demonstrate with a certain degree of confidence the relative probability that students' on- and off-task behavior occurred based on the presence or absence of Mr. Gupta's praise statements (prediction). Since Ms. Lim did not conduct a controlled experiment, she did not achieve knowledge of the relation between the two variables at the control level of understanding.

118. D) Variable ratio (VR)

Recall that the VR schedule specifies the average number of times a target behavior must occur to receive reinforcement. In other words, reinforcement is delivered after a variable number of responses have occurred. Thus, the occurrence of reinforcement is less predictable. In the scenario presented, reinforcement does not occur after a fixed or variable length of time. Students need to demonstrate a target behavior (complete an assigned task) for tickets to place in the box, and having one's name drawn from the box and receiving a reward may or may not occur for any particular student at the end of each week. This is an example of a system that uses a VR schedule of reinforcement. The other options (FI, FR, and VI) are distractors.

119. C) High-probability request sequence

Peyton is implementing the high-probability request sequence (high-*p*) procedure, which is a contingency-independent antecedent intervention that involves presenting a series of easy-to-follow requests for which the client has a history of compliance (i.e., high-*p* requests), and presenting the target request (i.e., low-*p* request) after the client has complied with the high-*p* requests. By starting with tasks Gabriel is likely to complete successfully, Peyton builds a pattern of compliance that makes it more likely he will comply with the more challenging request of brushing his teeth. This approach leverages initial successes to increase the probability of compliance with the target behavior.

120. D) Standardized

The behavior analyst is using a standardized test. Standardized assessments use uniform procedures and scoring criteria to measure an individual's abilities or skills. They are designed to ensure consistency and reliability in evaluating performance across different contexts and populations.

121. A) Descriptive

Descriptive assessment methods, which have been applied to evaluate potential consequences of problem behavior, involve direct observation of the target behavior in relation to other events under naturally occurring conditions. Eli used antecedent-behavior-consequence recording, a type of descriptive assessment, to record the occurrences of the target behavior and the environmental events surrounding it (i.e., antecedents and consequences).

122. B) Making eye contact with peers

Permanent product recording can be used when the behavior of interest produces effects on the environment that can be measured after its occurrence. Completed homework assignment sheets, toy-filled bins, and wet diapers are examples of permanent products that lend themselves to measurement. Eye contact, however, does not consistently produce effects on the environment that can be measured after its occurrence.

123. B) Determinism, selectionism, and parsimony

When explaining that all behavior possesses an identifiable cause and is to some degree determinable, the BCBA® advocates for determinism. Determinism is the assumption that the universe is rational, governed by discoverable laws, and that events are completely determined by previously existing causes. Relatedly, the BCBA espouses selectionism when encouraging the team to focus on explanations of the person's behavior based on the person's known experiences and the consequences of their behavior. The BCBA® advocates for the principle of parsimony when she encourages the team to rule out simple, logical explanations for the person's behavior before entertaining more complex or abstract explanations. As an applied scientist committed to employing the scientific method to understand and intervene in human behavior, the BCBA is certainly committed to the other four attitudes of science (i.e., experimentation, replication, empiricism, and philosophic doubt). However, she does not explicitly advocate for those attitudes in the team meeting.

124. C) Stimulus control

Stimulus control refers to behavior change based on whether or not some stimulus is present. In the scenario presented, Amy's response (reviewing discussion points and activities for 15 minutes) only occurs when a particular stimulus (event labeled "supervision meeting") is seen on her calendar. When the event is not seen on her calendar, the response does not occur. This is an example of a behavior that is controlled by a stimulus (i.e., stimulus control).

125. A) Recommend reinforcement rather than punishment whenever possible

The Code requires behavior-change interventions to prioritize reinforcement-based procedures. However, behavior analysts may recommend and use punishment-based procedures if other (i.e., reinforcement-based) procedures have been tried but failed to produce the desired results, or the intervention team determines that potential benefits of using a punishment-based procedure outweigh the risk of harm to the client.

126. C) Scratching a spot on your leg because it itches

Automatic reinforcement occurs when reinforcement is either a response product of a behavior or a product of the physical environment resulting from a behavior. Scratching a spot on your leg because it itches is an example of this as negative reinforcement (relief from itching) is a product of the behavior (scratching).

127. C) Shaping frequency within a response topography

When shaping within response topographies, the topography of behavior remains constant, but some other measurable dimension is changed. In this example, Kelly is intervening to increase Ian's use of vocal mands. Shaping frequency within a response topography is most appropriate.

128. A) Attempt to resolve the issue directly with the counselor; if it cannot be resolved, report it to the appropriate authority (e.g., administrator, supervisor)

When a behavior analyst experiences a problem with a nonbehavioral professional, they are obligated to attempt to resolve it. In the event Wanda is unable to resolve this problem with the counselor, the next step is to report it to the appropriate authority.

129. B) Echoic

An echoic is a verbal operant that is under the control of a vocal-verbal stimulus, with which it shares point-to-point correspondence (i.e., stimulus parts correspond with response parts) and formal similarity (i.e., stimulus and response physically resemble each other). In the scenario presented, Daria's vocal response of "apple" (vocal-verbal stimulus) evokes Milo's vocal response of "apple." Milo's response is an echoic.

130. B) Social positive reinforcement
The graph displays the results of an FA that included four conditions: alone, attention, play, and demand. The rate of yelling behavior is significantly higher in the attention condition when compared to all others. Thus, it is most likely that the function of the yelling behavior is access to social attention.

131. D) Interdependent group contingency
Mr. Caretto is implementing an interdependent group contingency, which involves providing reinforcement for all members of a group, in this case his students, based on each member of the group achieving a performance criterion that is in place for all members of the group (i.e., memorization of all multiplication facts).

132. A) Dr. Digable is not delivering feedback in a timely enough manner.
Dr. Digable is providing praise several days after Toni has performed the desired behaviors that she intended to promote. When delivering praise or other reinforcers, deliver it immediately following the behavior and verbally describe what the supervisee did correctly.

133. D) Ensure the intervention is being implemented with high fidelity
Sarah's periodic observations and data recordings are intended to ensure that the new intervention strategy is being implemented with high fidelity. By monitoring adherence to the protocol and providing ongoing feedback, Sarah helps maintain the integrity of the intervention. High fidelity in implementation is critical for the intervention's effectiveness and for achieving the intended client outcomes.

134. C) Rule-governed behavior
This is an example of rule-governed behavior, which is behavior that is under the control of verbal antecedents that are considered rules. There are two types of rules: those in the form of a simple request or instruction, and those that describe a behavioral contingency. In the scenario presented, the verbal antecedent ("Out of service for maintenance" text on the sign) served as a simple instruction that enabled Cooper to respond effectively without directly contacting any contingencies that would be harmful or inefficient to contact.

135. B) Response generalization
Response generalization occurs when the client emits an untrained response that serves the same function as the trained target behavior. In the scenario presented, Danielle was taught a response for obtaining permission to access the restroom but then began to emit an untrained response (waving her arms in the air and silently mouthing the word "bathroom") that serves the same function.

136. A) Administering checklists or rating scales at regular intervals to stakeholders who most frequently observe the problem behavior
Descriptive assessment involves observation of the target behavior in relation to environmental events and includes continuous antecedent-behavior-consequence (ABC) recording, narrative ABC recording, and scatter plot recording. Administering checklists or rating scales at regular intervals to stakeholders is an indirect assessment activity that can provide progress monitoring data.

137. C) The phrase, "at least 80% of the time."
The format of a goal statement can include the following components: condition, name of client, behavior to be increased or decreased, criterion, indication of how it will be measured, and date by which it will be achieved. The criterion defines how much, how often, and to what standard the behavior must occur in order to demonstrate that the goal has been reached. In the example presented, "at least 80% of the time" sets the criterion in the goal statement.

138. **B) Extinction of behavior maintained by negative reinforcement**
The behavior therapist is using an extinction procedure for escape-maintained behavior. By requiring the client to persist with tasks despite the yelling, they are eliminating the reinforcing effect of escaping the task. Thus, this is an example of extinction of behavior maintained by negative reinforcement.

139. **D) Notify his university and obtain approval from the institutional review committee before collecting any data**
It's not enough to obtain permission only from the context in which Hector would like to conduct his study. If this is a potential research project to be submitted to the university, Hector should notify relevant parties at his university (e.g., his faculty advisor), write a research proposal describing what the study will involve, and obtain approval from the university's institutional review board before proceeding. We do not conduct research until after it has been approved by a formal research review committee.

140. **A) Bar graph**
In the scenario presented, the BCBA® wants to display the number of activities that the student reported a preference for in each of the three activity categories. These categories are considered discrete variables (i.e., variables that are quantified by counting). There is no measure of performance over time. The most appropriate data display format for summarizing this discrete data is the bar graph (also known as the histogram).

141. **A) Response cost and time-out**
Procedures based on negative punishment are used to weaken responses by establishing contingencies in which targeted responses are immediately followed by the removal of reinforcing stimulus events. Among the answer options presented, "response cost and time-out" is the only answer that includes two negative punishment procedures. Response cost involves fining the client a specific amount of reinforcement, and time-out involves the withdrawal of opportunities to access reinforcement. The other answer options each include at least one positive punishment procedure.

142. **C) Provide a written description of the target skill**
The six steps to BST are (a) describe the target skill, (b) provide a written description, (c) demonstrate the target skill, (d) require the supervisee to practice the target skill, (e) provide feedback during practice, and (f) repeat step 4 (require the supervisee to practice the target skill) and step 5 (provide feedback during practice) until mastery is achieved. Martin did not provide an explanation of why a skill is to be targeted and the behavioral definition of it needs to be in written form. Ideally, a written description would be provided, and the supervisee would be given time to ask questions about it.

143. **C) Call a meeting with her supervisor and the client's parents to discuss how they can solve the issue; if parents fail to attend, it may be appropriate to begin terminating services**
If parents fail to comply with the program despite appropriate efforts to address barriers, then there is sufficient reason to move forward in discontinuing services. Note that the client is also no longer benefiting from services, which is also in and of itself sufficient for discontinuing services. Additionally, the family can be referred to other appropriate professionals (e.g., behavior analysts or counselors).

144. C) Selects a picture of a ball

In the scenario presented, the client observed a sample stimulus, the picture of a ball (A), and learned to match the comparison stimulus, a physical ball (B), to it. In other words, the client learned an A = B relation. Symmetry is indicated in the demonstration of reversibility of a sample stimulus and comparison stimulus. This means that a relation of symmetry would be demonstrated if the client was to perform the task in reverse, by observing a physical ball (B) and then selecting the picture of a ball (A), thus indicating the emergence of the B = A relation.

145. B) Saying "I like how you're following my directions" and giving tokens

A stimulus class is a group of stimuli with elements in common across formal, temporal, and/or functional dimensions. While the form of making the statement, "I like how you're following my directions," differs from that of giving a token, they are both consequences for desired behavior (i.e., following directions) and the most likely pair of stimuli to serve the same function (e.g., reinforcing following directions).

146. B) Negative punishment

This is an example of negative punishment and its effect on behavior. Negative punishment involves the removal of a stimulus immediately following a behavior, which decreases the future frequency of the behavior. In the scenario presented, Eddie's dad removes his video game controllers (i.e., his ability to play video games) immediately following Eddie's arguing behavior. This, in turn, decreases the future frequency of arguing behavior.

147. D) Generality

The seven dimensions of ABA are: applied, behavioral, analytic, technologic, conceptually systematic, effective, and generality. A change in behavior is considered to possess generality when it holds over time, across different settings, and/or spreads to other relevant and related behaviors. In the case example presented, Andy's social communication skills spread beyond the swing class environment and were evidenced to be durable over time.

148. A) Antecedent manipulation to decrease task demands

The persistent elopement behavior, despite the implementation of redirection and positive reinforcement for remaining in the activity area, suggests that antecedent conditions may need adjustment. By manipulating antecedents to decrease task demands, John can address the client's motivation to escape from these tasks, thereby reducing the occurrence of elopement more effectively.

149. B) Access to tangible reinforcement

In the scenario presented, Leslie's peers relinquish objects in response to her physically aggressive behavior toward them. When these objects are relinquished, Leslie then has access to and will engage in play with them. Thus, the likely function of Leslie's physically aggressive behavior toward other students at school during recess is socially mediated access to tangible reinforcement.

150. A) Access to a preferred activity after completing a reduced math assignment

The IV is the intervention. The IV represents the treatment variable that is used to intervene on the phenomenon of interest (i.e., target behavior). In an experiment, the IV is systematically manipulated to determine if alterations to it will produce reliable alterations in the dependent variable (DV). In this case, the most appropriate IV is providing Nic with access to a preferred activity to reinforce his completion of in-class math assignments (the DV).

151. D) Implement an intermittent schedule of reinforcement
Implementing an intermittent schedule of reinforcement can maintain the desired behavior (using the toilet) without the need for constant tangible rewards, which are unsustainable. Conducting an FA, teaching Sam to notify his parents, and talking with him about his reluctance to use the toilet may provide insights but are not direct solutions for maintaining the new toilet-using behavior.

152. B) It will enable them to further enhance their relationship.
Enabling Tiana to further enhance her relationship with Anders is not a good reason for agreeing to provide supervision. This reason may also be indicative of a slippery slope toward committing an ethics violation if it results in a romantic (i.e., dual) relationship. The reasons for providing supervision are that it is necessary for the delivery of quality behavior-analytic services, contributes to the professional development of supervisees and supervisors, is supported as best practice by the field's professional literature, and is required per the Professional and Ethical Compliance Code for behavior analysts.

153. B) Mid-level responding, high variability, increasing trend
The graph presented displays the data paths for three different behaviors, all of which can be visually analyzed across the characteristics of level, trend, and variability. Level relates to the position along the vertical *y* axis where a series of data points converge, variability relates to the amount of discrepancy between the values of a series of data points, and trend relates to the direction of a series of data points. When examining Behavior 2, the path of the data shows mid-level responding with an increasing trend. Furthermore, the data appears to increase in a relatively unstable, high variability pattern.

154. D) Refraining from taking a nap during the day
Manipulating MOs involves altering the environment or conditions that affect the value of a reinforcer and the likelihood of a behavior occurring. In this scenario, refraining from taking a nap during the day increases Grayson's level of sleep deprivation, making him more tired and likely to fall asleep at night. Other options like setting a reminder, only sleeping in the bedroom, and removing the television are strategies related to prompts or antecedent control, but they don't directly alter the motivation to sleep.

155. C) Multielement design
The graph presented shows the use of a multielement design. Also commonly referred to as an alternating treatments design, this type of experimental design involves delivering and measuring effects of two or more interventions in a rapid, alternating fashion. This allows behavior analysts to compare the effects of different interventions. It can also be used to compare the effects of an intervention with no intervention (i.e., baseline).

156. D) Decline to develop the program and recommend finding a professional with relevant experience
Bennett should decline the request because developing a program for adolescents with emotional and behavioral disorders falls outside his area of expertise in early intervention for children with developmental delays. Remember, the Ethics Code requires that behavior analysts work within their areas of competence. By recommending a professional experienced in working with adolescents, Bennett ensures the program will be designed and implemented by someone with the appropriate knowledge and skills, leading to more effective and ethical intervention for the targeted population.

157. A) Performance expectations for the supervisor and the supervisee in the form of a supervision contract

Performance expectations for the supervisor and supervisee should be clearly communicated at the outset of a supervisory relationship. When the supervisory relationship is between a qualified supervisor and a trainee acquiring fieldwork experience to meet Behavior Analyst Certification Board® (BACB®) requirements for the BCBA®, certification, a supervision contract must be established. The supervision contract is a written document that describes the supervisor–supervisee relationship and expectations for both parties.

158. A) Implement an emergency procedure to maintain his safety and refer him to an appropriate professional for assessment; programming can be placed on hold

The behavior analysts in this situation determined that there is a reasonable likelihood that the new behavior is influenced by medical or biological variables. Given this, a referral to an appropriate professional is necessary for ensuring that his medical needs are assessed and addressed. In the meantime, it is imperative that appropriate measures are in place to ensure the safety of the client. Programming can be placed on hold until after results of the assessment are obtained.

159. D) Function-based strategies

Behavior analysts use function-based strategies to improve personnel performance. To accomplish this, behavior analysts use performance diagnostics to examine relevant antecedents, behaviors, and consequences in the environment to identify possible reasons (i.e., functions) for performance deficits.

160. B) Rule

Using a rule involves the steps for delivering an instruction and extending it to include a contingency. If Suri was only providing an instruction, she simply would have said, "Wash your hands." But in this example, she established a contingency between a specific behavior ("Wash your hands") and a particular consequence ("Have a snack").

161. C) Directly requesting feedback

Directly requesting feedback from supervisees is the method that is most likely to enhance a supervisor's ability to tailor supervision to meet the specific needs of individual supervisees. Requesting feedback involves directly asking the supervisee the following questions: "Are you getting what you need?" and "Am I teaching [knowledge/skill(s)] in the most effective way for you?" Asking these questions can occur regularly as a part of supervision meetings.

162. C) Assess the implementation fidelity of the intervention

Before making changes to the intervention, fidelity of implementation should be assessed. Ensuring fidelity can be particularly challenging in situations involving multiple implementers. If the intervention plan was not implemented as planned, the lack of progress may be due to issues with fidelity rather than the intervention itself. Ensuring proper implementation by providing implementers with sufficient training and support to competently implement the intervention plan may help to resolve apparent issues with the intervention's effectiveness.

163. B) Contingent attention

In the attention condition of an FA, an experimenter withholds social positive reinforcement (i.e., attention) but will deliver it when the client engages in problem behavior. The purpose of this arrangement is to determine whether the problem behavior is maintained by access to social attention. Differentially higher levels of the problem behavior during the contingent attention condition when compared to the control condition would suggest that it is maintained by social positive reinforcement.

164. C) Immediate needs of the agency

When developing long-term goals for supervisees, supervisors need to consider the Task List items relevant to the supervisee's role, their performance across those Task List items, and the expected needs of the agency. Immediate needs, while important, are more relevant when developing short-term goals rather than long-term goals.

165. B) 6 months

A behavior analyst cannot accept as a supervisee an individual with whom they have had a romantic/sexual relationship within the last 6 months. The other answer options (3 months, 12 months, 24 months) serve as distractors.

166. B) Provide training on generalization strategies and monitor implementation fidelity

This approach supports the trainee in developing skills necessary for effective implementation across diverse environments. The other answer options (assign the trainee to work exclusively in a single setting, ignore the inconsistencies, revoke the trainee's supervision) do not effectively address the issue and may hinder the trainee's professional growth.

167. C) Backward chaining with leap aheads

Backward chaining with leap aheads is helpful when the client already has the prerequisite steps for a final behavior in their behavior chain. In this example, Clive only needs to learn the final step in the behavior chain: how to strap the velcro on his shoes. Since he already knows how to sit down (prior step), put his foot in the shoe (prior step), and take hold of the velcro with his hand (prior step), these steps do not require teaching. The behavior analyst can "leap ahead" to teaching the final step in the chain.

168. A) Applied behavior analysis (ABA)

ABA focuses on the application of behavioral principles and experimental methods to solve practical problems and improve socially significant behaviors. It uses data-driven approaches to identify and manipulate environmental variables to achieve desired behavior changes. The other options (behaviorism, EAB, empiricism), while related to the field of behavior analysis, do not specifically target the practical, applied aspect of enhancing behavior in real-world settings as ABA does.

169. C) Betty, a first-year college student with autism spectrum disorder, takes a ballroom dancing class with a BCBA® during which she learns and practices how to ask people to dance and make small talk. In her second year of college, Betty regularly asks questions in class and responds to professors' questions.

Betty is demonstrating response generalization. During intervention with the BCBA, she learned and practiced how to ask people to dance and make small talk. Then, without training, she used those skills in an alternative but functionally equivalent manner when asking questions in class and responding to her professors' questions.

170. B) Magnitude

Although Lincoln responds to in-class questions, his answers are not provided at an appropriate volume. This is an issue of magnitude, which refers to the strength or force of the behavior. The behavior analyst should focus on reducing the intensity of Lincoln's vocal responses to questions to achieve a socially acceptable volume level.

171. C) Click the clicker, then give the dog a treat; repeat several times

To create a CR using a clicker, Pat should instruct her students to repeatedly first click the clicker, then give their dog a treat. Pat is teaching her students to use classical conditioning to link the clicker (a neutral stimulus) and the treat (an unconditioned stimulus [US]) to transform the clicker into a conditioned stimulus (CS) that produces a CR. For this to be effective, the CS (the clicker) should occur before the US (the treat)—not simultaneously or after it. In this way, the clicker (CS) serves as a signal or cue to the dog that they are about to get a treat (US).

172. B) Function-based

Behavior analysts use function-based assessment (e.g., performance diagnostics) to identify variables affecting personnel performance. Performance diagnostics (or performance analysis) uses a function-based approach to identify variables affecting personnel performance. The primary model used for performance diagnostics at the individual level is the antecedent-behavior-consequence (ABC) analysis.

173. A) Access to social reinforcement

When examining the Antecedent column, we can see that each instance of the problem behavior is preceded by the teacher engaging in some activity that restricts Arya's access to the teacher's attention. When examining the Consequence column, the narrative data shows that the problem behavior is then followed by the teacher attending to Arya. Although limited, the data suggests that Arya engages in the crying behavior to obtain access to social reinforcement (i.e., teacher attention).

174. C) Objective measure of supervisee skill acquisition

Objective measures of supervisee skill acquisition should be prioritized when evaluating the impact of supervision on supervisee performance. These measures directly assess the acquisition and application of skills taught during supervision, providing concrete evidence of competence and progress. Feedback from supervisors is valuable but subjective, while the number of sessions and length of employment may not directly correlate with skill acquisition and improvement in performance.

175. D) Task analysis

Before behaviors can be linked in a chain, behavior analysts must develop a task analysis (TA) that breaks down a complex task into a series of smaller, teachable steps. Develop and validate a TA using one of the following methods: observe someone competently performing the task, perform the task yourself, ask for input from an expert, or use a systematic trial-and-error procedure. When determining the number of steps, consider the complexity of each step on the basis of what is manageable for the client. A treatment plan and an action plan are synonymous; both define the problem or diagnosis, prescribed treatment, treatment goals, planned actions to achieve treatment goals, a timeline for treatment progress, measurable objectives, and progress monitoring. Skinner's analysis offers a framework for language assessment and intervention.

176. C) Extinction

Abigail instructed Bexley's parents to use extinction, which involves no longer reinforcing a previously reinforced behavior. By ignoring Bexley's whining and not allowing her to watch TV, her parents removed the reinforcement that was maintaining the problem behavior, leading to its decrease.

177. D) Multiple stimulus without replacement
Liam presented multiple stimuli to Gus. When Gus selects an item, it is removed (i.e., not replaced in the array), which reduces the number of stimuli remaining in the array. This type of preference assessment, known as multiple stimulus without replacement, functions as a process that can be used to establish a preference hierarchy that indicates which stimuli are most preferred, which stimuli are moderately preferred, and which stimuli are least preferred.

178. A) They conduct assessments that prioritize reinforcement procedures.
Behavior analysts should prioritize reinforcement procedures when designing interventions, but this is a question about their responsibility in assessment. Behavior analysts are to select and design assessments that are consistent with behavioral principles; based on scientific evidence; meet the needs, context, and resources of clients and stakeholders; and focus on maximizing benefits and minimizing risk of harm to clients and stakeholders.

179. B) Function-based; contingency-independent; contingency-dependent
MOs and SDs are considered function-based. Those based on MOs are contingency-independent (i.e., do not rely on differential consequences for the target behavior), whereas those based on stimulus control are contingency-dependent (i.e., rely on differential consequences for the target behavior).

180. B) Utilizing culturally responsive performance management techniques tailored to each supervisee
Culturally responsive performance management techniques are designed to address the unique needs and backgrounds of each supervisee, ensuring that supervision practices are inclusive and effective. By tailoring supervision methods to the individual, Michaela can better support the development and success of her diverse team. Applying the same strategies or a standardized plan to all supervisees ignores these differences and can lead to inequitable treatment. Focusing primarily on those with the longest tenure does not address the needs of newer supervisees or those from different cultural backgrounds.

181. C) Avoid these social events and end the potential relationship before it starts; if Toby wants to pursue a relationship, he should wait at least 2 years after services have been discontinued
Engaging in romantic relationships with current clients is not permitted because such relationships can result in conflicts of interest and impaired judgment. Behavior analysts cannot engage in romantic relationships with former clients for at least 2 years from the date the professional relationship ended.

182. C) Implement a performance management plan that includes modeling, practice opportunities, feedback, and reinforcement
Conducting a function-based assessment helps identify the specific reasons for performance issues. By implementing a performance management plan that includes modeling, practice opportunities, feedback, and reinforcement, Alvin can provide Corinna with the necessary support and guidance to improve her skills in managing challenging behaviors. This approach addresses the root cause of her difficulties and promotes skill development through structured and consistent supervision practices.

183. A) Aziz neglected to incorporate a skill training component to help Malcolm acquire a functionally equivalent replacement behavior.
Aziz's implementation of a noncontingent schedule of reinforcement is appropriate as an antecedent-based strategy to reduce Malcolm's motivation to engage in exhibitionistic behavior. However, Aziz's intervention plan would have been more effective if he had not neglected to incorporate a skill training component to help Malcolm acquire a functionally equivalent replacement behavior (i.e., a response to garner attention from his fellow retirees without engaging in exhibitionistic behavior that made most members of the community feel uncomfortable).

184. A) Behavioral skills training (BST)
Behavior analysts utilize BST, which includes both performance and competency-based training elements, to teach trainees to competently perform intervention procedures with fidelity. BST involves a process of describing the target skill, providing a written description, demonstrating the target skill, requiring the trainee to practice the target skill, and providing feedback during practice. Didactic instruction, group-based training, and simulation training may offer some benefits, but they lack the comprehensive, interactive, and feedback-oriented nature of BST that ensures effective training.

185. B) "It may be helpful to try sensory integration therapy for addressing the motor skills problems. For the tantrums, however, I would suggest that we begin with a functional assessment."
It's important that behavior analysts respectfully collaborate with other professionals on treatment teams. This includes acknowledging the utility of other professionals' recommendations. However, there is no robust evidence to support sensory integration therapy as a sufficient standalone intervention for problem behaviors. As a behavior analyst, it is necessary to conduct a functional assessment to identify controlling variables and then proceed to design a function-based intervention plan for decreasing the tantrum behavior.

14

After the Exam

LEARNING OBJECTIVES

After reading this chapter, you will be able to:

- Describe the available opportunities for professional development.
- Identify options for obtaining continuing education credits.
- Search for career opportunities and critically evaluate them for goodness of fit.
- Plan for the job interview process.
- Understand the importance of and engage in self-care as needed.

Whether you passed the exam or not, we have some recommendations for you. Read on.

AFTER PASSING THE EXAM: SOME RECOMMENDATIONS

Congratulations! Your hard work has paid off! Passing the BCBA® Exam is a significant accomplishment and major milestone in your career as a behavior analyst.

There's a natural tendency to pass an exam like this, celebrate briefly, and then move on without taking time to process the experience. However, this can be a missed opportunity. Research suggests that acknowledging and savoring our positive experiences and successes enhances our well-being and resilience in the face of challenges. It took a lot of discipline, hard work, and intelligence to pass this exam. Let that sink in. Recognize and appreciate these positive qualities in yourself. Take a minute to reflect on and savor this positive experience. Imagine yourself installing it in your mind and body. Internalize your accomplishment. Life is often challenging, and it's not every day that you experience such a great success and sense of accomplishment. Enjoy it!

This can also be a good time for reflection. Fortunately, you'll never have to take this exam again; however, there may be other exams or tasks in your future that will require the same level of perseverance and focused effort to be successful. What can you learn from this experience? Consider the factors that fostered your success. Take note of the activities and practices that worked well for you as well as those that did not. What can you take from this experience to improve your performance and productivity in other aspects of your life?

As you move forward in your career as a behavior analyst, it's important to consider how you will continue to develop as a professional. Many behavior analysts find that membership activities through professional associations, attendance at behavior-analysis conferences, reading relevant books and materials, and participating in training events function to enhance their skills and continually reinvigorate their passion for the profession.

PROFESSIONAL ASSOCIATIONS

There are many professional associations that offer helpful resources for BCBAs. These include the Behavior Analyst Certification Board® (BACB®), Association for Behavior Analysis International (ABAI), and the Association of Professional Behavior Analysts (APBA), to name a few.

Behavior Analyst Certification Board

The BACB is more than just a website to visit to learn about certification/supervision requirements, apply for your credential, and make reports of ethical violations. The BACB also regularly publishes a newsletter available at bacb.com/newsletters containing important information about changes and resources related to obtaining/maintaining certification, conducting supervision, and adhering to ethics code requirements. The organization also now offers a podcast available at www.bacb.com/bacb-podcasts that discusses items that are presented in the newsletters, such as:

- Episode 7: The Autism Spectrum Disorder (ASD) Practice Guidelines
- Episode 10: Addressing Potential Ethics Violations With Others
- Episode 22: Helpful Ethics Resources

Association for Behavior Analysis International

The ABAI has been around for nearly half a century as a membership organization for those interested in the science, application, and teaching of behavior analysis. The organization hosts multiple conferences each year in locations in and outside of the United States. The ABAI also offers jobs placement services; access to special interest groups; many continuing education (CE) events; and six behavior-analysis journals:

- *Behavior Analysis in Practice*
- *Behavior and Social Issues*
- *Education and Treatment of Children*
- *Perspectives on Behavior Science*
- *The Analysis of Verbal Behavior*
- *The Psychological Record*

Association of Professional Behavior Analysts

The APBA hosts an annual convention that takes place in a different city each year. Members are given access to several helpful resources including the organization's newsletter, bibliographies of applied research, and materials on professional credentialing and health insurance coverage. The APBA also offers its members discounted subscription rates to several publications, including *Child & Family Behavior Therapy*, *Journal of Organizational Behavior Management*, and *Journal of Mental Health Research in Intellectual Disabilities*.

Beyond organizations with "behavior analysis" (or a functional equivalent) in the title, there are trade associations that focus on industries that may be relevant to you as a behavior analyst. For the many behavior analysts who work with clients with ASD, outfits such as the Council of Autism Service Providers (CASP) or the Association for Science in Autism Treatment (ASAT) hold professional conferences and offer resources that may be of interest to you.

PROFESSIONAL CONFERENCES

Attending professional behavior-analysis conferences can be a great way to connect with colleagues, grow as a behavior analyst, and obtain mandatory CE for recertification. In addition to the ABAI and APBA, there are numerous behavior-analysis organizations that hold professional conferences every year. Many state and regional associations are out there, including affiliated chapters of the ABAI and APBA. In California, we currently have the California Association for Behavior Analysis (CalABA). In Massachusetts, we have the Massachusetts Association for Behavior Analysis (MassABA) and Massachusetts Professionals in Behavior Analysis (BABAT). To start, conduct a web search of behavior-analysis association(s) in your area and consider what they can offer you if you elect to become a member.

For behavior analysts who reside outside of the United States or perhaps have a desire to engage in professional association activities in other countries, behavior analysis knows no borders. There are numerous behavior-analysis associations present in many parts of the world!

BOOKS

For BCBAs interested in translating their applied behavior analysis (ABA) skills into professional consulting work, Bailey and Burch's (2010) *25 Essential Skills & Strategies for the Professional Behavior Analyst: Expert Tips for Maximizing Consulting Effectiveness* is essential reading. In it, the authors teach the essential skills and strategies that foster success when consulting with leadership of human-service organizations and major corporations. The book is organized into five sections, covering essential business skills, basic consulting repertoire, applying your behavioral knowledge, vital work habits, and advanced consulting strategies. Within these sections, a wide range of essential skills is covered, from business etiquette and negotiation to using power effectively and becoming a trusted professional. It's a book BCBAs find themselves returning to again and again.

BCBAs new to the profession often seek resources related to supervision. Kazemi et al.'s (2018) *Fieldwork and Supervision for Behavior Analysts: A Handbook* serves as a helpful guide to fieldwork and supervision activities. This handbook couples core competencies with case scenarios and offers structured supervision guidelines for facilitating skill acquisition. Britton and Cicoria's (2019) *Remote Fieldwork Supervision for BCBA® Trainees* is another offering that aims to help prepare behavior analysts to provide high-quality supervision and mentoring to trainees, whether it takes place in-person or remotely. In it, the authors offer a clear framework and comprehensive guidance for the BCBA supervisor.

PODCASTS

Inside the Behavior Analyst Certification Board Podcast

These days, everyone has a podcast … even the BACB! You can find the podcast at bacb.com/bacb-podcasts. Episodes typically feature Drs. Melissa Nosik and Jim Carr along with other experts from the field discussing issues of relevance for the BACB and its members. For example, you'll find episodes focused on the role of subject matter experts (SMEs) at the BACB, the history of ethics at the BACB, the ASD Practice Guidelines, myths and misconceptions about examination development, and the Ethics Code for behavior analysts.

ABA Inside Track Podcast

This is a weekly podcast hosted by behavior analysts Robert Parry-Cruwys, Diana Parry-Cruwys, and Jackie MacDonald that discusses the latest articles in the field of behavior analysis. Episode guests include leading researchers and practitioners in the field of behavior analysis. The organization's aim is to serve as a professional community that helps to keep behavior analysts up to date through engaging, informative, and entertaining conversations about everything ABA. There are more than 200 episodes conveniently organized by topic (e.g., ethics, supervision, assessment, treatment, and skill building) on their website at abainsidetrack.com. Many episodes are centered around discussions of journal articles you'll likely want to read in advance of listening. ABA Inside Track is also a source for CE hours, some of which are free. Just listen to the episode (each of which is worth 1 CE credit), note the two secret code words shared during the episode, and then purchase credit for it on their website under the "Get CEUs" tab.

The Behavioral Observations

This is a popular podcast for behavior analysts hosted by behavior analyst Matt Cicoria, who conducts interviews with luminaries in the field. In each episode, an expert guest is invited to discuss a topic of interest, ranging from teaching functional communication and public policy to classroom management and advice on starting a private practice. You can access the podcast through the website at behavioralobservations.com or common podcast hosting platforms such as iTunes and Spotify. You can also earn CE credits; listen to certain podcast episodes, take the accompanying quiz to demonstrate that you were listening, and earn a CE certificate.

Other Podcasts, Including #DOBETTER, ABA on Call, and The Social ChangeCast

There are several other podcasts available that focus on behavior analysis, including #DOBETTER at collective.dobettermovement.us that is operated by "a community and network of forward-thinking, like-minded individuals dedicated to the pursuit of improving and expanding the field of behavior analysis" (Do Better Collective, n.d., para. 1). Their episodes cover a wide range of topics that address both practice as well as the critical sociopolitical dimensions of behavior analysis. The ABA on Call podcast hosted by behavior analysts Rick Kubina Jr. and Doug Kostewicz is another option that started in 2019 and explores topics in behavior analysis not often found in other podcasts, including the science of behavior and free will, ABA and creativity, future tech and ABA, and debunking ABA myths. And last, but not least, there is The Social ChangeCast podcast hosted by behavior analysts Denisha Gingles and Arin Donovan; they focus on bridging behavioral science and social justice to address critical social issues, current events, and all forms of oppression. Episodes have addressed topics such as privilege, power, and parenting; discussing systemic racism with children with autism; colonial research practices; and the ABA reform movement.

OPTIONS FOR CONTINUING EDUCATION

There have never been more ways for BCBAs to earn CE credits. Over the course of your career, you'll be presented with myriad opportunities for professional development. Given the ever-expanding proliferation of CE offerings, we recommend that you take time to carefully identify content that is (a) of interest and (b) will further develop your knowledge skills in relevant ways. The BACB's Authorized Continuing Education (ACE) Provider Directory at bacb.com/authorized-continuing-education-providers is a great place to search for potential CE providers for behavior analysts.

JOB HUNTING

After years of preparation, you're now a BCBA and ready to apply your knowledge and skills in support of clients. It's time to find a job and launch your career! The good news is that there has never been a better time to be a BCBA. Behavior analysis is used extensively in education, healthcare, animal training, and business management and has been shown to be effective in a wide variety of areas (e.g., parent training, substance abuse treatment, dementia management, brain injury rehabilitation, occupational safety intervention). Over the past two decades, the United States has witnessed significant growth. Between 2010 and 2020, the number of online job postings across a variety of fields and specialties requiring a BCBA, based on 50,000 sources, increased by 4,209%! Yowza!

When searching for a job, we recommend that you consider the type of setting, position type, and employer that will make the best fit for you. First, BCBAs work in a variety of settings, and learning about the different options (e.g., clinics, schools) and associated advantages/disadvantages can be hugely beneficial. There are also BCBAs who are moving into the growing field of digital behavioral health who offer a combination of in-person and remote support to clients. What setting is best for you?

Second, there are many position types. For instance, some BCBAs spend much of their time engaged in clinical work, whereas others are engaged in administration, teaching, research, and so on. There are also BCBAs who do salaried work and BCBAs who do contractual work.

Understanding how these forms of compensation differ can affect the consistency of your work as well as your bottom line, taxes, and benefits. What type of position is best for you?

Third, it's important to look at employer characteristics. When doing this, consider any signs of the organization's commitment to quality and excellence in the field. Given the rapidly changing nature of the field, does the employer support professional development for staff? This can take a variety of forms, such as offering CE credits, giving CE stipends, providing high-quality supervision, and enabling participation in professional conferences, training events, research, and other opportunities to enhance and further one's skills and knowledge. Engaging in ongoing professional development will ensure you're implementing best practices and facilitate career advancement. Also keep in mind that professionals these days tend to work for more than one agency and in more than one type of position over the course of their lives. While you may absolutely love one type of work today, it's sometimes difficult to predict what you'll enjoy or the level of compensation or responsibility you'll desire in the future. Put yourself in a position to grow your career, whether that means expanding your role, taking on additional responsibilities, moving into leadership, opening your own practice, or consulting with other organizations.

In addition to the extent to which an employer supports CE for staff, consider whether they (a) take active steps to support ethics and professionalism among staff; (b) have established policies related to health, safety, and emergency preparedness; and (c) support and take steps to promote diversity, equity, and inclusion. If the organization is accredited by the Behavioral Health Center of Excellence (BHCOE), the organization has demonstrated to an accrediting body that it meets standards for clinical and operational quality.

Throughout the job search process, be patient with yourself. It can take time, and everyone's experience is unique. While it may only take a week or less to find a position, it could take up to a month or two.

The time it takes to land a job can vary greatly based on how flexible you are on the type of position, whether you're willing to move or commute, how consistently you engage in searching, and your particular location, specialty area, and industry. It's important to remember that factors beyond your control, such as overall economic conditions and the job market, can also impinge on the time it takes to find a job. With optimism, patience, and consistent effort, you're sure to find a job that suits you well!

If you're not getting interviews or getting interviews but not the job, this should prompt reflection. Critically evaluate what's working for you and what is not. For instance, if you're getting interviews but not landing the job, it could be helpful to do some mock interviews with a friend or reach out for professional coaching. Perhaps you need to have a closer look at your résumé and to further refine it. Is everything you've shared accurate? Is it free of spelling and grammatical errors? Have you highlighted your achievements and distinguishing qualities?

You may also want to touch base with the people you've asked to serve as a reference to ensure they are able to provide a positive referral. You should contact each reference in advance to let them know that you are applying for jobs and ask if they're able to serve as a supportive reference that will provide positive commentary on your abilities, work ethic, and character. If they're not or seem hesitant, it's best to ask someone else. It's optimal to provide a variety of references that can offer observations of your work in different positions and roles and comment on different aspects of your character. Finally, it can be helpful to give your references a little guidance on the information it will be helpful for them to share.

Fortunately, BCBAs are in great demand, so you have every reason to be optimistic that you will find a position that's a good fit!

WHERE TO LOOK FOR JOBS

Reaching out to your professional network to alert them that you're looking for a job can be one of the most effective ways to find a position. A warm introduction by a colleague to an employer affords a significant advantage for job seekers. There are also a number of online job boards where BCBA job hunters can search for positions, post résumés, and apply for jobs. Recruiters often rely on job boards to source talent. Here are some suggestions to consider:

Association of Professional Behavior Analysts

The APBA has an online Career Center filled with helpful resources for job seekers available at jobs.apbahome.net/career-resources. In addition to its regularly updated job board, it features guidance on developing a winning résumé, preparing for job interviews, negotiating salary, working with recruiters, advancing your career, managing your online presence, and planning your career. APBA even provides personalized career coaching (for a fee).

Association for Behavior Analysis International

The ABAI hosts a Career Center at careers.abainternational.org where you can search for jobs by position type, location, company, experience, job title, job category, salary, and education. They also offer solid career advice resources, such as articles on conducting a job search, preparing for a job interview, and exploring nontraditional jobs for BCBAs.

State Associations for Behavior Analysis

Numerous state associations for behavior analysis feature job boards on their websites where recruiters can post open positions. For instance, the CalABA hosts a job board at calaba.org/career-center/employment-opportunities with daily job postings for employment and internships. Consider taking a look at the website for the state association for behavior analysis where you would consider applying and see if they might be able to provide additional leads for you.

Jobs in Education

If you're interested in pursuing a position in the field of education, EDJOIN is a leading education job site available at edjoin.org where you can search for jobs by region, state, and organization. While there are job posts from locations all over the United States, there is a disproportionately large number of them coming from California. If you're more interested in positions in higher education, consider checking out HigherEdJobs at higheredjobs.com where you can search for administrative, faculty, and executive positions in colleges and universities across the country.

If you're interested in working in schools around the world, connect with one of the reputable recruiting agencies matching educators with international schools abroad. These agencies hold job fairs and connect job seekers with openings in international schools. Check out International School Services at iss.edu, The International Educator at tieonline.com, Search Associates at searchassociates.com, Educators Overseas at educatorsoverseas.com, and Council of International Schools at cois.org.

Job Boards

There are also a plethora of general job boards used by employers and job hunters alike. Indeed.com is arguably the most well-known and popular job board; however, there are numerous others worth exploring. Google for Jobs at jobs.google.com combs the internet to assemble job postings from general job boards as well as websites overseen by small businesses. Employers share open positions on Ziprecruiter.com, which in turn posts those jobs on myriad other job boards. CareerBuilder.com is a well-trusted platform for job hunting nationally, while Craigslist.org is a good place to look for positions in your local area. Other job boards to consider utilizing include Lensa.com, which leverages artificial intelligence to match job seekers with the most relevant positions, and Ladders.com, which only features positions with salaries of $100k or more. If you are based in Canada, have a look at Talent.com (formerly Neuvoo); it began in Canada, so it is a good source for positions there. However, the platform has a global reach and a robust presence in the United States.

LinkedIn

LinkedIn, available at linkedin.com, is a networking tool for professionals that can serve as a good place to search for jobs and inform others in your professional community that you're looking for a job. You can search for positions and elect to receive notices about openings. Your profile on LinkedIn can also serve as an excellent online résumé; in fact, professionals are increasingly sharing their LinkedIn profile on physical résumés and CVs. You can even use LinkedIn to research potential employers and explore how you or a colleague may already have a connection with the company you could leverage for a warm introduction. If you have a profile on LinkedIn, ensure it is up to date and professional. LinkedIn has become an important place to define your professional brand and market your skills. Posting periodically on LinkedIn and responding in a professional manner to relevant posts can be a great way to raise potential employers' awareness. Expect that potential employers will check out your profile on LinkedIn and, perhaps, other social media platforms when considering whether or not to invite you for an interview or hire you.

MyABAJobs

MyABAJobs (myabajobs.com) is a job site for behavior analysis professionals where you can search by keywords and location, post a résumé, and subscribe to a weekly job email blast. The organization also has an active presence on Twitter and Facebook, regularly posting jobs for qualified behavior analysts.

Therapists in Tech

Although primarily focused on psychologists and therapists, Therapists in Tech (TNT) is a good resource for behavioral health professionals interested in careers in digital behavioral health (therapistsintech.com). TNT also hosts a community for posting jobs, networking, and information-sharing on the *Slack* communication platform.

Many Other Agencies

There are many agencies seeking BCBAs that may only post opportunities on their own website. Consider searching for agencies in the area you would like to work in using an online search engine or directory listing and visiting the "careers" section of their websites.

PREPARING FOR INTERVIEWS

You've narrowed down the kind of position you would like and the type of setting you would like to work in, updated your résumé, applied for jobs, and landed some job interviews. Now it's time to put your best foot forward in the interview. A little preparation can go a long way toward facilitating your success.

Take time to study the job description, think about the position, and research the company in advance of the interview. Consider why you think it's a good fit for you and make a list of your reasons. This will facilitate your ability to demonstrate that you are familiar with the position and clearly explain how your skill set and experience align with its requirements. Consider writing out responses to the most likely questions and practice providing answers that are clear and concise. As a rule of thumb, aim to answer questions in under a few minutes. It can also help to have a friend conduct a mock interview so you can practice saying your answers and receive constructive feedback.

Your ability to articulate how your previous work experiences exemplify your skills and prepare you to be successful in the position can set you apart from other applicants. When answering such questions, employ the acronym STAR.

- **S**ituation: Provide a detailed description of a specific situation or task.
- **T**ask: Explain what role you played and the goal of the task or project.
- **A**ction: Describe the actions you performed to successfully address the situation, solve the problem, or complete the task. Focus on the contributions you specifically made to achieve the outcome.
- **R**esult: Describe the result of your actions and how they made a critical contribution to achieving success or a positive outcome.

It's common for potential employers to ask applicants about their résumé, so be familiar with yours. Since you're used to writing SMART goals, use the same approach to provide **S**pecific, **M**easurable, **A**ttainable, **R**elevant, and **T**ime Bound descriptions of your achievements and accomplishments detailed in your résumé. For example, avoid giving a general comment on a previous position you held; instead, articulate how your specific actions in the job drove particular positive results, such as how an intervention you created and delivered enabled a client's improved behavior at school and how this, in turn, generated additional positive outcomes for the student.

Since job interviews often begin with an open invitation for the applicant to introduce themselves, you'll want to prepare for this in advance. Remember, the interviewer isn't looking to hear your life story. They just really want you to share a little bit about who you are and why you're interested in, and a good fit for, the position. So, take this opportunity to briefly introduce yourself and share some background on your training, credentials, and relevant experience. If you wrote a cover letter when applying for the position, you can likely revisit some of the highlights you shared there. Your goal is to share experiences and information about yourself that will transform the interview into a conversation and persuade the interviewer that you're a promising candidate for the position.

It's also rather common for employers to ask applicants to comment on their strengths and weaknesses, so it helps to have an answer ready for this question as well. Aim to craft a response that shares how your specific strengths will facilitate your success in the position's requirements. Turn this into an opportunity to share additional details about how your skills and related experience prepare you to be successful at performing your duties in the role. In terms of skills, consider commenting on your writing, leadership, communication, technologic, or organizational abilities. In terms of character, consider emphasizing your initiative, flexibility, honesty, empathy, patience, or ability to build rapport with others. Refrain from describing weaknesses that dissuade the interviewer from hiring you, such as your misanthropy or difficulty meeting deadlines, paying attention, or arriving at work on time. Share a weakness related to a strength, such as how your commitment to doing things well can occasionally impact your work-life balance, or a weakness related to the duties of the position that you're endeavoring to improve, such as practicing managing anxiety when delivering hard news to parents or learning a software program you'll use on the job.

Remember, job interviews are also a time for you to learn more about the position, setting, and company. Employers typically invite applicants to ask questions during the interview, so use this as an opportunity to not only gather the information you need to make an informed decision but also impress the employer by demonstrating you've done your homework and are well prepared for the interview. Come prepared with the questions you have about the job, such as those related to (a) caseload, (b) working hours, (c) workplace culture, and (d) other things that matter to you.

Caseload

Given the high demand for services, it is important for BCBAs to ensure that their caseloads are feasible and, therefore, ethical. If your caseload is too high, it can negatively impact your ability to provide high-quality services and potentially result in burnout. To determine appropriate caseload size, consider the complexity and needs of the cases as well as your skill level and availability of support staff.

Possible questions to ask include:

- How many clients can I expect to have on my caseload?
- How many client hours will I be responsible for?
- What is the expected amount of case supervision to be provided?

In addition to asking about how many clients you may carry on your caseload, asking about client hours and amount of case supervision needed is necessary for understanding what your workload will really look like if you take the job. Service delivery hours vary by client; one client may require only a couple hours per week while another requires 40 hours per week. The greater the number of treatment hours needed for a particular case, the more time you will need to dedicate to it. Exactly how much? Well, that depends on the amount of case supervision (i.e., what you do as a BCBA to support the case, including direct and indirect supervision activities) that is to be provided. If you have a client who is receiving 40 hours of treatment per week and your expected case supervision activities is 2 hours for every 10 hours of treatment (i.e., 20% of treatment hours), that equates to 8 hours of work each week for you on that case. And when you do the math, don't forget to consider other time-consuming work-related activities you may need to engage in, such as attending agency meetings, driving, and so on.

For those BCBAs engaged in the treatment of clients with ASD, you can refer to the Council of Autism Service Providers' (CASP's; 2020) *Practice Guidelines for Healthcare Funders and Managers* at casproviders.org/asd-guidelines for some general recommendations under section 6 on caseload supervision.

Working Hours

BCBAs can provide services to a wide variety of clients. As a result, companies that employ BCBAs are often open as much as possible to be available for their clients. This can mean companies open early in the morning, close late at night, and are open on the weekends. Consequently, it is important to be clear upfront about the company's expectations for working hours, limits on daily working hours, scheduling flexibility, and overtime compensation.

Workplace Culture

We recommend that you ask questions that will help you to assess your goodness of fit with the organization. Learn what you can about their values and what they care about, and how all of that translates to how you will operate within and for the organization. Possible questions to ask include:

- How would you describe the organization's culture?
- What are the organization's core values?
- How do you ensure that clients receive high-quality care?
- How do you support the growth and professional development of staff?
- How do you ensure the quality of care for the clients you serve?
- Is your organization accredited by the BHCOE?

Other Things That Matter to You

This is about you—finding a job that is a good fit for you. Are there considerations we have not covered that are important to you and will weigh heavily in your assessment of a job's fit for you? What other questions might you have?

Also consider bringing a professional portfolio or binder with your questions written down on a notepad so as not to forget any in the moment.

Get a good night's sleep the day before the interview. On the day of the interview, take time to get yourself centered in a manner that works for you (e.g., exercise, meditation, positive affirmations). Have a nutritious breakfast. Put on professional attire and groom with care. Avoid wearing a fragrance that is too strong. Give yourself ample time to get to the interview on time. While you wait for the interview to begin, focus on taking long, deep breaths and relaxing your shoulders and jaw. Think to yourself: I've got this!

Remember: Sending a tailored thank you note to every interviewer within 24 hours of the interview can go a long way. You can also use the thank you note as an opportunity to briefly reiterate your enthusiasm for the position and your qualifications and share something you learned about the position or the company during the interview. Take time to carefully proofread your note and consider asking someone with strong editing skills to do so as well.

AFTER NOT PASSING THE EXAM: WHAT NOW?

It's disappointing. You immersed yourself in the material and prepared for the exam but didn't pass. It may help to know that you're not alone. Remember, a lot of people *don't* pass it on their first try. According to the most recent testing data published by the BACB®, just over one-third of first-time examinees need to retake the exam.

But facts and figures can only do so much to soften the hit of a failed attempt at the exam. Failing the exam is failing the exam, and you're likely to experience a range of challenging emotions, ranging from disappointment and sadness to frustration and embarrassment—all of which are completely normal and to be expected. Instead of denying what's going on in your inner world, give yourself permission to feel your feelings and notice your thoughts. Breathe and give yourself time to process the situation.

This is a good time for self-care, and honestly recognizing how you're feeling is the first step. We all cope with challenges differently. Reflect on the strategies you've used in the past to cope with stress and difficulties successfully. What works well for you?

Take a comprehensive approach to self-care that addresses your thoughts, feelings, and behavior.

Bring your attention to the present moment. Deep breathing exercises and tuning into your five senses can be helpful. Focus on what you can control. You can't change the results of the exam, but you can control how you react. It's painful enough that you didn't pass the exam. Don't make it worse by punishing yourself.

BE KIND TO YOURSELF

Our own inner voice can be our harshest critic. Instead of beating yourself up or judging yourself, give yourself grace and support. Practice self-compassion. Think about what you would say to a friend, loved one, or child if they were in your shoes and feeling how you're feeling. Say those kind and comforting words to yourself. Recognize and accept how you're feeling. Instead of criticizing yourself and worrying unnecessarily, tell yourself that you're okay and that it's going to be okay. Think about the things in your life that are going well, that bring you joy, and for which you're grateful. Dr. Kristin Neff, an authority on self-compassion, offers free guided practices and exercises that you try on her website at self-compassion.org/self-compassion-practices/#self-compassion-exercises.

PUT THINGS INTO PERSPECTIVE

Remind yourself that it is only an exam. While it may feel like a big deal right now, in the grand scheme of things it's a minor setback that you can overcome. Now is a good time to critically evaluate how you approached preparing for the exam so you don't make the same mistakes twice. What did you do that worked? What didn't work? Which content areas did you know well? Which content areas were you weaker in? Which approaches to studying worked well and which didn't? Which study skills did you not try? Which test-taking strategies did you practice and use? Did they work? Are there test-taking strategies you didn't use?

GIVE YOURSELF PERMISSION TO START AGAIN

Perhaps you found it difficult to put in the time studying that's really required to pass the BCBA Exam. If that's the case, you'll want to consider steps you can take to bring more structure to your exam prep. Using a strategic planner like the one included in Chapter 2 of this book can help you maintain consistency. Consider working with a study buddy or a study group at set times to help hold you accountable to studying. Building in ways to reward yourself for studying consistently can enhance your motivation.

Instead of worrying or engaging in self-blame, take what you can learn from this experience and allow the emotions you're feeling to motivate you. Your best bet is to accept the situation, use problem-solving to devise solutions, build these solutions into your strategic plan, and start moving forward. Believe in yourself! You can do this!

CONCLUSION

In this final chapter, we offered some recommendations on what to do after the exam. For those who passed the exam, we encourage taking time to process the experience, savoring the success and accompanying positive emotions, internalizing the accomplishment, and reflecting on the factors that fostered success. We also encouraged making a professional development plan and shared a number of different options for CE. This chapter also provided sound guidance on job hunting and preparing for job interviews. For those who did not pass the exam, we reminded them that a lot of people don't pass it on their first try, shared some tips on coping with the disappointment and regrouping, encouraged reflection on what to do differently, and then suggested they put those solutions into a strategic plan and move forward.

REFERENCES

Bailey, J. S., & Burch, M. R. (2010). *25 essential skills & strategies for the professional behavior analyst: Expert tips for maximizing consulting effectiveness*. Taylor & Francis.

Britton, L. N., & Cicoria, M. J. (2019). *Remote fieldwork supervision for BCBA® trainees*. Academic Press.

The Council of Autism Service Providers. (2020). *Applied behavior analysis treatment of autism spectrum disorder: Practice guidelines for healthcare funders and managers* (2nd ed.). Author.

Do Better Collective. (n.d.). *The Do Better Collective – scholar membership*. Retrieved February 7, 2025 from https://collective.dobettermovement.us/do-better-scholars.

Kazemi, E., Rice, B., & Adzhyan, P. (2018). *Fieldwork and supervision for behavior analysts: A handbook*. Springer Publishing Company.

BIBLIOGRAPHY

Behavior Analyst Certification Board. (2020). *Professional and ethical compliance code for behavior analysts*. http://bacb.com/wp-content/uploads/2016/03/160321-compliance-code-english.pdf

Behavior Analyst Certification Board. (2024). *US employment demand for behavior analysts: 2010–2023*. Author.

Plantiveau, C., Dounavi, K., & Virués-Ortega, J. (2018). High levels of burnout among early-career board-certified behavior analysts with low collegial support in the work environment. *European Journal of Behavior Analysis*, *19*(2), 195–207. https://doi.org/10.1080/15021149.2018.1438339

Glossary of Terms

A

AB design. Experimental design that involves repeated measures taken during a preintervention baseline condition (A) and then again during an intervention condition (B).

ABA design. Reversal design that involves repeated measures taken during an initial baseline condition (A), then an intervention condition (B), and again after returning to the baseline condition (A).

ABAB design. Reversal design that involves an initial baseline phase (A), followed by an intervention phase (B), followed by a withdrawal phase (A), followed by a final intervention phase (B).

ABC design. Experimental design that involves repeated measures taken during a preintervention baseline condition (A), intervention condition (B), and second intervention condition (C).

ABC recording. A type of descriptive assessment in which behavior is viewed as a function of the antecedents that precede it and the consequences that follow it. Continuous ABC recording involves recording occurrences of the target behavior and specified environmental events as they occur. Narrative ABC recording, on the other hand, does not specify environmental events and involves recording only when the target behavior occurs.

Accuracy. The degree to which the observed value approximates the true value.

Analytic. Core dimension of behavior analysis that means control over a target behavior can be demonstrated (i.e., can be turned on and off), evidencing the existence of a functional relationship between the manipulated event and occurrence/nonoccurrence of the target behavior.

Applied. Core dimension of behavior analysis that means the variable of interest is important to an individual and/or society; that is, changes that improve an individual's quality of life (i.e., socially significant behaviors) are targeted.

Applied behavior analysis. A science in which behavior analysts apply techniques derived from the principles of behavior to change behavior (e.g., increase behavior, teach and maintain behavior, reduce problem behavior, etc.) and positively enhance socially significant areas (e.g., classroom management, generalization and maintenance of learning, communication, etc.). It utilizes experimentation to clearly identify the variables driving changes in behavior, and applies principles derived from the experimental analysis of behavior to change behavior.

Automatic contingencies. Environmental contingencies that can affect behavior without the mediation or deliberate actions of another person.

Automatic negative reinforcement. Termination or postponement (i.e., escape) of aversive stimulation that results directly from the behavior.

Automatic reinforcement. Reinforcement produced by a behavior or physical environment resulting from a behavior.

B

Backward chaining. A method of chaining that starts with the training of the last behavior in the chain before moving to the second to last, and so forth, until all the links of the chain are joined and emitted as a single interconnected performance.

Bar graph. A graph that is used to display discrete sets of data (e.g., performance of an individual or group of subjects during different conditions).

Baseline logic. A form of experimental reasoning that calls for prediction (anticipated outcome of an unknown/future measurement), verification (demonstration of a functional relationship between the intervention and target behavior), and replication (repeating of independent variable manipulations and obtaining outcomes similar to those of a previous study).

Behavior. An organism's activity that results in a measurable change in its environment.

Behavioral. Core dimension of behavior analysis that means that a study or intervention analyzes observable and measurable behavior in a precise and objective manner.

Behavioral skills training. An instructional method that involves describing the target skill, providing a written description, demonstrating the target skill, requiring the supervisee to practice the target skill, and providing feedback during practice. The last two steps (requiring the supervisee to practice the target skill and providing feedback during practice) are repeated until mastery is achieved.

Behavior-altering effect. A momentary increase or decrease in the frequency of a behavior that has been reinforced or punished by the stimulus whose value has been changed by the motivating operation.

Behavior-change goals. The product of goal-setting, which involves establishing criteria for behavior change after identification of a socially significant target behavior.

Behaviorism. A philosophy of the science of behavior and its various forms. It assumes that a science of behavior is possible, and that behavior can be studied and changed in a manner similar to other sciences (e.g., biology). Behaviorism primarily looks to causes in the external environment for explanations of behavior. As an intervention, behaviorism holds that it is often most effective to organize the environment in such a way that certain behaviors are more or less likely.

C

Chained schedule of reinforcement. A schedule of reinforcement that requires completing a series of behaviors in a specific sequence, with each behavior associated with its own cue. Reinforcement is given only after all steps in the chain are completed.

Chaining. A process of linking specific sequences of stimuli and behaviors. Chaining is used to teach more complex behaviors that are to occur as a single interconnected performance. There are several methods, including forward chaining, total-task chaining, backward chaining, and backward chaining with lead aheads.

Changing criterion design. Experimental design in which the initial baseline phase is followed by a series of intervention phases with successive/gradual criteria for change.

Checklist. An indirect measure that lists specific behaviors with a description of the conditions under which each behavior will occur.

Codic. Verbal operant that is under the control of a verbal stimulus without point-to-point correspondence but with formal similarity, and has a history of generalized reinforcement. Codics include textual and dictation types.

Collaborative teaming. A process for collaborating with others to serve clients. Collaborative teaming strategies include developing and using a shared language, employing the same data collection process, displaying results in an understandable way, and working together to develop and implement a behavior-change program.

Comparative analysis. A type of analysis that compares two or more distinct interventions (e.g., multielement experimental designs).

Component analysis. A type of analysis that evaluates the relative contributions of the parts of an intervention. A drop-out component analysis involves implementing an intervention and then systematically removing parts of it, whereas an add-in component analysis involves systematically assessing parts individually or together before implementing the intervention.

Compound schedules of reinforcement. Schedules used for investigating a single response in which two or more schedules of reinforcement alternate, appear in succession, or occur at the same time. As such, a compound schedule consists of two or more types of schedules of reinforcement. Compound schedules include concurrent schedules, discriminative schedules, nondiscriminative schedules, and schedules combining the number of responses and time.

Conceptually systematic. Core dimension of behavior analysis that means all the interventions or procedures are grounded in the basic behavioral principles of behavior analysis in a manner that fosters integration and systematic expansion of the procedures.

Concurrent schedule of reinforcement. A schedule of reinforcement involving two or more reinforcement contingencies operating at the same time for two or more behaviors.

Conditional discrimination. Emission of a differential response that is controlled by a single stimulus when it is in the presence of another stimulus.

Conditioned motivating operation. Motivating operation that requires learning to produce value-altering and behavior-altering effects. Conditioned motivating operations include surrogate, reflexive, and transitive types.

Conditioned motivating operation reflexive. Stimulus that has acquired its effects as a motivating operation as a result of it preceding the onset of unpleasant/painful stimulation.

Conditioned motivating operation surrogate. Stimulus that has acquired its effects as a motivating operation as a result of being paired with an unconditioned motivating operation.

Conditioned motivating operation transitive. Stimulus that establishes or abolishes the reinforcing or punishing value of another stimulus.

Conditioned punisher. Stimulus change that decreases the future frequency of the behavior that it immediately follows as a result of its previous pairing with one or more other punishers. It is the product of ontogeny.

Conditioned reinforcer. Stimulus change that increases the future frequency of the behavior that it immediately follows as a result of its previous pairing with one or more other reinforcers. It is the product of ontogeny, varies across individuals, and changes throughout the individual's life span.

Contingency contracting. A procedure involving the establishment of a document that specifies a contingent relationship between the completion of a specific task and access to a specified reinforcer. The contingency contract should provide a detailed description of the task and all relevant rules and describe the reward to be provided upon completion of the specific behavior.

Contingency-shaped behavior. Behavior that is learned through experience with contingencies.

Continuous reinforcement schedule. Schedule of reinforcement that requires the delivery of reinforcement after every occurrence of a target behavior.

Control. Level of scientific understanding derived from the discovery of functional relations in controlled experiments that demonstrate that a specific change to one event (independent variable) reliably produces a specific change in another event (dependent variable).

Cost-benefit analysis. A systematic process for assessing the potential benefits and costs of a procedure or treatment plan to determine if the benefits justify the costs and if the decision is economically sound.

Criterion-referenced measure. A direct measure that evaluates a client's performance against some predetermined standard.

Cultural humility. This refers to an approach to understanding and interacting with people from diverse cultural backgrounds that involves recognizing and addressing one's own biases, being open to learning about others' cultural perspectives, and actively seeking to understand and respect their experiences and values. It emphasizes ongoing self-reflection and learning rather than assuming expertise in other cultures.

Cumulative record. A graph that is used to display the running total of responses over time. The cumulative total is represented on the vertical axis.

Curriculum-based measure. A direct, criterion-referenced measure that is used to evaluate performance on tasks that a client performs as part of planned instruction.

D

Dependent variable. The target behavior that an intervention is designed to change.

Derived stimulus relations. Emergence of untrained responses indicating a relation (e.g., the same as, opposite of, different from, better than) between two or more stimuli following a history of related instruction or experience. The properties of equivalence are derived from the logical relations of reflexivity, symmetry, and transitivity.

Description. Level of scientific understanding derived from systematic observations which enable individuals to describe events in quantifiable terms that can be examined for possible interactions with other known facts.

Descriptive assessment. A method of assessment involving direct observation of the target behavior in relation to other events under naturally occurring conditions. Descriptive assessments include continuous ABC recording, narrative ABC recording, and scatter plot recording.

Determinism. Attitude of science that assumes the universe is rational, governed by discoverable laws, and that events are completely determined by previously existing causes. As a result, all behavior possesses an identifiable cause and is thus predictable and to some degree determinable.

Differential reinforcement. Reinforcing specific responses and placing all others on extinction.

Differential reinforcement of alternative behavior. A differential reinforcement procedure that involves reinforcing a targeted alternative behavior for the problem behavior and withholding reinforcement for the problem behavior.

Differential reinforcement of incompatible behavior. A differential reinforcement procedure that involves reinforcing behaviors that are incompatible with the problem behavior and withholding reinforcement for the problem behavior.

Differential reinforcement of low rate behavior. A differential reinforcement procedure that involves providing reinforcement when the targeted behavior occurs below a predetermined criterion.

Differential reinforcement of other behavior. A differential reinforcement procedure that involves providing reinforcement when the problem behavior is absent for a predetermined amount of time and withholding reinforcement for the problem behavior.

Dimensions of applied behavior analysis. The core dimensions of behavior analysis: applied, behavioral, analytic, technologic, conceptually systematic, effective, and generality.

Dimensional quantities. Features of behavior that can be measured. Dimensional quantities include repeatability, temporal extent, and temporal locus.

Direct assessment. A method of assessment to discover the skill strengths and deficits of a client. Direct assessment involves the use of direct measures.

Direct measure. A measure that involves an observer recording the target behavior as it occurs. Direct measures include standardized tests, criterion-referenced measures, curriculum-based measures, and direct observation.

Discrete-trial teaching arrangement. An instructional procedure that breaks down behavior into discrete steps (i.e., learning trials) with a clear beginning, middle, and end. Trials are repeated with the client receiving reinforcement for correct responding.

Discrimination. Emission of a differential response when presented with two or more stimuli.

Discriminative stimulus. A stimulus that, when present, signals that a particular behavior is likely (or not) to be reinforced.

Dosage. The amount or frequency of a treatment or intervention prescribed to achieve the desired change in behavior.

Duplic. Verbal operant that is under the control of a verbal stimulus with point-to-point correspondence (i.e., stimulus parts correspond with response parts), formal similarity (i.e., stimulus and response physically resemble each other), and has a history of generalized reinforcement. Duplics include echoics, mimetics, and copying text.

Duration. The length of time that behavior occupies; time elapsed between the onset and offset of the behavior.

E

Educational records. Data related to the client's education (e.g., transcripts, academic program, and disciplinary file). Educational records may contain documents that evidence the use of behavioral interventions and include functional assessment reports, behavior intervention plans, and progress monitoring data.

Effective. Core dimension of behavior analysis that means the intervention has altered the target behavior to a significant degree, is meaningful or socially important, and promotes long-term positive changes in the client.

Emergent relations. Stimulus relations that arise indirectly from related instruction or experience, rather than being taught directly.

Empiricism. Attitude of science that requires the practice of objective observation of an event of interest. Systematic measurement and accurate quantification are empirical methods used to develop scientific knowledge.

Equal-interval graph. A graph with both the vertical and horizontal axes divided into equal distances between marks to indicate the addition or subtraction of constant amounts. Equal-interval graphs include line graphs, bar graphs, cumulative records, and scatter plots.

Equivalence-based instruction. The process of forming equivalence classes (i.e., interchangeability between stimuli), which can be taught using matching-to-sample procedures with a minimum of two interrelated conditional discriminations.

Event recording. Recording the number of times that a behavior occurs.

Experimental analysis of behavior. A natural science approach to research that defines and clarifies the basic processes and principles of behavior. It was founded by B. F. Skinner with the publication of *The Behavior of Organisms* in 1938, which identified two types of behavior (operant and respondent). The operant three-term contingency is the primary unit of analysis. It is primarily a laboratory-based experimental approach that established the foundational principles of operant behavior.

Experimentation. Attitude of science that requires investigation to determine whether a functional relation exists between events. In an experiment, the independent variable is systematically controlled and manipulated to clarify its effects on the dependent variable.

External validity. The degree to which the results of the intervention (i.e., functional relationship demonstrated in an experiment) can be generalized to other behaviors, environments, and individuals/populations.

Extinction. Removal of reinforcement for a behavior.

F

Free-operant observation. A type of stimulus preference assessment that involves observing and recording the length of time (i.e., duration) that a client approaches, contacts, or engages with the stimuli when they are "free" to emit any responses. Free-operant observations can be contrived (with prearrangement of the environment to include items/activities the client may like) or naturalistic (without an prearrangement of the environment prior to observing).

Free-operant teaching arrangement. An instructional arrangement that allows for the client to freely emit one or more responses. A discriminative stimulus is sometimes present but not required. Reinforcement is not specifically programmed but the client may engage in responses that produce reinforcement continuously or intermittently.

Frequency. Count of a behavior or behavior class. Frequency is calculated by adding up the number of occurrences.

Fixed interval. Schedule that specifies the duration that must pass before the first occurrence of a target response will be reinforced.

Fixed ratio. Schedule that specifies the number of times a target behavior must occur to receive reinforcement.

Forward chaining. A method of chaining that starts with the training of the first behavior in the chain before moving to the second, and so forth, until all the links of the chain are joined and emitted as a single interconnected performance.

Functional analysis. A type of functional assessment that involves the manipulation of antecedents and/or consequences to observe and measure their separate effects on problem behavior. There are multiple types, including the basic functional analysis, brief functional analysis (BFA), trial-based functional analysis (TBFA), interview-informed synthesized contingency analysis (IISCA), latency-based functional analysis (LBFA), and functional analysis of precursor behavior.

Functional assessment. A variety of methods used to gather data related to the cause (i.e., function) of a problem behavior. Functional assessments can include functional analyses, descriptive assessments, and indirect assessments.

Functional communication training. A contingency-independent antecedent intervention that involves the use of differential reinforcement of alternative behavior to teach communicative responses that compete with problem behaviors evoked by a motivating operation.

Functional response class. Group of responses defined by their function (i.e., the outcome they produce in the environment).

G

Generality. Core dimension of behavior analysis that means a change in behavior holds over time, across different settings, and/or spreads to other relevant and related behaviors.

Generalization. Spreading of the effects of some operation (e.g., reinforcement, punishment, or extinction) on one stimulus to other, different stimuli.

Generalized punisher. Conditioned punisher that has been paired with many other punishers.

Generalized reinforcer. Conditioned reinforcer that has been paired with many other reinforcers.

Generative performance. This refers to the ability to apply previously learned speaking and listening skills to quickly acquire new, related skills without the need for direct teaching or additional reinforcement.

Group contingency. A contingency in which reinforcement for the entire group is dependent on an individual (dependent group contingency), a set of members drawn from the larger group (independent group contingency), or each member of the whole group (interdependent group contingency) achieving a performance criterion.

Group experimental design. Research design in which the analysis is conducted at the level of the group, not the individual.

H

High-probability request sequence. A contingency-independent antecedent intervention that involves presenting a series of simple requests followed by a target request.

Historical records. Data related to the client's history that may be learned through the review of many different possible types of records available.

I

Imitation training. Process for teaching imitative responses. Imitation training includes preassessment, training, postassessment, and probes for imitative behavior.

Independent variable. The intervention that is used to intervene on the dependent variable (i.e., target behavior). In an experiment, this is systematically manipulated to determine if alterations to it will produce reliable alterations in the dependent variable.

Indirect assessment. A method of assessment to discover the skill strengths and deficits of a client. Indirect assessment involves the use of indirect measures.

Indirect measure. A measure that does not involve direct observation but requires the client or others to recall and report information about the target behavior. Indirect measures include interviews, checklists, and rating scales.

Instruction. A verbal discriminative stimulus that specifies the response and contingency in a rule statement. It is often viewed as an instance of a rule.

Intermittent schedule of reinforcement. Schedule of reinforcement that does not involve reinforcing every occurrence of a target behavior. Intermittent schedules of reinforcement include fixed ratio schedules (with the exception of FR1), fixed interval schedules, variable ratio schedules, and variable interval schedules.

Internal validity. The degree to which the changes in the dependent variable (i.e., target behavior) can be attributed to the manipulation of the independent variable (i.e., intervention) and not the result of uncontrolled/extraneous factors.

Interresponse time. The length of time between two responses; time elapsed between the onset of one response to the onset of the next response.

Interval recording (or time sampling). Collection of procedures for observing and recording behavior, including whole interval recording, partial interval recording, and momentary time sampling.

Intraverbal. Verbal operant that is under the control of a verbal stimulus without point-to-point correspondence and has a history of generalized reinforcement.

Interview. An indirect measure that involves meeting with significant others to obtain relevant information about a behavior of interest.

L

Latency. The length of time from the onset of a stimulus (e.g., verbal instruction, cue) to the initiation of a behavior.

Level. Position along the vertical axis where a series of data points converge.

Line graph. A graph based on the Cartesian plane (i.e., two perpendicular number lines) that is used to display change over time as a series of connected data points. Each data point represents a relationship between some dimensional quantity of behavior (i.e., dependent variable) and time and/or environmental condition (i.e., independent variable).

M

Magnitude. Intensity of the behavior.

Maintenance. The degree to which a client continues to perform a behavior when some or all of an intervention that evokes it has been removed.

Mand. Verbal operant that is under the control of a motivating operation and has a history of specific reinforcement.

Matching law. A principle stating that the proportion of responses directed toward a particular choice or behavior will match the proportion of reinforcements received for that choice or behavior.

Matching-to-sample. A discrete-trial procedure that starts with the client making a response to the sample stimulus (i.e., conditional sample). The sample stimulus may or may not be removed before presenting the comparison stimuli, one of which matches with the conditional sample. When the client selects the comparison stimulus that matches with the sample stimulus, reinforcement is delivered.

Medical records. Data related to the client's health (e.g., clinical findings, diagnostic test results, care plans, and medication).

Mixed schedule of reinforcement. A compound schedule where two or more reinforcement schedules alternate, usually randomly, without any cues signaling which schedule is active. Reinforcement is provided when the response criteria for the active schedule are met.

Model. An antecedent stimulus presented to evoke an imitative response. Models can be planned (i.e., prearranged) or unplanned (i.e., antecedent stimuli that occur in everyday social interactions).

Momentary time sampling. Recording procedure in which, at the end of each interval, the target behavior is recorded as having occurred if it occurred at only the end of the interval. Momentary time sampling may over- or underestimate the occurrence of the behavior when intervals exceed 2 minutes.

Monitoring client progress. Process for tracking and evaluating responsiveness to intervention as evidenced by behavior change over time. Steps to monitoring client progress include operationalizing the behavior, developing a progress monitoring plan, selecting a measurement system, collecting baseline data and defining goals, setting intervention goals, collecting progress monitoring data, analyzing/summarizing/visually presenting the data, and evaluating/utilizing data for decision-making.

Motivating operation. An environmental variable that produces value-altering and behavior-altering effects.

Multielement design. Experimental design that involves delivering and measuring effects of two or more interventions in a rapid, alternating fashion. The design can be used to compare the effects of different interventions or the effects of an intervention with no intervention (i.e., baseline).

Multiple baseline design. Experimental design that involves establishing two or more independent baselines and introducing the intervention in a staggered fashion for each baseline. This design can be used to compare responding across different behaviors for a client, a behavior across different clients, or a behavior across different settings.

Multiple control in verbal behavior. There are two types of multiple control in verbal behavior (convergent and divergent). Convergent multiple control occurs when a single verbal response is influenced by multiple antecedent variables, and divergent multiple control occurs when one antecedent variable affects the strength of multiple responses.

Multiple schedule of reinforcement. A compound schedule where two or more reinforcement schedules alternate, typically in a random order, each with a unique cue signaling which schedule is active. Reinforcement is given when the response criteria for the active schedule are met.

Multiple stimulus preference assessment. A type of stimulus preference assessment involving the presentation of an array of three or more stimuli at a time. Multiple stimulus preference assessments include multiple stimulus without replacement (MSWO) and multiple stimulus with replacement (MSW).

N

Naturalistic teaching arrangement. An instructional approach that uses procedures recommended for programming of generalization to promote the development of verbal behaviors. There are a variety of naturalistic teaching approaches available which tend to be described as loosely structured with no planned order of instruction. Activities are chosen and paced by the client, and loose shaping contingencies are used to reinforce desirable behaviors.

Negative punishment. Removal (or reduction in intensity) of a stimulus immediately following a behavior, which decreases the future frequency of the behavior.

Negative reinforcement. Removal (or reduction in intensity) of a stimulus immediately following a behavior that serves to increase the future frequency of the behavior.

Noncontingent reinforcement. A contingency-independent antecedent intervention that involves delivering reinforcement on a fixed or variable interval schedule.

O

Ontogeny. How an individual's behavior develops over its lifetime based on their experiences with the environment.

Operant conditioning. Type of learning that occurs as a result of rewards and punishments. This concerns operant behavior, which is behavior individuals have control over. Operant behavior is modified by its history of consequences, which can be reinforcing (thereby increasing the frequency of a behavior) or punishing (thereby decreasing the frequency of a behavior).

Operant extinction. Reduction in behavior resulting from the discontinuation of reinforcement for it.

Operational definition. Objective, clear, and complete description of an observable and measurable target behavior.

P

Paired stimulus preference assessment. A type of stimulus preference assessment involving the presentation of two target stimuli at a time. Each stimulus is randomly paired with all other stimuli, but every possible pair must be presented. The client's selection between the two target stimuli presented at each trial is recorded.

Parametric analysis. A type of analysis that compares different levels of an intervention. It involves examining the effects generated by manipulating one or more dimensions/levels of the intervention.

Parsimony. Attitude of science that suggests that an explanation of a thing or event ought to be based on the fewest possible assumptions or unobservable constructs. It encourages scientists to prefer the simplest, logical explanation supported by experiments or reason.

Partial interval recording. Recording procedure in which, at the end of each interval, the target behavior is recorded as having occurred if it occurred at any time during the interval. Partial interval recording usually overestimates the total duration of the behavior but may underestimate the rate of high-frequency behaviors.

Percentage. A ratio expressed as a fraction of 100. This is calculated by multiplying the numeric value (e.g., count of a response divided by the total number of responses or opportunities/intervals in which it could have occurred) by 100.

Philosophic doubt. Attitude of science that assumes scientific knowledge is tentative and continually developing. Consequently, scientists remain skeptical about the validity and truthfulness of all scientific knowledge and open to modifying their beliefs based on new knowledge and discoveries.

Phylogeny. How a species' behavior has evolved over evolutionary time as it slowly makes changes necessary for survival.

Positive punishment. Presentation (or increase in intensity) of a stimulus immediately following a behavior, which decreases the future frequency of the behavior.

Positive reinforcement. Presentation (or increase in intensity) of a stimulus immediately subsequent to a behavior that serves to increase the future frequency of the behavior.

Prediction. Level of scientific understanding derived from repeated observations that demonstrate that two events systematically covary (i.e., correlate).

Product measure. A measure of behavior through examination of its effects produced on the environment. Measurement takes place after the occurrence of the behavior.

Professional practice. A domain of behavior analysis that is guided by the science of behavior analysis and involves delivering behavior-analytic services to human subjects grounded in the principles of behaviorism, research from the experimental analysis of behavior (EAB), and applied behavior analysis (ABA). It is a hybrid discipline informed by various mental health fields, education, communication disorders, physical therapy, and criminal justice.

Progressive schedules of reinforcement. Schedules in which each successive reinforcement opportunity is thinned regardless of a person's behavior.

Punisher. Stimulus change that decreases the future frequency of the behavior that it immediately follows.

Punishment. Basic principle that describes a functional relationship in which a behavior immediately followed by a stimulus change (i.e., consequence) decreases the future frequency of the behavior.

R

Radical behaviorism. Conceptual system developed by B. F. Skinner that seeks to understand behavior in all its forms and collapses the distinction between private events (i.e., thoughts and feelings) and public events (i.e., behavior that is observable and measurable). It assumes all behavior are influenced by the same kinds of variables and result from an individual's experiences and environments.

Rate. Count of behavior or behavior class per unit of time (e.g., per minute/hour/day). Rate is calculated by dividing the number of occurrences by the unit of time in which observations were conducted.

Rating scale. An indirect measure that lists items that a respondent can rate on a numerical or ordinal scale.

Reflexivity. Stimulus-stimulus relation is indicated in the selection of a comparison stimulus that matches the sample stimulus (e.g., A = A) without training to do so.

Reinforcement. Basic principle that describes a functional relationship in which a behavior immediately followed by a stimulus change (i.e., consequence) increases the future frequency of the behavior.

Reinforcer. Stimulus change that increases the future frequency of the behavior that it immediately follows.

Reliability. The degree to which the measure will produce consistent results.

Repeatability. The concept that behavior can be counted as it repeats across time. Measures based on repeatability include count, rate, and celeration.

Replication. Attitude of science that requires that experiments be repeated to determine the reliability of results. The validity, reliability, and usefulness of scientific findings are increased when experiments are reproduced, and the basic pattern of results is replicated numerous times.

Respondent conditioning. Type of learning whereby new stimuli develop the capacity to elicit responses through the pairing process. Respondent conditioning focuses on responses that are inborn, automatic, and involuntary. Pavlov, with whom this type of learning is most associated, focused on the connections between stimuli and responses (i.e., reflexes).

Response. A specific instance (i.e., occurrence) of behavior.

Response class. Group of responses defined by its form or function.

Response generalization. The degree to which a client emits an untrained response that serves the same function as the trained target behavior.

Response prompt. Antecedent stimulus that operates directly on the response (e.g., modeling, physical guidance, and verbal instructions) to assist the client in the emission of a target response. Response prompts include prompt delay (constant and progressive), system of least-to-most, system of most-to-least, and graduated guidance.

Reversal design. Experimental design that demonstrates the effect of an intervention by alternating its presentation and removal over time. ABA and ABAB designs are reversal designs.

Rule. Verbal antecedent that is in the form of a simple request or instruction, or describes a behavioral contingency.

Rule-governed behavior. Behavior that is under the control of verbal antecedents that are considered rules.

S

Scatter plot. A graph that is used to display the relationship between the variables depicted by the horizontal *x* and vertical *y* axes. The data points do not form a data path, but they can form patterns on the plane that suggest certain relationships.

Scatter plot recording. A type of descriptive assessment that involves recording when the target behavior occurs. Time is divided into shorter intervals and different marks are made on the observation form to indicate the extent to which the behavior occurred for each time interval.

Schedule of differential reinforcement. Schedules in which reinforcement is made contingent upon responses occurring at a predetermined rate of responding.

Schedule of reinforcement. Rule or protocol that specifies the requirements for reinforcement.

Selectionism. Attitude of science that assumes behavior is selected to continue or to be extinguished based on an individual's experiences and the consequences of their behavior. The environment affects living things through selectionism at the individual level (ontogeny) and the species level (phylogeny).

Self-instruction. Overt or covert prompting of desired behaviors and guiding oneself through a behavior chain or sequence of tasks.

Self-management. This refers to the personal application of behavior change tactics to produce a desired change in behavior. There are a variety of approaches to self-management that differ in the degree to which they emphasize antecedents or consequences for the behavior targeted for change.

Self-monitoring. This involves observing and recording one's own behavior. Self-monitoring is often taught in conjunction with self-management strategies.

Semilogarithmic chart. A graph that has a horizontal *x* axis that is divided into equal distances between marks, but the vertical *y* axis uses a logarithmic scale.

Setting/situation generalization. The degree to which a client emits a trained response in a setting that is different from where it was trained.

Shaping. A process of establishing a target response that involves the use of differential reinforcement for a progression of responses that are more like the target response (i.e., successive approximations of a terminal behavior).

Simple discrimination. Emission of a differential response that is controlled by a single stimulus.

Single-stimulus preference assessment. A type of stimulus preference assessment involving the presentation of target stimuli one at a time in random order. Each item is presented several times, and the client's response to each item is recorded.

Single-subject experimental design. Research design used to determine whether changes in the independent variable are driving changes in the dependent variable. In single-subject experimental designs, the subject is the unity of intervention and data analysis, the subject provides its own control for comparison, and the target behavior is measured repeatedly across different levels or conditions of the intervention.

Social positive reinforcement. Reinforcing reactions from others (i.e., attention).

Socially mediated contingencies. Environmental contingencies that can affect behavior with the mediation or deliberate actions of another person. Behavior analysts have primarily focused on socially mediated reinforcement.

Socially mediated reinforcement. Reinforcement produced by the actions of another person resulting from a behavior.

Social negative reinforcement. Termination or postponement (i.e., escape) of unwanted interactions with others as well as unpleasant tasks/activities.

Social validity. This refers to the degree to which targeted behaviors are appropriate, procedures are acceptable, and behavioral outcomes are meaningful.

Standard celeration chart. A graph that is primarily used to display the fluency and accuracy of a target behavior. The vertical *y* axis uses a logarithmic scale that allows individuals to record data points representing 0.001 to 1,000 times per minute.

Standardized test. A direct assessment measure with specific procedures that must be followed for its administration.

Stimulus. An event that affects the behavior of an individual. It involves a change in energy that affects a living organism through one or more of its sense organs.

Stimulus class. Cluster of stimuli with shared formal, temporal, and/or functional elements (i.e., physical features, timing of occurrence in relation to a behavior of interest, and/or effect on behavior).

Stimulus control. Alteration of the frequency, duration, latency, or magnitude of behavior by the presence or absence of an antecedent stimulus. This is established when a response is only reinforced when a specific stimulus is present, and not reinforced when other stimuli are present.

Stimulus generalization. The degree to which a client emits a trained response in the presence of a stimulus that is physically similar to the stimulus that was used to train it.

Stimulus prompt. An antecedent stimulus that operates directly on the antecedent task stimulus (e.g., movement, positioning, and redundancy) to assist the client in the emission of a target response. Stimulus prompts include stimulus shaping (gradually altering the form/topography of a stimulus until it eventually resembles the target criterion) and stimulus fading (making some feature of a target stimulus more salient, and then gradually fading it).

Symmetry. Stimulus-stimulus relation is indicated in the demonstration of reversibility of a sample stimulus and comparison stimulus (e.g., if A = B, then B = A) without training to do so.

T

Tact. Verbal operant that is under the control of a nonverbal stimulus and has a history of specific reinforcement.

Tangible reinforcement. Reinforcing materials or other stimuli.

Task analysis. Systematic process of breaking down a complex behavior into smaller, more manageable components in order to better understand and target the behavior for change. It facilitates clear and measurable goals, effective interventions, and identification of barriers to treatment.

Technologic. Core dimension of behavior analysis that means all procedures of an intervention are clearly detailed and described and that data and results of an experiment or study are clearly presented in an understandable and replicable manner.

Temporal extent. The concept that behavior can be timed as it occurs during some amount of time. The measure of duration is based on temporal extent.

Temporal locus. The concept that the timing of behavior can be measured as it occurs at a certain point in time with respect to other events. Measures based on temporal locus include latency and interresponse time.

Time sampling (or interval recording). Collection of procedures for observing and recording behavior, including whole interval recording, partial interval recording, and momentary time sampling.

Timing. Recording the passage of time with the use of a timing device (e.g., stopwatch).

Token economy. A behavior change system characterized by a set of contingencies that specify how tokens are earned/distributed and exchanged for reinforcers. It has three core components: a list of target behaviors to be reinforced, a generalized conditioned reinforcer, and a menu of backup reinforcers.

Topography. Physical form of the behavior.

Topographical response class. Group of responses defined by their form (i.e., what they look like).

Total-task chaining. A method of chaining that calls for the provision of training on each behavior in the chain during every training session until the client competently performs it.

Transitivity. Stimulus-stimulus relation is indicated in the demonstration of a derived stimulus-stimulus relation following the training of two other stimulus-stimulus relations (e.g., if A = B and B = C, then A = C and C = A).

Treatment integrity. The degree to which an intervention is implemented as designed.

Trend. Direction of a series of data points.

Trials to criterion. A measure of the number of response opportunities (i.e., trials) required to achieve a predetermined level of performance (i.e., mastery criterion). Trials to criterion data can be reported in terms of count, rate, duration, or latency.

U

Unconditioned motivating operation. A motivating operation that does not require learning to produce value-altering and behavior-altering effects.

Unconditioned punisher. Stimulus change that decreases the future frequency of any behavior that it immediately follows independent of the individual's learning history. It is the product of phylogeny and is naturally undesirable.

Unconditioned reinforcer. Stimulus change that increases the future frequency of the behavior that it immediately follows independent of the individual's learning history. It is the product of phylogeny and satisfies the basic life needs of an organism.

V

Validity. The extent to which an assessment measures what it is designed to measure. Valid measurement requires that a socially significant behavior is directly measured, its relevant dimension for answering the question is measured, and the data represents its occurrence under relevant conditions for answering the question.

Value-altering effect. A momentary increase or decrease in the reinforcing effects of a stimulus.

Variability. The amount of discrepancy between the values of a series of data points.

Variable interval. Schedule that specifies the average duration that must pass before the first occurrence of a target response will be reinforced.

Variable ratio. Schedule that specifies the average number of times a target behavior must occur to receive reinforcement.

Verbal operants. Types of expressive language (i.e., verbal behavior), which include duplics, mands, tacts, intraverbals, and codics.

W

Whole interval recording. Recording procedure in which, at the end of each interval, the target behavior is recorded as having occurred if it occurred throughout the entire interval. Whole interval recording usually underestimates the occurrence of the behavior.

Index